POLAND AND RUSSIA

The Neighborhood of Freedom
and Despotism in the X–XXI Centuries

The time will come – and with pride, you will say to yourself:
Let me be a slave, but a slave of the tsar of the universe.

Mikhail Lermontov, *Ishmael-Bay. Vostochnaya povyest'* [Eastern tale]

Oh Lord, let your spirit descend
and renew the face of the land, this land.

Pope John Paul II, Warsaw, June 1979

Białystok, Tomb of the Unknown Siberian Exile/Prisoner at the Church of the Holy Spirit. A reminder of the countless Poles who perished, most often namelessly, in the vastness of Siberia for the "crime" of being Poles. Photo: Adam Bujak

Andrzej Nowak

POLAND AND RUSSIA

The Neighborhood of Freedom and Despotism in the X–XXI Centuries

POLSKA FUNDACJA HUMANISTYCZNA IM. WINCENTEGO KADŁUBKA

Translation
Jan Czarniecki

Editing
Eoin Kavanagh

Supervising publisher and editor
Leszek Sosnowski

Preparation of graphics and cover
Studio Białego Kruka
Monika Starzyk
Paweł Lipa

Photographic editing
Mateusz Bednarz

References
Monika Makowska

Ilustrations
Adam Bujak: 2, 379, 437; BK Archive: 45 („Dzieje Polski", vol. I), 89 (by Marcin Sobiech), 267, 329, 383, 387, 407, 418, 419; East News: 415 (Maciej Macierzyński), 445 (Ukrainian Presidential Press); IPN: 365, 371, 375 bottom, 391, 397 (Andrzej Stawiarski); Jakub A. Maciejewski: 445; MNK: 41, 125, 155, 165, 171, 189, 219 top, 211, 223, 263, 277, 299, 367; MNL: 125 top; MNW: 22, 43, 68, 103, 151, 179, 201, 205, 206, 209 top, 227, 230, 243, 247, 251, 252; The Lenin Museum in Poronin: 319; NAC: 285, 324, 335, 364; PAP: 375 top, 387 top, 402 (bottom photo by Damazy Kwiatkowski), 411, 423 (bottom photo by Jacek Turczyk), 431; Polona: 25, 27, 31, 100, 162, 191, 257, 345; Wikimedia: 19, 37, 38, 49, 53, 57, 59, 69, 71, 74, 80, 85, 92, 93, 96, 105, 110, 113, 118, 121, 128, 131, 135, 136, 137, 144, 147, 159, 173, 188, 192, 195, 209 bottom, 215 (by Krzysztof Machocki), 209 bottom, 231, 234, 238, 239, 274, 280, 289, 293, 300, 303, 307, 313 (by Krzysztof Machocki), 321, 332, 333, 339, 340, 357, 353, 356, 349, 370, 376; ZKW: 115 bottom, 184; The Royal Castle of Wawel: 139.

Printing and binding
Skleniarz Kraków PL

1st edition
Krakow 2023

ISBN 978-83-7553-375-0

Cover photo from the picture
"Skirmish" by Wojciech Kossak.

Table of Contents

 **ANDRZEJ NOWAK**, a native of Krakow born in 1960, is a Polish historian and a public intellectual. He is a professor at the Institute of History in Poland's oldest University, the Jagiellonian (UJ). He also serves as head of the Comparative Imperial Studies Section at the Institute of History in the Polish Academy of Sciences. Prof. Nowak has lectured as a visiting professor at several universities around the world. In the United States (including Columbia University, Harvard University, Rice University), Great Britain (University of Cambridge, University College of London), Canada, Ireland, Japan and the Republic of Czechia. Between 1980 and 1988 Andrzej Nowak was personally involved in anti-communist journalistic and educational activities. He was a regular contributor to underground publications then in circulation. After the political transformations of 1989, he served as editor-in-chief of 'Arka' (1991–1994), co-founder and editor-in-chief of the bimonthly 'ARCANA' (1994–2012), as well as the editor of Poland's oldest academic quarterly: 'Kwartalnik Historyczny' (2020–2023). He still regularly writes for the monthly publication 'Wpis'.

An author of more than 30 books on Polish and Russian history (sold in over 400 thousand copies), among them: the multivolume *History of Poland* (in Polish, of which 5 out of a planned 12 volumes have been published), *History and Geopolitics: A Contest for Eastern Europe* (2008), *Imperiological Studies. A Polish Perspective* (2011), *Metamorphoses of the Russian Empire (1721–1921). Geopolitics, Odes and Nations* (2018), *The Fall of the Evil Empire. 1920* (2020), *Between Disorder and Enslavement. A Short History of Political Thought* (2020), *Poland and the Three Russias. A Study of Piłsudski's Eastern Policy* (expanded edition, 2021), *Jak postawała „imperija zła"? Doswid centralno-schidnoj Ewropy* (in Ukrainian, 2021), *Poland and Russia. The Neighborhood of Freedom and Despotism in the X–XXI Centuries* (2022), *The Forgotten Appeasement of 1920. Lloyd-George, Lenin and Poland* (Routledge, 2023).

Prof. Nowak has been the recipient of many awards and honors, ranking among the most distinguished of Polish scholars. For his *History of Poland* and other works, he was awarded the Order of the White Eagle by Poland's President Andrzej Duda in 2019, the Polish State's highest order of merit.

A Short Clarification
of Concepts

The names used in the title to this book Poland and Russia are not eternal nor unchanging concepts. They have evolved and indeed changed their meanings through the ages.

The word Poland was used for the first time in the year 1000, as evidenced in the historical sources. That name has been consistently used up until the present day to describe a specific political community. A wider political community was formed from the 15th century onwards by the Polish-Lithuanian State which as of 1569 was formalized into a Political Union, the Commonwealth with the Act of the Union of Lublin in 1569. This later concept of the Commonwealth encompassed most of the lands of modern-day Poland, Lithuania, parts of Latvia, Belarus, some territories of today's Russian Federation, and most of modern-day Ukraine. The ennobled inhabitants of these lands (including some city dwellers) were referred to as 'Szlachta' and were conferred with rights and also electoral and voting privileges, they were shall we say 'empowered citizens' of the Commonwealth. These citizens were primarily Lithuanians and Poles though also other ethnic groups were encompassed by Szlachta rights and privileges. Until the end of the 18th century, the terms Poland and the Commonwealth were used interchangeably to refer to this multiethnic state.

Russia is quite a different story. In the 9th or 10th century there was no Russia. The first Slavic State to emerge in the east was 'Rus' often referred to as Kyivan Rus. One must not confuse this Rus state with Russia. Sharing in the legacy of old Rus are in fact three separate nations and political communities: Belarus, Ukraine, and Russia. This last entity only begins to emerge, centered around a new settlement in the 13th and 14th centuries, located northeast of the original Rus state, a settlement that will become Moscow. This was indeed the name this state took and was known by at least until the end of the 16th century: Moscow or the Duchy of Moscow. The term 'Russia' was not in use and the lands which were under the dominion of the dukes of Moscow, Moskwa or in Latin Moscovia (in this meaning the state and not the city) did not reach as far as Kyiv, Smolensk or the Dniester River.

Moscow by conquering Veliki Novgorod in 1478, a competing center of political power in the north of what is now Russia, and then subsequently subjugating the Tatar (Mongol) lands of Kazan and Astrakhan began the process of creating its imperial identity, which would later take on the name Russia. Only with the ultimate subjugation of the eastern half of Ukraine (on the basis of the peace treaty of Andruszowo in 1667) could Moscow now justify its claim to the name Russia, which was emblematic of its desire to secure dominion over the lands of the former Kyivan Rus. Formally the name Russia comes into use when Tsar Peter I takes on the title of Emperor of all Russias.

By using the name "Russia" in the title of this book I refer through it, to these imperialistic ambitions by means of which the lords of the Kremlin in Moscow and later in St. Petersburg reach back to claim the heritage of Kyivan Rus.

It should therefore be acknowledged that the common tendency in the languages of the West to equate the words Rus and Russia is a falsehood. This distinction must be remembered. This term Ruś (Rus' or Ruthenia), Kyivan Ruś or old Ruś, for the historical lands of the 9th-century Slavic state and its various principalities up until at least the 16th century. We should also add that the concept of Ukraine as a state name also emerges in the 16th and 17th centuries in parallel with the term Russia. This is the moment in time when old Ruś ceases to serve as a form of state identification.

Introduction

There is a war taking place in Europe. A war for the independence of Ukraine, a war for the security of its neighbors, for the future of Europe, and the future of liberty in Europe. This is also a battle for the future of Russia. Can it be imagined – without imperialism? Can there be a Russia without a Russian Empire? Can Poland truly exist without liberty? What is the heritage of the *Rzeczpospolita (The Polish Republic or Polish-Lithuanian Commonwealth)*, and what is that of Moscow, did it ever achieve its own vision and self-ascribed mission to become the 'Third Rome'? In this book, I seek together with my readers, answers to these questions. I seek them in the history of the states themselves and in the history of the lands that historically lay between these two rivals. I seek them in the distant past before the names of Poland and Russia even came into being right up to the present momentous moment in our common history.

Freedom and Liberty or despotism and autocracy. These are not concepts separated by geography. They are impulses inscribed by human nature regardless of where it resides. In retrospect, however, and this is visible through the centuries, the progress of history creates or more accurately lends itself to the creation of forces that shape the conditions under which freedom and liberty can develop and flourish or where they can be suppressed and replaced. Conditions that strengthen the power of despotic techniques or embrittle them. This is just one of the ways in which we can try to conceptualize the history of Polish-Russian relations.

I have been working on these relations for more than forty years, since a 1981 publication in the Krakow-based underground publication *Po Prostu-bis* up to the time of my Master's thesis on the 'patron saint' of Russian imperialists, Nikolai Danilevsky, defended a year later in 1982 under the watchful gaze of Professor Władysław Serczyk's seminar at Krakow's now over 650 years old Jagiellonian University. Subsequently in a series of books, beginning in 1994 with a study of *Russia in the political thought of the Great Emigration*, and continuing on to this very day. *Poland and the*

Three Russias (2001), *Histories of Political Traditions. Piłsudski, Putin and Others* (2007), *History and Geopolitics: A Contest for Eastern Europe* (2008), *Putin. Sources of Imperial Aggression* (2014), *Metamorphoses of the Russian Empire* (2018), *The Defeat of the Empire of Evil* (2018), *How did the 'empires of evil' arise? The Experience of East-Central Europe* (a book that was to be published in Kyiv in March 2022). These works of mine and others you will find referenced in the appendixes and footnotes of this book.

However, here I am, not creating another scholarly work of research but attempting to collect thoughts and emotions that have been with me since I first came into contact with this history in the days of 'Solidarity' and Brezhnev. These thoughts have never left me from those first steps in academia up to these dark days of the Putin regime and now the heroic defense led by Ukrainians against this new wave of aggression. An aggression rooted in the Kremlin's concept of historical inevitability. I find myself once again grappling to comprehend this history – and I invite you my readers to join me in this attempt.

I dedicate this book to the memory of Natalya Gorbanevskaya, Vladimir Bukovsky, and Georgy Vladimov – three brave Russians I was privileged to meet on my academic journey, and to the memory of all the people who dared to speak out and to fight for freedom, both in their homeland, and for the freedom of others in the lands of their historical neighbors.

Andrzej Nowak
30 March 2022

Two Questions by Way of Introduction

Q 1. *What is the purpose of the English language version of this book?*

In January 2022 the US State Department published a list of 5 common disinformation narratives used by Russia to achieve its foreign policy aims. In this book, first written for Poles, you will find many references to such narratives they are respectively: (1) Russophobia, (2) Historical Revisionism, (3) The Collapse of Western Civilization, (4) US (foreign) Sponsoring of Popular Movements and finally (5) Reality is what the Kremlin makes it. All these narratives are aimed at discouraging any response to malign Russian actions. The aim of this book in its revised English edition specifically for the international audience, is to aid the reader in uncovering and counteracting such Kremlin methodologies. Because only through a deeper understanding of the past, including just how that past, or a version of it, continues to be relived and retold, can we move forward. Penetrate and better comprehend the often falsely or incompletely presented stories about the universally tragic histories of the people still inhabiting and those who once inhabited this beautiful yet troubled neighborhood. Only in this way can we build a lasting peace, give a perspective of a life in liberty and opportunity, not merely just a chance at survival for those who remain in these lands. While honoring the often-tragic deaths and life-affirming legacies of the people who once lived here.

Q 2. *A difficult history to grasp and why should one begin, at the beginning?*

With the above in mind, allow me to impart a few words of counsel based on the personal experience I gained while trying and I hope to some degree succeeding, in making this excellent book, originally written for Poles, a little more accessible for the foreign reader.

Firstly, you will find several "TN" references in the book as you read. These are points where I have endeavored to render Professor Nowak's work, originally written for his wide and growing Polish audience, a little more familiar and relatable for an international reader (these TNs will be available in full online at the following address). I trust these notes of mine will not hinder and only aid you on this journey. Additionally, to prepare the book for a non-Polish or perhaps non-Slavic audience the text of certain chapters, in particular chapters 1 to 6 those dealing with early less well-known periods of history in these lands, have been expanded somewhat with supplemental background information.

You will note that the last hundred years of history take up some 40% of the pages in this book. The 20th century is probably a period of Polish & Russian history that will be more familiar to many of you. If you started to read this book from that date point onwards (and I did so myself), you'd certainly gain a wider and deeper appreciation of 20th-century history. Especially in this still somewhat opaque and remote part of Europe. The challenge for the non-Polish reader when approaching this book is considerable. This is after all a thousand years of history of the Great Central and East European plains. Few from outside the region possess the historical mental maps of these lands prior to the 19th century. Yet here in just some 400 or so pages the author will try to at least stir your imagination, perhaps a desire to learn more while at the same time acknowledging that the scale here can be overwhelming as can be the detail.

Yet if you seek answers to the deeper sources of the current conflict. Ways to avoid the potential pitfalls that may lie in wait for those who would negotiate and implement a lasting peace. Then I am obliged to inform you that it is precisely in those proceeding thousand years of history, the years prior to WWI where you will discover many of the patterns that have shaped the why and wherefore of this region. It's nebulous history. Perhaps even the reasons why that history is so little known to us, even though it has somehow always been in front of us, in plain sight throughout the centuries…

Perhaps though, the most convincing argument I can offer you to start your journey at the beginning would be in the shape of a small town in

Southern Poland. A place not far from the old Polish capital of Krakow. A town with 800 years of multi-ethnic and multi-denominational history. A town in which the basic rights of its citizens and the rule of law were enshrined in its founding charter 750 years ago. A place settled by Poles but to which other Slavic nations Czechs, Rus or Ukrainians as well as Germans all flocked to and flourished in different periods down the centuries. A town that overcame religious intolerance and overthrew its local 16th-century antisemitic ban on Jews to then become one of the largest centers of Hasidism in Poland, indeed in Europe. A location which later during the Polish partitions would become the gateway to the West for emigrates from the impoverished lands of the Eastern Austro-Hungarian Empire. A town with a small railway hub to which those seeking a better life traveled in their thousands. Disembarking there in hope and waiting patiently for the right to transit to continue their journey onward towards to the West, perhaps even, to America. All of them seeking a new and potentially more prosperous life. Perhaps a life of freedom and not just from poverty. A town on whose territory an invading German Reich would visit with unspeakable horror. Human suffering on an unimaginable scale. A sacred place, above all for the Jewish nation and those of other nations whose lives were extinguished there. Today it's a town to which a new wave of migrants from the east has come. Where a thousand, or more, displaced Ukrainian women and children all found shelter within the first few weeks after Russia's all-out invasion of Ukraine in Feb 2022. It's a place that we all know, it is called Oświęcim, though most of us know it by another name.

Dictionary of Geographical Names and Terms

Brenna – Brandenbourg
Chanat Krymski – Crimean Khanate
Czechy – Czechia
Częstochowa – Czestochowa
Dniepr – Dnieper River
Dunaj – Danube River
Gdańsk – Gdansk
Głogów – Glogow
Halicz – Halych
Hospodarstwo Moldawskie –
    Principality of Moldova
Chocim – Khotyn
Kowno – Kaunas
Kijów – Kiev
Kołobrzeg – Kolobrzeg
Królestwo Węgier –
    Kingdom of Hungary
Królestwo Czech – Kingdom of Czech
Królewiec – Kaliningrad
Księstwo Bawarii – Electorate of
    Bavaria
Księstwo Saksonii – Duchy of Saxony
Kwedlinburg – Quedlinburg
Łaba – Elba River
Lwów – Lviv
Małopolska – Lesser Poland
Miśnia – Meissen
Morawy – Moravia
Moskwa – Moscow
Nowogród – Novgorod
Obodrzyce – Obotrites
Odra – Oder River

Ołomuniec – Olomouc
Zakon Kawalerów Mieczowych –
    Livonian Brothers of the Sword
Płock – Plock
Poznań – Poznan
Praga – Prague
Pregoła – Pregolya River
Prusowie – Old Prussians
Prusy – Prussia
Psków – Pskov
Radogoszcz – Retra
Ratyzbona – Regensburg
Republika Pskowska –
    Republic of Pskov
Rosja – Russia
Ruś – Rus
Ruś Czerwona – Red Ruthenia
Ryga – Riga
Sącz – Sacz (Old or New Sacz)
Sala/Soława – Saale River
Słowacja – Slovakia
Toruń – Torun
Twer – Tver
Warszawa – Warsaw
Wiedeń – Vienna
Wielkopolska – Greater Poland
Wilno – Vilnius
Wisła – Vistula River
Włodzimierz – Volodymyr
Wrocław – Wroclaw
Ziemia Nowogrodzka – The Lands of
    Novgorod

Poland and Rus: Neighboring Civilizations with Contrasting Origins and Experiences (X–XIV Centuries)

T his book will represent an attempt to review the history of Poland through the lens of its relations with Russia. In this very first chapter, we will examine the period when one of our protagonists is still somehow missing, when it is not yet possible to talk about a tangible Russian state or political entity. We will instead cover the first five centuries of relations between the Polish state (also referred to as the Lechitic or Piast dynastic state). A state which finds its formal origins in the middle of the 10th century when the ruling Piast Duke accepted Baptism at the hands of either a German (from Regensburg) or Czech (from Prague) Cardinal. In the initial absence of a Moscow or a Russia, we shall instead examine Poland's interactions with what many Russian historians of the past would have considered to be the 'precursor' states of Moscow, namely Kyivan Rus, or Novgorod Rus. Other historians often referred to these lands simply as Ruthenia, a Latin word used to describe Eastern Slavs. The term 'Russia' only entered into widespread use in the 17th century and achieved real significance with the declaration of a Russian Empire by Peter the Great in 1731. However, regardless of such historical semantics, I will undertake to persuade you my readers, that as a specific political-civilizational form, Russia was already taking tangible shape from the end of the 15th century, despite its then still ongoing vassal status to the Mongols. In my opinion, already by the end of the 15th century, we may refer to the Grand Duchy of Moscow as a nascent Russia, still decades before Ivan the Terrible would proclaim the first Tsardom of Russia.

Prior to the full-scale war in Ukraine, the default topic or viewing glass for many Poles regarding Polish-Russian relations, were the tragic events related to the Smolensk disaster of 2010. Coupled together with the ongoing disputes regarding Russia's monopolization of evidence, including the plane wreckage, relevant to the 'investigation' of the event. However, for many Poles far deeper, generational wounds are the primary drivers of their historical emotions regarding Russia. The recent history of World War II, the joint Nazi-Soviet aggression and partition of Poland in 1939, the occupation of the historical eastern Borderlands of the previous Polish state and systematic 'de-Polonization' of these territories through murder and forced migration. When Poles reflect on the role of their Eastern neighbor in these conflicts, they sometimes ask themselves the related questions just to what extent can historical guilt be attributed to the Soviet state, to the legacy of the Russian Empire, and indeed to the Russian nation?

We also ask ourselves another question. To just what extent were Russia and the Russians themselves merely additional victims in the astonishing list of crimes against humanity perpetrated by the brutal communist system in the years 1917–1991? The years when that specific ideological creation Soviet Russia existed. The intimacy and immediacy of these events of the 20th century compel Poles to often view Polish-Russian relations in a very painful, vivid way. This leaves many Poles prey to the accusation of Russophobia. Such sentiments rise with particular force when, for example, only two years after the Smolensk plane tragedy Poles gathered in the Warsaw Royal Castle and listened to the words of a joint letter by Polish Catholic bishops and the Moscow Orthodox Christian Patriarch Kirill I on the reconciliation of the Polish and Russian peoples. This beautiful poignant, though rather difficult, message was unfortunately compromised by the rather peculiar career of its co-author. The fact that Patriarch Kirill I has been a KGB agent since 1972 (code name: 'Mikhailov'), meant the words of the Orthodox church were largely denuded of any legitimacy or authority except that of the Kremlin's already then ongoing aggressive and coercive imperial agenda.

History precisely exists to allow us to reflect on the burden placed on us Poles and on the Russians resulting from this joint neighborhood that we must share, the meaning of a mission in this regard perhaps still unfinished, still ongoing in bilateral relations. When we reflect on this challenging historical and geographical legacy, one which was also touched upon by the bishops in the aforementioned letter read out at the castle in Warsaw. We should notice that the letter purposely did not pronounce any end of history or a finality of reckoning. Instead, they thankfully left the judgment of this legacy to us historians. However, we historians are hesitant to quickly issue a verdict on such a complex history, for the thought often plagues us 'Could things have been different'? Could we have found a better accommodation with the Russians, in whom, after all, we Poles can sometimes perceive the same reflections of ourselves as we can also see in other Slavic brother nations? Many Poles know this from personal experience when meeting Russian citizens in everyday life. We generally have no problems communicating linguistically, in everyday situations, or in friendly social contact. Above all, we are brought together by language; we are 'Slavic brothers' in the cultural heritage of a language with common roots. So, the question is often raised that maybe it would be possible to arrange our common relations differently, and then perhaps our history would turn out better?

Poles often ask themselves the same question in the context of their country's difficult relations with their other neighbors, especially Poland's German neighbor to the West. Though there can be no claim of Slavic brotherly relations in this context, Poland does share with Germany many common roots. For example, in Latin civilization the actively lived experience of the Renaissance and prior to the reformation, a shared Roman Catholic faith. The eminent Polish historian Feliks Koneczny (1862–1949) would though disagree with this statement, he would claim that Germany's civilizational roots are in fact more closely linked to the Byzantine civilization, we will reflect more on the civilizational roots of Poland and its neighbors later in this book. Moreover, Poles in the European context have an exceptional, unique even, long-lasting and enriching relationship with their old 'internal neighbor' the sizeable Jewish presence in historical Polish lands prior to WWII. A presence that flowed into Poland shortly after the foundation of the original Piast state. (TN Start) Many of these Jews fled centuries of recurrent antisemitic sentiment in other European countries even pogroms in Germany and elsewhere during the assembly and transit of the first crusades to the Holy Lands. These agile and erudite internal neighbors deliberately chose to settle in the lands of the future Polish-Lithuanian Commonwealth and in doing so benefit from the religious tolerance they found there. Further waves followed during the Reformation and Counter-Reformation in the 16th to 17th centuries. (TN End) This Jewish community had constituted a vital co-creative element within the Polish state, while at the same time, it

The Princes Boris and Gleb, sons of Prince Vladimir I the Great oh Kyiv, saints of the Orthodox Church. An icon from around the year 1300, probably from Tver in Northeastern Russia found in Veliky (Great) Novgorod.

posed a challenge unique to Poland due to its sheer size and vibrancy. (TN Start) For non-natives to these lands, the tragic events of WW II and the unimaginable horror, that genocidal holocaust orchestrated and perpetrated by the 3rd Reich and its accomplices throughout the region, overshadow those long centuries of Polish-Jewish co-habitation of these lands. (TN End)

It is in this context that we often consider the burden of our relations with Russia. Perhaps if we were not so divided by the conflict with Russia, then all our other relations with our neighbors could have turned out better? Were these 550 years of conflict, inevitable? Could events have been managed differently, more wisely, or at least better interpreted and understood?

Let me start our historical journey with a fundamental question facing Poles: could we as a nation, with full accountability, defend the thesis that the Russians are our brothers? There is no easy answer to this question. We may begin our search by looking in the books of our earliest historians and then search in the realms of pre-recorded history among the clues discovered by archaeologists or uncovered by modern historians. A good first starting point could be the first recorded observations of an outsider. So let us turn to the writings of an 11th and 12th centuries chronicler the monk we call Gallus Anonymus, who probably came from northern Italy. The very earliest recordings of Polish or rather 'Piast', the ruling family, history seldom came from a Polish pen. Sitting down at the turn of the 11th and 12th centuries to write a chronicle of the reign of Bolesław the Wrymouth (Pol.: *Bolesław Krzywousty*), at whose court he found himself, this foreign monk quickly realized that in order to fulfill his appointed task, to eloquently and accurately represent Bolesław's recent and glorious military achievements, he had to provide some historical background for his readers. He thus writes: 'But since the country of the Poles is far from the pilgrimage routes and little known to anyone except those who travel to Rus in search of trade, therefore, let it not seem ridiculous to anyone if I say a few words on the subject [of Polish history before Bolesław].'

This is why at the beginning of his chronicle, Gallus Anonymus clearly states that Poland lies far away and that yet another even more prosperous land lies further still to the east, where great trade is concentrated. Poland is thus presented as a land of transit. The land that one traverses to reach Rus (or Ruthenia) – an area of crucial trade routes at the turn of the 11th century indeed already centuries earlier. Interestingly, we find Gallus Anonymus's concept of Poland as a transit land somehow familiar even today. It is a role that has in many ways been perpetuated down the centuries. Even now, in our modern era, when someone from a more distant country wants to clarify where Poland lies, he often locates it precisely near Russia, perhaps nowadays beside Ukraine as its 'neighboring suburb' or its access point. In the United States, in Germany, or elsewhere in the West, we may hear it said by travelers to Russia and Ukraine, that they will pass through Poland along the way.

This point of view is worth recalling as it helps us conceptualize a certain difficulty in Polish-Russian relations, which Gallus Anonymus already recognized. This relationship is presented in an entirely different light by other chroniclers, those of Polish descent. Here we find the charming fables and stories that comprised the subsequent great native Polish chronicles (I will, for now, omit Master Wincenty's 'Kadłubek's' work). Firstly, among the domestic sources of Polish origins, we have the *Chronicle of Greater Poland*, written around 1295 by an author who, unfortunately, remains unknown to us. Then less than 200 years later we have Jan Długosz and his *Annals, or chronicles of the famous Kingdom of Poland*. Why is it worth recalling these two earliest sources of ethnic Polish chroniclers, works so essential for the historical awareness of Poles already from their childhood stories? Well, it is in the *Chronicle of Greater Poland*, that the fabled account of the three brothers Lech, Czech, and Rus appears for the first time. A fable that the chronicler treats as part of the true history of the region. This highly descriptive event was supposed to evoke the founding history of the various Slavic families and explain their choice of home for their respective permanent places of settlement.

This fable is a quite instructive, if romanticized representation of history. For it is worth realizing that in those lands where Poland lies, Slavs have been known to reside since, at least, the turn of the 5th and 6th centuries after Christ. With regard to this minimal time span, there is consensus among researchers. Meanwhile, many historians, especially archaeologists, argue to this day on the maximum time span and origins with an intensity rivaling the intransigence of today's Polish or indeed US political factions. Whenever I read archaeological texts from conferences on this topic, where

The legendary progenitor of the Poles – Lech – who was to have ruled over the Polan tribe dressed in princely robes according to a woodcut from 'Chronica Polonorum' by Maciej Miechowita. Krakow 1521.

the two schools of thought are at odds with each other, a lively, indeed fiery debate erupts. Representatives of one say that the Slavs have been in this region since the end of the pre-Christian era, perhaps even as early as 300 or 400 years before Christ, and that they originated here from Polish lands. Without going into the details of this dispute, I will only say that the Krakow school, represented primarily by the late Prof. Kazimierz Godłowski and the equally eminent archaeologist Prof. Janusz Kozłowski, propose a different concept. One becoming more and more prevalent today. According to them, the Slavs came from lands a little further to the east – from the area of today's western Ukraine, arriving to the land of modern-day Poland only at the end of the 5th century after Christ. Thus, according to them, the ancestral soil of the Slavs was located between the Bug and the Dniester Rivers.

Regardless of ethnographic origins, in keeping with the legend of the three brothers from the aforementioned Chronicle: Czech, considered the younger brother, stayed in the area of today's Czechia. The eldest brother, Lech, went further north to the lands of modern-day Poland, and the second of the younger brothers, Rus – went east. This tale of Lech, Czech, and Rus is familiar to almost every Pole being the basis for many fairy tales and fables from children's books, even the books of my own childhood under communism.

However, and this is crucial, let us note that in the later domestic telling of the story by the chronicler Jan Dugosz this legend is presented quite differently. Here for the purpose of this book it is worth posing the following question. Why is Rus depicted as our brother in the earlier *Chronicle of Greater Poland* and in the later writings of Jan Długosz, this is no longer the case? In this telling that for Długosz Rus is no longer a brother. The writings of the earlier book *Chronicle of Greater Poland* appeared during a period that we need to contextualize. This earlier chronicle appeared during a period of intense contact indeed a cultural-political clash (it could be thus called, with some caveats) that was Polish-Germanic in nature. Though at this time the concept of true national consciousness was still evolving. The clash encompassing not only the landed gentry and knights, many of whom had already developed the foundations of such consciousness earlier, but also many people living in the cities and towns who perceived the different customs and languages of their town neighbors up close. Such mixed settlements where, as a result of the peaceful migration during the 12th–13th centuries, Poles, came into quite intense interactions with a dynamic and populous German presence (including very many of the Jewish faith). But also in the smaller villages, of which hundreds were then settled under the so-called Magdeburg laws.

All this served to bring the 'locals' into direct contact with colonists-settlers from German lands. Sources from this era attest to the intensity of these processes: the peasants identify themselves as Polish-speaking, an intelligible, more or less common language, and on the other side are located what Poles refer to as the 'mutes,' [Pol.: *niemi*] that is, the migrants, who speak a foreign, unintelligible language, who socially stick together, cooperate, yet also compete with the 'locals' for the same resources, in time for domination, for a place in the symbolic and material hierarchy. There is a struggle for the primacy of language, its place in church services and sermons. The Church, the Polish episcopate, and some religious orders (the literate) feel obliged to stand up for the Polish language. This is undoubtedly a time of cultural and political conflict in this area. In such a context, a certain awareness of the Slavic community, a sense of it, and a desire to tell oneself a familiar origin story (the story of the 3 brothers) naturally persists. It is also worth adding that while at that time there was a strong political rivalry between the Piast and Přemyslid (Czech Bohemian) dynasties, with the apparent dominance of the latter, there was no such sense of any fundamental political national conflict with the eastern Rus principalities at the end of the 13th century. At the time, it was easy to imagine 'Rus' such as it then existed, as the brother of the Polish 'Lech.'

Further south, in the east, the settlements of Slavic tribes were organized into a political structure by Rus (I will say more about them in a moment). The center of this structure was on the Dnieper River in modern-day Kyiv, that is, far to the east of the places where the state of the first Piasts was formed. In fact, the lands of the first Christian Piast ruler, Mieszko did not extend much beyond the Vistula River which flows through Warsaw. Thus, over a thousand kilometers separated the original Polish capital of Gniezno from the city of Kyiv We should remember that it is only in the later part of the first Mieszko's reign that the region of 'Little Poland' (Pol.:

Jan Długosz (Coat of Arms: 'Wieniawa' 1415–1480), the eminent chronicler and author of *Annales seu cronicae incliti Regni Poloniae* in his workshop as rendered according to the artistic vision of the Krakow painter Antoni Gramatyka, a pupil of the celebrated artist Jan Matejko.

Małopolska) around the city of Krakow, was incorporated into the state of the first Piasts. Nevertheless, we recognize the region around Krakow as indigenously Polish, also historically. In those days the region 'Little Poland' covered the territory of today's Krakow and also the present-day Subcarpathian region or voivodeship centered around the city of Rzeszow.

Jan Długosz a tutor to the sons of the then King of Poland, Casimir Jagiellonian, had a different variation on the tale of the 'founding brothers' one in which Rus was not a brother, arriving on the scene later and in not such a friendly guise. He thus gave the temporal and geopolitical distance between Poland's origins and its eastern neighbor Rus, a different, intriguing expression. A kind of political lesson. According to Długosz, the descendants of Lech, the first Poles. lived modestly and with simplicity under the rule of the Lechitic dynasty. A dynasty that allegedly in Długosz's tale preceded the Piast dynasty. When that Lechitic dynasty expired, 'dignitaries and nobles' were said to have met at a rally near Gniezno, abolished the monarchy, established new laws, and elected 12 men entrusted with power in the country. According to the fable, the Poles 'freed from the princely yoke would now stand on the side of liberty and freedom mindful of their former oppression. Submitting their lives to the whims of a new absolute ruler would henceforth by no means be allowed.' [...] According to Długosz the Poles rightly decided to base their new political system on freedom on liberty and rights enshrined in law. Firm in the conviction that it was better to obey laws than to instead obey the whims of kings. Their new fabled Republic would have grown happier if they had been able to protect and preserve their newly won freedom. However, the newly liberated Poles he writes, quickly began to abuse their freedom, disputes and tribal conflicts broke out between the chieftains (oligarchs) between them and the people. The neighboring lands around Poland took advantage of this internal weakness, invading and ravaging the country of the Lechites. It was then, according to Długosz's chronology, that 'Rus' entered the arena of our history. While the Poles were fighting a civil war among themselves, as well as external wars with neighbors, the Rus state arose and grew in strength. Preoccupied with their republican concept of freedom, the Poles did not notice that during their moment of weakness, a strong and threatening neighbor was emerging in the east. The answer to this challenge was the appointment of a new monarch, the fictional Krak. To cope with both the internal turmoil and the difficult neighbors from the west but also to face down this new Rus threat from the east. The new Polish monarchy thus created by Krak was based on the rule of law on the law given by Krak to his subjects, yet it was a legal system that also placed limits and counter obligations on Krak the ruler.

The lesson for Poles from this revised origin tale from Długosz was this, if we focus too much on our personal freedoms and their assurance, we can overlook the emergence of serious geopolitical threats. In this case, on our eastern border, this theme would still echo strongly in Polish political

According to the tale of the chronicler Master Wincenty (often referred to as 'Kadłubek'), Prince Krak was a brave warrior. For his bravery in his mythologized fight against the Gauls, the forebearers of the Poles elected him king, and the city of Krakow was named after him. Krak, bassed on an engraving from 1554.

debate in the inter-war years of the 20th-century. Długosz, who brought his chronicle up to the threshold of the 1480s, almost to the time of his death, noted in the final pages of his text the tremendous growth of Moscow's power. He does not call it Russia, but precisely Moscow or 'Muscovy'. In that entity he already perceives a powerful rival, and future enemy that could threaten the Polish Kingdom.

So, when we try to weigh up whether this 'Polish-Russian' or even 'Lechitic-Rus' neighborhood was a historically significant fact already from the beginning of our history, regardless of whether the neighbor was Rus, Slavic, or someone else altogether, we can see already this ambiguity in these very first accounts of Polish historians. Ambiguity, though of a different kind, is also visible at the turn of the 12th and 13th centuries in the more mythical yet no less instructive writings of the chronicler Wincenty called 'Kadłubek' (ca. 1150–1223) a lawyer and Bishop of Krakow. His writing rich in historical factuality also contain episodical accounts of a clearly fictional nature. At a time when cultural and political relations with the neighboring Rus entity, an ever-closer neighbor with whom disputes over land were becoming a regular occurrence, Master Wincenty curiously did not write about Rus, the lands at that time centered around Kyiv. For Wincenty (Kadłubek) Rus was not a factor for the genesis of Polish statehood. On the other hand, he is the first to introduce the notion of the proud 'Lech' and the invincible nation of the Lechites (the alleged Polish forefathers), who are ready to face down any power. The historian presents this vision of Polish origin; not as defined by one man a monarch, as in Gallus Anonymus account, and not merely as a state but as something far broader in scope. A brave nation, one that is the master of its own destiny.

In Master Wincenty's narrative, there is a clear emphasis on the anti-imperial tradition of Polish statehood. The essence of this narrative is the defense of liberty and the invincibility of the proud Lechite nation. I want to remind you that the legends cited by Wincenty, though they have often been ridiculed, have coherent and thoughtful eloquence. The many fictionalized accounts serve to underscore the author's conviction that the Polish nation represented above all liberty. The chronicler talks for example about the 'battles' of the Lechites (Polish forefathers) with the Gauls, with the Parthians, there are also fables of confrontations with the legions of

Julius Caesar, and finally even with Alexander the Great himself. What is important instructive even is not of course the veracity of these tales but in the manner in which they are told and the symbolism within them. Perhaps the most intriguing and instructive tale is that depicted by a letter quoted by Master Wincenty describing the fictionalized response of the Lechites to Alexander the Great who has sent his envoys to collect tribute from the Lechite community. Their answer to him is sharp, graphic, yet also instructive for our journey and the recurring themes in this book:

"'Are you only emissaries/delegates or are you also questors/administrators of the royal treasury? They answered: "We are both delegates and questors." To this, the Lechites replied: "Then first, we must show our most sincere respect to the delegates, so that we may honor those magnificently received with equally magnificent gifts. Then to the questors, we must pay the appointed tribute/their due. For one must render to Caesar the things that are Caesar's so that we do make any undue affront to His Majesty. Thereupon, the principal emissaries/delegates were seized, their bones broken and torn out from their living flesh. Following this, their skins were stripped from their bodies and stuffed partly with gold, partly with the flimsiest of seaweed. This ore, humanly skinned but inhumanly clothed, was sent back with a letter reading as follows: "To the King of Kings Alexander – from the royal ruler of Poland. It is improper for one to command who does not yet have mastery of himself. For he is not worthy of victorious glory the one over whom his own emotions hold sway. Your own particular desire will never be sated nor find moderation. Moreover, since the limits of your avarice are boundless you will sow your poverty of spirit everywhere. Although the world entire cannot satiate the voracity of your appetite, we ourselves have found the means to somehow satisfy the hunger of at least these your fellows. Now let it be made known to you that we have no leather money pouches/purses; that is why we have put these gifts in the pouches of your most faithful emissaries/delegates. Let it also be made known that the measure of a Pole is not his wealth but by the valor of his spirit and the fortitude of his body. Poles thus possess no source from whence to satisfy the violent voracity of such a great king, nay so great a tyrant/monster. Do not doubt, however, that Poles are imbued in abundance with the true treasures of youth, by means of which they may not merely sate but put an end to the avarice of your character and to you along with it.'"

This letter is worth recollecting as it seems to capture something of the essence of Poland's response throughout the centuries to any tendencies towards empire that ever appeared on its horizon, a response to any imperial, insatiable greed. This letter was not a subtle message to any Rus or Russian empire, for no such aggressive empire of that kind existed at the end of the 12th-century. Still, it is the answer that Wincenty Kadłubek pens in an effort to distill the essence of the Polish national character. We will not let ourselves be ruled by anyone; we will not bow down to any empire. The same characteristic is also referenced by the aforementioned Gallus Anonymus, stating that it is precisely this adherence to liberty enshrined in Krak's succession that distinguishes the Polish state. A state which in its entirety has never been subjugated by anyone.

For now, let us leave aside these somewhat fictionalized tales of the chroniclers and instead focus on actual history as best we know it from the current state of research. On this basis we must confirm that the documented history of Rus is indeed older than that of the Lechitic or Polish state, dating in fact back to the middle of the 9th century. The state of the first Piasts is established nearly a hundred years later in the first half of the 10th century. Let us add, however, that this Polish state-forming initiative came from a native almost certainly Slavic dynasty. This native character of Polish state origin contrasts with the origins of Rus.

Both Gallus Anonymus and later chronicles attest to the names of Mieszko I's four predecessors, to which almost all historians agree today. As late as the 19th century, Franciszek Piekosiński and a few other historians, among them some German revisionists, endeavored to tell an alternative origin history to prove that Mieszko I was in fact of Norman, Danish or indeed Germanic origin. With the exception of a Papal deed called the *Dagome iudex* pointing to another, perhaps a second name for Mieszko, no other traces either archaeological, (with all available sources thoroughly verified) nor traces in any historical documents, exist to support a theory that the original Polish ruling dynasty was of foreign origin. In contrast, it was the representatives of the Piast dynasty who as their state crystalized now repelled non-Slavic external attacks and even made multiple military

Mieszko I – the first Polish ruler to be baptised – embraces a cross with his hand symbolizing his recognition of the Catholic faith. At the same time, he places his foot on a pagan idol. Next to the prince/duke is his Czech wife Dobrawa.

incursions into neighboring lands. Expanding state territory, at the cost of German and other rulers.

Meanwhile, in the case of Rus, the first elements of its statehood, if that term can be applied, are formed some 100 years earlier than the Piast state. This event is clearly the result of the incursion by a foreign power. The Rus state of Kyivan Rus, is in fact the byproduct of this foreign invasion. Norman Viking invaders established it as a means to effectively rule over a conquered local people and the state itself was initially organized for the instrumentalization of this Viking power. The fact that this was not a Slavic initiative is also indisputable for historians. These Scandinavian northern peoples taking advantage of the sea routes from the Baltic to the Black Sea and then onward to the Mediterranean, conquered nearly all of Europe's waterways for trade from the west, east, and south at the time. Those Normans specifically of interest to us here marched (or rather, sailed) across Lake Ilmen near the Baltic Sea, on which the settlement of Veliky Novgorod was then built. Subsequently headed towards the sources of the Dnieper River following its route southwards to the Black Sea coast. The warriors ferried their troops in shallow-bottomed boats floating down rivers and lakes; and in the places where these bodies of water could not sustain them, the boats were simply carried across.

Disputes over the very origin of the name 'Rus' are still not conclusively resolved. Most often, its source is found in the proto-Finnish term for the Swedish tribe: Ruotsi, which, according to some researchers, is supposed to derive from the words 'people who row.' It was from Sweden, from the area of Gotland, whence the tribe who conquered the East Slavic lands and trade routes, was supposed to have come from. Some historians also refer to the Proto-Germanic tribal name of the Rossomans. The historian and co-author of the now influential Eurasianism theory in Putin's Russia, George Vernadsky, links the name of the Rus to the language of the ancient Iranian steppe people, the Alans, among whom the word 'Ruxs' supposedly means 'shining', whence the name Roxolani – 'bright Alans' alluding to the fair hair of the invaders was said to have originated. The Roxolani, on the other hand, is also a name for a Sarmatian tribe. It is to this Sarmatian tradition, that centuries later the Polish nobility will attach themselves. Specifically in the 15th and 16th to set themselves apart from other inhabitants of the Commonwealth. At the same time, the name Roxolan and Roxolanka will be referred to as Ruthenian inhabitants of the Polish Crown lands, including their most famous representative a young woman captured by Turkish forces from the region of Rohatyn, the later beloved wife of Suleyman the Magnificent: Roxelana.

We may never fully untangle this knot of the etymological mystery of 'Rus.' However, we must reiterate that regardless of their name it was these Varangians – the Rossomans or the Rus, definitively a non-Slavic tribal group, who dominated the eastern north-south trade route from the Baltic to the Black Sea. Moreover, they laid the foundations for the political community of the eastern Slavs already in the middle of the 9th century. The earliest Ruthenian chronicle, known as the *Novel of Bygone Years* or *Nestor's Primary Chronicle* (written in the 11th century), depicts the beginnings of this political community as the result of a request addressed by the Slavic inhabitants of the area to their Scandinavian overlords: 'Our land is great and abundant, and yet there is no order in it. Come, therefore, to govern and rule over us.' This is indeed an important distinction when compared to the foundations of the Polish state which is the result of actions by an indigenous dynasty, a part of that society over which it claimed to rule and later came to organize. One can read from Gallus Anonymus, from *the Chronicle of Greater Poland*, but especially from Jan Długosz, a literal once again fabled description outlining the birth of this first indigenous Polish dynasty. 'After Popiel, who was eaten by mice, came Piast – a simple burgher from the town of Kalisz, or perhaps a peasant chosen according to the typical peasant rite'. The anointment of this commoner to become ruler of the new Polish state allegedly came about after the miraculous intervention of two messengers who stood in Piast's humble dwelling and signaled him out as a proper, worthy successor to the unworthy precursor Popiel. These two heavenly messengers bore the names of John and Paul. Perhaps this founding myth also had relevance for Karol Wojtyła when he made his choice of papal name after his election as Pope in 1978?

In any case, insofar as the Piast dynasty was made up of 'locals,' or 'our kin' – in Rus, the state would have its roots more in foreign conquest. The initial primary objective being profits from control over trade rather than any strict state organization and development. This center of the Slavs on the Dnieper River, inhabited by the East Slavic tribe of the Polans, was located in the 9th century on the vital trade route *iz Variag w Grieki* (i.e. of the Varangians – from the warlike Scandinavians of the Baltic Sea – to the Greeks, that is, to Byzantium). From 862, one can already speak of the formation of a Rus state and structures when the Scandinavian Varangian chieftain Rurik captured the northern regions of the East Slavic settlement zone (Veliky Novgorod would arise there). Then his successor (from 879), Oleg, subjugated the entire trade route south down to the Black Sea for his followers, with a central station at Kyiv on the Dnieper River (captured in 882). Like other nomadic empires of the Eurasian steppe, it was called a khaganate.

With the help of his Scandinavian followers, Oleg conquered more East Slavic tribes, narrowing the gap that initially separated the Rus Khaganate from the seats of the Western Slavs. He conquered the strategically important settlement of Smolensk in the north and made an expedition to Constantinople, from where he left at the price of a ransom together with a trade treaty favorable to the Rus Khaganate. Subsequent rulers of the Rus khaganate, Igor (912–945), his wife Olga, and his son Svyatoslav (945–972) continued this line of conquests. Svyatoslav suppressed the revolts of the Polesya Drevani and also conquered land in the north in 966 the territory of the Viatichi tribe, living in the basin of the Oka and Moskva Rivers, the area where the current Russian capital lies. Interestingly, these Viatichi were called Lakhs by the first Russian chronicler Nestor and were considered to be Slavs, not of eastern but western origin, a fact that also seems to be confirmed by recent genetic studies of their burial artifacts, showing the Central European features of their genotype. Were then the Lakhs of the Moskva River in fact genetic brothers, or at least close relations of the Poles? Conquered and annexed to the emerging East Slavic empire in 966? Yet another fascinating story of origin? A story this time of Polish-Moscow historical links? Like Oleg and Igor, the later Svyatoslav also conducted unsuccessful sacking expeditions against Byzantium, even temporarily moving the capital of his state from Kyiv to the Danube area.

The objective of these Norman conquerors was to get south towards the true center of Eurasian civilization at the time. For we must understand that the wealthiest civilizations also in terms of culture in the 9th to 10th centuries were by no means located in the west of Europe. It was instead to be found in Byzantium. The Roman world of Latin material and spiritual culture seemed at that time rather rudimentary and crude in comparison with the direct descendent of Imperial Rome's glory and the legacy of Greeks, the Byzantine civilization. A Byzantium that stood in direct competition to Baghdad's then Abbasid caliphate, a recently established yet flourishing state. It was these centers that focused the attention, the plundering and/or commercial appetites of the Varangians/Rus.

Prior to the arrival of the Normans or Scandinavians in the future seats of the Eastern Slavs, there had been two more powerful state organizations – or khaganates (khanates). In the middle of the 6th century, the Avars had appeared in eastern Europe, these people spread and reached as far as the central plain of the continent and were only beaten back by Charlemagne (747–814). After the Avars came the second pre-Rus organization the Khazars. Another people of Central Asian origin, who came to settle in the area between the Volga and the Don Rivers. What is vital in the history of the Khazars, who consolidated and maintained their state for at least 300 years until the beginning of the 11th century, now as a neighbor to Rus, is that the Khazars adopted (as the only state in the world) the Mosaic religion as their ruling religion. Most of the population, of course, was not of Jewish origin. However, with the intermediation of Jewish merchants fleeing persecution first from Persia and then later from Byzantium under Emperor Leo III (680–741), in the mighty merchant emporium created by the Khazars on the lower Volga River, on the shores of the Caspian Sea, this religion Mosaism [named after Moses, a variation of Judaism – *ed. note*] became the ruling religion. The Khazars expanded westward toward the Black Sea, coming into contact with the eastern Slavs. To the north of their state was the Kamsk or Volga Bulgars' khaganate, whose rulers, in contrast, adopted the Muslim faith, which was then undergoing a period of extraordinarily rapid expansion, both culturally and geopolitically.

The battle-scarred Prince Svyatoslav of the Rus tried to sack Constantinople several times – without success. He did, however, accomplish two other very critical military feats. First, he struck Khazaria (956/966), and though he did not completely destroy this state he weakened it severely. Yet Khazaria, however unpleasant a neighbor it was, (living off the trade in Slavic slaves) actually shielded Rus from something potentially more dangerous still: the Great Steppe beyond the Volga, from where successive waves of aggressors and conquerors had traditionally attacked from, out of Asia. The opening of the Great Steppe due to the destruction of Khazaria (eventually in the mid-11th century) would mark a significant turn in history. As from now on, the Rus lands and its neighbors in the west would have no Khazarian bulwark to guard against the effects of successive migrations of Asian nomads from Asia's Great Steppe to the west. Moscow and latterly the Russian Empire would much later become the first political entity to reverse this migration direction; starting in the 16th–17th centuries, reversing a millennial old tide of nomadic expansion. In what was a seismic turning point for Asia as it developed its land empire from west to east, deep into Asia, and eventually all the way to the Pacific.

Ruthenia or Rus, notably, was already expanding southward into the area of today's Balkans, the Danube area, where in the following centuries, it would lead one of the most significant geopolitical directions of expansion towards Constantinople through the areas inhabited by the southern Slavs. It was here that for the first time, the Eastern Slavs come into direct contact with the Southern Slavs, the peoples we identify today as Bulgarians or Serbs, among others, people with whom they would share a common alphabet. So, in this respect, too, it was a critical movement, which additionally had great direct significance for relations between Rus and emerging Poland, the state of the first Piasts.

After a betrayal by the Pechenegs and the death of Svyatoslav, Rus lost any realistic chance to conquer Constantinople. Subsequent battles for the throne of the Grand Duke were eventually won by Svyatoslav's younger son, Vladimir, who had settled in Veliky Novgorod. This was that same Vladimir or as he is known in Ukrainian "Volodymyr" who is feted both in Ukraine and in the Russian Federation, as the historical father of Eastern Slav state then in its Kyivan cradle. He reunited Veliky Novgorod near modern-day St Petersburg with Kyiv and sought to expand the trade routes leading south, where his father had already reached. He also struck against the Cherven settlements, an area that can be identified with villages stretching along the upper Bug River to the San, from today's Parczew and Chełm in the north to Sanok in the south. A relatively narrow strip of land yet one that was particularly important for east-west trade. The town of Cherven itself is identified today with the fortified settlement and studied by archaeologists in the village of Czermno in the Tomaszów district, a dozen or so kilometers from the Ukrainian border. This place is of significance as it constitutes the first record of direct relations between Rus and inhabitants of lands we associate with the state of the first Polish Piast rulers. Moreover, the geographical line of conflict broadly corresponds with the modern-day southeastern border of the Polish state.

The Rus chronicler Nestor recorded in the year 981: 'Vladimir or Volodymyr went towards the Lakhs and seized their strongholds: Przemyśl, Cherven and other strong points, which are under Rus to this day.' Nestor,

A picture symbolizing the early Viking origins of the original Rus State, the leader of the Varangian troop, the progenitor of the Rurik dynasty – Prince Rurik in Staraya Ladoga close to modern day St. Petersburg. He is accompanied by his brothers Syneus and Truvor. Painting by Viktor M. Vasnetsov.

who, from his entire narrative, clearly disliked the Lakhs, stated unequivocally that the Rus Prince seized the strongholds of the 'Lakhs.' So, this starting point, in the first historical record, the Rus side is undoubtedly one of an attack against the Lakhs or Poles and the pillaging of their strongholds – Przemyśl and Cherven. At this time in 981, we should note, that these lands were most likely not yet formally united with Mieszko's expanding state but were actually under Czech (Czech-Moravian) rule, like much of today's southern Poland in those years. This rule, however, would recede rather quickly and it seemed forever (returning only in a hybrid form with Habsburg participation in the partition of Poland in 1772). That is why the date of 981 could be considered the beginning of a long-lasting territorial

The Ruthenian prince Sviatoslav son of the Kyivan princess Olga, receives a weapon. Painting by Boris Olshansky 'The Trial (appraisal) of Svyatoslav – the donation of arms'.

dispute over the border between Poland and the Slavic nations to the east, initially Rus, latterly as a new eastern Slave state in the form of Moscow and ultimately Russia. Much of this disputed territory would, many centuries later be absorbed into The Soviet Union as part of Western Ukraine.

Thus, we see the echo of the ancient in the modern period of living historical memory. During the Stalinist period, that dictator's rule of thumb had been simple. Everything that was ever historically Rus meant it was Russian, and everything Russian meant Soviet, and so it was inevitable that these lands had to be taken. As an interesting aside in the historiographical records of the post-WWII People's Republic of Poland, a state that was of course subordinate to Moscow, attempts were made for a while to promote the rather far-fetched, indeed fairytale like Kremlin interpretation that Prince Vladimir, had come into possession of these borderland strongholds 'as a guest and ally, as a friend to the Piasts'.

Abandoning these dubious historical ideas, let us state for the moment this much: the entire disputed area between the Piast and Rurik states was not an especially large territory. Certainly, it did not merit being a starting point for centuries of conflict. Instead, it was a dispute over a small elongated swathe of land, and just as such disputes usually do, it also encompassed emotions of inter-'unneighborly' hostility. After all, this was certainly not a geopolitical dispute to the death. It was not an area that Poland or Rus depended on for existence or that either state especially prioritized. Yes, it was a material component of the economic activity of both countries. The area concerned a trade route that strengthened contacts from the south along the eastern slopes of the Carpathian Mountains to the European colonial city-states (Italian and Greek) that had been appearing on the northern shore of the Black Sea. However, this local dispute between neighbors was quickly followed by an increase in the pace of action. As early as 1018 when Mieszko's successor, the Polish ruler Bolesław the Brave (Pol.: *Bolesław Chrobry*) (967–1025) recaptured the Cherven Cities, having earlier installed on the throne in Kyiv Iziaslav, the elder son of the now deceased (1015) St. Volodymyr the Great. According to legend, Bolesław the Brave ushered Iziaslav into Kyiv as its new ruler by striking and notching his sword against the Golden Gate of the great city.

Bolesław the Brave deserved the title of Great, and we Poles often fail to give him his due. However, the most important fact for the purpose of this book is that he apparently illustrated no desire to involve Poland more deeply or dynastically in Rus affairs. Yes, he left Iziaslav on the throne and took out massive amounts of treasure from Kyiv as 'compensation', as Gallus Anonymus eagerly points out. However, his only objective in terms of territorial achievement was to reconquer the Cherven Cities, as 'what is ours and what has to be ours.' As for the fate of Kyiv, it was already to be decided among themselves by the candidates for Kyiv's rule from the Rurykovich family. The ruler of Gniezno (Poland's first capital) may have been the 'playmaker' in this rivalry, but he certainly did not intend to conquer or annex Rus to his state.

This feeling existed that the Poles were separate and the Rus had already developed a strong cultural and political identity in their own right. There was no question of a potential smooth unification: neither by conquest nor by a political or marriage-based union. At the beginning of the 11th century, Bolesław the Brave and his opponents or counterparties on the other side, the rulers of the Rus principalities, never envisaged an outcome in which there would be any such unification or union. This attitude made itself known, as it were, soon after by Rus. When the Piasts experienced a monarchical crisis under Mieszko II, son and successor of Bolesław. As it turned out the nascent Polish society could not bear the tremendous strain placed upon it by the astonishing logistics of Bolesław's military campaigns. These ranged from the lands of Luzyce and Milsko where the Elbe River flows to as far east as Kyiv on the Dnieper River, in just one year. Following Bolesław's death, as is well known to Poles, there followed the so-called pagan, or popular revolt in Poland. One that developed into a countrywide crisis in which Poland's neighbors from the east were also actively complicit. In Kyiv, Yaroslav, called the Wise, another son of Vladimir the Great, and a man who had now in turn usurped Bolesław's puppet, Iziaslav. Yaroslav eager to weaken The Polish state, which had so imperiously triumphed over Rus 13 years earlier, now supported Bezprym, Mieszko II's half-brother, as an alternative candidate for the Polish crown, in 1031.

However, the interesting thing is that this intervention by Rus, which increased the difficulties of the Polish state, was followed just seven years later by a reverse intervention. The same Yaroslav the Wise now sent actual military support to a new Polish King Casimir, 'the Restorer' (Pol.: *Odnowiciel*), a son of Mieszko II who ruled from 1016 till 1058. The Prince of Rus thus helped Casimir to rebuild the Polish state. For he in turn had no intention of seizing more than a piece of frontier land, the so-called Cherven settlements. Why? He perhaps recognized that the Piast state served a useful role in maintaining the balance of power beyond the Rus Khaganate's western border. In any case, a viable Polish state on one's border was preferable to the chaos that would have ensued in the event of a complete collapse of the achievements of Mieszko and Bolesław. He, therefore, supported the rebuilding of Poland at this point in time. Truthfully a somewhat diminished, and weakened version, but still a Polish Piast state separate from Rus. Yaroslav provided very effective assistance to Casimir the Restorer, who was also supported at that time by the Emperor, the German king, incidentally his very close relative (via his mother Richeza, who was a sister of Otto III).

Master Wincenty known as 'Kadłubek', bishop of Krakow, eminent historiographer and a blessed of the Catholic Church – rendering based on a 19th-century engraving.

A weakened Poland would present no rival to its Teutonic neighbors. As a buffer, though, it could be helpful to the emperor just as it would be for Rus. Moreover, Poland and Rus were by then neighboring states with close to a hundred years of relations. They shared many cultural and linguistic similarities yet possessed distinct national identities and differing political origins. Neither could thus conceptualize the thought of replacing or conquering the other.

Let us remember here, of course, the disproportion of forces. At this time, around 1050, Rus had between 4 to 8 million inhabitants, according to various estimates. Poland, afflicted by terrible defeats and internal strife from the pagan revolt, had a population that certainly did not exceed one million inhabitants. Rus was thus a much more populous country. Kyiv was at that time, one of the largest cities in Europe, with a population of about 40,000. Larger than either Paris or London in the 11th century. Its prosperity was based on the hugely profitable trade between Asia and Europe, in particular with Constantinople and the Abbasid caliphate's Muslim rulers.

Despite this disparity, however, a belief was forming that these two countries, the two centers of statehood, although occasionally disputing borders, were mutually sovereign. They were in this sense, equal. The later disintegration of the Rus state after the death of Yaroslav the Wise (1054) into an ever-increasing number of rival principalities would laterly offset this disparity. The energy with which a new Bolesław, the Generous (Pol.: *Szczodry* or *Śmiały*) (ca. 1042–1081 or 1082) returned to the military-led expansionist policy of his earlier namesake was to be a reminder in 1069 and later in 1077, of the ambitions and potential of the Piast state. In these years that Polish king twice visited Kyiv, at the head of a military force, each time with the aim of installing a Prince on the throne there. One whom he supported from among the now many internal rivals of the Rus princely families. While, by the by, taking liberty with the treasury of the Rus capital… This same monarch recaptured Przemyśl and (possibly) also the Cherven settlements. However, his second expedition to Kyiv and somewhat prolonged (reportedly also debauched) stay there ended unhappily for Bolesław the Generous. Upon his return to his capital Krakow, there was a violent dispute between the king and Bishop Stanisław of Szczepanów. As is well known to all Poles the Bishop was accused of treason and killed on the orders of the King. This led to outrage across Poland and indeed Europe-wide. The result was a tragedy for King Bolesław, also known as the Bold (*Śmiały*), and for the Polish state. Bolesław was forced into exile. His younger brother Władysław Herman now oversaw another defeat to the Rus principalities and loss of the Cherven settlements and Przemyśl, for a prolonged period. Though they will never fall out of their circle of interest and under future Polish rulers this land will be reclaimed.

When speaking of the first territorial disputes, I have not so far mentioned perhaps the most critical issue of all for the historical relations of

Bolesław Chrobry at the Golden Gate during his entry into Kyiv in 1018. The 19th-century painting by Wincenty Smokowski does not accurately reflect the reality of the 11th century; this gate did not yet exist at that time, moreover Bolesław's followers are clad in plate armor (a much later development), while the Polish ruler himself holds in his hand… a sabre popular in Poland only since the 16th century.

Poland with its eastern neighbors, the issue of religion. This is because the importance of religion for a whole host of disputes for Polish-Rus and later Polish-Russian relations actually develops only gradually; it does not make itself known at once. This dispute regarding the respective religious faiths, Catholic and Orthodox, adopted respectively by the rulers of Poland and Rus will prove to be key in time but not immediately. In 966 (or 965), Mieszko is baptized with his entourage. Over the next few decades under his reign, his son Bolesław and his grandson Mieszko II adhere to a steady process of Christianization, moving down through the Polish social hierarchies. Despite the protests of pagans in the years following, Christianity is after a time accepted unequivocally throughout Poland: in its Latin version.

We should recall that the schism, the final split between the Roman Church and the Orthodox Christian church of Byzantium, the Patriarchate of Constantinople, would not occur until 1054. So, some 50 or 60 years earlier at the end of the 10th century, for the rulers of Poland and Rus, there was still essentially one Church: from the shores of the Atlantic and the North Sea to the Dniester River and the Black Sea. Although there are, of course, significant cultural and ritual differences within it. However, it will soon become clear that the difference in rituals, rites and perhaps above all, the sources from which Christianity and religious authority would be drawn will be of great importance in the future. Mieszko's Christianity drew on sources from the West for himself and future Poles from papal Rome, via Czechia, Germany, the Italian & German monks even it seems some Irish; the Polish road to Christianity and baptism in the faith would always lead west and south to the waters of the Tiber, to the Vatican.

Rus, on the other hand, chose differently. This choice was described by the chronicler Nestor in the year 988. Prince Volodymyr now decides 22 years after Mieszko I to adopt one of the great monotheistic religions, finally giving up the paganism of his Scandinavian cohorts. He chooses from among four options: the Jewish religion, with which he neighbors to the southeast (Khazaria); the Muslim faith, with which he neighbors to the northeast (the Volga Bulgarians); to the south, Byzantium offers in turn an Orthodox version of Christianity. Yet Latin missions have also already reached Kyiv. In 961 and 962, Bishop Adalbert of Prague was hosted there, and then more Latin missions appeared. Let's add that in 1006/1007, Bishop Reinbern of Kołobrzeg also came to the Dnieper River. (Kołobrzeg or Kolberg in German, became part of the Polish ecclesiastical organization established in 1000 at the Congress of Gniezno; the bishopric lasted however only until 1015). Then St. Bruno of Querfurt arrived in Kyiv, also sent by the Polish state and church organization. He tried to convert not so much the Rus as they had already formally accepted baptism, but the aforementioned Pechenegs, who were neighboring them to the south.

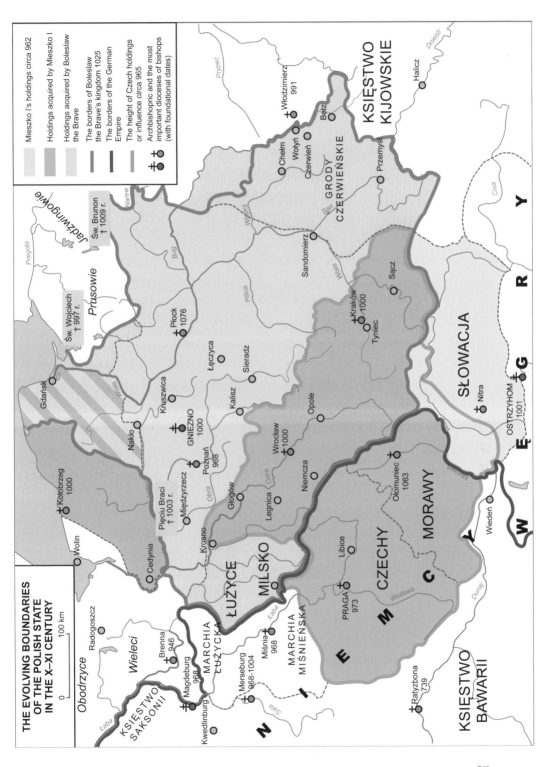

THE EVOLVING BOUNDARIES
OF THE POLISH STATE
IN THE X–XI CENTURY

0   100 km

Mieszko I's holdings circa 962

Holdings acquired by Mieszko I

Holdings acquired by Bolesław
the Brave

The borders of Bolesław
the Brave's kingdom 1025

The borders of the German
Empire

The height of Czech holdings
or influence circa 965

Archbishopric and the most
important dioceses of bishops
(with foundational dates)

KSIĘSTWO
KIJOWSKIE

Dniestr

Halicz

Prypeć

Włodzimierz
991

Bełz

Chełm

Wołyń

Czerwień

Przemyśl

GRODY
CZERWIEŃSKIE

San

Cisa

Narew

Wkra

Bug

Sandomierz

Wisła

Sącz

Kraków
1000

Tyniec

SŁOWACJA

Nitra

OSTRZYHOM
1001

Św. Brunon
† 1009 r.

Jadźwingowie

Pregoła

Prusowie

Św. Wojciech
† 997 r.

Płock
1076

Łęczyca

Sieradz

Pilica

Kalisz

Opole

Gdańsk

Wisła

Kruszwica

GNIEZNO
1000

Poznań
968

Wrocław
1000

Niemcza

Ołomuniec
1063

MORAWY

Wiedeń

Nakło

Kołobrzeg
1000

Pięciu Braci
† 1003 r.

Międzyrzecz

Głogów

Legnica

Obra

Odra

CZECHY

Libice

Morawa

Dunaj

Wolin

Cedynia

Krosno

ŁUŻYCE

MILSKO

PRAGA
973

Wełtawa

KSIĘSTWO
BAWARII

Ratyzbona
739

Radogoszcz

Wieleci

Brenna
946

Magdeburg
968

MARCHIA
ŁUŻYCKA

Miśnia
968

Merseburg
968-1004

MARCHIA
MIŚNIEŃSKA

Łaba

Sala

Obodrzyce

Łaba

KSIĘSTWO
SAKSONII

Kwedlinburg

Volodymyr eventually opted, and this is significant, for the Orthodox version of Christianity offered by Byzantium a choice that would later carry all the way to Moscow when that city was established over 160 years later. He was baptized, it is believed, on the shores of Crimea before returning to Kyiv to oversee the baptism of his family and then the wider population. Imagine what would have happened if Rus had chosen as its religion – Islam or – Judaism. The world's fate, and indeed Rus' relations with its immediate western neighbors, would have evolved quite differently. Poland with a substantial Islamic neighbor, just across the Bug River, from the beginning of the 11th century? Or perhaps a Poland neighboring a sovereign empire of the Mosaic religion while simultaneously hosting in future centuries the largest diaspora of Jews in Europe west of the Dnieper. Prince Volodymyr considered all these possibilities seriously, including the option of taking the model of Christianity from the emissaries of Latin Rome. How different the unneighborly relationship between the Western Slavs (Poland) and the Eastern Slavs (Russia) would have been: one religion, one culture, one broadly similar linguistic neighborhood. At most, there would have remained a dispute over some borderlands. Yet Rus chose Orthodoxy, the Christianity of Byzantium as the most attractive option available. It was an offer of rapid spiritual advancement. The alphabet created especially for the Slavs by the Thessalonian brothers, Cyril and Methodius, accepted in the Christian mission by Byzantium, now facilitates and accelerates the development of an indigenous literature in native Rus language forms. In the Piast state, in contrast, Latin will be the language of high culture and writing. However, this factor will also closely link Polish cultural development to what we broadly refer to as the European model providing a common language of communication including for the communication of ideas and laws. Rus will be separated to some extent from this development, by the choice made by Volodymyr in 988. The Polish-Rus border will become the border not only of two states but of two increasingly distinct cultures spiritually and politically. Two civilizations, based respectively on Byzantium and Rome, Orthodox and Catholic, Latin and Cyrillic. As a result, both states will experience and process the Renaissance era including the traditions and norms that flow from it quite differently.

As we have already mentioned, the symbolic date of the split in the Christian church is taken as 1054, although contemporary commentators of the event did not yet see any reason to talk in terms of a schism. There was not yet the pervading sense of absolute alienation between the two branches of the faith, especially in the 'Lechitic-Rus' borderland. There was (and in some way still remains) a sense of ritual distinctiveness cultivated from the beginning primarily by the Orthodox hierarchy. The first Orthodox monastery to be established on Rus soil was the Kyiv-Pechersk Lavra, or, as we would translate it, the Kyiv Monastery of the Caves. This holy monastery of Rus and later Russian Orthodoxy (during Putin's current war with Ukraine we could perhaps simply call it FSB Orthodoxy) has perpetuated a written tradition from the dawn of its history and an unusually strong sense of "otherness" from the Latin tradition. It was here that the first texts in the Rus language were written, reinforcing the Orthodox-based identity of the Rus, and fostering the sentiment that the main threat to this new faith could be that of 'Latinism' as represented by the 'Lakhs' or Poles subservient to it. The immediate neighbors to the west. As early as the end of the 11th century there are records of dreams of pious monks, in which Satan himself haunts them in the form of a 'Lakh'. Centuries later in Poland defenders of the Catholic faith would conjure up similar dreams of the devil who would appear in 'Lutheran hose (leggings)' or in 'German frock coats'. This over tracing of anthropological divides with additional religious divisions would create a shared experience of inter-unneighborly distrust and disdain facilitating future outbreaks of violence.

This was especially the case after the Fourth Crusade of 1204, which resulted in western crusaders' sacking of Byzantium, the capital of the Orthodox world, desecrating its symbols and carrying off its treasures.

It is worth noting the characteristic viewpoint on the Polish side with regard to the drawing of religious, or rather denominational, borders. Here we can reference a letter written in 1147 by the then Bishop of Krakow, Matthew. A letter, written in response to an appeal by St. Bernard of Clairvaux. Bernard had made a call to the Polish princes that they take part in the Second Crusade against the Moslems occupying the Holy Land. Matthew in turn crafted an exceptionally richly argued letter in response. It was lavishly laced with ancient erudition, references to Ovid, and Horace, among others. A letter giving evidence of an education resulting from the choice of Rome as the center of spiritual identity for Poland. However, he did not write merely to show off his learned background before his Pope and peers. He wrote to put forward the idea of another great mission that Poland could perhaps undertake, one to the east towards Rus. This spiritual mission was linked to his harsh assessment of the spiritual state of the Rus' neighbors. *Gens illa Ruthenica, multitudine innumerabili ceu sideribus adaequata* [...] *verae religionis instituta non-servat* [...] *Ruthenia quasi est alter orbis* (This Rus nation, with its innumerable numbers, comparable to the stars [...], does not observe the regulations of the true faith. [Rus is like another world]). This other, Rus world is 'permeated with an utterly heretical perversity'; it 'confesses Christ in name only, while in its deeds it completely renounces Him; it does not want to be compatible with either the Latin or the Greek Church, but to be something apart, and separate from both.' This dramatic vision of Bishop Matthew is not just a literary image for its own sake it is an affirmation of duty to the mission. Where does this idea of spiritual conquest of a neighboring but 'other world' come from? Did Bernard of Clairvaux himself impose it in his original appeal?

Nevertheless, in the end, Bishop Matthew apparently accepts it. He appears to hint that Poland could be helpful in such a mission, indeed perhaps it could be Poland's vocation because we are also Slavs. Like the Czechs, we inhabit the same 'icy zone' as Rus. However, to undertake this mission, the inhabitants of this Latin periphery, the western part of this icy zone, needed a more substantial tangible presence of the light and warmth coming from the center of Latin civilization. This last word is not abused here. It perhaps best expresses the rhetorical significance of the invitation that Matthew's letter finally addresses to St. Bernard himself: 'Deign, therefore, dear father, you who have illuminated other countries and bring light to our darkness; deign to instruct the unlettered Slavs in the way of customs and principles of life; deign to make Your presence known in the icy zone, so that [...] the terrible cold of the north be tempered by the breath of the south wind and the flame of the Volcano soften it, so that the unrepentant barbarism may find salvation in Your teachings, so that the uncultured people by Your skill may be placated, so that under the grace and guidance of the Lord they may be subdued.'

The Grand Prince of Rus, Volodymyr The Great, is being baptised. Visible on the left is the Byzantine princess Anna Porphyrogenita, sister of Emperor Basil II and fiancée of the Ruthenian prince. Fresco by Viktor Vasnetsov from St Volodomyr's Cathedral in Kyiv.

Poland, directly bordering this Rus 'otherworld', connected to it by a common geography, Slavic origins, and climate, is called to (or at any rate, could be called to) a great spiritual, civilizing mission in the East. However, Bishop Matthew's letter betrays a lack of conviction that Poland could carry out such a mission independently. He seems to assert that Poland still lacks a sense of its own power in this regard. Instead, it is a manifesto of cultural Occidentalism, a conviction that Poland needs to lean on the West or, more precisely, as we see it, the warm South perhaps directly the Southwest of Rome. To be able to undertake this challenge beyond our eastern border in the icy East, we must first be well fortified by this Latin Southwest, drawing strength from Rome, Monte Cassino, Clairvaux. Then Poland can transform the Rus otherworld and bring it closer to ours.

Meanwhile, a more significant chill was blowing from the East from the depths of the Asian steppe. A tragic time was approaching, especially in the history of Rus, the time of the Mongol invasion. When the first expedition of Genghis Khan's empire fell on Rus in 1223, the latter was divided into many quarrelling principalities. Although it tried to unite forces, Rus could not stand against the invaders from Asia. In 1238–1240, these lands finally succumbed to a terrible *pogrom* by Mongol armies. The harsh rule of the descendants of Genghis Khan, precursors of the so-called Golden Horde, now ruling over all of Rus, western Siberia, and part of present-day Kazakhstan, served to further isolate Rus from developments in Western European civilization. Although the Mongols also defeated the Polish and European knights at the battle of Legnica and ravaged the lands of the Piasts more than once, the associated cost in military losses against the better-prepared and resolute forces of the Poles and Hungarians meant that the Mongols never imposed their occupation over Polish or Hungarian territory. There was devastation but never subjugation. In contrast, the occupation, or at any rate, the Mongol (later called Tatar) sovereignty over the Rus lands, lasted as long as 250 years. Twice as long as the Partitions of Poland did and such a long period of subjugation would leave an indelible mark on Rus.

Yet this Mongol rule was just as recently as the last century referred to as 'blessed' by perhaps the most famous Russian historian of the last four decades, the late Lev Gumilyov. The son of the great Russian poet Anna

Akhmatova. A man who spent 25 years in the gulags, where he became the great renewer of 'Eurasianism', an important ideological trend in Russian thought, initially inaugurated in exile in the years 1920–1921. It is an ideology of explicit hatred directed towards the West, emphasizing how the West has always hated Russia. Eurasianism treats Russia as the last defender of freedom and pluralism in a world subjected to Euro-Atlantic colonization. In his top-rated history books in Russia, published in circulations perhaps already totaling millions of copies, he advanced a unique argument. That the Mongols, despite the atrocities of their invasion and rule, actually saved Russia from inevitable domination by the West. In the centuries following the Mongol invasion, Byzantium weakened, and Latin Europe grew in strength. Mongol rule thus, effectively shielded or separated Rus from the West; from the growing supremacy of Latin civilization in places like Poland. Thus, Rus was not overrun in the north by the crusader warrior monks known as the Teutonic Knights. Nor in the south by the encroaching Genoese colonies in Kaffa on the Crimea, Kilia on the Dniester River and Belgorod at the mouth of the Boh River.

I cite these declarations by Gumilyov to illustrate just how differently the role of the Mongols and their ruthless rule is viewed in certain Russian circles especially when viewed through this unequivocally anti-Western looking glass. The same perspective that pervades in contemporary Russian historical and political discourse. Its most explicit testimonies can be found in the Mongolian linguistic legacy that is still present in the Russian language. A legacy which later also passed into the Polish language during the time of Russian rule – including *kandały* (handcuffs), *dyby* (stocks), *opała* (political disfavor). This Mongolian heritage also includes the lessons of how to exert imperial control over a vast Eurasian territory through innovations in civil service. This concept also finds its expression in Russian vocabulary through words such as *tamozhnya* (customs office) and *yamshchik* (mail courier).

The reinterpretation of the Mongol invasion as beneficial to the future of Russia because it provided an Asian shield against the evil West seems to have clearly triumphed under the current Putin regime. Proof of this can be seen in perhaps the most significant referendum or public survey poll in the history of modern Russia, the poll on the *Imya Rossiya* – the question of which historical figure in Russian history represents the best, most worthy symbol of Russia. It was officially won by none other than Prince Alexander Nevsky (1220–1263), a man who was a model Russian collaborator of the Golden Horde overlords. Nevsky was at the same time, a hallowed warrior and victor over invaders from the West. Yet, before I devote more lines to Mr Nevsky let us take a moment to review the full results of this rather enlightening survey.

This was a survey of historical consciousness the largest of its kind ever undertaken in Putin's Russia, conducted in 2008–2009, and some 50 million respondents took part. Nevsky was followed in second place by the Tsarist prime minister, oppressor of the Poles, and vanquisher of the 1905–1907 revolution, Pyotr Stolypin; in third place came Stalin subsequently; in fourth – Pushkin; in fifth – Peter the Great; in sixth – Lenin, in seventh – Dostoevsky, in eighth – the butcherer of Warsaw's Praga District (among many other civilian massacres) Marshal Suvorov, in ninth Dmitry Mendeleyev (popular, however, not due to his advances in the field of chemistry, but for his later ideological work promoting Eurasianism); in tenth position, another butcher, though mainly of his own subjects (like Stalin and Lenin) – Ivan IV the Terrible. The architect of the Commonwealth's destruction and Poland's partition, Catherine II, is in turn ranked 11th. Curiously missing from the top 12 were Tolstoy, Chekhov, or any of the other great Russian composers. Above all, Russians, it seems, were and are perhaps still proud of their most successful murderers, autocrats, and architects of imperial autocracy, hard and occasionally soft power including those who are the most fervent admirers of such methods with certain writings by unquestionable literary giants such as Pushkin and Dostoevsky to the fore. These official results announced in 2009; were surrounded by some speculation at the time that Stalin actually came first though perhaps Putin somehow was not yet ready, at that time, to acknowledge Stalin as the leading figure of Russian statehood…

But why did Alexander Nevsky win? A semi-mythical figure from the 13th century when Moscow was little more than a village. According to a legend already popularized by chronicles from the late 13th century, Alexander Nevsky first 'defeated' the Swedes in a battle reported to have taken place on the Neva River. He also bested the Order of the Knights of the Sword in a battle that certainly did take place on Lake Chudskoye near the

The Mongol invasion of Rus in 1238–1240 proved to be a terrible tragedy for the country. At the Battle of the Kalka River, the Russo-Polovian army suffered a devastating defeat. Painting by Sergey Ivanov.

present-day border with Estonia. Crucially Nevsky was later immortalized in film by Stalin's brilliant propagandist, the supremely gifted film director Sergei Eisenstein (Dr Goebbels himself signaled him out as a model for the filmmakers of the Third Reich), who made the 1939 film 'Alexander Nevsky'. Celebrating an anti-Western orientation in the first realm it portrays the choice of subjugation to the Mongols as the lesser evil for Russia. Every child in Russia learns at school the final words of the film's protagonist, directed at the West: 'He who comes to Russia with the sword will die by the sword.' This work of Stalinist propaganda is the principal reason for Nevsky's popularity.

However, it is hard to deny that the two-and-a-half-century Mongol rule imbued the political culture of the Rus lands with an ingrained, absolute fear, of superior authority. Authority, which is capable of decisions to level entire districts or cities to the ground whenever it encounters the slightest sign of disobedience or resistance. From this perspective, that trait was perpetuated in the lands of the Rus *ulus* (this was the name given to the territorial domain of the heirs of Genghis Khan, who ruled over the Golden Horde): in the face of the khan's absolute power of *wsye kholops*: everyone is a servant, a slave, a serf, even the Rus princes. Princes who would make regular servile pilgrimages to the khanate's capital to obtain a 'title', that of leading collaborator (the so-called *yarlyk*) or drink a goblet of poison should they. In this culture, power and authority exist only and explicitly to trample down society and the populace, permanently. Moreover, society tries to bear this condition patiently and penitently. As a form of rule, it was to some extent aligned with the nature of the original foreign Viking conquest of the region, the 'Varese' power over the Slavs. Yet intensified under Mongol rule during the first centuries of Kyivan Rus's subjugation. Moreover, this will form the third axis of tension between Rus and neighboring Poland, in addition to historical territorial disputes and the religious-civilizational divide between Orthodoxy and Latin Europe. Poland would develop its political culture at this time in completely the opposite direction: the privileges of freedom and liberty were being guaranteed in the Polish state. Firstly, to the holders of clerical state, then latterly to those of knightly or of noble state, to be followed by the development of a basic civic culture and legal code. Republican for some, for other commentators, oligarchic, but most certainly not autocratic, and absolutely not one to favor those who would be meek and eager to grovel to centralized authority.

We should add, however, that this specific political culture of Tsarist Autocracy based on the fear of subjects and the terror of authority did not develop evenly across the territory of Greater Russia. In the far north, where Mongol influence and reach was minimal, the powerful merchant republic of Veliky Novgorod (and the similar vibrant Pskov Republic) flourished from the 12th century. There was no autocracy or militarism present there. Instead, a combination of Orthodox religious identity together with a spirit of trade and openness to exchange with Western partners across the Baltic Sea. The symbol of this tradition in such North Rus city state republics was the bell, summoning all the free citizens of cities like Novgorod to a rally, or a general assembly where decisions would be taken one might say (with some reservations), democratically on all matters of importance to the community.

In the southwest, on the other hand, at the extreme edge of Mongol authority, the juncture of Piast statehood in the region around Lviv, Volhynia, the so-called Red Ruthenia areas, also commonly referred to as Galicia-Volhynia; here dynastic contacts, trade, and sometimes military clashes with the Piasts continued. Shortly after the Mongol invasion, around 1250, Prince Daniel originally founded the city of Lviv – so named in honor of the prince's son, Lev.

At the same time in the northeast after Batu Khan's invasion, a new population center emerged from which the future Russia would grow, located in a zone of dense forests, difficult to traverse. During this period, tens of thousands of refugees from the desolated Rus lands sought shelter there from the Mongols. The initial main center there was Vladimir on the Klyazma River. Next to it, a tiny settlement would take shape: Moscow. First recorded in the sources in 1147 when its wooden *kremlin* (fortress) was founded by Prince Yuri Dolgoruki. Dolgoruki's son, Andrei Bogolubsky, had earlier invaded other Rus lands sacking Kyiv before the Mongols. He had wanted to destroy this alternative southern alternative to benefit his own emerging northeastern center of power and rule over all Rus. A crusading goal his successors will share.

As a separate principality, the heirs of Alexander Nevsky will take over Moscow, along with an inherited program of zealous service to the khans of the Golden Horde in the role of tax or tribute collectors from the other surrounding principalities for subsequent delivery to the khan. In Moscow, the core of a future autocratic Rus or Russia will take shape, in Russian: a culture of Tsarist Autocracy, samodzierzawa, *самодержавие*, based on violence against one's own subjects at once insidious, at once resorting to open terror, all to ensure the subjugation of neighboring lands and peoples.

Meanwhile, by the end of the 13ᵗʰ century, Poland had begun to overcome the period of 'kingless' crisis or interregnum that it had experienced shortly after (the first) Bolesław the Brave's victorious reign and the later abdication in disgrace of his descendent and namesake Bolesław the Bold. Now at the turn of the 13ᵗʰ and 14ᵗʰ century a renewed crowned

Piast monarchy, under King Władysław 'Łokietek' (1260–1333) and his son King Casimir the Great (Pol.: *Kazimierz Wielki*) (1310–1370), would return to the eastern territorial program of the first Piasts: the recovery of the area associated with the name *Grody Czerwieńskie* (Cherven settlements), which had been lost once again at the end of the 11th century. Of course, it was also a matter of strengthening the economic basis for the development of the state. A state that had been rebuilt and reunited with great difficulty by opening it up to the lucrative trade going through Red Ruthenia also towards the Black Sea. King Łokietek skillfully took care to ensure the best possible relations with his most powerful Rus neighbor: the new Duchy of Galicia-Volhynia centered around Lviv. He even received some direct military aid from this region's rulers the brothers Lev and Andrew, during Łokietek's struggles for Polish independence against the Bohemian Luxembourgs in 1321. However, honor and harmony in this neighborhood have not always been the guarantors of a long life. Two years later, in a letter dated 21 May 1323, King Łokietek would regretfully notify Pope John XXII that the two princes, 'an impregnable shield' protecting Poland from the Tatars, had died. They were in fact his nephews, for the foresighted Łokietek had 28 organized his sister Euphemia's favorable union with their father Prince George of Galicia-Volhynia back in 1290. In 1323, the ruling Lev and Andrew, were killed (either by members of their court or in battle, it is unclear from sources). Regrettably, neither of them left any male descendants. King Łokietek did not attempt to occupy and rule Halych-Volhynia on his own. This would certainly have caused conflict not only with Lithuania, encroaching ever more boldly on the territory of the former Kyivan Rus. It would have also spoiled relations with Hungary which had for more than a century been claiming 'Galicia and Lodomeria' (i.e., Halych and Volhynia, indeed the powerful Hungarian ruler Andrew II had temporarily imposed a new king there in the form of his son Coloman, in 1214). So, King Łokietek now made a deal with Lithuania and won its approval for a compromise ruler-candidate. This was Bolesław, the son of the Piast prince of Mazovia, Troyden, and Maria, the sister of the late or slain in 1323, princes of Halych-Volhynia. This Bolesław Troydenovich, after adopting Orthodoxy as his religion took the name of Yuri II. Proving to be the most clearly entitled to inherit rule in Lviv and

The prosperous and independent trading town of Veliky Novgorod, in the oldest part of the city, are the remains of the earlier settlement of Rurikovo Gorodische. A painting by Apollinary Vasnetsov.

the adjacent region of Volodymyr he was brought to the Halych-Volhynia throne by his patron the Polish King Władysław Łokietek.

It is at this time that onto the great scene of our history emerges, a vigorous tribe (a proud medieval nation) the Lithuanians. This pagan principality of fearsome Baltic warriors during the reign of Gediminas (1315/16–1341) through force of will, of arms and some clever diplomacy with the Pope, made a great leap forward, extending its dominance in Rus, by taking advantage of the slackening grip of the Golden Horde in the west and north. Lithuanian supremacy was preferred by the western and northern Rus princes to the continuance of the Tatar yoke. So almost without a struggle, the Lithuanians smoothly extended their rule to encompass virtually all of modern-day Belarus, extending their influence as far south as Kyiv, as well as east to Tver, and Vyazma. The 'younger brother' of the Grand Duke of Lithuania now becomes the Duke of Smolensk. Veliky Novgorod accepted Prince Narymuntovich, another appointment by Gediminas, as protector of its borders. Gediminas already used the title *Rex Litvanorum et multorum Rutenorum* in 1323, and later simply: *Letphinorum Ruthenorumque rex* – king of the Lithuanians and Rus. Let us note, however, that all this would not have been possible, at any rate not on this scale, had it not been for the involvement of the Teutonic Order in a war against Łokietek's Poland. A war that continued into the early reign of Casimir the Great. Without the presence of the feared knightly order, perhaps Moscow, or another principality of the former Kyivan Rus, would have been quicker to take the lead in this process of 'consolidating the lands of Rus.'

Peace was achieved on the Lithuanian-Polish border, again thanks to King Łokietek's wise decision to ally with Gediminas and marry his young son Casimir (who would die without a male heir) to the Lithuanian princess Anna. This was the harbinger of a future Polish-Lithuanian dynastic union that would follow the extinction of the male royal Piast line. Through this alliance, Lithuania was able to act as a unifier of the Rus lands, gradually taken from the rule of the Khans of the Golden Horde, already in retreat in the first half of the 14th century. (TN Start) Gediminas would himself be ultimately succeeded by two of his issue, Kestutis and Algirdas who would rule the Western and Southeastern parts of the greatly expanded Duchy and their respective heirs, Vytautas and Jogaila would both play major roles in the next chapter of our story. (TN End)

Shortly after Łokietek's death in the spring of 1340, the rule of his protégé Prince Boleslav Troydenovich, in Halych and Volhynia, where he had taken the name Yuri II Boleslav, also came to a brutal end. He was poisoned by his subjects. What was the reason for this crime? The aversion of the local, Orthodox presumably, elites for the prince? Perhaps his too frequent contacts with the Catholic, Latin world? Under his rule, the Franciscan monks had developed their missions in the Halych principality. The chancellery of Yuri II Boleslav did not speak Rus but instead used Latin. It is known that Prince Yuri II Boleslav founded the town of Sanok under the Magdeburg Laws on 20 January 1339 (probably the first city under the Magdeburg Laws ever located in a Rus principality). For comparison: Lviv received recogni-

Ivan I Kalita (c. 1288–1340), a Ruthenian ruler and collaborator with the Mongols, from 1325 Duke of Moscow, grandson of the Russian national hero Alexander Nevsky. Kalita moved the seat of the Metropolitan bishop of the Orthodox Church from Volodomyr to Moscow, where he also established the first wooden fortress to be called the Kremlin.

tion for its land holdings from the hands of Casimir the Great only in 1356, Kyiv will also adopt the Magdeburg Laws in 1492, and Minsk in Belarus, in 1499). The privilege of organizing the community in Sanok was granted to a townsman from Sandomierz in east-central Poland, Bartholomew, as witnessed by the town heads of Bochnia and Warsaw, Adalbert and Bartholomew respectively. Already this early influx of Polish (but also Czech and German, according to sources) settlers into urban centers of historical Rus lands may have worried the Rus Orthodox population. Perhaps, however, the real power stakes were not any abstract or episodical sense of social resentment and religious-ethnic-cultural conflicts. Perhaps instead a real and tangible security dilemma, the civil violence driven by a cadre of elites still basing their power and authority on agreements with the distant, but still formidable lords of all Rus? Specifically, the Mongols and their Tatar Khan descendants of the Golden Horde?

Yuri II Boleslav was, in any case, indeed poisoned in his capital, Volodymyr (Volyn). Casimir as King Łokietek's heir, and the closest relative of the now deceased Halych Prince, entered the principality by force of arms and, in the words of a chronicler of the time, Traska, 'subjugated it to his own advantage.' Thus thwarting the attempt of the Uzbeg Khan to bring those West Rus lands back under (his) Mongol sovereignty. As depicted in the bull of Pope Benedict XII, issued in that same year of 1340, and the information from King Casimir contained therein, the Polish Crown at this point took on the role of an active Christian bulwark, against the Tatars on the Rus frontier of Western or Latin civilization, establishing dominion over these lands for the Polish crown. The interesting thing is that in this papal narrative, Poland did not receive any help from the West of the kind Bishop Matthew had alluded to in his earlier letter. Instead, Poland comes to an accord with the successors of Rus. It forms an alliance, in truth unequal and burdened by mutual suspicion, yet, nevertheless, Poland concludes an arrangement, in which the people of Rus are to be preserved 'in their rites, laws, religion and customs.' Another chronicler Janko of Czarnków also emphasized the voluntary, (though not without an undercurrent of clear Polish superiority), nature of the oath, then taken by the social elite of the Halych Rus to the Polish King. So, was this conquest, crusade, or union by consensus? Preserving Rus autonomy with security for all?

Poland entered Rus in 1340, a land that had been disputed since the inception of the Piast state, neighboring the Rurikids from Mieszko and Volodymyr the Great. Casimir III the Great is in many ways perpetuating a concept that had already begun 180 years previously. He is continuing the 'eastern policy' of his predecessors. It was pre-empted by a carefully built base of influence in the region of Galicia-Volhynia Rus, the construction of which was commenced by another Casimir. This was the earlier 'Casimir the Just', then followed by his sons Leszek the White and Konrad of Masovia, by his grandsons, led by Bolesław the Chaste, and finally by his great-grandsons, led by King Łokietek. This was certainly not a 'hostile takeover', but a gradual unwavering expansion of political, economic, and cultural relations over centuries. When the dynasty around which centered the state structure of Galicia-Volhynia Rus, was snuffed out, it being descended from Prince Roman (a onetime 'protégé' of the future prince Casimir II the Just) this western part of Rus, now found itself at a geopolitical crossroads. It had many alternative choices before it. Firstly, it could attempt to have renewed its historical control now weakened by the hand of the Tatar overlords. It could and indeed wanted to seize on the authority of Lithuania, impressively developing its expansion already into dozens of other principalities at the expense of Tatar rule. Finally, Hungary, with the title of the kingdom of 'Galicia and Lodomeria', belonging to the Arpads at the beginning of the 13th century, could have also been encouraged to come forward and claim the land for its own.

But the year 1340 revealed yet one more, a very distant and, it seemed extremely ambitious candidate for sovereignty over all of Rus, and thus also over Volhynia's towns Volodymyr, Lviv and Halych. This was the moment when the still-distant Duchy of Moscow revealed the extent of its ambitions. The reigning grandson of Alexander Nevsky, Prince Ivan I (or Kalita ca. 1288–1340), decided, just like his grandfather, to build his career and Moscow's legacy on the principle of being the closest possible collaborator with the Mongol overseers of Rus. He obtained the associated *yarlykh title*, and the khan's designation as Grand Prince of Rus, in 1328. Despite having previously covertly provoked an anti-Tatar uprising by his chief rival, Prince Alexander of Tver, northwest of Moscow, Khan Uzbeg now entrusted Ivan Kalita with the honor of completely ravaging those land of Tver and smaller principalities of northern Rus sympathetic to Tver. In this way Ivan garnered for himself the nickname Kalita (kaleta in Polish) which means money pouch, by means of his policy of buying slaves from neighboring principalities of the Tatars and then resettling them in his expanding Moscow lands. There is perhaps a somewhat poetic analogy here with the mythical story of the Lechite's letter and 'gift' of pouches to Aleksander the Great in the tale of the chronicler Kadłubek that we referenced earlier.

Most importantly for the geopolitical progression of our tale, Ivan Kalita brought about the transfer of the earlier established Orthodox seat of the Metropolis of all Rus from its seat in Vladimir-on-Klyazma to Moscow. Thus, since 1325 that settlement now became the new spiritual capital of Rus Orthodoxy, and the Metropolis added to the Moscow princes' spiritual power and political influence over their Orthodox Rus neighbors. Kalita used this power immediately against his rival Prince Alexander of Tver, who took refuge from a punitive Tatar expedition in Pskov close to the current Estonian and Latvian border. The Moscow Metropolitan then denounced both Alexander and Pskov. Facing such a dilemma Alexander now turned to the Lithuanians for support against Moscow and the Tatars.

In 1339, Kalita also initiated an expedition of Tatar-Moscow forces against Smolensk as the prince in control of that city had earlier allied himself with Lithuania. This clash between Moscow and Lithuania over the sovereignty of Novgorod, Pskov, and now over Smolensk (a settlement of strategic and symbolical importance for centuries to come) finds a peculiar echo during the time of Ivan Kalita's stewardship, in the Tatar expedition to the Kingdom of Galicia-Volhynia of 1340. The idea pervading all of these incursions, was to prevent the historical lands of Rus, including the westernmost among them, from passing under Polish or 'Latin' rule.

Thus, a centuries-long Gordian knot of geopolitical rivalry was in the process of being tied. The seizing or 'protection' of the Rus inheritance from the waning Golden Horde with Moscow was an instrument of this policy. Moreover, Moscow itself was gaining in importance, especially with the religious blessing of the new Moscow Metropolitan for its political conquests and the now holy mission conferred upon Ivan I Kalita: the task of 'collecting the Rus lands' for his successors. All Rus lands, so also those lands that Casimir the Great 'had encroached upon' in 1340. Though naturally, Lithuania would remain the first and most significant rival in Moscow's early work of 'collecting Rus lands' for the next century and a half. Crucially Ivan Kalita also managed to secure from the Khan the inheritance right and so he could now pass on the title of the grand prince to his son. Moscow's dynasty was thus able to legitimately continue the pursuit of Kalita's holy mission even after his death in March 1340 (or 1341, the Rus *letopis* chronicles do not definitively clarify the date).

In 2001, two years after Putin came to power in the Kremlin on the back of a new holy war, this time against Chechen terrorists and the mysterious bombing campaign against tower blocks in Russian cities, the Orthodox Church of the Moscow Patriarchate officially recognized the historical figure of Ivan Kalita as a saint The feast of St. Ivan Kalita now falls on 13 April. This is the feast of the founder of Moscow's seat of power. Ivan Kalita's grandson, Dmitry Donskoy (1350–1389), 40 years after the death of his notable grandfather, had already dared to defy his Tatar overlords for a moment during a symbolically significant gathering of a large part of the Rus' princes around him. Dmitri's great-grandson, Ivan III (1440–1505), will finally consolidate the ever-expanding Moscow empire. He will boldly take over the political and ideological legacy of the now fallen Byzantium, laying the foundation for Moscow to proclaim itself the 'Third Rome'.

In the way of Ivan III's initial mission, that of collecting 'Rus lands' will then stand the legacy of the union by the marriage of Algirdas of Lithuania's son, Jagiełło, to the Angevin great-granddaughter of Władysław Łokietek, Queen Jadwiga (or Hedwig) of Poland. This marriage in 1386 with Jadwiga (the last of the Piast line) earlier crowned a female 'King' together with crucial pre-nuptial provisions of the Union of Krewo (by which Jagiełło and most of his followers would be baptized) would be the foundation stone for the emerging Polish-Lithuanian Union. Partially conceived to fight against the Germanic power of the Teutonic Knights, this union will swiftly break the Order's strength in the great battle of Grunwald only to later find itself locked in centuries of conflict with Kalita's heirs in Moscow.

Our two centers of power are both now coming into sharper focus and contact. One, with its foundations in a relatively equal, nascent union of two separate nations both now adopting Latin tradition, ceding spiritual authority to an external power, in Rome, while also learning the art of compromise by joining forces against a common foe to achieve a great victory and the common benefit and prosperity of their peoples. The second power center in contrast, would absorb the civilizational methods of an external Mongol oppressor, assuming for itself the right to shape, unilaterally, its own spiritual and religious vision of its neighborhood. A state with both secular and religious authority centered in Moscow in the hands of one ruling dynasty, one with a legacy of trading human life for purses of money.

I ended my Second Volume of *Dzieje Polski* (The History of Poland) with words referencing King Łokietek's renewed legacy of Polish involvement in Rus and the new line of Polish rulers brought forth by the marriage of his great granddaughter Jadwiga. Here they serve as the closing of this first introductory chapter on several centuries of historical relations and the perceived inevitability of Russia's historical mission, now realized in the present-day by Putin's tanks driving into Ukrainian territory. In Ukraine's hour of need and ongoing struggle for independence, this Polish and Lithuanian power must rally once again and rally Europe along with it.

The Concept of Commonwealth (*Rzeczpospolita*). Novgorod – Moscow and Lithuania's Dilemma (XIV–XVI Centuries)

The events I will discuss in this chapter are tied together by the dilemma of a growing fear of geopolitical revisionism. Revisionism centered on an aggressive emerging Moscow. Fear of such a nature or on this scale did not exist before. When Poland and the Rus principalities lived side by side for several centuries, intermingled, as it were, each influencing the other, occasionally skirmishing along a relatively small borderland area. An area which did not constitute a major strategic determinant for the day-to-day livelihood of either side. Neither entity presented an existential threat to the other, although civilizationally, they were diverging. The situation changed when it seemed that Poland was at the height of its power, thanks to the personal union by marriage with Lithuania in 1385. This proved to be a wise undertaking by the lords of Krakow and Lesser Poland driven principally by the elites based in that city. For they decided to offer the hand of Queen Jadwiga of Anjou, a young girl bearing the proud title of King of Poland to the then pagan Prince of Lithuania, Jagiełło (Lith.: *Jogaila*) (1362 or 1352–1434). The decision to unite in matrimony Poland and Lithuania (with a suitably politically orientated pre-nuptial agreement) ushered in a state dynasty under the scepter of Jagiełło that would assume the name of the Jagiellons or Jagiellonians, creating at the same time the largest state, territorially, in Europe.

At that time, Moscow was still a relatively small country, quite distant from the borders of the original Piast state. However, it was a far closer neighbor of Lithuania. Moscow in the second half of the 14th century, occupied a territory smaller than today's Poland, under 250,000 sq. km. Thus, it seemed that following the union of Poland and Lithuania and the breaking of Teutonic Knights' power at the historic Battle of Grunwald in 1410 this Polish-Lithuanian state now occupied a privileged geopolitical position in the struggle for dominance over Eastern Europe. The most critical strategic problem facing the Poles and Lithuanians thus far, had been the expansive tendencies of the Teutonic Order's state. The Knights, backed up against the shore of the Baltic Sea and its trade routes which they greedily monopolized, had repelled the advances of Poland and Lithuania for years. However, the Teutonic Knights were now defeated and diminished. After the Grunwald defeat, the monastic state was never to rise again to its former power. Nevertheless, factors of a religious and civilizational nature made the true balance of power in the region look somewhat different from what a glance at a map or a brief assessment of measurable power alone would suggest. These more subtle and opaque factors were to put the far smaller and weaker Moscow of that time at a significant advantage.

Moscow and the separate lands of Rus, the latter now largely under Lithuanian sovereignty, were united by a shared Orthodox faith and culture and, perhaps even more profoundly, by an association with Byzantine civilization, the association which had evolved around this faith and its imperial-religious tradition. The Muscovite state on the northeastern edge of Rus, however, should be interpreted in this period as an area where the cultural influence and political traditions of the Mongols (dominant there for two and a half centuries, though no longer prevailing) had already left an indelible civilizational mark. Feliks Koneczny, the eminent Krakow-Vilnius historian, referred to this specific Moscow historical experience as that of a Turanian civilization [i.e. the steppes, camp civilization with its cradle in central Asia (on the vast Turanian Plain) – *editor's note*]. In modern-day Russia, this model is now referred to as 'Eurasian'. These differences would reinforce themselves, those between the Rus state initially established around Moscow (together with its later iterations which emerged in time out from under Mongol domination), and the Rus lands under Lithuanian dominion or directly ruled via the Polish Crown (Red Ruthenia). The region's entry into the circle of impulses and influences of Poland's Latin civilization, only accelerated this divergence. During the next four centuries of history, subsequent to the initially marriage-based 1386 Polish-Lithuanian union (for only in 1572 would a formal union of the two states be conducted, then renamed as the Polish-Lithuanian Commonwealth), these other Rus lands would now emerge. These lands would be something culturally and politically apart and later become known as Ukraine and Belarus. Entities

The Christianisation of Lithuania according to a painting by Władysław Ciesielski. Clearly rendered are the Polish royal couple Queen Jadwiga of Poland and her Lithuanian husband now King of Poland, Władysław Jagiełło, surrounded by the members of their court. In the background on the left, Bishop Andrzej Jastrzębiec blesses the assembled with his right hand.

differing in a civilizational sense from a future Russia, having developed outside the orbit of a still distant, at that time, Moscow. A state, a Moscow, burdened with an entirely different historical experience.

The role of the Church and the establishment of seats of higher learning are just some of the symbols of these western, Latin influences in the original Rus lands, already largely absorbed into the Lithuanian state when Jagiełło and his people were baptized (1387–1388). It is worth recalling that the second rector of the Krakow University was Jan Wajduta, Duke of Drohiczyn, one of Jagiełło's Lithuanian cousins. A man Lithuanian by lineage, and yet Rus in culture. Interestingly, this seat of higher learning had already existed earlier, but it was now revived by Jadwiga and Jagiełło and flourishing after the renowned Stanisław of Skarbimierz became its rector

The Battle of the Blue Waters in 1362 ended in a brilliant victory for courageous and celebrated Lithuanian Grand Duke Algirdas Gediminas (father of Władysław Jagiełło) over the armies of the western (blue) Khanate of the Golden Horde. Painting by Artur Orlonov.

in 1401. This is accurate testimony to the inclusivity of purpose evident in the work of this Poland's first ever university. Indeed, it's an example of the broader approach of the Polish state towards Lithuania, not just the ethnic population of Lithuania, but the state of Lithuania including its laws, its significant Rus population, and the associated cultural legacy already inherent in that state.

Did Poland have enough strength and capacity to change all of Rus? This question was a fact that faced the rulers of both Poland and Lithuania. I purposely use the plural 'rulers' here, because from early on in the union there were two men in charge, so to speak. Though at odds, often extremely vehemently so, Vytautas Alexander (the second name he had taken at baptism), a cousin of King Jagiełło, finally came to an agreement on a form of co-government that would be effective for the two still formally separate

69

states over which Jagiełło now ruled in title. To this agreement that ceded authority in Lithuanian lands to Vytautas, Jagiełło would remain faithful till the end of that cousin's life. In practice one could even refer Jagiełło consenting to the Stewardship of Lithuania under the lifetime rule of Vytautas, who was son of Jagiełło's uncle Kestutis (1354–1430). For despite the later reformulations of the Polish-Lithuanian union, the details of which we will not go into here, Vytautas was in return subsequently consistently faithful to Jagiełło and the union with Poland from the end of the 14th century and for three more decades, till his death in 1430. In 1399, however, the more youthful Vytautas also contemplated more ambitious goals. Opportunities were opening up before him for an advance in the east with the support of the Polish Crown. He and the entire Gediminovich family from which he and Jagiełło were descended were bound by ties of kinship to various Rus princes descended from the original rulers of Kyiv the extensive Rurikovich family, which had grown since the 9th century. In the Gediminovich family, ties were particularly close to Tver, a leading principality that then competed with Moscow during the 14th century for leadership of that remaining part of Rus not now under Lithuanian dominion. Thus, the prospect of a dispute, an element of permanent conflict with Moscow, was shall we say somehow embedded in the family tradition. This family element in fact applied more so to Jagiełło who was a son of Lady Juliana of that same principality of Tver.

Jagiełło's father, Algirdas (Olgierd) Gediminovich (1296 or 1304–1377) and husband of Lady Juliana, had twice earlier stood with his armies at the walls of Moscow, close to achieving domination over that city. However, each time he relented, conscious of the fact that Lithuania's forces were not yet sufficiently powerful to subsequently control all of Rus, and the Duchy of Moscow, thus, doubtlessly disappointing his wife's brethren in Tver. Yet, Vytautas would now return to this great gambit though differently in the last years of the 14th century. He would seek to subjugate all of Rus between the Baltic Sea and the mouth of the Volga River and the Caspian Sea in one conclusive campaign. To this end, he allied himself with Tokhtamysh, a rightful' claimant to sovereignty over the Golden Horde. Tokhtamysh had come to seek support in Vilnius and win back the throne of the Horde. However, to achieve his aims Vytautas would now first have to turn south, not east and defeat Edigey, the *de facto* current ruler of the Great Horde. Edi-

Vytautas the Great (Witold in Polish), Grand Duke of Lithuania, cousin of King Władysław Jagiełło and *de facto* steward of the Lithuanian and Rus lands.

gey was a man nominated to that role by Timur or Tamerlane (1336–1405), the world's greatest conqueror at that time. The decisive battle took place on 12 August 1399 at the Vorskla River, a river in what is now eastern Ukraine. There, Vytautas' army and his allied Polish reinforcements were taken by surprise and utterly defeated. Many of the Rus knights supporting Vytautas died in this battle, but also Poles, the governors of Krakow, Płock, Mazovia, Czersk, and many of the Polish knights that they led. It was a crushing defeat.

However, was this battle, when viewed from the perspective of the following centuries, truly a defeat for Poland? If Vytautas had won the Battle of Vorskla, he would have been the master of all the great rivers and trade routes of Eastern Europe, Lithuania would have probably afterwards also absorbed Moscow. Yet the population of native Lithuanians in that new realm would have been less than 5% of the overall population in such a united Rus land. Over time the Lithuanians simply would have dissolved into it, just as the Scandinavian Varangians had done once before in Kyiv. With such a negligible minority, it would have been rule in name only and even then, not for very long. Neither Vytautas nor any of his successors could have hoped to consolidate their rule based on any elemental Lithuanian supremacy. He and his brethren would have had to assimilate completely into the Rus element, which, by the strength of its traditions, would have triumphed in the civilizational sense, also culturally, and ultimately politically. He would have triumphed by transforming Lithuania into a Rus state. It could not have been otherwise. Only by the maintenance of a zone in Rus, the political organizer of which was effectively a more populous Poland; a Poland in turn united by dynastic union with Lithuania, could the Latin, and European cultural impulses be made to work and spread effectively. Only in this fashion could the cultural synthesis that would help to bring forth the countries that we today call Belarus and Ukraine, have succeeded over the centuries. These two East Slavic countries remained largely within the Orthodox rite, but existing over time within a Lithuanian state structure, subject to its code of laws they became lands apart. Latterly in combination with, and increasingly under the direct influence of, the Polish state in its Republican or Commonwealth form [Pol: commonly referred to as *Rzeczpospolita*] a different identity began to emerge.

Simply by being exposed to Polish culture, and then via this 'transit land' to European culture, the lands of Belarus and Ukraine in terms of character continued to evolve along a trajectory different to the one set in Moscow and those lands still ruled by the Golden Horde, developing over time a new identity unto themselves.

Vytautas' defeat near the Vorskla River and, at the same time, the fact that he managed to survive the battle, had thus in a curious fashion, actually saved the Polish-Lithuanian union. Vytautas had to put aside his dreams of conquest for many years, if not forever. Poland now became an indispensable ally for him, a necessary crutch upon he could lean and rebuild his own position in Lithuania, indeed the position of Lithuania itself – *vis-à-vis* the Order of the Teutonic Knights, as well as *vis-à-vis* Moscow. After all, besides the Polish-Lithuanian union, the other more visible beneficiary of the Battle of Vorskla would be Moscow. After the battle, seeing the defeat of the Prince of Lithuania, the then Moscow Prince Vasily I, a great-grandson of Ivan Kalita (and as we will explain below, the actual son-in-law of Vytautas), could now breathe a sigh of relief and plot anew the rivalry with Vilnius for these borderlands, for the stronghold of Smolensk, for supremacy over the rich trade of Novgorod and Pskov, for the future of Rus. Vorskla in fact would prove to be one of the first major milestones on Moscow's path towards establishing an Eastern European empire. Just as 310 years later, at Poltava near where that same river flows, the crushing victory of Tsar Peter I over the Swedish King Charles XII and the Ukrainian Cossack Hetman Mazepa, would become the keystone for the Russian Empire's proclamation and its continued expansion for a further two and a half centuries.

At the dawn of the 15th century, the alluring power of the Orthodox faith was of paramount importance to the Rus population in Eastern Europe. Please note that this time the modern concept of national identification did not exist. That concept of nationality as we now know it would develop far later. In the late Middle Ages, the most important feature for a person's identification was religion and in this neighborhood, whether he or she was a Catholic or an Orthodox Christian. Even if one attended a church, sometimes very far from one's place of residence, if once a month or once a year at that time (parish networks were not as dense as today), the essential issue was which church one attended and with which Church was one associated.

Grand Duke Dmitry Donskoy of Moscow (1350–1389) defeats the Tatars led by Mamai at the Battle of Kulikovo Field (1380) symbolizing the first efforts by Moscow to rid itself of the Mongol overlordship. Painting by Adolphe Ivon.

From this point of view, of great importance was the fact that well before the battle of the Vorskla River as early as 1326 the heart of East Slavic, Rus Orthodoxy would come to be located in a still relatively small town, that of Moscow. Through the efforts of Ivan Kalita, mentioned in the previous chapter, a Metropolis of the Orthodox Church was established there. Shaped by Kalita and now supporting him with the authority of this new Moscow Metropolitan, the ideological program of 'collecting' all the lands that once belonged to Kyivan-Novgorod Rus began to take tangible and spiritual shape. Precisely because of the powerful support for this expansionist program in the Moscow-based Orthodox Metropolis. It was from here that incredibly effective propaganda originated that set the stage for the brief gesture of defiance against the Mongols. A gesture led by Vasily's father, Dmitri called Donskoy, against the Golden Horde, with whom Moscow had collaborated closely for centuries. Indeed, Moscow had in fact risen on that very collaboration. It was a fleeting yet important victory the battle that followed, in which Dmitry Donskoy fought against the Tatars on the Don River at Kulikovo Field in 1380.

The battle did not bring an immediate or lasting strategic gain, as just a year later the Tatars invaded and ravaged Moscow, Dmitry had to flee his capital, and the unquestioned sovereignty of the Golden Horde over Moscow was restored for another 100 years. Nevertheless, the Battle of Kulikovo Field was, from a propaganda point of view, brilliantly exploited by the Moscow Kremlin. Thanks to it, it could shake off the odium of being little more than the 'key collaborator' of cruel Mongol power. Dmitry Donskoy collected such propaganda assets for the future, his son Vasily was however a prince who knew how to judge current opportunities. He now saw a great opening to further his interests in the geopolitical game and tie himself to the much more powerful Gediminovich dynasty. Seizing his chance in 1391, he then married Vytautas' daughter, Sophia. Thus, it had come to pass that subsequent Moscow rulers would be tied by blood to the Gediminovichs and descendants of Vytautas. Though this by no means would make them automatic allies of Lithuania or Poland.

Lithuania paid for its defeat at the Battle of Vorskla with substantial losses among their frontier strongholds and territories. In 1401, Smolensk rebelled against Vytautas, restoring the rule of the local, Moscow-allied branch of the Rurikovichs in the crucial stronghold. Another border principality, Ryazan, then tried unsuccessfully to wrest the Bryansk lands from Lithuanian rule. More forces, however, would be needed to recapture Smolensk. An expedition was launched against the mighty fortress in 1404, with all the Polish King's Lithuanian brothers taking part. The three-month siege, however, saw the forces literally bounce off the walls of fortress Smolensk. As Długosz's writing confirmed, Polish knights were also taking part in this siege. However, when the prince of Smolensk departed his stronghold for Moscow, Vytautas returned to the attack once again and this time, on 26 June 1404, Smolensk surrendered to Lithuania and would remain under Lithuanian rule for the next 110 years. Under Lithuanian rule, though, at least initially, with a Polish garrison. As the Rus chronicles confirm, Vytautas now erring on the side of caution decided to garrison the mighty fortress with Polish knights (or at least with a Polish command) to minimize the risk of the fortress slipping again to Moscow.

In 1405, King Władysław Jagiełło forced Vytautas to pledge that Smolensk and other new conquests in the east would henceforth be subordinated to his successors and the Polish Crown. Yaroslav Nikodem, a contemporary biographer of Vytautas, believes that this act, renewed in 1406, did not so much signify Vytautas' acceptance of some kind of 'Polish sovereignty' over Smolensk but was in fact an attempt by the Lithuanian steward to entice the Poles (Polish lords) and the King himself, thus fortifying Vytautas for his inevitable future confrontations with Moscow. The war's first installment came to an end in 1408, with Vytautas concluding a peace treaty with Moscow confirming the stalemate. Lithuania and Poland now had to, in what would be a regular theme in Polish history, face a more significant, direct threat from the west, or rather from the north. The great decisive war now began with the Teutonic Order and the Holy Roman Empire supporting it (with an avowed enemy of Poland, Sigismund of Luxembourg, now on the imperial throne). Peace in the east would last only as long as it would take to defeat the Teutonic Order in a series of battles culminating in the aforementioned great battle of Grunwald.

(TN Start) Grunwald, the greatest military engagement of that age anywhere in Europe with consensus estimates pointing to an engagement of some 60,000–70,000 men at arms, would occupy a foundational place in the history of Polish and Lithuanian state but also their respective national legends, akin to that of the battle of the Teutoborg forest or the Siege of Orleans for the German and French nations. It should though be noted that the war against the Teutonic Order was not only concluded with a victory by military means. It was supplemented by successes in the field of diplomatic relations and theology. This was best illustrated at the Council of Konstanz (thanks to the erudite oratory of among others the Krakow-educated Paulus Vladimiri, or Paweł Włodkowic). This Polish scholar and jurist would face down and effectively counter John of Falkenberg's argumentation in favor of the Teutonic Knights. The Order's advocate claiming, they had the right to slay peaceful pagans (Lithuanians) simply on account of them being pagans. Włodkowic's argumentation prevailed in what could be considered one of the first international debates on genocide and the concept of a 'Just War' in the annals of 2nd millennial Europe. The victory over the Teutonic Order was thus comprehensive also in the political and ecclesiastical sense and it would cement Polish-Lithuanian political and civil authority in the region for centuries to come. (TN End)

The religious factor also made itself known during the long reign of the Jagiełło, sovereign over the united Lithuania and Poland for nearly half a century. In 1440, Prince Casimir, Jagiełło's younger son, took the grand ducal throne in Vilnius at a very young age. Seven years later, having waited three years for the return of his brother, Władysław, from the Battle of Varna (1444), he would then also take the Polish throne in Krakow. It would thus be King Casimir Jagiellon (1427–1492) who would be the first to solely exercise sovereignty over both states in the union. He would reinforce the underlying framework of the Polish-Lithuanian Union and, at the same time, Lithuania's defense of its eastern lands. The most eloquent testimony to this was the so-called 'Perpetual Peace' treaty concluded in 1449 between King Casimir of the Jagiellonian dynasty and Prince Vasily II of Moscow (the son and successor of Vasily I) known as the Blind as a result of a cruel mutilation he suffered during a civil war in Moscow.

The peace treaty demarcated spheres of influence in Eastern Europe in a way favorable to Moscow. Under the peace terms to be included in Moscow's sphere of influence was Veliky Novgorod, a vast, rich, and traditionally strong merchant republic extending its dominion as far as the

Ob River on the border of Asia to the Baltic Sea. Moscow would also have some dominion over Pskov, a strong merchant republic on Novgorod's western periphery. A third disputed city, which was still outside the formal authority of Lithuania and Moscow, namely Tver, that birthplace of King Jagiełło's mother, was to remain within the sphere of Lithuanian influence. Thus defined, the spheres of influence of the two rivals for future dominion in Eastern Europe were so divided. Lithuania was clearly setting its sights on merely defending its current influence and holdings.

King Casimir having succeeded to Jagiełło, directed his policy towards the weakening of separatist Rus sentiments aroused in the lands of Lithuanian Grand Duchy, sentiments often grounded in Orthodox identity. This was the aim of the new great privileges he granted to the local Lithuanian elites prior to his departure for coronation with the Polish crown in Krakow, on 2 May 1447. These unprecedented freedoms of Casimir were granted not only to the 'great lords' but also to the boyars of the entire Grand Duchy, regardless of their religion. They thus undercut the possibility of building opposition to his rule on a broader social or religious (Orthodox) basis. Casimir also abandoned attempts to permanently subjugate Moscow and instead decided to make an accord with its Grand Duke, Vasily II. The immediate benefit of this was to be the solemn resignation of the Muscovite prince from any future support in fermenting rebellions in Lithuania. Indeed, military reinforcements from Moscow, as paradoxical as it may look from today's perspective, now actually assisted the armies of the King of Poland and the Grand Duke of Lithuania to regain Kyiv from the hands of a rebel uprising in the summer of 1449. On 31 August of that same year, a 'perpetual peace, covenant, and friendship' agreement was entered into between Casimir Jagiellon and Grand Duke Vasily II of Moscow. The existing borders were unchanged. Both rulers pledged not to support the internal enemies of the other and to help each other defend against the Tatars. The treaty also delineated the aforementioned, and relatively favorable for Moscow, spheres of influence.

Now just for the sake of example let us view the eternal Lithuanian-Moscow peace accord of August 1449 from the perspective of another August accord signed 490 years later. Here I refer to the Nazi-Soviet pact of 1939. In this accord, Moscow's geopolitical successor, the Soviet Union, would also divide spheres of influence with a different western partner, Nazi Germany instead of Lithuania. Indeed, Lithuania and Poland would now be the 'objects' to be divided. Perhaps the best Polish researcher of the grand Duchy of Lithuania in the 15th century today, Lidia Korczak, correctly notes that the earlier accord was similarly rooted in the concept of Great Power politics. After all, it involved the dealing out of spheres of influence with regard to the territory of separate 'independent states, none of whom actually accepted the treaty's provisions.' Of course, Casimir was no Ribbentrop nor was Vasily the Blind a Molotov. Yet the very principle underlying this treaty, how different it was in nature from, for example, the earlier Polish-Lithuanian agreements with Jagiełło and Jadwiga's marriage, is striking. Here though there was only cold geopolitics with some ruler family ties at play, no ideology. In addition, notes the same researcher, it proved to be a most unwise and poorly constructed move from the Lithuanian side. For Tver, birthplace of Casimir's grandmother (Jagiełło's mother), included in Casimir's sphere of influence, geographically actually stood on the road from Moscow to Veliky Novgorod and to Pskov, the two territories to which that same treaty granted dominion over to Moscow. It was clear that since Vasily and his successors had been effectively given the 'go-ahead' to subjugate the two great merchant republics, which had previously whetted the appetites of the Lithuanian princes, Tver that quite literally stood in the way of Moscow's future dominions would also be in play.

Certainly, Casimir did not react at that moment to other serious threats from Moscow, which would grow over time to become the main foundation of its perceived 'ideological' superiority, leading to subsequent Moscow conquests at the expense of firstly the Lithuanian 'sphere of influence' and latterly Lithuania itself only to culminate finally with the entire Polish-Lithuanian Commonwealth. One such threat was the increasing dependence of Moscow's Patriarch on the secular ruler in Moscow matched by increasing religious independence from Constantinople. In December 1448, just a few months before the 'perpetual peace,' was signed a 'council' of Orthodox bishops convened by Vasily thet elected a candidate who was now designated by Vasily to be the new Metropolitan, not just of Moscow, but of 'Kyiv and all Rus.' Kyiv, a city let us note for more in the sphere of Polish influence at the time. The man chosen to serve as the new Metropolitan

Views of Moscow by Apollinary Vasnetsov. Top: The fortified walls and the Kremlin dating from the 14th century. Bottom: In the early days of the reign of Daniel of Moscow (son of Alexander Nevsky), Moscow was little more than a wooden fortress town incomparable to Kyiv or Krakow.

was the Bishop of Ryazan, Jonah. The first but not the last time Moscow would independently choose a Metropolitan without sanction from the Patriarchate in Constantinople.

Vasily II rejected the attempts at union between the Orthodox Church and the Roman Catholic Church made by the Constantinopolitan Patriarchate at the Council of Florence in 1439. The Uniate Metropolitan Isidore, sent from Florence to mediate, was instead imprisoned by the Muscovite prince. Simultaneously Vasily claimed that Tsargrad (Constantinople) had lost the purity of the Orthodox faith and only in the Moscow Kremlin could a sure foothold in the world for spiritual Orthodoxy now be found and within it, salvation. At first, Casimir Jagiellon ignored Jonah's elevation, but in January 1451, he recognized him at a solemn convention of princes, boyars, and bishops in Vilnius. Thus, the Metropolitan in Moscow under the thumb of his Grand Duke, became the religious superior not only for all Orthodox states and states beyond Lithuania's eastern border – for Novgorod, Pskov, Ryazan, Tver – but also for the Orthodox inhabitants of the Grand Duchy of Lithuania. It was not until later, in 1458 at least, that Casimir would attempt to protect his state from the subsequent consequences. Then in an agreement with Patriarch Gregory III of Constantinople (a supporter of the Florentine Union aimed at bridging the Schism), who was in Rome at the time, he obtained the nomination for Kyiv to be a separate Metropolis of the Orthodox faith in the lands of Rus. From 1458, therefore, there would now be two Orthodox Metropolises: one in Moscow and the other in Kyiv. However, the former will maintain its previously won dominance over all non-Moscow Rus' principalities outside of Lithuania. Moreover, it would remain a powerful tool for the spiritual and secular 'reconquest' of the lands of all of Rus by the Moscow grand princes, later facilitated by both the fall of Constantinople in 1453 and the agile exploitation of Orthodoxy in the creation of Moscow's imperial strategy especially by the son and successor of Vasily II, Ivan III, a ruler rightly called the Great, and no less justly the Harsh.

The most significant change in the geopolitics of this dispute in the coming years was the resolution of the question of just in whose hands Veliky Novgorod, the wealthiest state in this part of Europe, many times wealthier than Moscow or Lithuania, would fall. This merchant republic, which had functioned independently practically since the 10th, or at least since the 11th century, had become one of the most important economic centers in north-eastern Europe during the later Middle Ages. It dominated trade not only on the White Sea but also on parts of the Baltic Sea as a significant partner and rival of the Hanseatic League, the powerful union of German merchants.

Territorially, Novgorod was still about four times the size of the Grand Duchy of Moscow. However, its character, that of a free merchant republic, and its economic strength were simultaneously a source of political weakness. For the ruling merchant oligarchies could be easily played off against each other, dividing them into factions favorable to Lithuanian influence and others favorable to Moscow.

While important in the political realities of Novgorod, the religious issue (fear of Latin Catholicism stoked by Moscow propaganda) was not the only concern and may not even have been the most important one. What mattered to the merchant elites was whether they could preserve their freedom in trade, from which their power grew. The wealthy merchants of Novgorod realized it would be easier to maintain this freedom with Lithuania than with Moscow. Hence, they readily invited Lithuanian princes from lateral lines with links to the Gediminovich family thusly ennobled to hold the position of a titular prince (though in Novgorod, the prince/*knyaz* was only titular).

When the struggle for the future of Novgorod began to enter its decisive phase, there was a significant change on the Moscow throne. Following Vasily II, a reign plagued primarily by civil wars, restricting any initiatives by Moscow, his young son, Ivan III (reigning 1462–1505), now took the throne. He is indisputably the greatest of Moscow's rulers. However, we hear of him less often, and he certainly captures less of our imagination than his grandson Ivan IV, the Terrible, or his distant descendant of Peter the Great. Yet it was this Ivan III who truly established the power of the Moscow state and was the founder of a future Russian Empire together with its imperial ideology. Ivan III's most important goal was to carry out the will of Ivan I Kalita, to 'gather together' (i.e. 'conquer' or 'redeem') all the still-scattered Rus principalities and finally strike against Lithuania, his main rival. Ivan III intuitively knew how to make the most of any opportunities that came his way to thus strengthen Moscow's position.

A symbol of Lithuania's defensive policy at the time was the outcome of the aforementioned efforts to establish a second formalized and rival Orthodox Metropolis in Eastern Europe. This was to re-establish in Kyiv the historical center of Slavic Orthodoxy as it had existed prior to the Mongol invasions. The Orthodox Church of the Eastern Slavs thus gained or regained a second capital next to Moscow, this time in a location under the secular rule of the Lithuanian princes. Lithuania no longer aspired to a union with the Moscow Orthodox Church and no longer wished to occupy Moscow or its lands, instead contenting itself to take autonomous spiritual care of its Orthodox Christians, whose spiritual and by default political ties with Moscow would now be cut. For the Lithuanian state, and later for the Polish-Lithuanian Commonwealth, the persistent problem remained how to manage the majority Orthodox population, make them the same loyal subjects as Lithuanians in Lithuania, as Latin Catholics in Poland? As we know, political rights in the Polish-Lithuanian union were guaranteed to those who would be baptized under the Latin rite. From 1433 onward, most of the major personal and political rights were now also allowed to those believers in Lithuania who had been baptized in the Orthodox fashion.

As a testament to the power of Orthodoxy in Lithuania, I offer the following exemplary case of religious conversion among the magnate or ruling families of Lithuania. In the mid-16th century, just before the *en masse* conversion of Lithuanians to Protestant religions (primarily to Calvinism), out of the 54 prominent princely/magnate families controlling Lithuania, 20 had still retained the Orthodox faith, and 34 had adopted, voluntarily of course, within the first 150 years since Jagiełło's baptism in Krakow Roman Catholicism. There was still thus an influential role for Orthodoxy in the demographic structure of Lithuania's ruling elite. Lithuania's drive to make its Orthodox Christians independent of the Moscow metropolis would eventually culminate in dramatic changes at the end of the 16th century. For in 1589, Moscow gained a prestigious success, by elevating its Metropolis to that of a fully independent patriarchate. After Jerusalem, Antioch, Alexandria, Constantinople, Moscow would then become the fifth ecumenical, or universal, patriarchate, now clearly emerging at the forefront of the Orthodox world for religious and political reasons.

Ivan III ascended to the Kremlin's throne in 1462 and proceeded very quickly with an energetic agenda. The first success unexpectedly fell into his hands; it was his marriage, with which he was assisted. He owed it to the age-old policy of Rome, its efforts to attract Orthodoxy into a union with Catholicism. This often incorporated a far higher political price for the potential spiritual gain. It would be a hefty one this time and those states neighboring Moscow would have to pay it. For it was on Rome's initiative that the idea of marrying Ivan III to Princess Zoe or Sofia, the niece of the last emperor of Constantinople, was proposed. After the Turks' assault and the tragic fall of Byzantium in 1453, seeing the subsequent liquidation of her father's Peloponnesian rule, Princess Zoe took refuge in Rome. It was from there, in the name of the great idea of unifying the two Churches, that she was sent to Moscow. Of course, nothing came of Ivan III's conversion to the Christian faith or the Latin rite; in fact, under her husband's domination, Zoe became the most vocal spokeswoman for the Orthodox tradition, linked, after all, to her upbringing in the Byzantine tradition. Some historians even credit Princess Zoe for bringing to the Moscow court the tradition of the two-headed eagle, the symbol of the Byzantine Empire.

It must be reiterated that this was the time of the seemingly inevitable decline and fall of Byzantium (Constantinople). In the 15th century, numerous attempts, culminating in the Council of Florence, were made to unite the Eastern and Western Churches. However, efforts to save Byzantium from the Turks failed. Indeed, some efforts only strengthened the conviction of many Orthodox Christians that 'a turban is better than a [cardinal's] *galero* [hat]', and all attempts to communicate with the Latinists end up in such a way that the latter would not give any real political help, but instead would steal away the soul. Thus, after the fall of Byzantium, Princess Zoe was married in the Kremlin to Ivan III in 1472; Moscow had already openly claimed the role of heir to Byzantium. For as long as it had endured, if only at the end as a tiny state surrounded by enemies, Byzantium had nevertheless possessed undisputed primacy in the Orthodox world. There was only one Orthodox Emperor, in Byzantium. When that Emperor died in heroic battle against the Turks on the walls of Constantinople, into the political vacuum that was then created in the Orthodox world, stepped Moscow, the heir to that fallen Empire.

Sculpture depicting the head of the Byzantine princess Zoe Palaiologina, niece of the last Byzantine emperor Constantine XI Palaiologos, who died when the city fell to the Ottoman Turks. In 1472 in a initiative of the Catholic church seeking to convert Moscow from Orthodoxy she became the wife of Ivan III of Russia and Grand Duchess of Moscow; her grandson was to be Ivan IV the Terrible.

In this way the doctrine of Moscow as the 'Third Rome' was gradually born. Rome had seen its title as the world's leading city pass from the Tiber over to the Bosporus, to Constantinople. When that city fell a thousand years later to the Muslim Turks, Orthodoxy 'naturally' moved its imperial capital to Moscow, the Third Rome. In fact, it simply moved to the last viable and then vibrant state where Orthodoxy was the ruling religion (if utterly dependent on the ruler) aiding in this way the consolidation of the motherland and from whence the great reconquest of lands lost by the Orthodox faith would take place.

The idea of Moscow as a Third Rome and a Second Jerusalem was announced in its original form as early as 1492. However, it was not until the years 1523–1524 that the monk Philotheus of the Pskov monastery (Moscow had then recently conquered Pskov), fully expressed this idea in a passionate letter he addressed to the new Tsar, Vasily III: two Romes have fallen, the third is Moscow and it will not fall as long as it remains faithful to the Orthodox mission. A mission thus emerged, one of hatred of the Latin or Western world, a mission to liberate of all fellow Christians groaning under the weight of the 'Latin' yoke. This was how the program of imperial conquest against the lands of the Polish-Lithuanian state would be first sanctified. For in those lands were to be found the closest Slavic relations, 'our brothers', those who yearned to be 'liberated.'

Ivan III appreciated the importance of symbols that would elevate his power to the heights of a universal empire. But he didn't think only in terms of symbols or ideological influence. Three years after his marriage to Zoe, in 1475, he formed an important alliance with a new political entity created after the breakup of the Golden Horde, the so-called Crimean Khanate. Of course, this alliance was naturally against the Polish-Lithuanian state. Ivan III's Moscow diplomacy also takes him into contact with the wide-open area of European politics for the first time. Firstly, he made contact with the then largest and the most dangerous direct rival of the Jagiellonians' in Central Europe, namely Hungarian King Matthias Corvinus (1443–1490), a man who had restored the power of the Hungarian state after conflicts over succession arising from defeat at the battle of Varna in 1444, where young King Ladislaus (Władysław) Warneńczyk, heir to the thrones of both Poland and Hungary, had died while leading a cavalry charge at the age of just 20. In the mid-15th century Corvinus had emerged and now stood in the way of perpetuating the continued rule of the Jagiellonian dynasty in the Hungarian capital.

The power of the Hungarian state and the allure of the Buda court, highly civilized and playing a leading role in the emerging Renaissance (Hungary stood culturally supreme in this part of Europe), attracted the attention of Casimir Jagiellon. Holding the dual title of Polish King and Grand Duke of Lithuania he aspired to place one of his sons on that throne, as he likewise did on another throne, that of Prague, a throne then held by George of Poděbrady, a man unrecognized by most European courts. Ivan III in Moscow could grasp the map of Europe and with the swift recognition of a two-headed eagle he saw that it was to the west and south of Poland's capital in Krakow, that allies could be sought to crush, or at least undermine, the power of the Polish-Lithuanian state. For he recognized that power and would not challenge it alone.

After securing his first ally, Matthias Corvinus, in 1484, two years later Ivan III reached out further west, to the imperial court of the Habsburgs, where the future main rivals of the Jagiellonian dynasty in the struggle for supremacy in Central Europe were to be found. Diplomatic feelers were sent to Vienna via Nuremberg and back again to Moscow. In 1486/87, Moscow-Habsburg diplomatic exchanges began. For Ivan, it was essential not only to have an anti-Jagiellon alliance with the Habsburgs but also to satisfy his aspirations to be recognized as 'Emperor in the East' and so be taken seriously by his 'peer' in Western Europe. He directly sought recognition of his title of Tsar or Emperor. It is at this time that the title of Tsar enters into Ivan III's titulary though it is not yet consistently or permanently applied. His grandson, Ivan IV, would later permanently adopt it.

Moscow's diplomatic preparations to surround the Jagiellonians, and their Polish-Lithuanian state, from the south and the west, gain additional significance if we realize that it was at this time that Ivan III made a decisive move on the geopolitical map of Eastern Europe, the annexation of Veliky Novgorod. This happened in 1471 though it was later by force of necessity conquered again in 1478/79. The annexation took place under circumstances that still to this day arouse the emotions of some historians and many purveyors of alternative history.

Novgorod, clearly realizing the growing threat and its virtual encirclement by Moscow, sought support in Krakow and Vilnius from Casimir
Jagiellon. A representative of the pro-Jagiellonian orientation in Novgorod,
Marfa Boretskaya, known as Posadnitsa (the wife of Isaac Boretsky, head
of Novgorod's merchant's guild), wanted to bring about a formal alliance
with Casimir Jagiellon, obliging the Polish King to help Novgorod in the
event of a Moscow invasion. 'We do not want the Grand Duke of Moscow!
We are not his patrimony! We are a free people!' These shouts resounded at
a Novgorod rally called by the famous town bell in 1470. Then in defiance
of Ivan III, the independent politicians of Novgorod elected King Jagiełło's
grandson, Mikhail Olelkovich, one of the Orthodox Gediminas, as the new
prince of Novgorod. However, Lithuania did not provide Novgorod, then
threatened by a Moscow invasion, with any assistance. The Novgorodian
'army' such as it was would be annihilated by the forces of Ivan III, at the
Battle of Shelon, in July of 1471. A just punishment for their 'treachery' with
the Latin King of Poland

Here we foreshadow the methods used in later years, right down to
the present day, each and every time Moscow would reach out to make an
imperial conquest to annex additional territory. Ivan III cunningly first
applied these methods specifically to Novgorod: he led the executions of
the most prominent representatives of the elite hostile to his rule, accusing
them of 'treason.' A much larger group was then deported to Moscow. Ivan
strengthened his pro-Moscow party that was already in place (assisted by
the orthodox church) making it more closely subordinate to his will, yet
still not directly incorporating the territory into the Moscow realm. In the
words of his Russian biographer, the great Muscovite prince cemented in
place of the previous republican tradition a political culture of despotism
based on the psychology of the poor.' A republic does not provide a tangible
sense of freedom to the poor; despotism does not either. However, despotism 'justly' takes that freedom away from everyone, both poor and rich.
The victorious and cruel tyranny, would punish the representatives of the
elite harshly, giving in this way, a twisted sense of equality: the equality
of fear. Fear of the court of the Grand Duke. In deference to this poverty
psychology, Ivan, during his visit to the northern metropolis in late 1475,
readily took advantage of denunciations made by the poorer members of

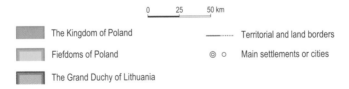

Poland & Lithuania 2ⁿᵈ half of 15ᵗʰ century

```
0      25      50 km
```

The Kingdom of Poland	⎯⎯⎯⎯ Territorial and land borders
Fiefdoms of Poland	◎ ○ Main settlements or cities
The Grand Duchy of Lithuania	

Novgorod's population against the remnants of its elites. At the end of 1476, Ivan's officials deported yet another batch of such 'unruly' occupants from Novgorod to Moscow for 'trial'. A prototype for the 20ᵗʰ century trial of sixteen leaders of Poland's underground WW2 State and Home Army, duped into captivity by Stalin's hatchet men in 1945. The humiliation of

Ivan III's earlier show trial led to a secondary anti-Moscow uprising by Novgorod, ruthlessly suppressed.

In January 1478, the Novgorodians once again surrendered their city after this 2nd uprising. Symbols of the city's independent stance and status were taken to Moscow including: the brave Marfa Boretskaya (along with her grandson, as her sons had already been imprisoned or executed by Moscow's henchmen) together with the great bell, used to call the population of the city to assembly and voting. That symbol of more than three centuries of Novgorod's independence. Another symbol of independence was the diplomatic archive of the merchant republic, also taken to Moscow, to provide evidence of Novgorod's 'treachery,' i.e. accords with Lithuania and the Polish King. This time, there were mass deportations of the entire population and settlers loyal to Ivan III now took their place. Veliky Novgorod, by means of salami tactics, was eventually fully incorporated into Moscow between 1471 and 1478. More 'slices' in the form of other settlements would quickly follow. The cities of Tver (incorporated into Ivan's rule in 1485), Ryazan (practically as early as 1483), and later Pskov. This last city also saw its inhabitants revolt, although Ivan's governors had actually ruled there from 1461; finally, the symbol of the rally to freedom and liberty, the bell of Pskov was also brought to Moscow though only in 1510. This was the model of Moscow's imperialism. This was how northern Rus, a centuries old republican alternative to Moscow's despotic, political culture of enslavement, was extinguished.

In 1480, Ivan III finally rid himself of the 'protection' of the Mongol overlords that had been weighing down on him. The former Golden Horde, which had been sowing fear in Rus principalities for nearly two centuries, no longer by that time existed as a coercive force. Having collapsed under the weight of internal feuds and into separate khanates: the Kazan khanate, the Astrakhan khanate, the Siberian khanate, the Nogai khanate, and key to our area of interest the Crimean khanate. This Crimean khanate had been solidifying since the mid-15th century on the northern shore of the Black Sea under the Girei dynasty. To the east in the center of the former Golden Horde lands, with its capital at Sarai on the lower Volga, Batu Khan tried unsuccessfully to maintain power and legacy of the Great Horde. It mobilized to 'protect' Novgorod from Moscow but when it was clear there would now be concurrent Polish-Lithuanian mobilization the initiative petered out. Thus, in 1480, after the unsuccessful intervention of the Kazan Khanate, the Mongol rule over the eastern Slavic lands of Rus, which had lasted two and a half centuries, effectively expired. A dozen years later, the remnants of the Golden Horde would be finally swept away by Moscow.

Why did Casimir Jagiellon act so passively at this critical turning point in Eastern European history? We must recall that these events occurred just after the Peace of Toruń in 1466, which had ended yet another war with the Teutonic Knights, this time of Thirteen Years'. A war now conclusively resolved. Gdańsk & Pomerania had finally been recovered, a diminished Teutonic Order had been made *de facto* dependent on the Polish state; it was no longer any threat. Finally, Casimir Jagiellon's strategic eye could now turn to the south towards Prague and Buda, to the courts and the rich and cultured capitals so much closer to Krakow. Cities where he wanted to install his sons, as these cultural capitals attracted him much more than wealth in Novgorod. They appealed to him with the level of their civilization, economic, cultural and political allure. This was also the opinion of the Polish elites and, above all, those of the Lesser Poland (Pol.: *Małopolska*) of Krakow region. The decision to turn to the south instead of north, was a confirmation of Poland's Latin orientation.

The distance from Novgorod (just south of modern-day St. Petersburg) to Vilnius is similar to the distance from Vilnius to Krakow. Any intervention of Casimir thus presented obvious logistical challenges and flanking threats to his military arising from such a remote northeastern campaign to liberate the seized lands Thus, whether it was the aspirations for and preoccupation with the southern thrones of Buda and Prague, military logistical concerns, or an expression of the more profound, fundamental, Latin orientation of the Polish-Lithuanian elite, towards the southwest rather than the northeast the decision was taken. Perhaps it was indeed a logical logistical and strategic calculation. Or perhaps was it Moscow's effective malign diversionary tactics of the time, which were decisive in this case. Playing a crucial role in the Polish-Lithuanian state's failure to engage. Novgorod's ultimate fate was largely a geographical geopolitical fait acompli. The Moscow diversion that I allude to above consisted primarily in organizing a conspiracy of Rus boyars with the Jagiellonian state against Casimir Jagiellon. This led to an

The wedding of Grand Duke Vasily II the Blind of Moscow to Princess Maria daughter of Jaroslaw the wise of Kyiv. The bridegroom's mother Sophia Vitoldovna rips off a belt from Vasily the Cross-Eyed that once belonged to Dmitry Donskoy. Painting by Pavel Chistyakov.

assassination attempt on the King during one of his trips to Lithuania. The timely detection of the assassination attempt ended with the execution of two of the most critical conspirators. Yet as a harbinger of future conflict a third conspirator, Fyodor Bielski, fled to Moscow, and there his daughter married Ivan III's son, Vasily, to became mother to Ivan the Terrible.

This conspiracy in the late 1470s, at the time of Novgorod's second subjugation by Moscow, shook the foundations of Casimir IV Jagiellon's rule in the Rus lands. It brought to light once again the problem I have mentioned here many times. The rule over the Rus lands inside the Lithuanian state was neither secure nor stabilized. There were still internal tensions between ethnic Lithuanian and Rus elites, now excellently played off against each

Ivan III "the Harsh" of Russia throws off the Tatar yoke and orders the killing of the Khan's deputies. An artistic vision by Nikolay Shustov.

other by Moscow's center of imperial expansion. The initial stage of these destabilizing operations took advantage of pre-existing internal divisions in the enemy's lands and thus prepared the ground for future conquest and annexation by Moscow. This would become the playbook for future Russian expansion. The second stage, the transition to open aggression, occurred immediately, after Casimir Jagiellon's passing. His half-century-long reign, which nevertheless inspired respect in the Kremlin, now came to an end. At this point, the personal union between Lithuania and the Crown, never formalized as a legal union of states instead merely by means of a common ruling succession, started to fray and in some ways even collapse. Alexander Jagiellon (1461–1506) ascended the throne in the Grand Duchy, while his older brother Jan Olbracht (1459–1501) in turn took the throne in Krakow.

Casimir Jagiellon's eldest son, Vladislav (1456–1516), was already occupying thrones in Buda and Prague at the time but was a man lacking in initiative. For Ivan, this Jagiellonian division was a dream-like opportunity.

In 1492, Moscow thus went on a direct offensive against the Lithuanian state. A series of six wars in total waged against Lithuania (and later also against Poland who would, after a time, back the Lithuanian state) now began: 1492–1494, 1500–1503, 1507–1508, 1512–1522, 1534–1537, 1563–1570, in fact they lasted throughout the century until Ivan IV the Terrible and his clashes with the Polish elected King Stephen Bathory (Pol.: *Stefan Batory*): 1577–1582, when Moscow's momentum was finally halted, though at the cost of massive military and economic losses for both sides throughout the 16th century.

At the outset Ivan III simply launched his traditional 'acquisition' operation, the snatching of more Rus lands from Lithuania. Immediately after King Casimir's death in the summer of 1492. Ivan ordered armed expeditions up to the border territories of Mezetsk, Sierpetsk, Masalsk, and Vyazma. There was also a threat of an attack on Lithuania's key stronghold in the east, Smolensk. In 1493, Moscow was unexpectedly offered a type of alliance with the ruler of the emerging city of Warsaw, Duke Konrad the Red of the original Piast dynasty. A man who wanted to consolidate the surrounding Mazovian lands under his rule, Piast rule, once again. In playing against the Polish Crown's tenuous hold on Mazovia, Ivan sought agents of influence, breaking up the forces of the Polish and Lithuanian states from within, and not by Instrumentalizing the Orthodox faithful. He found some willing agents who, like Duke Konrad, through their own ambitions, allowed themselves to be turned into tools of Moscow's policy. This opportunistic tactic, well remembered in the Kremlin, would be another key element in Moscow's future geopolitical strategy.

Of course, the Kremlin continued to seek an ally in the Western Empire, with the Habsburgs. Fortunately for Poland, the new ruler, Maximilian (from 1493), was temporarily more preoccupied with his efforts to try and control Milan, so Ivan's offer to partition the Jagiellonian monarchies was, at this point 'put on hold' for two and a half centuries. Therefore, in February of the following year, a new 'perpetual peace' was concluded with Moscow. Lithuania finally renounced all its rights to sovereignty over Novgorod,

Tver, Ryazan, and Pskov, all already either incorporated into Moscow or fully subordinated to it. It was losing a relatively small part of its actual territory for the time being, with Vyazma sharing the border 'principalities of Verkhovsk' with Ivan. Peace was to be sealed by the marriage of Lithuanian Grand Duke Alexander to Ivan the III's daughter, the beautiful Helena. She turned out to be a good wife, but, as we shall see, she was only a tool for her father to legitimize later incursions into Lithuania.

Alexander's older brother Jan Olbracht, the King of Poland, urged Alexander to settle relations with Moscow peacefully as soon as possible. From the very beginning of his reign, Jan Olbracht like Casimir before him thought of reorientating the entire effort of Poland but also of its natural, as it seemed to him, Jagiellonian allies (specifically Lithuania and Hungary) towards the south. In keeping with the geographical aspirations of Casimir, he wanted to regain lost access to the Black Sea, Kiliya, and Belgorod, to separate the Ottoman Empire anew from the Crimean Khanate, and indeed as a first step to regain effective control over the Moldavian fiefdom. His efforts however ended in his defeat in the forests of Bukovina in 1497.

During the war, which was interrupted in 1494, (a conscious prelude to a decisive showdown), Ivan III had begun to regularly use the title 'lord of all Rus,' targeting the very basis of the Grand Duchy of Lithuania's territorial legitimacy. Alexander as ruler of the Duchy could thus never agree to the recognition of this title. In 1500 taking advantage of the weakening prestige and real power of the Jagiellonian monarchies, Moscow again sent out its armies, prepared for many months, against Lithuania. The pretext for the new war, the second already in just eight years that Ivan III imposed on his western neighbor, was the alleged 'persecution of the Orthodox Church' under Alexander Jagiellon. At least according to Moscow's interpretation. Ivan himself explained the precise nature of this oppression for Alexander had allowed the construction of a *Latin rite place of worship* (i.e. a Catholic Church) in Polotsk. Thus, the mere existence of a Catholic place of worship in the Rus lands of Lithuania was regarded by Ivan as an act of 'oppression' of Orthodoxy. The Moscow ruler also stressed the 'malign' aspirations of the Orthodox archbishop of Kyiv who wanted to renew the Florentine Union on the territory of the Grand Duchy of Lithuania, meaning religious authority in the lands for the Pope. However, most Orthodox lords, boyars,

Constantinople, as rendered in a 14th-century French miniature.

and townspeople in Lithuania did not feel oppressed many having reached the highest echelons in the Grand Duchy's power structures. The wealthiest among them, Prince Konstanty Ostrogski, was, in fact, Hetman (Field Commander) of the entire Lithuanian army.

However, one great Lithuanian lord, that Prince Semyon Bielski, whose brother Fyodor, had been beheaded nearly 20 years earlier for his involvement in a plot on the life of Casimir Jagiellon was tempted by Moscow. He decided to go over openly to Ivan's along with his borderland holdings in Belaya, located about 150 km northeast of Smolensk. Ivan had been waiting for just such an opportunity for a long time. Though he knew that by accepting Alexander's subject into his service, he violated the 1494 peace treaty with Lithuania, which forbade either side from so doing. He also knew that several other princes were already following in Bielski's footsteps, among them Vasily Ivanovich Mažaisky (who ruled over a large area from Kursk to Severovo Novgorod) and Semyon Ivanovich Shemichev, who ruled over Starodub, Gomel, and Chernihiv, all key strongholds on the road from Smolensk to Kyiv. This was the goal of Ivan, to capture Smolensk and later Kyiv.

But let's emphasize once again the relevance of these Moscow methods for the present day. Methods innovatively practiced by Ivan III as a pretext for war and as a road map for the destruction of the intended victim from within and without. Here, in 1500, for the first time towards the Lithuanian state, then against the Polish-Lithuanian state, the Kremlin began to formally instrumentalize the religious argument. Presenting himself as the political 'guardian' of Orthodoxy, Ivan demanded recognition of his right to evaluate the fate of Orthodox Christians abroad and intervene on their behalf. In contrast, however, not even modest freedoms for Catholics, less still for followers of Judaism, could be mentioned in Moscow. It is difficult not to reflect, unfortunately, in such a historical context, on the 'message of reconciliation' of 2012 that I referred to in the first chapter. An initiative dictated by Ivan's 21st century successors in the Kremlin and foolishly adopted by their compliant, perhaps complicit political 'counterparts' of the time in Poland. That declaration signed by the Moscow Patriarch Kirill I (a long-time KGB agent code named: 'Mikhailov') read out in August 2012 at the Royal Castle in Warsaw. The site of the declaration was intentional by Moscow, for in the minds of many Poles the

Royal Castle of Warsaw shares a dual place in history. It was also the seat of the Tsar's governors in the 19th century. There was also a clear if subtle messaging for Poles taking place. As Moscow has always used Orthodoxy for political interference, a means to sow disunity, to weaken its western neighbors. In the 17th and 18th centuries, this 'defense of religious rights of minorities' was used repeatedly, especially by the 'Enlightened Monarchies'. Not only against the Polish-Lithuanian Commonwealth it would also be instrumentalized and imposed on a weakening Turkey in the 18th and 19th centuries.

In 1500, Ivan wanted, to deal a fatal blow to the Lithuanian state with the aid of a new alliance with the Crimean Khan. That year while Lithuanian possessions in Kyiv were ravaged by the Crimean Khan Girey, the troops of Ivan decisively defeated the Lithuanian army in the great Battle of Vedrosha, taking prisoner the most prominent Russo-Lithuanian leader of the time, the Orthodox prince Konstanty Ostrogski. Fortunately, Poland and Lithuania had finally begun to collaborate militarily that year. Alexander came to an accord with the Polish King Jan Olbracht. Jointly they now launched a broad diplomatic offensive, a distinctive strength of the Jagiellonian states during this difficult moment. Support gathered, ranged from France in the west (important to stem the threat of Turkey joining in coalition against the Jagiellonian states) to the remnants of the Golden Horde in the east the so-called Great Horde from the Volga River, which supported the Lithuanians militarily.

Thus strengthened, King Olbracht sent the first-ever Polish envoy to Moscow in the early months of 1501, an envoy who faced down Ivan jointly with delegates of two other Jagiellon states: Alexander of Lithuania and also Ladislaus of Bohemia and Hungary. This manifestation of fraternal solidarity was simultaneously a veiled threat to muster Hungarian and Polish aid in the event of any further aggression by Ivan against Lithuania. Unfortunately, the impending death of Jan Olbracht and the subsequent distractions resulting from the succession process of a new Polish King paused any preparations for a counterstrike in the east. Thankfully though following in the footsteps of Casimir's dual reign, the union of Vilnius with Krakow was restored, with Alexander now additionally taking up the Polish royal throne. Smolensk thankfully withstood a siege of close to three-months by

Ivan's army in the fall of 1502. Moscow, however, still retained all its gains from the previous two years, amounting to almost a third of the Grand Duchy of Lithuania's total territory before the war.

After negotiations from January to March 1503, a six-year truce was concluded in Moscow. Ivan's state was expanded by an area of more than 200,000 square kilometers (an area the size of today's Belarus). The Chernihiv and Severian lands, with such strong strongholds as Chernihiv, Starodub, Gomel. Severian Novgorod, the northeastern territories around Kyiv, with Lyubichy and Putivl, the southern part of the principality of Mstislavl, a large part of the Smolensk lands, with Bryansk, Trubchevsk, Dorohobuzh and Toropets, and even part of the Polotsk land already adjacent to the Lithuanian capital Vilnius, including Nevel, all came under Moscow's rule. Alexander also reluctantly recognized Ivan as the ruler *gosudar* of *Vseia Rus* (ruler of all Rus), which only reinforced Ivan and his successors' sense of entitlement and destiny to continue their efforts to banish Lithuania from the Rus lands. Under the truce of 1503, Moscow also established its rule on the trade route of the Dnieper River, near Gomel and Chernihiv, driving a wedge at that location deep into the remaining territory of the Grand Duchy of Lithuania.

After the death of Ivan III in 1505, the young Vasily III temporarily appeared to be a less threatening opponent. On the Polish throne, too, there was a change Sigismund the Old (1467–1548) again reunited the thrones of Vilnius and Krakow succeeding to them in 1506. This concurrent succession obviously strengthened the Polish-Lithuanian state. However, the Polish Lithuanian attempt to undo the result of the two previous wars by means of a third war in 1507–1508 failed with no territorial gains. A significant change was brought only by the diplomacy of Sigismund the Old, who crucially now won the Tatars to the Polish side after they had spent some thirty years participating in opposing alliances. This greatly strengthened Poland's geopolitical position in its rivalry with Moscow. Please still note that only thirty years earlier, Lithuania had seven neighbors to the east including the Pskov and Novgorod Republics, the Grand Duchy of Tver, Moscow, the Grand Duchy of Ryazan, plus the Great Horde and the Crimean Khanate. Now there were only two, the Crimean Khanate and an expanding Moscow.

The coronation of Alexander Jagiellon as represented on a miniature in the Roman Pontifical of Bishop Erazm Ciołek from around 1510.

Then, in 1512, the next and longest of the Kremlin's wars with the Polish-Lithuanian state began. It lasted ten years. Vasily III directed his armies at Smolensk wanting in this way to finally open the road to Vilnius and Kyiv. This war became the first occasion for an attempted partition of the Polish-Lithuanian state, a partition by Moscow and remnants of the Teutonic state, Monastic Prussia. Prior to the conflict, the more dangerous, earlier concept of a Moscow alliance with the Habsburgs and the Holy Roman Empire began to take shape. The Habsburgs were still the main rivals of the Jagiellonian dynasty in the struggle for the Hungarian and Bohemian thrones. This rivalry promoted the renewal of Emperor Maximilian's contacts with Vasily. At the end of February 1514, the terms of a first treaty of the two double-headed eagles, both Catholic and Orthodox, were negotiated in Moscow.

The date for a joint attack by Moscow and Vienna on Poland was agreed to be the day of its patron saint, Saint Adalbert (Pol.: *Św. Wojciech*), that is, 23 April of the following year. Emboldened by the deal with Maximilian and with renewed hope of breaking Polish-Lithuanian resistance, Vasily III threw a huge army, reportedly as large as 80,000 strong, into Lithuania in April 1514. The main thrust, was led by Prince Glinsky, went again towards Smolensk. On 31 July, the overwhelmed defenders surrendered Smolensk to Moscow's rule. One hundred and ten years after Vytautas had recaptured this stronghold (with the help of Polish knights) for Lithuania. Thus, the key stronghold for strategic supremacy in Eastern Europe fell into the hands of Vasily. No longer referred to simply as grand prince, but 'Tsar Vasily'. The Moscow *hospodar* triumphed doubly at this point. Not only because he had finally gained the coveted fortress. Having proclaimed himself Tsar for some time and thus equal in power to the other Emperors (Byzantine, which no longer existed) the Khans of the former Golden Horde (also no longer in existence), Vasily crucially also obtained recognition of his new title from the 'Latin Emperor', Maximilian, a condition of the alliance with the Habsburgs that the ruler of Moscow had set. Maximilian accepted this condition. On 4 August 1514, still unaware of the capture of Smolensk by the Moscow army, Emperor Maximilian signed the text of the 'eternal alliance' with Vasily, 'by the grace of God Emperor and Ruler of all Rus,' and had it delivered to him by his envoy Schnitzenpaumer. (TN Start) This was the commencement of centuries of close collaboration between Vienna and

Moscow marked by among other events the partitions of Poland in the 18ᵗʰ century and Russian support in suppressing the Hungarian revolt against Hapsburg rule in 1848. (TN End)

Three and a half centuries later, the geopolitical horror of this moment was captured in a painting then envisioned by the Krakow artist Jan Matejko. The 24-year-old at the time painter, was the son of a Czech man and his German wife, people who chose Poland as their homeland and lived there under Habsburg rule as Poland at the time no longer existed on the map of Europe. Matejko gave this strategic horror embodiment in the atypical shape of the grizzled figure of *Stańczyk*, the court jester of the Jagiellons. The full title of the famous work, painted in 1862, is somewhat misleading: *Stańczyk at a ball at Queen Bona's court when news comes of the loss of Smolensk*. In the summer of 1514 when Smolensk fell, Bona Sforza was not a queen of Poland; Sigismund's beloved first wife, Barbara Zápolya, was still alive. What is essential, however, is that gloomy stare that the wise *Stańczyk* casts into the future: he understands the implications of that fateful breakthrough made at Smolensk's gate. Though, more than a thousand kilometers from Krakow's Renaissance court he knows that further defeats will follow it, giving way step by step, slice by slice, to Moscow's advances, leading ultimately to the final partitioning of Poland and for Matejko's lifespan at least, foreign Hapsburg rule in Krakow.

In August 1980, the popular Polish signer-songwriter of the time, Jacek Kaczmarski again conjured up these visions in his popular song about *Stańczyk*. In both these artistic expressions, painting and song, we can see a harsh reproach against the political elite of the era being repeated. Not only did they not understand this threat, they make no attempt to avert the danger, and were simply too busy with their idyllic Renaissance pastimes. It is not a just reproach, but an echo of the past repeated in the political teachings of the historical school of Krakow, which took on Matejko's *Stańczyk* as its patron. Already, there in this moment at the beginning of the 16ᵗʰ century, lay the source of the future Polish partitions, it is the Poles themselves. Their own nativity, selfish hedonism, their internal weaknesses are the origins of their own downfall.

Poland, or more precisely, the Jagiellonian dynasty, now had to pay dearly to avert the mortal danger through a major strategic concession towards

Stańczyk – the court jester of Jan Olbracht, Aleksander Jagiellończyk, Zygmunt Stary and Zygmunt August – in Jan Matejko's painting 'Stańczyk during a ball at the court of Queen Bona in the face of the loss of Smoleńsk' The great fortress was stormed and captured by Moscow's troops in 1514.

the Habsburgs. The Empire thus was drawn away from its alliance with Moscow by a treaty concluded in Vienna in 1515. Sigismund the Old and representatives of the Jagiellonian elite in Bohemia and Hungary agreed to such a deal with the Habsburgs that in the event of an heirless death of the unifying thrones in Buda and Prague, Ludwig Jagiellon would assume both thrones. Of course, no one could have predicted at the time that 11 years later, this Ludwig (1506–1526) would follow in the footsteps of Ladislaus (Władysław) Warneńczyk and die heirless on the battlefield of Mohacz in 1526, at the age of 20. The thrones of Buda and Prague would thus slip irrevocably from Jagiellonian hands.

Although the Habsburgs gave up their alliance with Moscow, after such a concession by the Jagiellons, the very fact that such a Moscow-Vienna deal had been concluded a year earlier showed the new diplomatic and geopolitical capabilities of the Kremlin especially in its anti-Polish dealings with potential Western partners. One now had to win alone in the field in order to defend oneself. Diplomatic concessions to the Empire were not enough. When a Moscow army of 45,000 men moved westward out from the captured fortress of Smolensk, an approximately 25,000-strong Polish-Lithuanian-Rus army now marched against it from Minsk. They were led by Hetman Konstanty Ostrogski. The proud, Orthodox Rus wanted to finally wash away the disgrace of his defeat and capture 11 years earlier at the Battle of Vedrosha. The two armies met on 8 September 1514, near Orsha, on the Dnieper River, in the same place where Vasyl's and Sigismund's armies had already faced each other six years earlier. The Polish and Lithuanian forces, with their masterful horsemen utterly defeated the army of the would-be Tsar of All-Rus. His battle aspirations were shattered during this great Battle of Orsha. In Belarus to this day patriots commemorate the day. September 8th is a holiday celebrating their national pride with the chosen patron the victorious Hetman Ostrogski: an Orthodox Rus who refused to be a subject of the Moscow *hospodar*. Novgorod had perished, but another Rus embodying an alternative to Moscow's rule triumphed in this battle: a place in history for Belarus and Ukraine as political and cultural entities separate from Moscow was now assured both in memory and in history.

The essential geopolitical loss of Smolensk, however, could not be reversed during the course of this war. Likewise, Moscow's goals of eradicating all Lithuanian rule over the Rus lands were also, fortunately, not achieved. Although Vasily III did not resign fully from them. In 1517, he made a deal with Albrecht Hohenzollern, the last Grand Master of the Teutonic Order and precursor of the later Prussian dynasty that Bismarck would later harness and lead to German unification. Albrecht struggling to maintain the viability of the Order, was ready to ally with Moscow and strike a combined blow against the Polish-Lithuanian state, thus carving out a larger piece of land for his rule. On 10 March that year, Albrecht's envoy Dietrich Schönberg signed a formal alliance with Vasily against the Polish-Lithuanian state in the Kremlin. This was the first, but not the last,

Battle of Orsha – fought on 8 September 1514 – a great victory for the forces led by Konstanty Ostrogski now a celebrated hero of Belarussian national independence movement. Painting from the first half of the 16th century by a painter from the circle of Lucas Cranach the Elder. The view depicts the crossing of the Polish artillery over an improvised pontoon bridge over the Dnieper River.

as we see from today's perspective, a political union between Moscow the Hohenzollerns and their political inheritors, built around the common project of eradicating Poland and Lithuania from the map. The 1517 version of this alliance, though controversial, involving an accord between an arch-Catholic crusading Order, under the formal patronage of the Pope in Rome, and the schismatic 3rd Rome of Moscow. To explain away this paradox a most daring yet surprisingly effective 'clarification' was sent by Albrecht from Königsberg to Rome: explaining that the Order's talks with the ruler of Moscow were, of course, directed ultimately at converting Vasily to Catholicism…

Thus, was born the first project of the Russian-German (as opposed to Russian-Habsburg) partition of Poland dating from 1517. As it was in every subsequent partition project, with the possible exception of the

Molotov-Ribbentrop Pact, in this alliance it was the Russian side that was the initiator and also the stronger party. It was Moscow that sponsored Albrecht Hohenzollern, giving him a considerable sum of money to field an envisaged force of 12,000 troops. Fortunately for us Poles, the master of the Order took the money, even with these funds his weakened state could not field the adequate number of soldiers. Poland managed to secure victory in this new conflict with the Order, fighting on simultaneous fronts. At that point, the future doom of Poland had not yet coalesced as it would in the later embodiment of such alliances between Russia and Prussia under their future German rulers, Catherine and Fredrich the Great. The true lesson of the war of 1512–1522 was that it illustrated the geopolitical threat posed by an offensive Moscow operating in conjunction with western neighbors of the Polish-Lithuanian state with both sides discerning the geopolitical gains inherent for them in the weakening of Polish-Lithuanian power. As it was, this threat will be inherited by Sigismund the Old's successor, Sigismund Augustus, and by subsequently elected kings, as the Polish-Lithuanian Union takes on its new formalized nature as the Polish-Lithuanian Commonwealth or 'Rzeczpospolita'.

CHAPTER III

The Great War. *Rzeczpospolita*: Europe's First Imperfect Union, Cast Aside by Moscow (XVI–XVII Centuries)

The turn of the 16th and 17th centuries was perhaps the period when Poland (latter as the Polish-Lithuanian Commonwealth) enjoyed the most significant advantage in its history of conflict with the Grand Duchy of Moscow (which would also, though somewhat later, change its name, to Russia). Therefore, whenever we Poles experience such moments of advantage, strength, success, or an increased sense of responsibility among nations for what happened in the past, a legitimate question always arises. Did we not waste our opportunity to emerge triumphant in this troubled neighborhood? Before we consider this question in depth I would like us to first return to our chronology, which appears at first sight to be a simple continuation of earlier conflicts and wars fought between the Muscovite state, evergrowing in strength, and the Polish-Lithuanian state, retreating gradually westwards from Eastern Europe, under the onslaught by the armies of Ivan III and later Vasily III.

The reign of Vasily's successor in Moscow, Ivan IV, known as the Terrible (*Grozny*) (1530–1584), began with a significant symbolic gesture on his part. He formally inherited the throne when he was only three years old but could not begin ruling until he turned 17 i.e. in 1547. Ivan IV then promptly decided he would be the first ruler in the Kremlin to actually crown himself as opposed to simply proclaiming himself Tsar. Completing through this rite the dream of building a 'Third Rome', utilizing the future symbol of Moscow's monarchs referred to as the Monomakh's cap. Though in fact the cap had been gifted in the early 14th century to Ivan Kalita by his master, the Khan of the Golden Horde it was treated in the Kremlin instead as a symbol of Byzantine imperial heritage. Answering a diplomatic question addressed by the Polish King Sigismund Augustus regarding the significance of this coronation, Ivan the Terrible brazenly lied stating that whoever crowns himself with the 'Monomakh's cap' becomes a Tsar because this crown was offered to the rulers of Rus by the Byzantine Emperor Constantine IX Monomach himself (who reigned in the 11th century).

With this coronation of Ivan IV and the accompanying audacious lie now as the fundamentals of the state's imperial ideology, a new period dawned that would be marked by the renewed energy with which Moscow would embark on its conquests. Their first areas to be targeted were those of Kazan and Astrakhan on the Volga, the last two remnants of the former Mongol Empire. Eliminated in two successive blows: in 1552 and 1556 and though seemingly of no geographical or political relevance to the Polish state, these events are nevertheless very much related to the history of Polish-Russian relations for two reasons. Firstly, because of the ground-breaking significance of the annexation of the two khanates for the very essence of Moscow. A Moscow which certainly from that moment onward can no longer be merely called even erroneously just the heir of Kyivan Rus, or indeed a Rus state in general. Moscow was becoming an empire. At least in the geographical sense. Russia in the proper sense of the word. The principality of Moscow was certainly no longer a state only of the Orthodox Rus. In fact, it had already ceased to be one in 1478 when Ivan III incorporated Veliky Novgorod. For Novgorod was, after all, primarily populated by colonized northerners, representatives of the Finno-Ugric ethnic grouping in fact above all, Finns. They inhabited the forested and swampy areas from Novgorod to the mouth of the Ob River beyond the Urals. However, it was not until the absorption of Kazan and Astrakhan, those large dense areas along the central and lower Volga, with a decidedly non-Slavic and non-Orthodox population (comprising of Mongolians, Tatars, Buryats, Kalmyks) were included, a population with a predominantly Muslim religion, that an empire of differing nations was truly born.

I recall this event to bridge once again the gap between the old and the new Moscow and raise awareness of the enormous modernday challenge Russia now faces in the 21st century: that of a dual identity. It raises the same question that has recurred many times in Russian history, one which also faced the Soviet Union in its final years. Though this question often escapes the view of western observers. Will Russia be a state dominated by an Eastern Slavic element based on the Orthodox tradition, or will it not in time be overwhelmed by the influence of a more demographically buoyant Muslim

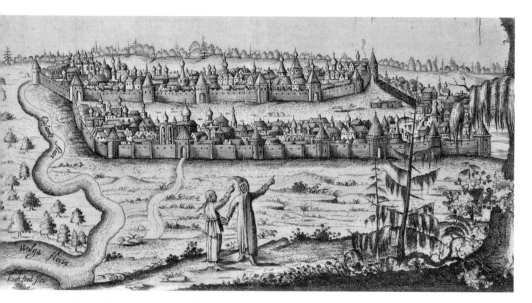

Top: After conquering Kazan, the capital of the Kazan Khanate, Ivan IV the Terrible, ordered that the entire Tatar elite there be either slaughtered or deported deep into Russia's new Siberian territories commencing Moscow's history or mass forced deportations of subjugated peoples. Bottom: Ivan later used the same method against Astrakhan.

population? Perhaps this is why, among other things, Putin has decided to subjugate and absorb slice by slice Lukashenko's Belarus as if it were a minor regional governorship. It's also why he's gambled on conquering Ukraine to push back against this specter of dual identity. The so-called '*Russky mir*' (Russian world), formed on such a basis, is to be the answer to this fear?

In the 16th century, the technique of absorption of new lands was applied on a massive scale to the inhabitants of Kazan, a method that Moscow's rulers first used, as we have already seen in relation to Novgorod. This technique involves deportations and the removal of local elites. (TN Start) It shared some similarities with the English pacification and re-settlement of the northern province of Ireland in the 17th century (TN End). After the capture of Kazan and then Astrakhan, all the more important Tatar families were removed from these cities of these rich fertile lands, either killed outright or deported deep into the infertile and harsh depths of the expanding Russian state. In their place were brought colonists from the center of the Russian state. Exceptionally the Tatars who lived around Kazan were not moved. The most important thing for Moscow was that the capital of the region should change its character and that the Tatars, who had already been indigenous to the land for two or three centuries, should now be demoted in rank and deprived of their elites. Ivan IV implemented this technique effectively against Kazan and on a large scale.

Four centuries later, Mikhail Muravyov, the infamous 'Hangman' who came to pacify Lithuania during the January Uprising of 1863, and his direct successor, General Kaufman, used this as an interesting comparison. They claimed that Lithuania, a remnant of the former Commonwealth, would not become Russian until the Poles in the area were reduced to 'selling soap' like Tatars in Kazan. So, the local intelligentsia should be reduced in their status; they were to become simply local merchants with no ambitions, no elite status. Or they could also choose the path of collaboration with the Empire. Then they would advance like many of the Polish elites and intelligentsia did during the post-WW2 communist era. Individuals building their own hierarchies and then lobbying to shape opinions and policy in the drawing rooms of the post-1989 new 3rd Republic of Poland.

Let us return now to the 16th century. Having accomplished the task of eliminating the elites from the Volga basin population, Ivan IV then experimented with a historical imperial technique to complete the conquest of Kazan and Astrakhan, one even older than Russia and Moscow. This was the practice of mass deportations of the indigenous population. Harking back to the practices of Assyria and ancient Babylon. In doing so, the Tsar made a breakthrough of sorts, as Moscow could now open up such potential migration 'destinations' deep into its recently claimed Asia and Siberian holdings. A grand march from Europe towards Asia, thus reversing the historical dynamics of the great steppe empires up until that date. The populace had always historically pushed from Asia towards Europe. It can be said, half-jokingly, half-seriously, that Moscow was, as it were, taking revenge for the past conquests of Genghis Khan, Attila, and other great conquerors of the Eurasian steppe. Eighty years later, after making this breakthrough, Cossacks, in the service of the Tsar, will make their way all the way to the shores of the Pacific Ocean.

It is this change in the vector of Eurasian expansion, initiated by Ivan the Terrible, that would make Russia a state that could no longer be conquered. At any rate, from the western side. This was simply due to the new strategic depth of its expanse, which will eventually open up as far as Vladivostok and Kamchatka. For this same reason, it will no longer be possible to place the Russian and Polish states side by side as two equal adversaries or even potential partners. The breakthrough for Russia, therefore, did not in fact arrive, as some assume, 80 years later in Ukraine when the Polish Commonwealth lost sway over that land and its people. Instead, it began with this geopolitical initiative born out of the misery of forced migration, opening Russia's way to penetrate and importantly persist in its presence, deep into the Asia landmass.

Ivan IV then turned to the north-western frontier of his empire to carve out a door to the Baltic Sea to which Moscow had no access at the time. It was cut off from it on one hand by Swedish rule, then encamped on the southern shores of the Baltic, on the other by the remnants of the Order of the Knights of the Sword, still occupying at that time the territories of today's Latvia and part of Estonia. The Teutonic Knights, had finally bent the knee to the Commonwealth and secularized in 1525, and everyone knew the days of this other earlier Order, of the Knights of the Sword on the Dvina River were also numbered. Ivan IV, therefore, decided to strike first destroying this state. In this way, he would secure a broad access to the

The cruelty of Tsar Ivan IV the Terrible still today exceeds the imagination of the civilized world. The ruler did not even spare his own son, Ivan, whom he personally murdered in 1581 in a fit of rage. Painting by Ilya Repin.

Baltic for Moscow and at the same time, encircle the Lithuanian capital of Vilnius from the north.

The dispute over the inheritance of the Order of the Knights of the Sword inevitably led to conflict with the Polish Republic. King Sigismund Augustus (1520–1572), one of the wisest rulers in Polish history, well understood the strategic importance of access to the Baltic Sea for Moscow's trade and its further expansion westward. He strove to prevent Ivan from securing this access to the Baltic, inhibiting Moscow's growth. A growth that could then potentially be reinforced by commercial sea-based trade links with new Western partners against the interests of the established Catholic 'transit land' of Poland.

Indeed, in the meantime, Moscow had already elaborated a 'workaround' for this route. England, interested in trading with Moscow and securing access to vital raw materials, opened a sea trade route north around Scan-

113

dinavia with the help of her northern trading company, later named the Muscovy Company. Open only in summer, it reached Arkhangelsk through the White Sea, where ships of English merchants could arrive. This was the same route the British supply convoys ran to the Soviet Union in 1941 and 42. Thus, thanks to England, which at the time, was also under the scepter of another ruler distrustful of the Catholic Church's power, Elizabeth I, who blazed with ideological fervor against a Poland which like Spain was another pillar of the 'papists'. Russia's sea trade with Western Europe was thus already opened and would fuel Moscow's expansionist agenda.

Ever since Martin Luther started the Reformation in 1517, England had been one of the main forces of Protestantism in an already confessionally divided Western Europe. This factor also led to a rapprochement, not just economically but politically, between Protestant forces seeking to undermine Catholicism across continental Europe and the offensive tendencies of an Orthodox Moscow. Ideologically, the Protestants and the Orthodox had little in common, only a common, powerful adversary: the Catholic faith and the political communities that sustained it. The Polish Republic was as Elizabeth pointed out in rather harsh terms one of the most important among these pillars supporting Catholicism on the continent. This anti-Catholic motive in 18th century Europe (which would later unite not only Orthodox and Protestants but also militant atheists) would play out, a significant role in the later vilification of Poland as a state of intolerance, eroding what we would call today Poland's reserves of soft power in the lead up to the period of the partitions. It's a tendency not without relevance for the modern era.

To prevent further expansion of these growing contacts across the Baltic, Sigismund Augustus in 1557 tried to put a stop to the offensive by Ivan IV against the Order of the Knights of the Sword. He countered Ivan's by bringing about the Treaty of Pozvol, in which the Order of the Knights of the Sword now effectively allied with Lithuania against Moscow. Thus began the great Livonian War, which lasted some 25 years, from 1558 to 1583, with a short break of several years after 1570. A war, which was led to a dazzling military conclusion under another newly elected King of the Republic, the resolute Hungarian, Stephen Bathory. Yet the initial stage of this quarter century conflict actually began with a successful Moscow offensive which took place during the earlier reign of Poland's Sigismund Augustus.

Sigismund Augustus, King of Poland by the Grace of God, Grand Duke of Lithuania, Ruthenia, Prussia, Mazovia, Samogitia, Livonia, Smoleńsk, Siewierz and Chernihiv, etc., last male descendant of the Jagiellonian dynasty, as depicted in a portrait from the workshop of Lucas Cranach from around 1555.

In the initial phase Lithuania could not field a significant force on its own and was not yet formally united by a state of union with the Polish Crown, this would take place only later in 1569 at Lublin. It was till that time only a union at the personal level (two separate states having the same ruler). The Grand Duchy of Lithuania denuded of much of its historical lands in earlier conflicts could not alone effectively resist the onslaught of Ivan the Terrible's troops. Gradually the more important strongholds in Livonia were occupied by Ivan's army. In 1563, Moscow troops launched a direct offensive no longer against Livonia but the actual Lithuanian state lands, seizing, among other things, the vital fortress of Polotsk, beyond which the road to Vilnius itself lay open. Here, however, Polish troops supporting the Lithuanians would stand in their way. The force was composed on one hand by the armies of the faithful Orthodox knights of Lithuania led by Filon Kmita, the other main segment was the troops of Mikołaj 'the Red' Radziwiłł, a Calvinist and one of the two prominent Lithuanian magnates as well as an outstanding military leader. Radziwiłł beat the Russian army at the Ula River in January 1564 and then again in February of that same year at Orsha.

After these two defeats of the Russian army, Prince Andrei Kurbsky (1528–1583) defected to the Lithuanian-Polish side. He had been Ivan the Terrible's closest associate and commander of the Moscow army in this section of the front. A characteristic and a symbolic figure. It is worth remembering that Kurbsky became later synonymous with the image of a traitor throughout the Russian state a role he's retained for the next 450 years. This vision of events was artistically, and, at the same time, most influentially recorded for Russian thought and imagination in the two-part film directed by Sergei Eisenstein's 1944–46 *Ivan the Terrible,* a film produced on Stalin's personal orders. The first part deals with the conquest of Kazan, and the second part is entirely devoted to the battle against Lithuania and the betrayal of Ivan the Terrible by the boyars. The film was and perhaps remains, the world's most astonishing cinematic apologia for the terror of Moscow's political police: the so-called *oprichnina.* A militia unit created with the task of simply murdering anyone suspected of disloyalty to the Tsar.

The film also features the stereotype of an effeminate Poland; the Wawel court is ridiculed as a symbol of the 'rotten West.' There is a scene set at Wawel in the film's plot line, informing of Kurbsky's betrayal, and his alleged desire to now partition Russia in partnership with Poland and the Jesuits. According to this image perpetuated by Russia's state propaganda from the time of Ivan the Terrible all the way down through from Stalin and on to Putin, anyone who flees from the Tsar's rule has to be a traitor in league with foreign elements. Any political emigrant is a servant of the rotten West. Prince Kurbsky justified his departure by engaging in an ideological polemic with the Tsar on the grounds of a dispute about his system of rule, about the way power was being exercised or indeed abused.

Prince Andrei Kurbsky has remained the symbol of the Russian political emigrant for so-called free Russians, being the first in a long line of like-minded men and women in Russia's subsequent history. He represented such a symbol in the 19th century for Alexander Herzen, a great friend of the Poles and for many Russian emigrants in the 20th and 21st centuries.

As a defender of absolute power or what would be known as Tsarist Autocracy, Ivan IV was not ashamed to speak of his despotism in his letters to Kurbsky, openly justifying that this was simply what the nation demanded of him: to shear it short like a sheep. 'If you are such a defender of the just cause,' Ivan IV writes to Prince Kurbsky, 'why don't you come to me and become a martyr? Only then will you be able to shine by example.' The cynicism that beats from the pages of Ivan the Terrible's letters makes us think about the cynicism of contemporary Russian political power and that of its disciples on so many levels. We Poles also know about this cynicism from the many texts and political commentaries published in Poland and overseas about Poland often by international and native Polish publicists. I draw attention to the ideological polemic between these two sons of Moscow not just because of its importance for the future of Russia. But its existential importance for the future relationship between the written word and the truth, between the written word and ideas of morality, in our part of Europe. It can serve as an instructive guide to navigate and aid our understanding of what actually happened, in this part of Europe in the centuries following Ivan's reign right up to the present day.

In Russia at that time, a boyar opposition movement was forming against the Tsar, specifically against the Tsar's autarchy. The Moscow Rurik state, now under the penultimate representative of that line, began to enter an era of crisis due to Ivan IV's violent and coercive rule that exceeded all

Prince Andrey Kurbsky (1528–1583) was one of Ivan IV the Terrible's most trusted men. In 1564, however, outraged by the cruelty of the Tsar towards his own subjects he went over to the side of Poland and Lithuania. He continued to reproach the ruling tsar for his cruelty also in their own personal correspondence with one another. A portrait of the prince by Pavel Ryzhenko.

limits of despotism. It was after Andrei Kurbsky left the country that the Tsar introduced the regime of the *oprichnina*, a system of control by so-called political police. This guard answerable to the Tsar was given absolute power over those parts of the state where Ivan IV expected more significant opposition to his rule. Each *oprichnik* had a dog's head attached to his saddle to symbolize loyalty to the tsar. An *oprichnik* could arrest and kill (without warrant or trial) any of the boyars, (that is representatives of the higher nobility) or members of the Moscow court, burn his dwellings and confiscate his land. The *oprichnik*s it is estimated murdered between a few thousand to perhaps even tens of thousands of people.

The eight years of *oprichnina* oppression became the most horrifying symbol of violence by the state directed against its subjects. However, it somehow did not leave a traumatic mark on the public mood of the elite in the Russian state. The aforementioned film of Eisenstein depicts the *oprichnina* as a triumph of the Tsar's wise power over the conspirators, over the oppositionists. For only through bloody repression could the Russian state be saved from the external enemy, that is, from Poland, from the (Latin) West, just as Ivan the Terrible states in the film's closing words. Through this image, Stalin spoke to his subjects, justifying not only his policy towards Poland but what was happening in the Soviet state in the 1930s and again after WWII, the Great Purges (the mass terror of 1936–1937, when nearly 700,000 people were executed and several million imprisoned): for us to win World War II, it was first necessary to cleanse the rear' of 'traitors,' that is, to murder hundreds of thousands of our fellow citizens.

Apologists of Joseph Stalin and Vladimir Putin repeat the same mantra to this very day: violence and murder are the necessary prices to pay for the greatness of our state, for its victories in the international arena. For we need to project fear upon our neighbors, regardless of the cost to our own citizens. These ideas were crystallized in the era of Ivan the Terrible and its subsequent retelling in the Russian tradition. However, I would like to point out another aspect. Over time it became increasingly difficult to govern the state in this way. Ever more opposition suppressed with ever more violence, eventually undermined the state's own resources. Four hundred fifty years ago, this opened the door to another innovative if perhaps ultimately an unrealistic approach towards resolving the Polish-Russian conflict. Namely, to overthrow the despotic power that a large portion of the Russian elites were either disillusioned with or simply terrified of. With the aim to then supplant it with a republican Polish-inspired political model, guaranteeing civil liberties and rights for the noble elite of Moscow.

There was indeed just a hint of such an auspicious moment in 1561 that could perhaps be seized. For as is common, when the war was already underway in 1561, peace feelers were simultaneously sent out. Ivan the Terrible put forward his offer to marry Anna Jagiellonica, the sister of King Sigismund Augustus, a means of suggesting to Polish citizens that the political conflict with Moscow could thus be resolved peacefully; he still demanded in return

119

'only' all of Livonia (i.e. today's Latvia and Estonia) and only made a reference to his 'rights' to Kyiv. The Polish monarch, of course, rejected all these suggestions. However, the nobility seized upon and fervently discussed the matter in the local Polish assemblies (*sejmiki*), paving the way for the idea that perhaps such a union could actually become a real solution after all, the Tsar would marry a Polish royal, or perhaps, alternatively, a king from Poland could go to reign in Moscow?

As the echos of the Oprichnina's activities began to reach the Polish nobility, their willingness to pursue such concepts temporarily cooled. However, they would continue to develop these ideas, especially in light of the euphoria and sense of strength that Poland, (especially the Polish nobility), gained when 180 years of efforts finally culminated in the conclusion of the formal legal Union of Poland and Lithuania in the so-called *Union of Lublin* in 1569. This was a shining example of collaboration among nations instead of conflict. The Union of Lublin which legally gave birth to the Commonwealth, held for some commentators outlines of a future European Union project. It certainly changed the shape of Central and Eastern Europe. It filled the Polish nobility with hopes that the great experiment that had now ultimately succeeded with regard to Lithuania, could possibly be repeated on a larger scale; what we had achieved with Lithuania and 'Lithuanian' Rus could also be realized in Moscow...

The temporary truce concluded in Szczecin (Stettin) in 1570 did not end the war but it did create a climate where similar ideas could now germinate and grow. Before analyzing the various concepts, I will briefly surmise the military settlement of this war. This occurred when Poland's second elected King, Stefan Bathory (1533–1586), came to the Polish throne. With his three energetic campaigns of 1579, 1580, and 1581 he would strike not into Livonia, where Moscow's power was already installed, but instead directly towards Moscow. First, Bathory recaptured Polotsk in 1579, in 1580 Velikiye Luki, and in 1581 he completed his offensive at the walls of Pskov. He did not capture this city, but the siege prompted the Tsar to open peace negotiations in earnest and sign the Truce of Yam-Zapolsky in 1582, a treaty that now allowed Poland to regain both Livonia and Polotsk.

This extraordinary, dazzling campaign (you can find an account of its fascinating organizational and military details in Volume V of the History

120

The main purpose of the *oprichnina* set up by Ivan IV the Terrible was to terrorize the Tsar's own people, and in particular to pacify the upper classes which could have represented a threat to his rule for the slightest sign of 'disloyalty' to the tsar. Image by Pyotr Pavlov.

of Poland *Dzieje Polski*) did not disabuse either Polish or Lithuanian political opinion of their desire, expressed in sejmiki, to seek a more permanent solution to Polish-Moscow-Russia conflict something other than ever recurring war. The last 15 years of the 16th century and the first 15 years of the 17th century was not in fact the time, that many Poles often assume it was. A time when Polish-Russian relations were at their worst. Actually, it was the time of greatest hope for finally closing this dispute peacefully. Starting in 1572, when Sigismund Augustus, the last representative of the Jagiellonian dynasty on the Polish throne, was already dying. Even before his death, inspired by the writings of Andrzej Frycz-Modrzewski, a man called Andrzej Ciesielski wrote a speech to the deputies of the Sejm, in which he presented the prospects for resolution of the Polish-Russian dispute (a truce was in force at that time). This plan was to be put in motion by Sigismund

Augustus, who not having a male descendant, would, take on and foster the younger son of Ivan IV the Terrible, Fyodor. Still alive at the time was also the Tsar's eldest son, whom Ivan IV would soon kill with his own hands, also alive was his youngest, Dmitry, who would be killed later by Boris Godunov, and advisor to Ivan IV and a future Tsar himself. The young Dmitry's name and memory though would live on through the intrigues of the future 'false successors' or 'Dmitriads' as they would be named.

The Polish initiative for a long-term settlement was based on the assumption that Tsar Fyodor, who having been taken to Poland for his upbringing, would then adopt the Polish political culture, based on the recognition and guarantee of civil liberties. He would then instill these ideas in his homeland, and finally ensure the return of territories that Moscow had taken from the Lithuanian state in the 16th century, namely Smolensk as well as the Chernivtsi and Severian lands. Such a fabled but unrealistic scenario was vividly discussed in the Commonwealth (though not in the lands of Moscow), by means of hundreds of printed and political writings that now followed Sigismund Augustus' death as the first *interregnum* began. It is instructive to note that by the end of the 17th century, that is over the course of the next 130 years, only a handful, literally three, prints relating to non-religious topics would be published in Russia. Meanwhile, in Poland, just in the period of the first two *interregnums. These periods of the 'vacant throne'* which took place in 1572–1573 after the death of Sigismund Augustus and again in 1574–1576 after the abdication from the Polish crown and flight to France of Henry of Valois. During this time, we know of more than 100 political pamphlets that were produced dealing only with the events of the vacant throne. We must underline this difference, this civilizational gap in the production and dissemination of the written word that existed between Poland and the lands of the Tsar at this time. Only in this way can we hope to grasp the magnitude of the task that the Polish elites were considering taking on. They themselves even wondered whether it would be possible to manage these differences, to overcome them with effort, and thus bring Moscow closer to (Latin, Renaissance) Europe by means of the power of Poland's example. In Moscow, however, it was firmly believed that they did not need any teachers from the West, certainly not from the Republic (the Commonwealth), which was considered as the arch enemy.

Regardless, in the Kremlin, they had long known how to live, how to die, and also how to kill for the Tsar.

During the first *interregnum*, Piotr Mycielski, among others, actually put forward in his political writings the potential candidacy of Ivan IV for the Polish throne. He argued that although this Tsar was known to be a terrible tyrant, his exposure to the political culture in Poland would have to have a transformative effect on him. Mycielski, buttressed his thesis by underlining the political triumph that was the Union of Lublin. Since it had been possible to unite the Lithuanian and Rus peoples together with the Poles in this glorious union, the people of Moscow would also change by following the Polish example.

And here we open a significant page in Polish political thought, indeed in Polish political thinking about Moscow, or later about Russia. I deliberately used the word 'page' here because the best-known symbol of this thinking is the poetic metaphor of the Russian man as a white or blank page to be written on. This metaphor was immortalized in *Part III* of Adam Mickiewicz's *Dziady* written in the 19th century (The Forefathers' Eve), in which this great Polish-Lithuanian poet writes about Russia and Russians as being an unwritten white page, as a void that will only be filled by civilizational work, or rather, work by others on the moral content of this page. In this Polish way, the page would be filled by the good of liberty and not the evil of despotism. Poland is, as it were, called here to fill this void or write the page with liberty. In 1573, however, a fundamental and practical objection was put forward against this rather noble vision being proposed by some. For a 'Muscovite' (as the Tsar was called) would not only fail to convert to our customs and political culture but would instead introduce his despotism to us and would also take any opportunity to incite against the Republic the 'peoples of his faith and language' those living in the lands of the Commonwealth that is, the Orthodox Rus in the lands we now call Belarus and Ukraine.

As can be seen in this argumentation, there appeared a relatively clear identification of the issue of national identity in the political debate of 1573. Referencing the possibility of using its essential elements, religion, and language to conduct a great political subterfuge by the Orthodox-Rus empire of Moscow. There also appears in this debate, perhaps for the first time, a theme that would develop centuries later in our reflection on relations with our imperial neighbor to the east, a theme of fear and a warning against 'Russian influences on the Polish soul', as the eminent historian of ideas, Marian Zdziechowski, philologist and rector of the Stephen Bathory University in Vilnius would so beautifully encapsulate in his so titled 1920 work.

Thus, as early as 1573, we can see that the exchange of arguments essential for the future of Polish-Russian relations centered on the question: can we 'convert' Russia? Do we have enough strength to change a country of this size? Or if we open up to Russia, could it dominate us with its strength and numerical superiority and terrorize us with its ruthlessness of thought and action, so that we would in the end simply 'lick the Tsar's feet' in fear? Can the metaphor of the 'white page' apply at all to a political-ideological structure that is already centuries old, has different civilizational roots and is encased in powerful symbols that have now been worshipped for generations (Nevsky, Kalita, Ivan the Terrible, the 'Monomakh's cap,' the 'Third Rome,' etc.)? Is it possible to now overwrite it with contradictory ideals which seems obvious and are undoubtedly good for us, despite a well-established despotic political tradition? This dilemma will recur many more times, as will the idea of reconciling with Russia through some form of personal union.

As we know, the naïve Polish supporters of Ivan the Terrible did not win out among the voters on the electoral field near Warsaw, and Ivan himself made it clear: he could only be King in the Republic if he took such lands as he wished. For Ivan Poland would have to simply to satisfy itself with the role of a western province of his Moscow empire. The victorious competitors in the election campaign for the Polish throne thus became firstly Henry Valois and then subsequently Stephen Bathory after the former's sudden return to France. (TN Start) It should be noted the decision to initially choose Henry, a Frenchman, was an early expression of a long-standing tradition in Poland to seek strong relations with the French state, something Moscow would observe with interest and subsequently do much to try and thwart. (TN End) While Bathory was still alive, upon hearing of the death of Ivan IV the Terrible, an imposing diplomatic mission was then sent to Moscow to probe whether it would be possible to resolve the Polish-Russian conflict. Resolve it by way of installing the newly elected Polish King as the Tsar of Russia and taking custody of tsarevich Fyodor. This son of Ivan IV had already come of age but was not considered completely mentally fit.

Top: Sigismund Augustus performs the act of swearing in of the Union of Lublin in 1569, which formally created the Polish-Lithuanian Commonwealth. Bottom: The courageous and resolute 2nd elected King of Poland, Stefan Batory, with his military prowess curbed the imperial ambitions of Ivan IV the Terrible. Paintings by Jan Matejko.

However, neither this mission nor the subsequent large-scale missions of the Republic to Moscow, sent under the leadership of Lithuanian chancellor Lev Sapieha, could have succeeded in Moscow. For the facts on the ground had quickly changed and the ambitious boyar, a former member of the *oprichniki* and one time advisor to Ivan, Boris Godunov (1552–1605), had already taken 'custody' of Tsar Fyodor and now moved quickly to replace him on the throne as the next Tsar.

Ambassadors from Vilnius and Krakow in Moscow at the time saw the resultant revolt of the urban population in Moscow and the weakening of the tsarist state itself, exhausted by wars and eight years of *oprichnina terror*. Witnessing this the idea of repoliticizing Moscow now returned with greater intensity in the discussions of the Polish senators at the time. It was carried on to the level of the Polish regional assemblies (Sejmiki). Since Moscow was internally divided with rebellion against Godunov, many of the elite the old boyar families looked with disgust at the career of this parvenu-*oprichnik*. Could these elites perhaps be persuaded to replace him with an external candidate? One that could guarantee a return of order after the expiry of the Rurik dynastic line. Hence, that earlier concept, that of a positive lasting resolution to the Polish-Russian conflict returned to noble Polish minds amid all this ferment.

There was also a new and growing geopolitical reason for cooperation, a joint struggle against the Crescent Muslim Empire now pushing ever harder from the south. Not long after the greatest of the Ottoman Empire's rulers, Suleiman the Magnificent's death in 1566, Ottomon power resumed its militarily advance against its northern neighbors. The Muslim empire was at the zenith of its power. Anti-Turkish cooperation thus seemed at the time a clear geopolitical basis for Polish-Moscow cooperation. With this offer, successive envoys were sent to Moscow. After the death of Stephen Bathory, and with Ivan's son Fyodor candidacy for the Polish throne, no longer arousing the same level of fear as his father's had. This Fyodor perhaps he could be easily led? Lithuanian deputies, in particular, now firmly opted for Fyodor's election. At the head of this and other lobby efforts of the now third free election was the bishop of Samogitia, Melchior Giedroyć (Lith.: *Merkelis Giedraitis*) a representative of a powerful family in Lithuania. His family descendent Jerzy would also play a key role in re-engineering

Poland's geopolitical pre-disposition some four hundred years later holding a leading role among the Polish emigrees of post-WWII Paris.

Returning to our story, at the time, there was a prevailing conviction that a peaceful resolution of the dispute with Moscow was necessary to prevent Lithuania from being further ravaged by its neighbors to the east. Bishop Giedroyć even went so far as to offer the throne to Fyodor in behind-the-scenes talks with Moscow's envoys and, at the same time, probed them as to whether Fyodor would agree to only accept the additional title of mitre the Grand Duke of Lithuania in the possible future event that he might lose the election for the Polish throne in Krakow. Such a suggestion bordered on secession, a betrayal of the Polish-Lithuanian Commonwealth on the bishop's part but it was an expression of the continued ferment of optimism still alive among certain Lithuanian magnates following the Union of Lublin.

Fortunately, nothing serious came out of the plans to detach Lithuania from the Republic. However, as we can see, a variety of forces were at work in Polish-Moscow relations. In Lithuania, these interests sought to advance their cases by various means. Sometimes considering the Polish cultural and, in a sense, political superiority within the relatively recently formalized Union as a more significant threat than the existential threat invoked by potential military domination by Moscow. However, the tendency to consolidate the Polish-Lithuanian Union definitely was the prevailing argument of the time among the majority.

The two most extensive proposals for a union addressed to Moscow were associated with the next two great diplomatic missions of 1590 and 1600. The second was the largest ever addressed to Moscow by the Commonwealth. At the head of the 1,500-person retinue was again the great Lithuanian chancellor, Lev Sapieha. The terms of this elaborate project are fascinating and worth recalling. For more than any of the previous initiatives, the proposals outlined would have served to secure the equality of the combined states, resembling in many of its more positive aspects some of the 20th century concepts elaborated for a united Europe. According to Lev Sapieha's outline, the two states would have a joint defense capability in the south and a common treasury in Kyiv to finance that defense (a concept with similarities to ongoing EU discussions on defense arrangements). In 1600, when Sigismund III Vasa secured election to the Polish throne (Having

At the turn of the 16th and 17th centuries, in the Tsarist state, unlike in the Polish Lithuanian Commonwealth, there appeared to be no schools providing education at a secondary level where the elites could be educated. Nor were books yet printed en mass. An engraving illustrating work in a Polish printing house of the time.

just recently lost his monarchical power in Stockholm,) the idea of Russian 'support' to counteract this new 'Swedish lobby' in Poland also came into play. In addition, Sapieha's project included, beyond *ad hoc* combinations and geopolitical concepts, a proposal for common societal and economic projects including: a unified monetary measure (as we would say today: a common currency), the right to establish trading companies between subjects in both states (an early form of common market) facilitating free trade arrangements throughout the combined territory of the Commonwealth and Moscow lands and also the right to acquire education anywhere. The latter one could be viewed as a pre-cursor of the modern-day Erasmus student programs, already at the turn of the 16ᵗʰ and 17ᵗʰ centuries.

Yet despite all these innovations the project proposed by Sapieha is today in Moscow regarded as a gross manifestation of discrimination against the then emerging Russian state. On what premise was this discrimination supposed to be based? Well, in fact on education for though scarcely believable by western standards at the time, there simply were no secondary schools or indeed any formalized school system in the then tsarist state, not even for the elites. Orthodox schools did not exist and the local Orthodox elite who sought to further any home tutored education they had received could only do so by travelling abroad. They thus received their education in Greece, or in the Polish-Lithuanian Commonwealth. It should be noted that between 1596 and 1636, some Orthodox schools were created and run in a limited way due to the provisions of the Union of Brest. Even if nascent in their nature, such Orthodox-based schools did lay the groundwork for future excellent schools such as the later-named Mohyla Academy in Kyiv, the Orthodox Academy in Ostroh, and the excellent Brotherhood schools in Lutsk or Vladimirall also areas of orthodox faith crucially under the jurisdiction of the Polish-Lithuanian Commonwealth and not of Moscow.

It was in this fashion that Sapieha and the other initiators of this plan envisioned future integration, in a gentle manner, led by trade and education. After all, no one would force boyar children to be educated in Polish schools, but whoever wished to acquire any knowledge would simply have to go to the University of Krakow or the University of Vilnius, as the Commonwealth already had these two well-established and recognized universities. Alternatively, they could go to other Polish run-schools, some of which were also of a very high standing. In a state so united by the various aforementioned institutional arrangements (security commerce and education), there was to be a transitional stage when the two monarchs would function side by side. They would wear two identical crowns that would be cast anew, and after their reign, there would then follow a union based on equality, with no changes to borders. The Lithuanian part of the new united Commonwealth would not have the right to reclaim Smolensk nor any of the other lands lost in the 16th century to Ivan III.

Thus, this was a genuinely far-sighted project rooted in compromise, a remarkable testimony to the mature political and civilizational thought processes that permeated the elites of the Polish-Lithuanian state. With its many ideas of union, it was far ahead of what many European schools of thought had accomplished even before the middle of the 20th century. This idea, however, obviously stood in the way of the political ambitions of the former oprichnik Boris Godunov. For in the meantime, after the death of Ivan IV's last son Fyodor, the last of the Rurikovichs, this former advisor and enforcer had crowned himself Tsar, hoping to establish his own dynasty. Tsar Boris decided to delay the receipt of yet another diplomatic delegation from the Commonwealth, for a month and a half, citing a deliberately demeaning pretext: that he had a sore toe... When he finally met with the delegation, the elaborate and groundbreaking union project was rejected because simply it was country to his own dynastic plans for the Moscow throne. At any rate, the foundations of this new dynasty would prove to be highly fragile. The other envious boyar families headed by the powerful old Romanov family (more senior than the Godunovs) plotted against him. The older boyar families of the Golitsyns, Belskys, and Shuiskys felt humiliated by the fact that a *nouveau riche* ex-*oprichnik* had risen to the rank of Tsar thanks mainly to his career of 'service', as we might say today.

From the circle of the Romanov house, a specially groomed candidate now emerged to lead the overthrow of Boris Godunov False Dmitry I (1581–1606). Crossing the border of the Polish-Lithuanian state in 1603, he first revealed himself at the courts of Lithuanian Orthodox magnates presenting himself as the youngest son of Ivan the Terrible, miraculously saved from political murder. The real Dmitriy, son of Ivan the Terrible, had, in fact, been assassinated much earlier by Boris Godunov's envoys in Uglich.

Soviet actor Nikolai Cherkasov in the title role of Tsar Ivan IV the Terrible in the biographical film directed by Sergei Eisenstein. Known for his cruelty, the ruler was the favorite historical figure of Stalin.

This man, well-educated (he spoke Polish and Latin), clever, perceptive, this False Dmitry I quickly won many followers, seduced not only and not primarily by his charm but also by the prospects that his career entailed. The Muscovite state was rocked by internal peasant revolts linked to poor crop yields caused by the regional cooling of the climate taking place at the beginning of the 17th century, and the great famine that ensued. There were also Cossack revolts. All this increased the instability of the Russian state, but it was also greatly tempting for many to try to seize upon this great adventure with Dmitry: and begin the march for the additional throne in Moscow.

Dmitry was received in Krakow in 1604 by King Sigismund III. Unofficially for the plotters most senators and all the *sejmiki* voted against supporting Dmitry, believing this ruse to be a form of adventurism unworthy of the

Commonwealth. This view was held above all by Jan Zamoyski (1542–1605), the most important of the senators, who, like most of the senate, believed that what the Commonwealth should above all obtain from contacts with Moscow was the return of the lands it had lost in the 16th century, above all Smolensk. Not any quest for the throne in Moscow or a union with it. Nevertheless, the King gave False Dmitry I his blessing, if you will, for the road. Dmitry, having also won over to his cause the bankrupt Sandomierz voivode Jerzy Mniszch, then decided to marry his daughter Maryna. Dmitry went on to hoodwink a circle of magnates into supporting him, not only Polish but above all Rus, Orthodox families from the Commonwealth (including the Sapieha branch, faithful to Orthodoxy and the Wiśniowiecki family, descended from a lateral line of the Rurikovichs Ivan IV's family line). His rising star would lead him on to Moscow and, eventually, see the city opening its gates to him in 1605.

False Dmitry I reigned in Moscow for a year with the help of Polish, Lithuanian-Rus 'assistance'. But he made it clear he did not intend to succumb to them, contrary to the notion of many defenders of Orthodoxy in Moscow. Moscow's Orthodox propaganda developed the false myth that Dmitry was actually being followed in by representatives of the Jesuits a covert spiritual and educational 'Catholic aggression' that would steal Moscow's soul and give it up to the 'papists,' the 'Latinists.' Dmitry had no such intentions. However, the close to a thousand Polish-speaking people in his entourage stung the eyes of many in this hundred-thousand-strong capital, those who wanted to continue to fight for the throne in the Kremlin, not for the benefit of some 'waif' returning from foreign lands, but for themselves. A conspiracy of the Shuysky princes led in 1606 to the overthrow of the False Dmitry I and the introduction of Vasily Shuysky to the throne. In the subsequent slaughter of Poles in Moscow the False Dmitry I himself was also murdered, his body burned, and his ashes then scooped into a cannon and fired in the western direction from whence he had come. That he and his ilk should never again return.

Yet return he did, the very next year. In fact, several pseudo-Dmitrys now appeared, more self-proclaimers. Among them, one even succeeded in being recognized, at least by historians as False Dmitry II. Though this one bore no resemblance to his predecessor, let alone to the real Dmitry Rurikovich. However, because of the promise that this man could succeed where his predecessor had failed, he was even recognized by 'his wife', Maryna Mniszech. He was also supported by several adventurers who led him further into the Muscovite Principality in search of treasure and adventure. A significant moment in this 'Dimitriad' became the siege of the holiest site of Moscow Orthodoxy. The Holy Trinity-St. Sergius Lavra, the siege of which lasted for more than a year and a half, between 1608 and 1610. The site located roughly 80 kilometers northeast of Moscow has a similar symbolic importance, as the Jasna Góra monastery in Czestochowa does for Poland. The Lavra did not surrender to the Lithuanian-Polish soldiers besieging it, led by Jan Piotr Sapieha with his *Lisowczyk*s the seasoned soldiers gathered around him. This siege became the most important symbolically for the mobilization of Moscow's Orthodox opinion against the Poles, a symbol of religious faith holding back the 'foreign invader'. This was indeed reminiscent of the far shorter siege of Częstochowa more than 40 years later (1655) by Poles resisting the Swedish invaders. To this day a great symbol in Poland of religious faith but also of national sovereignty.

This new Tsar Vasily Shuysky decided to ally with Sweden against Poland and yet another Polish-Russian war now began. This time, the *sejmiki* gave their consent (by approving war taxes) to the campaign because everyone understood that an alliance of Sweden and Moscow against the Commonwealth was a mortal danger. However, in the new Commonwealth and under its new statutes, without the consent of the citizens and their representation at the Sejm, then approved by the local *sejmiki*, it was impossible to wage war, because the citizens decided on all taxes including taxes raised to finance the army. In Moscow however, only the Tsar ultimately decided everything (at least until someone assassinated him). This fundamental difference and its implications for mobilization of forces in later years should not be forgotten.

Thus, in 1609, the war began again, and the one clear goal set before the King by way of the *sejmiki* was to regain Smolensk. The monarch headed there with his army, laying a long siege to this fortress. During this campaign, the outstanding commander, Hetman Stanisław Żółkiewski, achieved perhaps the most brilliant triumph in Polish military history. On 4 July 1610, at the Battle of Klushino, near Moscow, he beat an army seven times the size of his force. The Polish force involved did not exceed four thousand men, primarily Hussars, the famed mounted warriors of the Commonwealth. That success opened the way for him to take the Kremlin, facilitated this time not by military means but through a settlement with seven of the great boyar families. These seven wanted to oust the Shuyskys from power and prevent further chaos in the Muscovite state by finally offering the throne to a Polish candidate, who would be Prince Władysław. Though with no formal authority to do so from King Sigismund III, Hetman Żółkiewski hastily made a deal with the boyars, in which he promised that Prince Władysław would come to Moscow, be given an Orthodox upbringing there, accept Orthodoxy and become a Moscow Tsar and that thus Moscow would lose Smolensk or any other Lithuanian Rus land seized in the 16th century. The great military strategist obviously overstepped his authority and King Sigismund III on hearing of the 'deal' dismissed the proposal.

Some historians, especially publicists who are poorly acquainted with the realities of the era, are most critical of Sigismund's decision, claiming that it was his Counter-Reformational zeal that prevented the King from accepting Hetman Żółkiewski's wise and considered compromise. The hetman's compromise was generous but was also unacceptable from the point of view of the Commonwealth's strategic interests. The *sejmiki* had previously defined the goal of the war in their decision to allow taxes to be raised. Ordering the King to regain Smolensk. Sigismund III could not abandon this duty if he wanted to act under the law in force at the time, he was a sovereign answerable to his people in contrast to the absolute monarchs in the west. There was also another consideration, that of a father. Sigismund understandably could not reconcile himself to the thought of sending his son to an uncertain fate in Moscow. It was difficult for him to think of his firstborn son sharing the same destiny as those ashes earlier shot from a cannon. Nor did he want the new ruler of the Russian state, a young boy taken under control by Russian boyars, to become a hostage to geopolitical interests utterly foreign to the Polish-Lithuanian state and its political culture. Such a turn of events would have been all but inevitable. So, Sigismund III decided to change the arrangement negotiated by his field commander or Hetman: he would not hand his son over to the Kremlin until he had matured, and only then would Prince Władysław determine, for himself, if he would want to change his faith upon becoming Tsar. On

The False Dmitry swears an oath to Sigismund III Vasa to introduce Catholicism into Russia. Painting by Nikolai Nevrev.

The siege of Pskov by King Stefan Batory and his knights, although not ultimately crowned with success, it contributed for the favorable to the Commonwealth truce at Yam Zapolsky (15 January 1582), which forced Ivan IV the Terrible to cede Livonia to Poland. Painting by the Russian Frenchman Karl Briullov, 1843.

the other hand, Moscow must return the lands it seized in the series of 16th-century wars against Lithuania, including Smolensk.

The conflict was thus irresolvable, having gone on for far too long and with the additional complication of civil strife in Moscow between boyars with all the associated plunder and rape that war entailed. Under these conditions, Orthodox propaganda designed to inspire the defenders with the idea of 'Moscow the Third Rome' now naturally fueled hatred of the external Latinist or Lakhs invaders. This led to a national uprising against them in 1611 the only national uprising in the history of Russia and, in its second iteration of 1612 it finally achieved success. The Polish-Lithuanian garrison of Żółkiewski's soldiers that had entered the Kremlin in September 1610 and stayed there legally, also occupying the central districts of the vast city, was now under siege. It was primarily the Orthodox Church that pro-

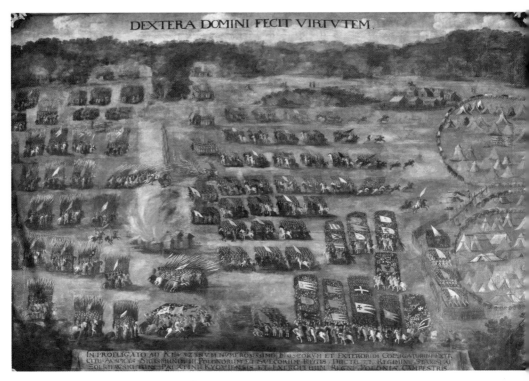

DEXTERA DOMINI FECIT VIRTVTEM.

IN PROELIGATO AD KLVSZYNVM NVMEROSISSIMO MOSCORVM ET EXTERORIDI COLLIGATORUM EXTR
CLAVASPICIS SIGISMVNDI III POLONORUM ET SVECORUM REGIS DRCTIS ET REGIMINE STANISLAI
ZOLKIEWSKI MINE PALATINI KYOVIENSIS ET EXERCITUUM REGNI POLONIÆ CAMPESTRIS

On 4 July 1610, Hetman Stefan Żółkiewski defeated the combined and numerically superior Muscovite and Swedish armies arrayed against him by Prince Dmitry Shuisky and Jacob Pontusson de la Gardie at Klushino by means of repeated cavalry charges of the Polish hussars, forcing them to make a panicked retreat. Image by Szymon Boguszowicz.

tested against its presence, calling for an uprising against the Latin troops of King Sigismund III, as well as the Moscow traitors who wanted to see Prince Władysław, the son of the arch-enemy and Catholic King of Poland, on the throne. After a year-and-a-half- in November 1612, the Polish garrison was forced to capitulate out of starvation they were already 'eating' the Kremlin walls, having eaten all the rats and mice beforehand. Also, some reported cases of cannibalism testified to the dire situation in which the beleaguered Polish and Lithuanian soldiers found themselves. In this pitiful fashion the optimistic hopes for a peaceful resolution of the Polish-Russian conflict were buried. Honorable conditions were set for the garrison to leave the Kremlin fortress, but they were not adhered to by the Moscow side; with many of the Polish garrison being murdered, and the rest being imprisoned.

Immediately after the surrender of the Polish garrison in the Kremlin, a *Zemsky Sobor* (an 'assembly of the land') was held in Moscow, a sort of analogous Polish Sejm, except that it was appointed from above, exactly the opposite of the Commonwealth. Its aim was to elect a new dynasty. Mikhail Romanov (1596–1645) was chosen, a young family representative who had been vying for the throne ever since the Rurik dynasty expired. He had sat quietly with the Polish army in the besieged Kremlin, together with his mother and 'other collaborators of the Lakhs,' but he was drawn to the banners of the victorious anti-Polish uprising because of his father who was the Patriarch of Moscow, a man imprisoned in Malbork by the Poles for duplicity. Yet above all, he secured support because the other families competing for the Tsar's crown hoped that the young, inexperienced boy would be easily ousted by them later. This would not happen, however. Although the male line expired under Peter I as early as 1725, the Romanov family would still formally survive on the tsarist throne until 1917.

Smolensk was recaptured for the Commonwealth in 1611 and just 6 years later in 1617, the Polish-Lithuanian army under Hetman Jan Karol Chodkiewicz once again stood directly before the Kremlin's walls, striking at Moscow militarily, with great help from a Cossack Rus army under Hetman Piotr Konashevich-Sahaydachnyy. This time, however, the Kremlin was not occupied. By 1619 it had already become clear that this war could bring no settlement other than a new line of demarcation and that there would be no true lasting peace let alone Union between Poland and Russia. On 3 January 1619, a truce was concluded at Dywilin (a few dozen kilometers east of Moscow). On its strength, the Commonwealth regained the Smolensk lands, part of Chernihiv and also the Severian lands. However, it was well known to both parties that Moscow would now only wait for an opportunity to reclaim these lands once again and return to its strategy to 'collect Rus lands' and crucially gain trade access to the Baltic Sea. Russia's first attempt at this after the death of Sigismund III Vasa in 1632, met with failure. This is because the Polish-Lithuanian state quickly mobilized for war with the swift election of Władysław IV and a victorious counterattack against Russia's designs.

I am already using the name Russia consciously here because the Moscow state had already geopolitically established itself on the edge of the Pacific Ocean by the beginning of the 17th century. Moreover, it had also elected

The Tsar Vasili Szujski together with his brothers pay homage to King Sigismund III the Vasa and Prince Władysław in the Great Hall of the Senate of the Royal Castle in Warsaw. An artistic vision by Tommaso Dolabella.

the new Romanov dynasty and was returning to the program of imperial restoration and expansion. It thus becomes difficult to maintain the previous name of Moscow, as it implies the initial 'local' nature of the Kremlin's power undervaluing the momentum and prospects of this expanding state. The Tsar still had ambitions to 'collect the Rus lands', all of them. Yet at the same time, it already ruled over an area several times larger that had never had anything to do with the original Rus (Kyiv or Novgorod). From the end of the 15th century to the end of the 18th century, the rate of this expansion continued, at an average of 60–70 thousand square kilometers annually. Roughly speaking, it was as if every year, for three hundred years in a row, Moscow swallowed Holland and Belgium combined. No longer 'just' Moscow. It was already tsarist 'Rossiya'.

The Treaty of Polyanovka concluded in 1634 summed up the state of affairs that had lasted since 1619: Smolensk passed to Poland and the Polish-Lithuanian state accepted the Romanov dynasty and it would not lay claim to the Moscow throne in the future. During the Polyanovka negotiations, a notable conversation took place with the Russians, led by Grand Crown Chancellor Jakub Zadzik, which Szymon Starowolski noted down in his chronicles: 'Moscow when they were told during the treaty discussions at Smolensk of the concepts to unite with our nation, casting off the yoke of tyrannical bondage from their necks having been laid down with us together to enjoy the freedom and pleasure of liberty, replied to the saintly memory of Father Zadzik the Crown Chancellor of the time: 'We do not want your freedom, Mr Bishop, keep it for yourself, because in our country there is only one tsar, who disposes of our nobility and estates, and in your country, every boyar is a tyrant, who knows how and who to take from, and advice and patience will not suffice.'

There was a perception that there was too much of this liberty and freedom in the Polish-Lithuanian state, and one does not know who to listen to... in Russia, on the other hand, there was only one Tsar, and all were obedient slaves to this one tyrant and thus there was order. This answer from 1634, discouraging further attempts at any peaceful settlement of the Polish-Russian dispute, leaves us with the history of Polish-Russian relations on the threshold of the even greater military conflicts that took place shortly after, starting in the middle of the 17th century.

From the Moscow and Swedish 'Deluge' to Russian 'Protection'. Ukraine the Hinge? The Kremlin's Race to the Seas (1648–1721)

In the 17th century the determining factor for relations between the Polish-Lithuanian Commonwealth and Moscow was to be the Cossack question which would also shape the Commonwealth's subsequent fate. This question developed in the Polish Crown lands of what we will from now on refer to as Ruthenia and latterly as Ukraine and Belarus as these names come into historical use. Let us state at the outset with the term 'Ukraine'. A word that only began to come into common use in the second half of the 17th century, and even then, still somewhat sporadically. The internationally recognized term generally accepted and used at the time to describe the land that today we refer to as Ukraine was this somewhat more nebulous term 'Ruthenia' – hence 'Ruthenians', earlier 'Rus'. On the other hand, 'Muscovites' lived under the distinct and separate jurisdiction of the Tsar's scepter at this moment in history. A fact that current Russian propaganda refuses to acknowledge, contrary to the evident historical facts.

The incorporation or transfer of the Ruthenian lands, hitherto belonging to Lithuania, into the Polish Crown itself, was accomplished by an act of the King who was legal heir to these lands. This was Sigismund Augustus, during the Lublin Sejm or Union of Lublin in 1569. It was, however, a transfer viewed by the Lithuanian lords with great bitterness, as Lithuania had acquired these lands in the 14th century and now lost title to them in favor of the Polish Crown. The local population, if we may make so broad a generalization, mainly comprised of Orthodox faithful, did not really notice this change when it was made or at least paid it scant attention. Hardly anyone cared in Kyivan Rus that they had now become part of the Polish Crown instead of Lithuania. They were part of the Commonwealth regardless; little had changed for them. However, this change would prove crucial for the future demarcation of the border between Ukraine and Belarus, that is, the Ruthenian land (Belarus) that remained formally within the Grand Duchy of Lithuania after 1569. The political traditions of this Belarus land and its inhabitants date back to the early Middle Ages and the Turov-Pinsk principality, then ruled by a separate branch of the now extinguished Moscow dynasty the Rurikovich family. However, the demarcation by Sigismund Augustus in 1569 would reinforce and really mold this separation anew during the next two centuries within the Grand Duchy of Lithuania.

A second factor in the development of the Cossack question was the ecclesiastical union, known as the Union of Brest, something to which we referred in an earlier chapter. This was concluded in Brest-Litovsk in 1596 by another act of the Sejm. It was intended to end the potentially divisive religious split within the Polish-Lithuanian state by making all inhabitants, Catholic and Orthodox now subject to the Pope's authority regardless of ongoing religious rights or practice. Contrary to these intentions, unfortunately, this Union in some cases contributed to an additional deepening of internal divisions and tensions.

From a security point of view, one can see a natural sense of desire in the Union of Brest to protect the interests of the Commonwealth for future generations. The inception point for the Union must also be associated with the earlier elevation of the Moscow Orthodox Metropolis to the rank of the Patriarchate, an event that took place seven years earlier. Moscows was now the fifth ecumenical, or universal, Patriarchate in the Orthodox world next to Antioch, Jerusalem, Alexandria and Constantinople. These first three patriarchal capitals immediately recognized the elevation of Moscow, suitably bribed by Boris Godunov the temporary 'usurper' Tsar. On the other hand, this new supreme rank as the capital of Orthodoxy granted to Moscow, as we've already alluded to, an ability to foster the danger of subordinating the Orthodox population within the Commonwealth to the 'expanded' spiritual authority of the Moscow Patriarch. A Patriarch *de facto* in the service of the Tsar. Especially in the conditions after the great uprising and bloodshed that commenced in 1648. The Patriarch in Moscow was, let us remember, wholly subordinated to the state power policy, just as is the case in modern-day Russia.

It was a potentially explosive religious mixture that fostered fertile ground for a conflict between the bottom of the Orthodox social class, to put it briefly and simplistically, and the upper, or dominant landed elites,

143

IAŚNIE WIELMOZNY HIPA-
ciusz POCIEY ARCY-
BISKUP METROPOLITA KIIOW-
SKI HALICKI Y CAŁEY RUSI
BISKUP WŁODZIMIERSKI
Y BRZESKI.

The Greek Catholic Metropolitan of Halych and Kyiv Hypatius (Adam) Pociej (1541–1613), one of the founders of the so-called Uniate (Greek Catholic) Church in the First Polish Republic or Commonwealth, as depicted by an unknown artist in a portrait from the 17th century.

which associated themselves more and more explicitly though also quite voluntarily, with Catholicism. These elites would become synonymous with the exploitative practices (especially of their intermediaries) carried out on many of the huge new agricultural estates established all across the Ukrainian lands in the decades following the Union of Lublin. Exploitation, fed by greed for a share in the huge profits earned by selling grain to a Europe then ravaged by the 30 Years War, which had devastated German agricultural production. Though the actual spark that would lead to outright rebellion by the population would come from the Ukrainian or Zaporizhian Cossacks.

Cossacks had already appeared on history's pages in the steppe borderlands with Crimea, in the Volga and Don River basins, in the Turkish empire and as far north as Moscow all since the beginning of the 16th century. Those in Ukraine traditionally settled in lands beyond the rocky *porohy* (Dnipro or Dnieper River rapids), in an area stretching from where the modern-day city of Dnipro lies, south towards Zaporizhia. This was a motherland open only to the courageous and the daring, calling themselves the Zaporizhian Cossacks or Nizhovets, from this point on. The word 'Cossack' itself, recorded as early as the 13th century, initially signified a watchman or a sentry. Our 16th-century Polish chronicler, Joachim Bielski, devotes a separate chapter to the Cossacks at the end of his narrative on Polish history. At that time, under Stephen Bathory, they were already clearly recognized as a force crucial to the future of the Commonwealth. 'There were not so many of them before, but now there are a few thousand, and they often inflict noticeable harm against the Turks and Tatars. […] It is good for them to be there, but that they be [disciplined] and paid; and that they live there on the [D]nipro River continually on islands or spurs, of which there are several and are quite defensible.'

This was also Bathory's policy to 'bring in line' the Zaporozhians so they could assist him in his crackdown on Ivan in Moscow. With a proclamation that he issued in Lviv in 1578, he established a Cossack registry of 500 men, the nucleus of a regular paid armed force, as a result of which the Zaporozhian Cossacks on that registry were to serve the Commonwealth, under a separate hetman appointed by the King. The Cossacks served the King and the Commonwealth well, while maintaining their internal, soldierly autonomy. Being on the list gave them many of the rights and entitlements normally reserved for the Polish Lithuanian elites of the Commonwealth. They distinguished themselves in battles against the Tatars, as well as against Moscow and the Ottoman Empire. The symbol of this highly efficient fighting force eliciting such admiration from Poland and Lithuania alike was Hetman Petro Konashevich Sahaydachnyy, who led the Cossack regiments to Moscow (including the 1617 incursion) and played a pivotal role at their head of defense during the first great battle of Khotyn, in which the Commonwealth held back a 120 thousand strong Turkish invasion force in the fall of 1621.

Unfortunately, multiple Cossack uprisings motivated by the aforementioned social and religious issues including unscrupulous efforts to monopolize the production of alcohol in the region, broke out over time. These were in parallel suppressed ever more bloodily by the Polish magnates, intolerant of disruptions to their lucrative grain trade from Ukraine to Western Europe. This state of play persisted until 1648. Then, 10-years after the last uprising, comes perhaps the largest ever (certainly by sheer percentage number of subjects mobilized) uprising known in history one celebrated in many of the great works of Polish and Ukrainian literature. The uprising of Bohdan Khmelnytsky. The disasters that this uprising inflicted on the Commonwealth were not only military and economic but also of a moral nature. The Commonwealth state, which had previously been able to defend its regional power position in a geographical area stretching from Bucharest as far north as Estonia would now be shaken to its very core. (TN Start) For the non-Polish reader unfamiliar with Polish military history of this time, let us note that in the preceding 50 years the Commonwealth had not only retaken Smolensk and occupied Moscow, but it had also repealed the aforementioned Ottoman Turk incursion at the first battle of Khotyn. It had additionally fought and defeated the Swedish army in multiple engagements, even besting Gustavus Adolphus in the field, a man considered the greatest military commander of 17th-century Europe. Adolphus tasted this defeat in the battle of Trzciana where he was defeated by Hetman Stanisław Koniecpolski. Yet this resolute Polish military with its famed Winged Hussars would now find itself, at least initially and to the amazement of many of its earlier foes, incapable of coping with a rebellion

Peter Konashevich Sahaydachny (1570–1622), Hetman of the Zaporozhian Cossacks, one of the most outstanding Cossack leaders of the 17th century. He repeatedly acted in loyal defense of the Commonwealth of Poland and Lithuania, against Moscow and Turkish armies. He and his Cossacks played a decisive role in the great Battle of Chocim in 1621. A 19th-century portrait by an unknown artist.

on its own lands. A rebellion spearheaded by the Cossacks' and ably led by Khmelnytsky. (TN End)

Khmelnytsky the man himself was an alumnus of the Jesuit college in Lviv, an earlier scribe for the Zaporizhian Army, but now frustrated and disappointed by personal grievances and the cancellation by the Polish king of a planned renewed great war with Turkey. That cancelled war, proposed initially by King Władysław IV who had with duplicity raised Cossack hopes of rich plunder and new glory in battle for this uncommonly brave and free-spirited warrior people. The Polish king now fueled the ferment that brought forth this new uprising in 1648.

Within months Khmelnytsky had triumphed over the Crown troops, at the battles of Zhoti Vody, at Korsun, and at Pilavets, and with the sudden death of the Polish King Władysław IV, Khmelnytsky's appetite grew, his struggle became one not just for better rights for his people but for the full independence of a Cossack-Rus state. All the while also eyeing the possibility of a tactical alliance with Tsar Aleksey Mikhaylovich, the second Tsar of the new Romanov dynasty. Among some Cossacks, the search for a patron in Moscow was popular not so much because of any ethnolinguistic affinity but due to religion. The 'Muscovites' themselves called the inhabitants of the Ukrainian lands of the Commonwealth, 'Cherkas' [an archaic name for the Cherkists, i.e. an ethnic group from the north-western Caucasus region – *editor's note*]. We should add that Khmelnytsky had to talk to Moscow envoys through interpreters as the two languages at that time were not as similar as they are today. However, the religious issue played a more important role here for identity in the 17th century. From Moscow came an initially very cautious response to these Cossack advances. The Kremlin had in its memory its failure to retake Smolensk in 1632–1634, which ended with the surrender of the large Moscow army before the troops of Władysław IV. Even when hearing of the defeats that the armies of the Commonwealth had suffered in their clash with the Cossacks, Tsar Aleksey and his advisors were cautious afraid to enter into open conflict with the still perceived as mighty Polish-Lithuanian state.

However, Moscow certainly intended to somehow take advantage of the situation and the internal weakening of the Commonwealth by the civil war with the Cossacks. It demonstrated such an aspiration, crudely, during the famous 1650 visit by envoys Yuri and Stepan Pushkin (brothers), both prominent Russian diplomats of the time. Their goal was seemingly 'trivial': they demanded the punishment 'at the throat', i.e. by death, of, among others, Prince Jeremy Wisniowiecki (for the crime of not listing all of the tsar's titles in a letter he had addressed to him), as well as complaints and calls for retribution against the printers and authors of texts, published in the Commonwealth, which did not describe Moscow or Russia and its ruler in a flattering enough manner. These included the works of Jan Aleksandr Gorczyn (*Memory of the Virtues, Happiness and Bravery of Władysław IV*, Krakow 1648) and the great poet Samuel Twardowski (*The Cossack War*, Leszno 1649). On top of this, the Commonwealth was requested to pay half a million red zlotys in compensation for the tsar's 'moral losses' and to return Smolensk and other cities recovered under Sigismund III. To all this, of course, the Commonwealth was not going to agree. The first delegation of 1650 had to satisfied themselves with a symbolic (yet still troubling) gesture: the public burning of 'offensive' pages from the works so incriminated by these tsarist diplomats in the courtyard of one of the palaces in Warsaw.

Agreeing to a foreign power's censorship of books in a country that prided itself on its freedom, the nobility's freedom of speech above all, this would have been the very definition of humiliation, which is often the first step to capitulation, to subjugation by any bully. The people of Warsaw gathered around the pyre watching some of the pages being burnt, even if not whole books, were perplexed and rightly protested: 'It would be better for the King to break the peace with the Muscovites or the contested cities to secede instead of disgracing the Polish Crown in this way. Here they are burning the fame of Sigismund and Władysław in the town square.' The senators who agreed to this solution wanted to avoid war at a time of weakness. They agreed to this dishonorable gesture, to avoid a war they could not evade. A lesson in statehood that should always be remembered.

In 1650 the Commonwealth was slowly recovering after the heroic defense of Zbarazh and the Zborov settlements from Khmelnytsky's forces and their Crimean Tartar allies. Therefore, the Pushkin envoys did not push any harder. In 1653, when the echoes of the great Polish victory over the Tatar-Cossack army at Beresteczko (28 June–10 July 1651) had already faded, and the impression again existed of a frail Polish state following

149

another great Polish defeat at Batoh a year later (1–2 June 1652). A defeat in which Poland lost many of its most experienced fighters. The Tsar now could no longer hesitate. He decided to support Khmelnytsky's ongoing struggle against the Commonwealth but on his own terms. In Moscow, on 11 October 1653, the *Zemsky Sobor* [an assembly of representatives of the Orthodox nobility and clergy meeting under the chairmanship of the Tsar, functioning only until 1684 – *editor's note*] now declared war against the Polish-Lithuanian state. At stake was to be, first and foremost, dominion over Ukraine, a giant leap in the historical process of 'collecting Ruthenian lands', and the realization of 'Kalita's testament.' Against such a backdrop, Khmelnytsky himself was now becoming a mere tool of the Kremlin's imperial policy, his Cossack-Ukrainian independence projects soon would be forfeited. A Moscow envoy was sent to Pereyaslav, Khmelnytsky's head-quarters. There, in January 1654, at a Cossack council, an agreement was approved, effectively bringing Ukraine under Moscow's dominion.

It is worth noting that this agreement immediately raised strong doubts on the Cossack-Ruthenian (Ukrainian) side. The moment the Cossacks swore to the agreement and called on the Russian deputy to do the same on behalf of their master, Tsar Aleksey, they heard the answer that the Tsar would never swear an oath to any of his subjects. This lack of reciprocity gave them much to ponder on for it soon turned out that they were now in fact the Tsar's slaves not citizens, and no deals could be made with slaves. The relationship of ruler and subject in the tsarist state was quite different from the one the Cossacks had become accustomed to in the free Commonwealth. Where the King had obligations to those he ruled over. The foreshadowing was ill for the future of the Ukrainian-Russian Union. Pereyaslav set the stage for the dramatic struggle of the present day. Indeed, that historical experience also helps to shape Kyiv's position with regard to negotiations with Moscow to end the current conflict.

Let us also recall that a significant part of the Orthodox bourgeoisie and even the clergy of Pereyaslav, Kyiv, Chornobyl, and other cities controlled by Khmelnytsky, actually refused to swear allegiance to the Tsar and were subsequently forced to do so. Some of the Cossack regiments (Bratslav, Human, Poltava) also spoke out against surrendering to Moscow, and there is no testimony that the Zaporozhian Sich ever swore allegiance to the Tsar.

150

The Cossack Hetman Bohdan Khmelnytsky with Tuhay-Bey (leader of the Crimean Tartars) near Lviv. St John of Dukla hovers in a cloud over the city. Painting by Jan Matejko.

However, Khmelnytsky had already gone so far that he could not turn back from this road to perdition. Perdition ultimately for the Commonwealth and initially for the cause of Ukrainian liberty. In the early summer of 1654, three Russian armies entered the Commonwealth. The poorly-supplied, poorly-defended yet still the largest stronghold in eastern Europe, Smolensk fell, and other strongholds fell along with it. In 1655, due in part to the conflict between the Grand Hetman of Lithuania, Janusz Radziwiłł, a man of great personal ambition, and King John II Casimir (*Jan Kazimierz*), the already weak Lithuanian army was unable to put up any effective resistance to the three Russian armies entering Lithuanian lands while simultaneously facing off against Khmelnytsky's Cossacks then advancing from the south. The culmination of the second campaign, in 1655, was the capture of Vilnius by Russian-Cossack forces in August of that year. A true *sacco di Vilnius*, meaning the destruction, ruin, and looting of this great city, the Lithuanian capital, something from which it would take 100 years to recover.

Tsar Alexis of Russia (1629–1676), who personally entered the ruins of Vilnius, now declared himself Grand Duke of Lithuania, White Russia, Volhynia and Podolya on 13 September. A Cossack-Russian army now besieged Lviv, and another occupied Lublin, Puławy and Kazimierz, reaching the Vistula River itself not far from Warsaw. Hundreds of thousands of residents of the Grand Duchy of Lithuania, mainly from the territories of today's Belarus, were now deported deep into the Russian state, not just to intimidate the rest but to exploit the labor and skills of the deported and drive economic development in the expanding Tsarist Empire. This was a massive operation of destruction and resettlement already on a scale analogous to Stalin's most extensive operations in these same lands three centuries later. The Grand Duchy of Lithuania lost between 20 and 30 percent of its population during this Moscow Deluge (1654–1660).

Yet despite the rousing successes of his army in the summer and early autumn of 1655, the Tsar now had to face the question: what next? For at the same time as his invasion a second 'deluge' the great Swedish invasion of the Polish lands began from the northwest. This was actually the renewal of a war between Sweden and the Commonwealth, put on hold with a ceasefire in 1629. The Swedish troops entered the weakened Commonwealth with King Charles X Gustav at the helm, driven by what he perceived to be a legitimate

Swedish claim to the Polish crown as well as the common 30 Years War staples, brigandage and plunder. He was conducting a similar incursion against Denmark at the same time. Gustav was also eager to preempt any further actions by the Tsar, concerned by the sudden emergence of too much Russian power along the southern shore of the Baltic Sea, perceived by some to be a Swedish lake. In contrast to the resolute fight by Polish forces on the eastern lands, there was the pitiful surrender of the western Poland lands, so-called Greater Poland districts on 25 July 1655 at Ujście. An event many would call a *de facto* betrayal it opened the floodgates for the Swedes to conquer Warsaw and march all the way south towards Krakow. In a matter of months on the threshold of autumn, there was hardly a patch of free land of the Commonwealth on which a sovereign power, independent of either Moscow or Stockholm, remained. On 20 October, in Kėdainiai, Lithuania, Prince Janusz Radziwiłł eager to preserve his standing in a new post-Commonwealth status quo, suddenly and without any legal basis, announced the rupture of Lithuania's Union with Poland and submission instead to Sweden. This was a duplicitous move to preserve himself and his holdings from the encroaching Tsarist troops. For many, it seemed to be the death knell for the Union and the Commonwealth, which would soon disappear from the map altogether.

The Tsar then sent a letter to King Carl Gustav, stating that the Russian armies wished to proceed with their advance onto Warsaw and Krakow. He was ready to 'accommodate' the Swedish King giving him 'only' Royal Prussia, i.e. Pomerania, as well as Courland so that the Swede could 'round out' his Baltic basin possessions. On the other hand, the then landlocked lands of Lithuania and Poland should come under exclusive Russian rule. The Tsar, in a policy ever repeating for centuries, began to gather around him willing collaborators from the Commonwealth's ruling elites. Some of the nobles indeed regarded the Tsar's supremacy as potentially the 'lesser evil' to a Protestant Swedish rule. In exchange for loyalty, for accepting the role of subject and facilitator of Moscow's policies in the lands of the Commonwealth the Tsar did not offer individual magnates anything new except the preservation of their offices and estates. This modest offer seemed at the time highly attractive to many who had heard of or indeed seen the aftermath of the great sack of Vilnius and several thousand representatives of the Polish and Lithuanian nobility in 1655 now swore allegiance to the Tsar. Among the 'leaders' of the Moscow party were the two regional governors of Troki, voivode Mikołaj Stefan Pac, and of Chernihiv voivode Krzysztof Tyszkiewicz; the offer of collaboration also came to the notice of Lithuanian field hetman Wincenty Gosiewski, who, however, was quickly taken prisoner by Sweden. Some of these magnates also held aspirations to play the role of the new power and representative of the Tsar following Russia's final occupation of the entire Commonwealth.

However, the proposal for the partition of the Commonwealth, which Tsar Alexei Mikhailovich actually submitted to the Swedish King in writing, obviously could not satisfy the appetite of the voracious, both figuratively and literally, Charles Gustav. A Russian-Swedish conflict to control the Baltic and its trade, a conflict between these two mortal enemies of the Commonwealth, was inevitable. However, the fate of the Commonwealth was not, as it turned out yet sealed. Faced with the oncoming Russo-Swedish cataclysm the spirit of resistance awoke in many, including the non-converted members of the nobility. The symbol of this resistance became the heroic defense of the Jasna Góra monastery at Częstochowa in southern Poland (18 November–27 December 1655). Events well known to many Poles, I will not elaborate on them here.

For Tsar Aleksey Mikhailovich, the interception of secret letters from of Karl Gustav to Bohdan Khmelnytsky in the east now became the pretext for an open pre-emptive strike by his troops against Sweden. Khmelnytsky clearly was not content to surrender to the Tsar but was still looking for other options to secure freedom and independence from a potential Tsarist regime a regime he now knew would restrain his liberty more so than the Commonwealth. This is why he sought an ally in the Swedish King. Of course, this proved that decisive immediate action against the Swedes was needed from the Moscow side. Thus, came about the intervention of Imperial (Habsburg) diplomacy, concerned about the triumphs of Charles Gustav at the head of a Protestant 'crusade' in Europe. Vienna would lead an attempt to conclude a temporary peace agreement between the Tsar and the Polish King John Casimir. Subsequent negotiations and the preparation for such a temporary agreement took place throughout 1656.

In the Tsar's first diplomatic mission, addressed to the supporters of King John Casimir, including Hetman Paweł Sapieha, (another character well

Only one monk from the handful gathered courageously faced down the Swedish attackers thus wrote Josef Ignacy Kraszewski of Father Augustyn Kordecki. Depicted Father Kordecki among the blessed defenders on the walls of the Jasna Gora Monestary. Picture by January Suchodolski.

known to readers of the second part of Sienkiewicz's trilogy of books, *The Deluge,*) the Tsar proposed that John Casimir could retain his reign until his death, but only in the Crown lands of Poland since the Grand Duchy of Lithuania in its entirety would immediately pass over unconditionally to Russia. After John Casimir's death, Poland was to reunite with Lithuania but now under the Tsar's scepter. The essential matter for the Tsar was to secure the Polish throne for himself. Along these lines, an armistice was concluded in November 1656 in Nemėža, a village near Vilnius (today it is already a district within the city limits). Tsar Aleksey was to be elected by the future Polish Sejm still *vivente rege* (during the life of John Casimir) as Polish King, while the Commonwealth did not renounce Lithuania (the Tsar did not renounce it either, this issue was to be left 'undecided' for the time being); in any case, in the end, Tsar Aleksey Mikhaylovich certainly understood he was to emerge as the ruler of both Lithuania and Poland.

The most important thing was that the truce in Nemėža broke the mortal danger for the Commonwealth of continued cooperation between the two invading powers Sweden and Moscow. Powers which had *de facto* already divided the lands of the Commonwealth by that time. Characteristically for its geopolitical strategy, Moscow artfully did not sign up to the Swedish-initiated formalization of this first known and rather elaborate 'Polish partition project' to 'legalize' or put in writing the perceived 'post-Commonwealth' order. This was called the Radnot (Transylvanian) Agreement, concluded in 1657. Under its terms Sweden, Brandenburg, Transylvania, Khmelnytsky's Ukraine and Prince Bogusław Radziwiłł would all participate and partition the Commonwealth, but Moscow chose to stand apart unwilling to commit in writing to the full extent of its territorial ambitions. This illustrates the value of Poland's written truce in Nemėža, concluded a little earlier, a truce where the Tsar did commit himself in writing to cease his aggression against Polish forces. Thus, allowing the Poles to focus their attention towards changing the facts on the ground through military means against one instead of against two invaders.

Over the next 4 years Polish forces in part with the help of the Austrian army, slowly pushed back the Swedish 'Deluge,' After the death of Bohdan Khmelnytsky in 1657 the Cossacks, now bereft of their leader and disillusioned with their relationship with Moscow, turned their hopes once again toward the Commonwealth. Khmelnytsky suffered a stroke upon hearing news of the defeat of his Transylvanian allies with whom he'd hoped to partner with in the partition of Poland. The new Cossack hetman, Ivan Vyhovsky, turned against Moscow and occupied Kyiv. In 1658 mindful of the disastrous impact of the initial 1648 rebellion on the Commonwealth's power, the now more foresightful elements of the Polish elite put forward proposals to re-integrate the Cossacks as formal members of a newly expanded Polish-Lithuanian-Ruthenian (or Ukrainian) Commonwealth. The so-called Hadziacka Union was concluded in September that year (from Hadziacz (Hadyach) in eastern Ukraine, where it was signed) with the aim of establishing a permanent union between the Crown (Poland), Lithuania and the newly separate, but equal 3rd member of the Commonwealth: This

3rd member would be called the Grand Duchy of Rus, with its capital in Kyiv and encompass three provinces – Kyiv, Braclav and Chernihiv and overturn the Pereyaslav settlement with Moscow signed 4 years previously. The Union was approved by the Polish Sejm and sworn in by King John Casimir.

Since the Hadziacz Union strengthened the position of the Cossack elders, opening wide the possibility of their promotion to the noble landed class, Moscow quickly undertook efforts to incite a section of the Ruthenian peasantry against this new Hadziacz settlement. It was not the first or the last time the Kremlin would indulge in such social engineering in neighboring territory, priming internal 5th columns to be sacrificed on the altar of its imperial goals. The still-potent Cossack army shortly after would inflict a devastating defeat on the Russian military at Konotop in July 1659. Yet ultimately all their skill on the battlefield was no match for Moscow's darker diplomatic and subversive arts. In time, Moscow engineered the overthrow of Hetman Vyhovsky and effectively undermined the Hadziacz Union shortly after. Doing so by intensifying its ongoing efforts to ferment discord among the Ruthenian peasantry and selected Polish nobles of wavering loyalty. A group that Moscow, after the events of the Deluge, now clearly perceived as an effective future tool to undermine the Commonwealth from within.

In the meantime, however, the Commonwealth finally began to rebuild and recover from the Swedish invasion and concluded the Peace of Oliva in 1660. It could now devote the remnants of its forces to deal with Moscow's ongoing occupation of the eastern half of the country. In 1660, two Russian armies were destroyed in a great strategic triumph. Firstly, on 29 June, the Commonwealth forces were victorious at the Battle of Polonka (today Belarus, Brest region), with Paweł Sapieha and Stefan Czarniecki in command. In the battle of Chudnov, fought from 14 October to 2 November, Hetman Jerzy Lubomirski's army then forced the surrender of Vasyl Sheremetev's Russian army, operating in the territory of Ukraine.

These were strong blows inflicted on Moscow, but the Commonwealth was utterly exhausted by this state of constant war. Importantly, and in a relatively new experience for Poland that war had been fought largely on its own territory and had lasted more than 12 years being waged continuously since 1648. Unpaid troops had for many months begun to show tendencies to mutiny some, forming so-called confederations, further pursuit of the Tsarist

157

army was impossible. Yet, the very fact of the Commonwealth's survival against all odds, bordered on the miraculous. This was also the impression the Commonwealth left on perhaps the most outstanding politician of the era, Prince Frederick William of Prussia, the man known as the 'Great Elector'. A man who would rule Brandenburg and Prussia with an iron fist for 40 years and lay the groundwork for future Prussian hegemony. He himself had taken advantage of the time of the 'Deluge' of the Polish-Lithuanian Commonwealth to finally shed the Hohenzollern (Teuton) fief dependence from the Polish Crown dating back to the defeat of the Teutonic Order several centuries before. Yet despite this seismic diplomatic success against the Polish crown Fredrich William in his testament to his future successors left a salient message. A warning based on the ultimate outcome of the Deluge that they should never underestimate the Commonwealth because, like the phoenix, it is reborn from the toughest oppression and cannot be ultimately defeated. After all, Frederick William had participated in the Treaty of Radnot that was to have wiped the Commonwealth *from the map, being* eager to carve out a piece of it for himself because, after all, there actually was no Commonwealth at that time. Yet 5 years before his death in 1683 the Great Elector would read reports of how a new Polish King Jan Sobieski with his army spearheaded by winged hussars would lead the coalition to smash the Turks and lift the great siege of Vienna. Through its inherent resilience founded in an adherence to the concept of liberty, Poland had pushed back against what seemed to be the inevitability of its own demise and partition by aggressive neighbors, all of whom collaborated to bring about that demise. Pushing back the tragic moment of the partitions by 120–130 years.

Now imagine what would have happened if Tsar Aleksey Mikhaylovich's plans, so close to realization in 1655/56, had been crowned with success. Who would the Poles be today if the Polish state had ceased to exist already at that moment? It was of primordial importance that Poland survived this crisis even though she no longer had enough strength to emerge from it fully victorious. She managed, however, to fend off this invasion (recapturing, among other things, Vilnius and Grodno in December 1661), but the ravages inflicted upon the land and people meant she could not fully regain her earlier power. Moscow was, unfortunately, assisted in its efforts by future internal divisions within the Commonwealth. King John Casimir wanted

'I swear to the Lord God Almighty and the Holy Trinity, that (…) in this Confederacy (…), according to my ability, I will do what is needed and will perform all that befits my office, according to God, my conscience and common law'. The Tyszowiec Confederation which led to the rallying of Polish forces against the Swedish invasion and that army's sacrilegious attack on the Monastery of Jaśna Góra in Częstochowa in the painting by Walery Eljasz-Radzikowski.

to push through a *vivente rege* election: that is, the election of a new King, a candidate promoted by the French state, before his demise. The opposition, led by the victorious leader of the battle of Chudnov, Hetman Lubomirski, did everything in turn to prevent this.

The Commonwealth was now beginning to enter a period of civil division and conflict. In a last attempt to gain a strategic advantage in relations with Russia, John Casimir's led an expedition to the left bank of the Dnieper beyond Kyiv 1663/64, but it failed. It would no longer be possible for Poland to challenge Moscow militarily from the South. The marshland of southern Belarus would inhibit such an expedition. Only by holding the solid ground east of Kiev or the great Smolensk Gate could any European rival challenge Moscow militarily. The exhausted Polish could not continue the fight. The Crimean Khanate and the Ottoman Empire's power behind it now claimed sovereignty over the south Ukrainian lands. The Commonwealth relented and the Tsar would now hold dominion over the other Ukrainian lands east of Kyiv. Thus ends this crucial stage in Polish-Russian relations with the Truce of Andrusovo, 30 January/9 February 1667. Though for the Commonwealth there would be no true respite as five years later Poland would again be attached this time from the South by the Ottoman Turks and forced to concede yet more territory before that conflict's end in 1676.

After these events, it is also clear now that without hesitation, one can now use the word 'Russia'. Moscow had made a decisive step in its westward expansion. The Truce of Andrusovo sealed this breakthrough: The Commonwealth divided up Cossack Ukraine to share in it with the Tsar. The so-called left-bank part of Ukraine fell under the tsar's rule. Zaporizhzhia further to the south was to be formally a Polish-Russian protectorate, a veil, so to speak, for both countries obscuring the true power in that land the Tatars and their Ottoman Turk supporters. Moscow would in fact increase its presence there over time. Just as it would not surrender Kyiv to Polish dominion as it had originally agreed to do within two years under the terms of the Andrusovo Treaty. A Moscow that has subjugated Ukraine, or at least half of it, is already the Russia that we can recognize from western school textbooks. Especially since it is from these lands, conquered by the invasion of the Commonwealth from Smolensk and Chernihiv to Kyiv, that now the very best-educated cadres the men, laying the foundation of the future

Orthodox modernizing Russian state of the Tsars, will emerge. Transforming it from medieval Mongol-influenced Moscow, into modern-day Russia.

The truce at Andrusovo was concluded for 13 and a half years. However, it proved to be a permanent demarcation line, depriving the Commonwealth of a *de facto* foothold in the Cossack realm and. As a result, making this separation from the Cossacks a permanent factor in the further division and weakening of the Commonwealth's earlier power. For let us remember that while Poland was losing half of the Cossack/Ukraine, Russia was gaining half of Ukraine and the Chernihiv, Smolensk and Siverian lands. Lands it had previously lost to the Commonwealth based on the Truce of Deulino, after the Time of Troubles and the Polish occupation of the Kremlin had passed.

Moscow also conquered Siberia at the same time while it was waging its wars in the west. This did not immediately add to her great strength; after all, these were primarily wild and empty territories. Yet the fact that the Cossacks now stood on the shores of the Pacific Ocean at the beginning of the 17th century and that they reached as far as Kamchatka and established a permanent border with China, gave Moscow a strategic depth now unmatched by any other country. Previously, fighting her as an equal was possible, even with slightly smaller numerical forces. Now though she had gained an advantage over all its western neighbors. This advantage would henceforth be the experience every Polish ruler in Warsaw, that of Sweden's Charles XII during the Great Northern War, and later Napoleon in 1812 in fact all of Russia's subsequent opponents, the advantage of strategic depth.

Few especially in Western Europe were as yet cognizant, in the second half of the 17th century, of the importance of this transformation. This was best demonstrated by how unimportant Russia seemed in European relations at the time. The most significant conflict of the 17th century, the Thirty Years' War, ended in 1648 with peace treaties concluded in two Westphalian cities, Münster and Osnabrück. Attached to them was a list of European states recognized as a kind of community of the new order of peace in Europe. Moscow is listed there in the penultimate, 48th place out of the 49 states mentioned in the treaty. Behind it was only Transylvania, a Turkish fiefdom.

At the end of this seventeenth-century story, it is worth adding that until the time of Peter I (1672–1725), the Commonwealth was, from the perspective of Moscow-Russia's foreign policy, still the most important direct rival.

Illustrations by Antoni Zaleski to the 'Memoirs' of the Mazovian nobleman Jan Chryzostom Pasek. Top: Pasek greets his father on his return from the expedition of the Polish contingent against the Swedish forces in Denmark. Bottom: Pasek and his companions stand up for the rights of a wronged widow.

An opponent, the enemy number one on the horizon, limiting the strategic goals of the emerging Russian Empire. In this regard, we have an indicator even more tangible than the roster of states of the Treaty of Westphalia. In the archives of the Russian Foreign Ministry, the books of the *Posolsky prikaz* as the ministry was called at the time records kept to this day. Reference to the Commonwealth fills as many as 256 such books from the 17th century, in contrast, other nations are far less frequently mentioned Sweden 129, Crimea 90, Austria 49, Turkey 28, Denmark 24, England 20, France 15, and Prussia 7. This shows eloquently, from Russia's point of view, the scale of the Polish-Russian struggle in the 17th century.

Today, perhaps because we have been somehow educated not to nurture our image abroad, the date of 12 September 1683 and Poland's role that fateful day has been disregarded in Polish political discourse. However, at that time in Europe, this victory was perceived as something significant. A testimony to the still unextinguished possibilities of the Commonwealth. Its inextinguishable strength, founded in the concept of liberty and Poland's adherence to Latin tradition. A strength which our ancestors regrettably did not fully harness. The army that confronted the Turks that day also consisted of imperial Hapsburg troops and other allies. Still, no one doubted at the time that this was a victory for Commander-in-Chief Jan III Sobieski and the Polish hussar cavalry, still unmatched in Europe. Immediately after the Vienna victory, and probably not in part unrelated to its publicity, a window in time opened up in the 1680s that was perhaps the only time in the history of Polish-Russian relations when the Polish language and culture actually started to become fashionable at the Russian court. Polish was now spoken there, painting styles for portraits were adopted, novels printed in Poland were acquired and read in Russia, and the Polish language was used as a model, for the first attempts to write verse and poetry in the Russian language. This was the time of the reign of Regent Sophia (1682–1689) after the death of Tsar Alexey. This short time ends when Sophia's ambitious half-brother Peter comes to power. A man who will go down in history as Peter the Great and who would play such a significant role in bringing the Commonwealth under Russian influence.

However, it is necessary to mention one more event that occurred before Peter gained real power (he had been formally co-ruler since 1682). In 1686, the Perpetual Peace, otherwise known as the Grzymułtowski Treaty, was signed. Concluded as a result of negotiations in Moscow by the Poznań based voivode Krzysztof Grzymułtowski (a man richly rewarded for his docility in the negotiations). The peace formally ended the war between the Russian Tsar and the Commonwealth, previously only paused by the Andrusovo truce. It already gave back eastern Ukraine and accepted the now permanent loss of the city of Kyiv to Moscow. Remember that the Kyiv provincial region, which Casimir Jagiellon had created, remained within the Commonwealth but simply without its natural capital. However, the most fraught point of the treaty was the one that recognized Russia's right to 'guardianship' over the Orthodox population of the Commonwealth. Opening up almost unlimited possibilities for Tsarist diplomacy to interfere in the internal affairs on the basis of perceived religious 'intolerance'.

At the end of the 17th century, King Jan III Sobieski, the great victor of Vienna was now a shadow of his former self. In the clash with the magnate opposition, to whom state affairs had become alien, he also began to pursue his private dynastic interests to secure the Crown for his rather unworthy successors, headed by Jakub Sobieski, to gain some 'foothold' for a future dynasty. He hoped that this could be in Moldavia, a fiefdom to be torn from Turkish hands. Therefore, the most important strategic objective for him became a continuation of the war with Turkey. However, a necessary condition, from the point of view of the Venetian alliance namely Rome, was Russia's participation in this war. The price for this participation would be constant pressure on Poland from the diplomatic forces of these countries, including from Vienna, to finally conclude a perpetual peace treaty with Russia. Jan III Sobieski opted thus to sign this peace treaty against the interests of the Commonwealth. Reportedly with tears in his eyes, he signed the Grzymułtowski Treaty in 1686 just three years after his great victory at Vienna. Symbolically however the Commonwealth did not ratify this peace treaty for some 60 years only doing so finally at the Sejm of 1764. This was the same Sejm at which the German-born Tsarina Catherine II, would sanction the power of her former lover, Stanisław August Poniatowski, as the Grand Pantler of Lithuania.

Regardless of how we judge the moral level of the Polish elites, it must be made clear that there was an awareness among them that the peace con-

'He was the last of the Polish kings, who left behind a heroic legend', thus wrote Józef Ignacy Kraszewski about John III Sobieski. King John leads the Polish knights and Hussar Cavalry against the besieging Turkish forces at Vienna 1683. Painting by Stanisław Chlebowski.

cluded by Grzymułtowski was extremely unfavorable to the Commonwealth and its long-term prospects. Although, simultaneously, it was a time when it still seemed possible for the Commonwealth having regained strength could continue to function peacefully and with mutual benefit alongside Moscow. There were no immediate major points of conflict from the Russian side. Indeed, there were even some signs of cultural rapprochement. This brief geopolitical pause was interrupted when the Tsarist Empire began to exploit the potential it had accumulated in the second half of the 17th century. This was done by Peter, who made his political and strategic debut with the capture (1696) of the fortress of Azov on the Black Sea. Thus, he directed his expansion towards the south, pursuing a Russian strategy that was apparently benign towards Poland. At the time, many spoke of the possibility of a lasting Polish-Russian alliance, whose common basis would be the struggle against the Crescent, the Ottoman Empire and the Tatars. Poland had not yet regained the lands it had lost to Turkey by the infamous

(Buczacz) in 1672, so it had good reasons to wish for a continuation of the conflict in this area.

However, upon reaching Azov on the Black Sea, Peter now radically changed Russian policy. He chose to 'smash through a window' for Russia towards Europe via the northern route rather than the southern one: this was the essence of this change and the genesis of the resultant Great Northern War. This decision and Peter's epic travel through western Europe in 1697–1698 coincided with an event of great importance for the Commonwealth. The Tsar was setting off *incognito* from Riga to reach Dutch and British ports and eventually through the German countries on to Vienna. He began this journey following the death of Jan III Sobieski when the election took place in Poland to choose a successor. A process which dramatically demonstrated the weakness and fragmentation of the Commonwealth.

It was then that Peter formulated, one can say, in short order, the goals of Russian policy with regard to this election. He already knew that the election would be characterized by divided opinions and that there would be multiple candidates. Peter clearly did not favor the French candidate, Prince Conti, who enjoyed the most popularity and was widely considered to be the favorite. This was because he realized that Conti's victory would mean the establishment of the Commonwealth's future on the shoulders of a strong French ally. It would also have the effect of easing the conflict with Turkey, thus strengthening the Commonwealth *in its rivalry* against Russia and a now emerging Prussia. Recognizing this as a potentially unfavorable turn of events, Peter made a somewhat peculiar and bold at the time move, oft repeated in subsequent elections. He sent a letter not only to his ambassador in Warsaw but through him also to the voters gathered in Warsaw to elect a new King. He warned them not to elect Prince Conti, and he threatened them with war if they chose the 'wrong', i.e. candidate not to Moscow's liking. This letter came late, just before the election itself, so it probably did not have a decisive impact. Prince Conti was in fact the victor, elected and proclaimed King by Primate Radziejowski. However, the supporters of another candidate, the Elector of Saxony, Augustus II the Strong, who had received fewer votes, (many through bribery by the Russian side), now decided to hold a second, alternative election. The Saxon proved to be faster on his feet or in his stirrups than the Frenchman and he arrived in Krakow, where the royal insignia were then by stealth tricked out of the cathedral treasury, and thus Frederick Augustus of the house Wettin was crowned King of the Commonwealth. The Elector of Saxony won through deception the battle for the Polish throne adding it to his earlier Saxon title. He would now rule both states simultaneously, most to Peter's satisfaction.

The young Tsar was, unlike the Saxon, a ruler not only bold but also consistent in his course. He had a clear vision of Russia as a superpower, a pillar of which was the swiftly formulated program of permanent intervention in the internal affairs of the Polish-Lithuanian Commonwealth. A program since implemented, almost continuously, for more than three centuries. Its basis was the belief that the Russian Tsar had the right to decide who would or could not rule in Warsaw. That he could use threats, intimidation, in this case, even military threats to do so. Such a 'nuclear option,' or rather the 'bogeyman' of military intervention was still a common custom in the late 17th century, and how often would it be repeated later with ever new means of terror?

After returning from a great and instructive tour of Western countries in 1698, Tsar Peter established direct talks with the new Polish King August II the Strong in Rawa Ruska. This was, in a sense, the first, as we would say today, Polish-Russian summit. It was the first time a Russian Tsar met a Polish King in a role other than that of a defeated captive we Poles fondly remember the homage of the Shuysky Tsars before King Sigismund III Vasa. In Rawa Ruska, the Tsar and the King now met seemingly as partners, holding a tournament of rulers in… the consumption of alcohol. Although Peter lost in this competition in other areas Peter was the clear winner. The two jointly prepared plans for war against Sweden, a war that would transform the geopolitical situation in Eastern Europe. Why did Peter need the Commonwealth, which formally did not participate in the conflict but would instead serve as its primary battleground and thus suffering the most? Poland's sacrifice was an expression of Augustus the Strong's ambition and gratitude to the Tsar, to whom he owed the throne in Warsaw. This war, called the Third Northern War or Great Northern War, began in 1700; Saxony the other realm of Augustus formally entered in it as an ally of Peter. The Swedes, led by Charles XII, promptly beat the Russian army at Narva (1700), followed by the Saxon army at Riga, and then moved hostilities into the formally still neutral Commonwealth.

In the confusion and destruction caused by the Swedish intervention, appear the first critical manifestations of the Commonwealth's direct subordination to Russian policy, as an 'ally' and 'patron.' This first became apparent in Lithuania, which had already been devastated by internal strife. There, the opponents of Sapieha's domination of the Grand Duchy organized themselves into a powerful faction of so-called 'Lithuanian republicans' who smashed Sapieha's opposing forces in the Battle of Valkininkai (18 November 1700). These victorious 'republicans,' defenders of golden liberty against the proclaimed absolutism of the Sapieha line then immediately turned for protection to the Russian despot, Tsar Peter. He would, it was thought, defend them against a possible revanchist attack by Sapieha's regathered forces supplemented with potential Swedish support. This was the means by which the 'Lithuanian republicans' became *de facto* the first Russian political force within the Commonwealth's borders. Thus, described by the most thorough researcher of the era, the Warsaw historian Jacek Burdowicz-Nowicki. They prepared two consecutive treaties with Russia 'on behalf' of the 'Lithuanian Commonwealth' in April 1702 in the suburban Moscow village of Preobrazhenskoye, where Peter resided, and then in July of the following year at the Tsar's camp at Nyenskans on the Neva River, renamed Schlotburg by the Russians. In return for financial subsidies, they effectively pledged to take on the role of the political and military arm of Peter's plans within the Commonwealth in the renewed fight against Sweden and its influence. However, in reality, they would at the same time serve Peter's ends in the struggle to establish a lasting Russian presence in the region.

The Commonwealth, coerced by the King's conduct, voluntarily signed a treaty with the Tsar in 1704 in Narva (the Polish negotiator was Tomasz Działyński). Under this curious treaty, it became a subordinate, in essence, an ally of Russia in the war against Sweden. Russian troops were granted by this untypical treaty the right to wage war without restrictions on the territory of the Commonwealth. Thus, it was up to Russia to decide when its troops would not only enter but also when they would ultimately decide to leave. Russia also financed the Polish side in the continued struggle against the Swedes. Peter did not push for any annexation conditions to be introduced into the Treaty of Narva, nor did he demand any territories what he wanted was to bind the entire Commonwealth with a treaty that would prevent it from becoming anti-Russian or simply: independent.

The tremendous initial successes of the Swedes allowed them in turn, to force the election of a new Polish King, or rather anti or counter king. Stanisław Leszczyński (1677–1766). An election, conducted at the barrel of Swedish muskets in July 1704. Two confederations were thus formed by opposing Polish sides: the first, pro-Swedish supporting the 'new' King and the second pro-Augustus II (and therefore, pro-Russian). Fueled from the outside by their 'allies', this new civil war in the Commonwealth was now destroying Polish sovereignty to its very core. The Swedes ravaged Poland, and then moved against the lands of Saxony also part of Augustus's realm. In the end, the Tsar defeated Charles XII's army, (TN Start) partially by exploiting Russia's new strategic depth. A campaign which saw Charles pursue the Tsar far across Belarus and into central Ukraine exhausting his men, though allow Charles to recruit to his cause Ukrainian Cossacks who had defected from Perter under a new Hetman Ivan Mazepa (TN End). The Battle of Poltava, fought in July 1709, proved to be a turning point. Soundly beaten Charles XII barely escaped with his life, accompanied by Mazepa, who remained loyal to him, and Stanisław Poniatowski (the future father of the last king of Poland). In the aftermath of the battle, Peter I now became the master of Eastern Europe including the greatest prize of all for Peter, the Eastern Baltic Sea.

Many of Leszczyński's earlier supporters now realigned themselves behind the original King, Augustus II who again succeeded to the throne thanks to the Tsar's military support. Peter had by now figured out the complexity of Polish political life, so he maintained a deputy to the king who formally would represent Moscow's interests. Not only that, he also knew that it was necessary to also have such a Russian resident attached to each of the four great field commanders or hetmans (grand and field, one of each in Lithuania and the Polish Crown lands) since each of these four men had their own separate policy and scope of interests. The Tsar played it so that each of his resident diplomats with the separate Hetmans would have individual instructions on how to maneuver, to manipulate this seemingly complicated machinery within the Commonwealth. The goal was simple: the King and the hetmans were never to join forces, so the Commonwealth

169

would now be internally divided, quarreling and, therefore, in perpetuity, weak. This goal has guided Russian power all the way to the 21st century and not only towards Poland.

Pausing for a moment one can see a reflection of such a policy in Moscow's present-day toying with Western European countries and the U.S. The relevant 'residents,' or agents of influence, try to shape the opinion of extreme right-wing formations, holding up President Putin as a '*katechon*' the last hope for saving the moral order destroyed by the decay of the West. The last defender of the Cross, etc., etc. Others, in turn, would present Russia as leftist and leftist opinion makers champion it as the only country that successfully opposes the hated imperialism of the U.S. A country which is always ready to 'liberate' more countries from the specter of 'fascism' Some agents of influence appeal to the 'pockets' of their trading partners where can one do greater business deals if not in Russia? Hence the employment opportunities for various Gazprom positions, with Russian banks, etc., often fronted by ex-politicians such as Chancellor Schröder, the ex-Prime Minister of France, the local 'republican' Mr. Fillon, politicians of Austria (Chancellors Schüssel and Kern) or in Italy, as well as numerous other countries even ex-secret service agents. The addressees of the Kremlin's diplomatic 'offer' are also separatist movements (similar to the Lithuanian republicans) the Catalans against Spain, Corsicans against France, Scots against Britain… For the 'realists' at the State Department in the U.S. and some of the influential American think tanks prior to February 2022, some apparently bought off or at least heavily influenced by Russia, quite contrary to American interests, there was a suggestion that only a partnership with Russia could ensure world stabilization. Provided the sphere of Russian 'natural influence' is respected. Not just Ukraine but also Lithuania, Poland, Georgia, the other Baltic states all the perceived 'orphans' of the former Warsaw Pact umbrella. Something for everyone. To stun and paralyze the enemy, the victim of this game, from within and without and enable Moscow's continued imperialistic activities. We have quite a few such residents even now in the Third Polish Republic. Peter I's policy has proven its effectiveness over time so why should it ever change?

The symbol of this era became the Silent Sejm of 1 February 1717. It occurred when Augustus II attempted to consolidate his power over the

The Battle of Kalisz (29 October 1706) between the supporters of Stanisław Leszczyński (supported by Sweden) and the supporters of Augustus III the Strong (supported by Moscow) was the largest clash in the Crown lands of the Polish-Lithuanian Commonwealth during the Third Northern War and included Poles fighting on both sides against one another.

Commonwealth through a *de facto* war against the nobility, with the help of Saxon troops introduced into the country. It was then, of course, that Peter acted as a peacemaker: between the disaffected members of the nobility and the King, between 'freedom' and the 'autocracy', all the while manipulating the parties to this tragic conflict. The anti-King confederation was led by Alexei Dashkov, and at the King's side was the Russian Ambassador Grigory Dolgorukov. The latter finally acted as an arbitrator, proposing a compromise of sorts at the Silent Sejm. It went down in history by that name because of the form of the session, as no deputies or senators were allowed to speak out only the activity of voting was allowed.

The Polish Sejm, as never before, barely lasting a day, approved everything in silence; only the rapporteurs reading the content of the law acts were heard. It was feared that the session would be broken up by the shouting of the *liberum veto* slogan (that still existing power of any attendee to unilaterally veto a proposal), so any discussion was forbidden entirely. Only the kissing of the royal hand and adoption of previously prepared laws was allowed. What facilitated the quiet of this extraordinary session? It was the 'allied' Russian troops gathered outside the walls of the chamber, of course. One of the first new laws passed would cap military spending, radically limiting the ability of Poland to field a sizeable army in the future.

Gradually, however, there was a sobering up among the Polish elites. It was not that no one had any foresight. That nobody thought about the implications or indeed failed to understand what was happening. However, the fact these things were taking place was a great paralyzing shock. The sense of threat of real Russian domination led to a temporary rapprochement between a large part of the opposition and the King, who then turned towards the Holy Roman Empire in Vienna. This move was perhaps the first attempt to save the country from the power of the Russian ambassadors by seeking a coalition with Western (and other) allies. The result of this initiative, the Vienna treaty, concluded in January 1719, was signed not only by Emperor Charles VI but also by the ambassador of the British King George I. Austria together with Great Britain, then already the most considerable power on the seas and a major European power. These two were then joined somewhat counterintuitively by Turkey now ready to support the Commonwealth that had so frequently in the past thwarted Ottoman ambitions in Europe all to limit Russian influence in the center of Europe.

The Great Northern War was still not concluded, with Russian troops still stationed in Poland. Based on the new treaty, the Commonwealth had a chance to remove this 'guardianship' from its territory. Yet it soon became clear just how effective the policy of internal decay pursued by Peter I's envoys had become. For all four of the Polish hetmans now voted against the Vienna treaty; the Sejm, which was called to ratify it, was canceled. Poland's ability to ratify an international treaty vital to its interests had been

Nevsky Prospekt in St Petersburg the monumental main street of the city established by Peter the Great and built under the supervision of Aleksander Menshikov at a cost of tens of thousands of workers' lives many from the lands of modern day Ukraine. Based on an 18th century engraving.

denuded and exposed for all its potential allies to see. The Commonwealth trapped by internal paralysis could not regain its sovereignty.

The Tsar won the Great Northern War. The symbolic victory of the new era of Russian strength its entry onto the European stage. Now additionally drawing from European models of modernization to help further its capacity for expansion. Perhaps, eventually to subjugate Europe itself. With strategy directed from its new capital, Saint Petersburg. Founded by order of the Tsar in 1703 on the marshes at the mouth of the Neva and the Baltic Sea, and on the bones of tens of thousands of slaves who built it (both Russian peasants Finns, Balts and prisoners from the Great Northern War), the city was established as the new capital in 1712. It took its name not from its founder, as is often mistakenly believed, but from St Peter, the patron saint of Rome. For this was to be the new capital of the universal empire, the new 3rd Rome. A reference repeated by the name under which Tsar Peter had the first masonry temple built in the fortress that lay at the heart of the new city: this was the Cathedral of Saint Peter and Saint Paul, henceforth the burial place of successive Tsars.

The center of this new world empire was to be Russia stretching from the Pacific all the way to what had once been Eastern Europe's greatest city, Kyiv. Russia's civilizational origins were, in turn, recalled by the name under which the new capital's first monastery was built, in tribute Alexander Nevsky the first crusader against the Latin West. Peter did not abandon this patron saint of Russia's holy war. As the Tsar-reformer himself was to say: 'We need Europe for a few decades [to modernize the state, especially the army] with her help, and then we will 'turn our backs on her' [*povyernyomsya zadom*]'. In 1721, when Peter triumphantly ended the war with Sweden by capturing the lands of modern-day Estonia for Russia, he simultaneously adopted a new title and name for his state. Henceforth it was to be *Rossiyskaya Impyerya* – the Russian Empire, and the Tsar now formally became an Emperor.

We shall bookend this chapter with one more ominous sign for the future, especially with regard to Poland's future fate all the way into the 20th century. This was the conclusion of yet another treaty or rather an alliance just one year earlier between old allies. Concluded in Potsdam 13 February 1720, at Potsdam outside Berlin, Friedrich Wilhelm (1688–1740), the famed Soldier King in Prussia, concluded with Tsar Peter the first treaty in history that would guarantee cooperation between St Petersburg and Berlin a treaty with echoes of the earlier failed alliance between Albrecht von Hohenzolleren and Vasily III. In contrast to later arrangements, this was no partition of Poland, instead it was designed to maintain the Commonwealth in its current anemic political state. 'Both rulers now and in the future will guard that the Polish Commonwealth will keep its liberties, customs, constitutions, laws and privileges intact. And if the royal court shows any hostile intentions in this respect, or will persuade the Commonwealth to join the alliance between the Emperor, the King of Great Britain, that the Polish King concluded in Vienna or will seek to gain sovereign and absolute power in the Commonwealth by stealth, then the King of Prussia and the Emperor of All the Russias will not only oppose this with their advice and deeds, but will strongly support the Commonwealth, so that this does not come to pass, and that everything in Poland remains as it was before'. This was the most crucial point of the Potsdam Agreement, guaranteeing Berlin's and Russia's support for any future opposition in Poland that would assist in maintaining the current (relatively new) state of paralysis. An opposition that would sabotage any return to the vitality of the old Commonwealth.

Empire Through Enlightenment, Techniques of Enslavement, Acquiescence, Accommodation and Resistance (1773–1797)

T he most straightforward technique for the Russian Empire to render the Commonwealth dependent and weak was by the corrupting its political class of the time by the Russian ambassadors. Simply put this meant bribing the most influential representatives of the magnate or noble families making up various factions (groups) which then would fight each other in the political sense, though not only. Such events took place in the Commonwealth both under the reign of Augustus II (1697–1704; 1709–1733) and following his death, when the election of his successor, Augustus III (1696–1763), conveniently coincided with the entry of two Russian army corps into the lands of the Commonwealth. During the previous *interregnum*, Tsar Peter had threatened to 'only' use the army if the citizens of the Commonwealth elected a candidate that Russia did not like. Now, for this next election, the new Empress, Peter's niece Anna Ivanovna, went from words to deeds to bring Polish liberty to its knees. She sent 32,000 soldiers not to the borders of the Commonwealth, but onto its 'sovereign' territory to ensure the continuation of a 'humble' or appropriate approach among the citizens of the Commonwealth in respect of the norms and values of the 'electoral process'.

In 1733, after an unbroken series of free elections of their rulers dating back three and a half centuries, the citizens of the still-existing Polish-Lithuanian Commonwealth now heard directly from a neighboring power that, this time, they could no longer choose the kind of King they wanted but had to choose the kind that their neighbors thought would be best for their interests. Polish citizens of course did not want to elect a king 'at the end of a musket muzzle' nor under the dictates of an instruction sent by a foreign Tsarina Anna Ivanovna, who forbade them to vote for Stanisław Leszczyński, now the most popular candidate among voters of the nobility. The primate-*interrex (Temporary Steward)*, Theodore Potocki, wrote in a journalistic response to the Tsarina's instruction, that Poles had to oppose this *diktat* and clearly inform the Russians of that intention: 'In our country, absolutism in Poland is not to reign as it does in her state.' The *interrex* urged 'that we should not be led by the nose and show that *gens libera sumus nemini servimus unquam* [we are a free nation, that is, never a slave to anyone].'

Outraged by this outside pressure, the citizens sovereignly elected their preferred candidate, Stanisław Leszczyński, already a much older man than when he had become the Swedish-enforced counter-king during the Great Northern War. Moreover, they did so unanimously. At that time, the army corps sent by Tsarina Anna Ivanovna was already approaching Warsaw. Of course, under the guise of 'defending' Polish freedom. This act of force was supposed to 'convince' the citizens of the Commonwealth of their error. There was indeed a group of those who allowed themselves to be won over by this unsubtle argumentation. They did not recognize the legally elected monarch instead, under the threat of Russian bayonets, they proclaimed King Augustus III as the new ruler. This represented of course for Russia a clear case for intervention in the affairs of the Commonwealth under the terms of the earlier referenced Postdam accord signed between Berlin and St. Petersburg 13 years earlier.

It was at this time that the word 'independence' started to appear in the Polish political vocabulary. The young priest Stanisław Konarski (1700–1773) wrote it down for posterity. The future founder of modern education in the Commonwealth and a supporter of political reform published a public polemic in 1733: *Listy poufne czasu bezkrólewia* (original Latin title: *Epistolae familiares… Secret correspondence from the time of the interregnum*). In it, he wrote these words: 'The Commonwealth is the supreme mistress of its own laws, independent of any power of foreign monarchs. [...] The Commonwealth rightly has by divine right the supreme power subject to no one and guards it like all other Kingdoms and empires. [...] One cannot command he who is not dependent on someone else. He who is subject to no one except God is not obliged to obey anyone except God. [...] It is, therefore, the greatest wickedness in any Kingdom and the well-organized republic for foreigners to publicly accuse citizens and offices and even the republic itself of contempt for the laws, as if boasting that they think better of the republic than its own citizens. [...] In any republic, one should first consider one's own *raison d'etat*, and only then someone else's. The dignity and benefits of the republic should not be subordinated to foreign interests. The worst method of persuasion is one that instills fear, suitable for enslaved minds, not free ones. Everything is lost in a free republic when freedom has been lost.'

Others followed these words to defend independence through actions. Local confederations began to form all over the country, in defense of the right to a free choice by the Poles. First, in the Sandomierz province, where in December 1733, citizens confederated 'by the independence and supreme majesty of the mistress of her rights, the Commonwealth, knowing no one but God Himself as its overlord [...], against our invaders and oppressors, who are so audacious to attack from the outside, and against the conscienceless traitors from the inside, who have entered into agreements and machinations against the Commonwealth with foreign courts...'.

Later, the General Confederation of the Grand Duchy of Lithuania, assembled 5 November 1734 in Dzików, united under the same slogan of defending independence. This was, in fact, the first Polish uprising in defense of independence. It did not resonate as strongly in Polish cultural memory as the subsequent ones. Still, it certainly left a lasting mark on the experience of that generation, whose children would later rise to arms during the later Bar Confederation. This uprising became the common experience of several thousand active participants in that struggle, the majority of whom were noblemen including the later initiator of the Bar Confederation Józef Pułaski, father to Casimir Pułaski. The struggle continued for 2 years until 1736.

After that pacification, and the approval of the new reign of Augustus III in accordance with the wishes of Russia and Austria, it became clear to all that independence was a form of liberty that differed greatly from the mere privileges of the nobility. The concept of liberty was now ringing hollow in Poland. With the uprising's defeat, Father Konarski undertook to invest all his efforts into laying the groundwork for a more universal concept of independence. A program for the construction of schools with the Collegium Nobilium placed at the top of the list, schools to mold a new patriotic elite, as well as the formation of a program for reconstruction of the state and

Stanisław Konarski (Coat of arms "Gryf" (1700–1773)) an eminent thinker, playwright, poet, translator, editor, educator, publicist, school reformer. He played an essential role in the reform and expansion of the Polish educational system prior to the partitions and was the founder of the Collegium Nobilium.

crucially to convince the brethren nobility to back this program. Konarski saw the sovereignty of the Commonwealth, so brutally trampled by Russia's armed intervention, as a task to which all other civic tasks and duties must now be subordinate. Such an approach opened the way for Konarski's new concepts: the need for reforms aimed at the economic strengthening of the state based on Western European models and a recognition of the fundamental role of the King as the initiator and protector of these necessary changes (*Rozmowa, na czym dobro i szczęście Rzeczypospolitej zaległo – 1757*).

By publishing his greatest, most important work *O skutecznym rad sposobie* (1760–63), Konarski placed the dot over the 'i' in the logic of just how to develop or re-engineer the patriotic concept. External freedom or independence would require the necessary limitation of what fellow citizens considered to be the essence of their civic freedom. For without civic freedom, liberty throughout the Commonwealth would be threatened. Yet where would liberty be if the Commonwealth itself would perish? This was the rhetorical question that Konarski posed to his readers encapsulating the dispute between the two contrasting models of Polish patriotism. These contrasting models would be displayed in stark form in the next historical period the so-called Stanislavian period.

Konarski's first appeal was for the abandonment of the parliamentary device of unanimity voting or *liberum veto* (the famous: 'I do not allow') something that for many Poles was still synonymous with their vision of liberty in their homeland. He blamed this device, with obvious evidence to back his claim, for contributing to the paralysis of the Sejm and leading to ineffective government. He pointed to it and the source of anarchy contained within it warning: 'Under anarchy, no state can last for a long period'. You misunderstand your freedom and misidentify threats to it, seemed to be Konarski's message to his contemporary Poles. However, he did not frontally attack the republican tradition; he referred to it with respect and with a deep historical understanding. Yet, he still wanted to change it. He warned that the 'protection' by powerful neighbors could not save the Commonwealth or its freedom but would only in time deepen the state of anarchy until the Polish-Lithuanian state itself having served its purpose would no longer be needed by those neighbors: 'neighborly protection can be the stepmother of our freedom, but the mother of it, that it cannot be.'

Unfortunately, the work on political corruption, on the moral and financial decay of the Commonwealth's elites did not stop either. Moreover, the resources of the Russian ambassadors were far greater than those at the disposal of the humble Piarist priest Stanisław Konarski. Of even greater importance were the personal ambitions and avidity in the 'civil cold war' between the King and the opposition in Poland, equally skillfully played upon by successive emperors (Elizabeth, reigning in 1741–1762, and later Catherine II, empress from 1762–1796) by means of their respective ambassadors in Warsaw. The clearest and most shameful example of such would be the Targowica Confederation at the end of the 18th century. This accord among certain Polish nobles in collusion with Russia against Polish independence would leave the saddest mark on the long history of internal corruption. Aimed at overthrowing the newly enacted 3 May Constitution of 1791 (more on this later) it was orchestrated by the great magnates Stanisław Szczęsny Potocki (1751–1805), Seweryn Rzewuski (1746–1811) and Franciszek Ksawery Branicki (1730–1819) though under the aegis of Empress Catherine II of All-Russia. The actions of these men showed a lack of elementary respect for the political community they themselves came from. They simply trampled on that community, their brethren, in a bid to satisfy their own ambitions politics and through their naivety, foreign agendas.

As it happens, those key Targowica leaders who formed the confederation (signed *de facto* in St. Petersburg) did not do it for material gain they did not care about money; they possessed enough of it. Szczęsny Potocki was regarded as the wealthiest man in Europe, and certainly in the Commonwealth. He believed he was saving the republican system from an 'absolutist' coup that of the 3 May Constitution. As such he did not hesitate to ask for help from such a defender of freedom as the despot Tsarina of St. Petersburg. Just as Seweryn Rzewuski believed sanctimoniously that he was defending the office of the hetman, without which the Commonwealth surely could not be free and therefore invited the foreign 'hetmans' of the Russian army to invade Poland. These men committed actual treason in the name of their own political ideals. Ideals, which in their view, were being trampled

181

upon by the hated May 3rd Constitution and the equally hated Polish King Staś who had ushered it in. On such viciousness and internal strife, Russia excelled and built the basis for its future eventual enslavement of Poland.

I deliberately made this leap forward in time between the eras of Peter I and Catherine II (1729–1796) to point out the hazardous element inherent in the attitude of a section of the Commonwealth's elites. Men who believed that based on the bayonets of a foreign army, and on the rulings of foreign courts, it was possible to realize their own vision of what was best for Poland. They thought that once this vision was realized, Russia would simply walk away from the Commonwealth as if by magic. It is worth adding that none of the aforementioned founding fathers of the Targowica Confederation later occupied positions of authority after the Russian army established control. There were other people for that, unrelated to these machinations who would be assigned those roles. People who only wanted to rule Poland on behalf of Russia to earn money while settling their private interests and scores.

However, what is worth remembering from this eighteenth-century lesson are not those scoundrels of Targowica in 1793, who consented to rule in Poland under Russian bayonets and distributed favors to its people. Such villainy occurs everywhere and is easy to judge unequivocally, there is no honest way to justify it. A more complex issue and an essential point for reflection, also in the present day, is that timeless bargain spelt out in the small print, that unending political dilemma of compromise that can in its worst embodiment lead to treason of oneself, of one's nation. After all, even today, some people believe that in the name of realizing their own political ideals (the Targowica members had in mind the republican ideal, but this, of course, can be subject to substitution), it is permissible to demand on the help of a powerful neighbor, one who'd play the role of a patron to their branch of the political spectrum representing internal divisions within a state or a Commonwealth. These peoples for the sake of these ideals pin their hopes on this external patron. Believing the patron can provide the embodiment of this ideal, nurture the value they hope to preserve. That in this way they will save 'freedom' at least their ideal of it, in one way or another. Save it for Poland and secure 'liberty' from those Poles who were simply unenlightened, ill-informed those who 'chose wrongly'…

Often this specific pattern of thinking is repeated, 'that a lot could be done for the Poles, but to succeed, it is necessary to resort to external aid' of Russia or another patron because those Poles themselves do not understand what is good for them. Only we understand, 'I, Hetman Seweryn Rzewuski', 'I, General of the Podolya lands', 'I, Szczęsny Potocki', 'I, Hetman Franciszek Ksawery Branicki' (the 3 Targowice leaders), and so on. The names can be exchanged for others, down to the present day, it is a pattern that repeats. The patron, Russia plays out these people and their ideals, uses them and then consigns them onto the trash heap of history. For the founders of Targowica, this was surely a very bitter experience. They found out that they were not destined to restore the republic of the Commonwealth, that they simply became reduced to the role of pathetic agents in a Russian intrigue that destroyed their own political community and took away their identity as citizens of the Commonwealth. This is perhaps the most important lesson that comes from the experience of collusion with Russian imperial policy. It consists of corrupting Polish political elites with the temptation that, based on the Empire, one can realize the good of the Commonwealth. Crucially, many such unwitting agents manage to convince even themselves with the story of their own exceptional foresight and the 'complex strategic nature' of such decisions that their fellow citizens, incapable of grasping the concept need not necessarily be consulted. It is instead simpler to achieve an understanding with the enlightened patron of St. Petersburg or Moscow for this purpose than with one's own citizens.

In the eighteenth century, Russia also rediscovered another way of realizing its imperial ambitions and goals towards its western neighbor. A method suggested at the court in St. Petersburg by the *hegumen* (prior) of the Vilnius Orthodox monastery of the Holy Spirit, Theophan Leontovich. Let's not forget that there was still Orthodoxy in the Commonwealth (TN Start) as despite the conflicts with orthodox Russia that religion had not been discriminated against in Poland. In fact, the Kings of the Commonwealth from the time of its first elected King Henry Valois, made a pledge at their inauguration to uphold religious tolerance throughout the Commonwealth (TN End). In 1758, during the reign of Peter I's daughter, Empress Elisabeth (1709–1762), the *hegumen* wrote a letter to the College (i.e. the Russian Ministry of Foreign Affairs at the time), in which he pointed out to

183

'He ascended to the throne out from under a skirt', so it was said maliciously of King Stanislaus Augustus. Although the king liked to pose for portraits cloaked in armor (top), he had little of the spirit or chivalry of a knight. His election (bottom) took place with the noteworthy assistance of Russian bayonets.

the enlightened administrators that 'after all, one can move the border by 600 versts (a verst is roughly a kilometer) of the best land with an Orthodox nation.' He referred to the fact that these lands, which became part of the Commonwealth after the Polish-Lithuanian union, were once inhabited by Orthodox Slavic people and that by the mid-18th century, Orthodoxy had deeply retreated in popularity eastward. This trend had to be reversed, the German Tsarina in St. Petersburg thus had the duty to carry out such an Orthodox "Reconquista" now being orthodox herself.'

We rarely realize it, but before 1772, the Orthodox faithful accounted for less than 5% of the Commonwealth's population just before the first Partition. For, while back in the 15th–16th centuries, the majority of the peasant population of the lands east of the Bug River professed Orthodoxy, the vast majority gradually converted to the (Brest) Union over the next two hundred years. They accepted this version of unity with Rome, which guaranteed them traditional rites and the Eastern liturgy despite the ultimate jurisdiction of Rome. This hurt the legitimate Orthodox elite in the Commonwealth and reminded them that there was still a battle to be waged for the governing of souls. Not only for souls in the literal sense of salvation, whether they would be saved according to the Orthodox or Catholic rite but also for their loyalty, should remain subjects of the Commonwealth or could they instead turn to serve the Orthodox Empress?

The aforementioned Theophan Leontovich was the first who suggested this Orthodox Reconquista concept, but four years later in 1762, when the unusually lavish coronation of Catherine II (1762–1796) was taking place in Moscow (following the earlier murder of her husband, either with her consent or by her design, Peter III). The Bishop of Mogilev, Grigory Konissky (1717–1795), no longer as the superior of a monastery, but as the most important Orthodox bishop in the Commonwealth, he now made a similar request from the lands of the Commonwealth directly to the Tsarina. In doing so, he actually used the phrase 'on behalf of the Belarusian nation,' although none of the local peasants had as of yet identified themselves with any true sense of a Belarusian identity. They identified themselves with their immediate neighborhood (with their own sense of 'localness' (Pol.: 'tutejsi') and, above all, with the orthodox faith they professed. At that time, national consciousness was still in its infancy. Nonetheless, the first top-down outline of a new project that of a nation, to be joined in Eastern Slavic-Orthodox unity under Moscow's rule, had now been formulated. It was no longer just an exercise in manipulation, paralyzing the Commonwealth by winning over magnate factions fighting against each other. Instead, this would be, a partitioning, a tearing away from the Commonwealth of all its eastern lands in the name of the old holdings of Rus, in the name of an Orthodox unity that should be restored. Moreover, it should be done so in the name of the patronage that Moscow exercised over Orthodoxy. This was the concept of the 'final solution' for the Commonwealth. Thus, Catherine II now invoked the foul provision of the 1686 Grzymułtowski Treaty granting the right of the Tsars to 'take care' of the Orthodox believers in the Commonwealth.

We have then, on the one hand, the prospect of further 'patronage,' or indirect rule over the entire Commonwealth, and, on the other hand, the desire to divide that Commonwealth, invoking the old titles of Rus to unite the Ruthenian lands in the name of the eternal struggle between Orthodoxy and Latinism, i.e. with the West. Catherine II was perhaps partially by right of her German origins very much a monarch of her age. The state in the embodiment of its monarchy still had its rights, and the peasants could not impose their will on the noble state, whose privileges still had to be respected. However, Catherine was also highly progressive in her thoughts, she could grasp the potential power inherent in the argument put to her by the Bishop of Mogilev, Konissky. She recognized this highly effective tool and yet still she hesitated.

The Empress's hesitations reflected the struggles between the various factions playing out at the St. Petersburg court at that time. Among them was the chairman of the War College, or, as it were, the Minister of Military Affairs, Zakhar Chernyshev (1722–1784) who advocated seizing Commonwealth territory to reward officers in the Russian army. Indeed, since 1756, the Commonwealth had been devastated by successive marches of the Tsar's armies on the route from Moscow to Berlin, which was then occupied twice by Russian armies, as part of the so-called Seven Years' War. A war during which Russia, in alliance with the Empire of Austria and France, fought against the English-backed Prussian monarchy of Frederick II. The Russians after some early setbacks inflicted several heavy defeats on the Prussians. They could have literally trampled Prussia, yet they didn't. Why not?

When Tsarina Elisabeth died, she had been initially succeeded in 1762 by Peter III (reigned only from 5 January to 9 July). This was a man who fanatically worshipped King Frederick II and the Prussian military regime and drill. The new Tsar decided to save Prussia from total annihilation and abruptly withdrew Russian troops from Brandenburg (this was the so-called Miracle of the House of Brandenburg, that Hitler dreamed of in his bunker in April 1945 upon hearing of FDR's death, fortunately, he did not live to see any such miracle). During this abruptly interrupted conflict, Russian troops were still marching through Poland. They saw how prosperous the Commonwealth was again becoming, how it had 'bounced back' after the destruction in the Great Northern War and the previous Swedish and Russian 'Deluges.' Tsarist generals, who saw this with their own eyes asked: just how much should we fight for this Empire and get nothing out of it? If we took the lands of the Commonwealth and incorporated them into Russia, you would be able to reward us, your highness, with peasant 'souls,' i.e. landed estates taken from their previous owners in Lithuania and the remaining Lithuanian Rus lands.

It was then that this lobby of those with direct self-interest in ruling Poland began to slowly gain the upper hand in the power game of Russian politics. This clashed with Peter I's old, broader vision, which Catherine was still trying to implement. She did not want to divide the lands of the Commonwealth but instead wanted to control and exploit them through Russian ambassadors, as a far less onerous objective for a hegemonic power and beneficial to Russia in the form of maintaining a "curated" Polish buffer from the west. From 1762, however, Chernyshev continued to bend the ear of Catherine with the suggestion that the lands of the Commonwealth must finally be taken away, by Russians because they have *de facto* already ruled it for fifty-some years, moreover, no one would even lift a finger in defense of it...

Catherine, however, remained undecided. Two years later, she appointed to the royal throne in Warsaw her former lover, Stanisław August Poniatowski (1732–1798). Like many before and after him, he deluded himself that he would be able to use his connections at the court in St Petersburg to implement his reformist plans for the good of the Commonwealth. He made many efforts in this regard, especially in the early days of his reign,

Casimir Pulaski commands the defense of Bar; though the youngest (and most talented) of the confederate commanders he actually fought in defense of the fortified monastery at Berdyczów; it was instead his father who remaining in Bar led that defense, Joseph, marshal of the military association of the Bar Confederacy. Painting by Korneli Szlegel.

but after just three years, it became apparent that his ability to act was utterly and deliberately paralyzed by those who initially "empowered" him.

As soon as Stanisław August was elected King by order of Catherine II, the Tsarina and King Frederick II of Prussia (1712–1786) issued a joint declaration on the rights of dissidents in the Commonwealth. They invoked the principle of freedom of conscience so cherished by the European Enlightenment, which neither of them (especially Catherine) practiced with as much zeal as they preached, especially, God forbid in their own country. In Russia, after all, conversion from Orthodoxy to any other faith was an action, punishable by death. This was the only sentence for apostasy from the 'true faith,' from Orthodoxy. There was no such persecution in Prussia, but the exclusive ruling religion was Lutheranism; other faiths were at best

The Bar Confederates during the defense of a minor hamlet of the nobility; the armed actions of the Confederates were primarily based on guerrilla warfare. Image by Józef Brandt.

grudgingly tolerated. Frederick and Catherine, meanwhile, hypocritically demanded total freedom and equality of faiths in the Commonwealth. The Tsarina could now begin to use this Orthodox charter, which Konissky had suggested to her, and Leontovich had earlier hinted at. The legitimacy for any intervention provided to Russia by the terms of the 1686 Grzymułtowski Treaty that Jan Sobieski had wept over. This program of 'equality for the dissenters,' implemented with exceptional brutality in Catherine's plan, would now plunge the Commonwealth into ever-increasing chaos.

A faction of the old magnates headed by the most powerful Lithuanian magnate Karol Radziwiłł aka *Panie Kochanku* ['My Beloved Sir'] (1734–1790) came out against the hated Stanisław August Poniatowski, with the collaboration of, among others, the Bishop of Krakow, Kajetan Sołtyk (1715–1788). They were ready to do almost anything to remove the hated 'Ciołek', as Stanisław August Poniatowski was referred to from the throne.

Ciołek was a name derived from the designated name of his coat of arms. On 23 June 1767, at the instigation of Russian ambassador Nikolai Repnin (1734–1801), the Radom Confederation was formed against the King, which was also intended to paralyze the King's reformist agenda and put a stop to his positive intentions for the Commonwealth. However, neither Karol Radziwiłł nor, even more so, Bishop Kajetan Sołtyk could agree to a curious demand put forward under the guise of this Radom Confederation, to give up the primary position of Catholicism, as the ruling religion in the Commonwealth. They hesitated, too attached to the Catholic faith, too attached to that vision of Polishness that could not be separated from it, to agree to the "equality" of those of a different denomination. Tolerance of other religions, yes, by all means, but equality of religions no.

This is the moment when Catherine and her ambassador to the Commonwealth, Nikolai Repnin, young, ambitious, and later so infamously important in the history of the Commonwealth, decided to push matters right to the edge. They forced through the idea of equality of religion by means that were formally deemed to be extra-constitutional. When the Sejm resisted pressure from the Russian ambassador on the issue, Repnin simply ordered the kidnapping of several Commonwealth's senators from the very center of Warsaw by a special unit under the command of Osip Igelström (1737–1823) a colonel of Swedish origin. Such special units common in the days of the Soviet Union were a rarity, Igelström's group though proved to be specialized in their craft. They started by kidnapping Polish senators, then they abducted the Crimean Khan, and finally threatened to seize the Swedish king. When Catherine delegated Igelström in 1790 to negotiate with the Swedish king, the latter immediately signed a peace favorable to Russia so he could have the comfort to die in his own bed without being abducted.

But let's return to the aforementioned kidnapping and the years 1767–1768, when Repnin, on behalf of Catherine, decided on this act of unprecedented humiliation for Poland. The Bishop of Krakow, Kajetan Soltyk, the Bishop of Kyiv, Józef Andrzej Załuski (1702–1774), Hetman Wacław Rzewuski (1706–1779), and his son, the young envoy Seweryn Rzewuski (1743–1811), the later a future infamous hetman and Targowica member, were all dragged from their beds, in their Warsaw palaces. The three senators and one envoy of the Commonwealth thus abducted by the

A British etching depicting the First Partition of Poland. Tsarina Catherine II, King Frederick II of Prussia and Emperor Joseph II single out on a map the lands of the Polish-Lithuanian Commonwealth that they intend to seize. King Stanislaus Augustus (with his hands tied) watches on helplessly.

Russian army were imprisoned deep in Russia, in Kaluga. The terrorized deputies (elected to the Sejm under the control of the Russian military) agreed not only to restore the rights of Orthodox Christians and Protestants to sit in the Sejm and Senate but also agreed to sign the 'treaty of eternal friendship and guarantees' signed with the Empress of All-Russia on 24 February 1768. The Commonwealth was officially becoming a Russian protectorate, and Catherine II was to be the guarantor of its political powerlessness.

Such a blatant humiliation of the Commonwealth and the attempt to impose the 'equality of religions' demand by the 'teachers of tolerance' from St Petersburg and Berlin led to a revolt that would become known as the Bar Confederation. This was in fact a great mass uprising, the first on this scale in Poland, in defense of Polishness and Catholicism. The first Polish national uprising and the first European counterrevolution against the trampling of the faith of the Cross by absolute despots. The Confedera-

The famous protest of the Nowogródek MP Tadeusz Reytan, trying to prevent the Polish partition bill from being voted through in the Sejm, is observed by the Russian ambassador Nikolai Repnin (up in the balcony). The Marshal of the (Sejm) Confederation, Adam Poniński, the main actor in this traitorous political pageant, calls in the guards. Towering over the entire scene is a portrait of the Empress… Painting by Jan Matejko.

tion fought for its ideals over a prolonged period of nearly five years, from February 1768 through to the fall of 1772.

Unlike the earlier Dzików Confederation (1734–1736), the Bar Confederation left a rich cultural legend in living memory as well in terms of its political legacy. Therefore, I will dispense with providing all the details here. I will only remind you that this confederation was founded by a conspiracy co-initiated by Princess Anna Jabłonowska, the great patroness of the independence movement of that time. A symbolic beginning for the significant role Polish women would play in this and later Polish uprisings, a most recent follower being another Anna, Walentynowicz, the 'Mother of Solidarity', who would die in the 2010 Smolensk tragedy.

Let us also recall that the Bar Confederation plunged the country's entire territory into hundreds of battles and skirmishes, in which blazed the fame of such heroes as Józef Pułaski and his son Casimir, Józef Zaremba, and Sawa Caliński forging their places in history. It also left thousands of crosses marking the remembrance of the Confederates' deaths in battle. The most important symbols of their sacrifice Lanckorona, Tyniec, Częstochowa, and the heroic six-week (February–April 1772) defense of Wawel Castle against Alexander Suvorov's troops the later butcher of the Warsaw district of Praga. Nothing more eloquently defines the determined attitude of the Confederates, an attitude of defiance against the yoke of subjection than the Speech of Mr Pułaski to his Soldiers before battle: 'let posterity know that if we did not know how to defend our Homeland, we at least knew how to die for It.'

These were not idle words, their truth was attested to by the actual sacrifice of thousands, such as Horsztyński, immortalized by the poet Słowacki. As the historian of the Bar Confederation, Władysław Konopczyński wrote eloquently that the average confederate 'set off into the field, not yet knowing well what he had to fight for so that in the cleansing baptism of blood he learned in the face of death that he was suffering and dying not for the *liberum veto* or the right to oppress peasants or the faithful of other faiths, but for the wholeness and the independence of the Homeland. Through such an inferno of initiation, successfully passing through various social spheres and neighborhoods of Poland, and certainly not only aristocratic Poland, one became hardened by the experience. This was because the armed resistance lasted as I stated earlier not just a few months, as it did in 1792, but for over fifty months. That wall, impenetrable from the side of the most dangerous Russian deluge, stood and solidified in Polish souls. Poland, fenced off by it, and despite the tragedy of multiple partitions, awakened, rejuvenated, hardened just as [Grand Lithuanian] Chancellor [Michał Fryderyk] Czartoryski had predicted to the Russians – Poland endured.'

During the ensuing guerrilla warfare, nearly half of the active Confederates were killed or wounded in the fighting, and thousands lost their estates, being either seized or ravaged by the Russians. Catherine directed, among others, a young but already prominent commander to fight the Confederates, the aforementioned Alexander Suvorov. She also incited the masses of Ruthenian peasants in the Commonwealth's southeastern borderlands to rise against the Polish nobility and against the Jews. Tens of thousands

193

of people were slaughtered during this so-called *koliivshchyna*. First, the Ruthenian or Ukrainian peasants murdered the nobility, Catholic priests and Jews, and then they themselves were murdered in a pacification operation jointly conducted by the troops of Catherine and those still loyal to King Stanisław August bathing the whole region in a bloodbath of all the faiths. The base treachery of this 'class' policy of Catherine II was appreciated years later by Karl Marx in his analysis of this *koliivshchyna*...

In the arena of European propaganda to legitimize the bloodshed in Poland, Catherine's goals were well served by one of the foremost Enlightenment writers, Voltaire, generously rewarded by Catherine for his letters and enunciations on the matter of the "intolerant Poles". In a series of pamphlets, he described the Confederates as sinister Catholic fanatics, 'bloody genocidaires' who dared to shoot at the 40,000 Russian soldiers sent by Empress Catherine into Poland to 'guard peace and tolerance.' King Frederick II of Prussia also popularized a similar image in his personally written satirical poem, *The War of the Confederates* (they were characterized simply as the embodiment of 'Polish fanaticism, darkness and barbarism'). This image, supported by the propaganda of the powers dominating the Commonwealth and consistent with the previously prepared and disseminated stereotypes, was now adopted in the political imagination of a significant section of Western European elites.

After the Confederation was crushed by the forces of the young Alexander Suvorov's soldiers (a man later feared throughout Europe as the conqueror of the French armies, the conqueror of the Alps, but also the 'butcher' of Warsaw's Praga District in 1794), several thousand participants in the uprising were sent to Siberia. This should be highlighted because after all this was Russian military repression inflicted on the citizens of what was after all formally an independent sovereign country! These new deportations opened for the first time on such a scale, a new Siberian chapter in the history of Polish-Russian relations. It is worth adding that recently, researchers from western Siberia (Svetlana Mulina and Anna Krich, in cooperation with Polish historian Adam Danilczyk) published a brilliant dictionary of the deportee-Confederates of Bar, including even such minute details as their exact height and age. Such issues were important for evaluating the usefulness of these 'Polish slaves' by the tsarist authorities. Concerning the

Nikolai Repnin, the Russian ambassador in Warsaw, exercised *de facto* authority over the Commonwealth (he referred to Stanislaus Augustus as a 'wax puppet (doll))'. He was a faithful executor of Empress Catherine II's policy.

Commonwealth, Catherine began to use the same methods that Ivan the Terrible used earlier against Veliky Novgorod or Kazan. First, the abduction of the elites, then mass deportations, resettlement, terror and for the rest a kind or a coercive word of encouragement, to collaborate.

It was not however, the Bar Confederates uprising that was the main reason for the First Polish Partition that followed, but the political games being played out between St Petersburg, Berlin and Vienna. Games, ultimately decided upon at Catherine's court. Moreover, there had been constant pressure from the Prussian monarch Frederick II, long awaiting the Tsarina's decision on the First Partition. One which would allow him to unite the geographically separated West and East Prussian lands, and there was the consideration of Russia's difficulties in its war with Turkey. Russia wanted, by means of this first Partition, to clear the playing field for pursuit of that war to expand its territories to the south and west. This is how Chernyshev's (the aforementioned Minister of Russian Military Affairs) partition plan ultimately triumphed. Almost on the second day after Russia incorporated the lands of today's eastern and central Belarus, as this was the area annexed to the Russian Empire in the First Partition, the Tsarina gave away 80,000 peasants 'souls' in a single decree to her faithful military enablers. This was the actual dimension of this decision for those who had been awaiting it for so long. In total more than a quarter of a million peasants 'souls' would be distributed as a reward to Russian generals and officials in the subsequent partitions. Henceforth, as disposers of the property created by the partitioning of Poland, they will become the most fervent anti-Polish 'lobby' in Russian politics. They, their families and their heirs, will defend the policy of liquidating the Commonwealth, to the bitter end.

Without diminishing the role of Frederick II, who constantly pushed for Catherine's decision to make the Partitions a reality, it must be mentioned here that she, and only she, could make this move because she was the one who was the decision maker for the Commonwealth. Immediately after the First Partition, Catherine tried to pacify Poland, now truncated by its three neighbors, to return to the old policy of controlling what remained of Poland's 'hollowed out hull'. This was handled by the new ambassador, Otto Magnus Stackelberg, who subjugated both the court of King Stanisław August and oppositionists still openly critical of the King. Nevertheless, the 'hollowed out hull' of the Commonwealth woke up to life, shaken by this First Partition, reborn anew by the blood sacrifice of the Bar Confederates, the memory of the thousands of fallen, exiled and disappeared.

It can be said that after the defeat of the Bar Confederates, this kind of organic work set off with redoubled force. It gave birth to the Commission of National Education, the Four-Year Sejm, and the great repair project of the Commonwealth. This was work not against the existing though still rather new insurrectionary tradition, it was in fact work in conscious reference and reverence to that tradition. So that the sacrifice of those who died, lost property or were sent to Siberia, would not be in vain; so that the Commonwealth would find within itself the reserves of strength that would allow it to be independent. The very same Sejm that approved the First Partition now initiated the work of reforming the educational system. Between 1782 and 1791, the secondary schools of the Commission of National Education would be attended by an average of 6,000–7,000 students a year, while those run by the Piarist order (already modernized in Konarski's time) had attendances of about 4,000 a year each, with a further 4,000–5,000 in the remaining secondary schools, primarily run in the Ruthenian lands by the Unitarian order of Basilians. It can be estimated that in the twenty years between the First and Second partitions, nearly 100,000 young people would have received a modern education in the Commonwealth in more than thirty secondary schools and at the academic level (there were about 2,000 graduates out of the two main schools (the universities in Krakow and Vilnius).

Limiting the previously dominant role of Latin in education was combined with an emphasis on the importance of the Polish language as a standard tool for the education of the Commonwealth's population. In this language, the university printing house in Krakow published nearly a quarter of a million copies of school textbooks in just over a dozen years. The fundamental goal of education was to make students good citizens, serving their Homeland – the Commonwealth wisely (these words: 'Motherland' and 'Commonwealth' were often repeated in the Commission's instructions to teachers).

The elites of the Commonwealth, educated in the last two decades of its existence in the spirit of 'modern' pride in the 'Motherland' and its Polish-expressed culture, would prove to be indigestible to the multi-ethnic empires that were intent on dividing the state among themselves. In his *Notes* on Polish Government (written at the request of the Bar Confederates), the great French philosopher Jean-Jacques Rousseau prophesied in 1771 that after twenty years of national, patriotic education, Poland would no longer be a nation that could be eliminated, even if it were to lose its statehood in the future. Moreover, the elites educated in just such a spirit during those twenty years would remain active for another 30–50 years, decisively influencing the profile of Polish identity in the 19th century. This is the generation of Julian Ursyn Niemcewicz, Joachim Lelewel, Tadeusz Czacki, Adam Jerzy Czartoryski – teachers and patrons to the future great writers of the Romantic age Mickiewicz, Słowacki, Mochnacki…

The cultural strength and sheer size of this new elite can be judged by comparing data on book production and readership in Poland, with similar such activities in the Russian Empire. An Empire which de facto occupied the lion's share (area-wise) of the Commonwealth and still enjoyed a reputation of being among the most 'enlightened' of nations, at least under Catherine II. The average annual production of books in Catherine's Empire for the years 1776–1780 was – 240 titles; in 1786–1790 – 390; in the last five years of Catherine's reign (1791–1796) – an average of 375 titles. In the Commonwealth in the same periods we have, for 1761–1780, the average annual production was 484 titles; for 1781–1785 – 482 titles; in 1786–1790, due to the political revival in this period, the average rose to 765 titles (in 1790 alone, 1,086 titles were published in the Commonwealth); in the years 1791–1795, due to the effect of the Second Partition, the average drops to 465 titles per year and then decreases dramatically after the liquidation of the state, in the five years 1796–1800 – to just 225 Polish titles (the same number that was published in the Polish-Lithuanian state before 1640).

Thus, in the Commonwealth in the last years of its existence, on average, twice as many books were published annually as in the Russian Empire during the same period. Nearly 2,000 titles of books and pamphlets with political content were published during the Great Sejm (1788–1792) the period of greatest intensity of debate in and about the Commonwealth. Anna Grześkowiak-Krwawicz, the most prominent expert on the subject, points out that the circulation of some political publications amounted to between 5,000 and 10,000 copies. In 1780–1792, the number of subscribers to various periodicals amounted to 196,000 in the Commonwealth, incomparably ahead of the number of 'enlightened' Russian readers.

It is worth realizing this when we still hear the exclamations of praise among Western scholars and researchers delighting in Russia's enlightened monarchy and the level of culture that was achieved by Russia under Catherin's rule. Yet, in reality, this was still an Empire based more on the plunder and exploitation of its liberty loving, more culturally dynamic neighbors, than on its own internal or generic creative forces.

However, Russia's entanglement in the war with Turkey meant that Poland could still for a time at least begin to rebuild the institutions required to reassert its sovereignty. The Four-Year Sejm was called and confederated, and it thus could not now be dismissed by the power of the liberum veto. It was then that Catherine began to consider the possibility of a final settlement of the Polish question. Her principal advisor in this matter was, at the time, the most enlightened Prince Grigory Potemkin (1739–1791). He was not only her erstwhile lover but also her morganatic husband (they had secretly married without inheritance rights for any descendants) and her closest advisor. Having latterly fallen out of her closest circle, that is, out of her bed, Potemkin was eagerly thinking of a way to still secure a permanent position for himself. He thus recalled his childhood origins in the lands of Smolensk, which had of course once belonged to the Commonwealth. He was ready to accept the indignity of cloaking himself in his Polish origins, in other words nobility, in order to now carve out a state for himself in Ukraine. His considerations went in the direction of a limited partition that would allow him to create his own state in Ukraine, connected to a second state that was to be created due to Russia's expected conquests of Turkish possessions, the so-called Dacian kingdom.

Catherine allowed Potemkin to play with these plans and, in part, commence their realization. He was the enforcer of the plan implemented in 1785 to incorporate Crimea into Russia and the designer of the truncated Commonwealth's ultimate dependence on Russia. He stipulated that if Poland caused any trouble, it should be partitioned immediately. He put this in words by penning a 1788 memorandum on Poland: 'It would be better if we did not divide her [except, of course, for the Ukrainian piece, which was to be destined for Potemkin]. However, if we are to divide it, let us divide it immediately and with finality.'

Future Targowica adherents felt attracted to Potemkin, believing that he was the man with the most significant influence in St Petersburg, who at the same time also understood Polish affairs best, as he had been interested in them for years. Stanislaw Szczęsny Potocki, Seweryn Rzewuski and Franciszek Ksawery Branicki went to visit him at his court. Old Potemkin, however, was already dying at the time without the vitality to see through his plans to the end. Now orphaned by their "patron", the future Targowica adherents, therefore, went on to St Petersburg and sign their confederation, later so-called (for the sake of its own obscurity) the Targowica and not the Potemkin Confederation.

Russia decided on the Second Partition as soon as the Commonwealth tried to stand on its own two feet. The moment when the legislation of the Great Sejm bore ripe fruit in the form of Europe's first constitution, making the bourgeoisie more citizen-like, taking the rights of the peasants under its protection and, above all, introducing a governmental system of power in the Commonwealth in the new form outlined in the 3 May Constitution. The Polish King's alliance with the reform-minded part of the opposition, led by Ignacy Potocki, had led the Sejm to practical results. Potocki persuaded the King and most of the Sejm to accept an offer of alliance with Prussia in March 1790. The King resisted, for he feared (and rightly so) that Prussia would want at least Gdańsk and Toruń from Poland in return for such an alliance. If they did not get them, they might instead turn to Russia with a new proposal for a partition: Russia could always offer more territory at the expense of Poland. The alliance with Prussia, however, did encourage them to enact new rules for the political system in defiance of Catherine. Citizens 'free from disgraceful foreign orders of violence,' as the preamble to the Constitution of 3 May proclaimed, were proud of the breakthrough. The Commonwealth was to be a well-governed efficient state, opening the prospect of further gradual social and political change: toward a modern universal, no longer merely a noble (Pol.: *szlachecki*) dominated electorate.

Catherine II simply could not allow this to happen. She had to wait until her entanglements in the successive wars with Turkey and Sweden were over to then organize anew an armed intervention against 'rebellious' Warsaw

Top: A view of Warsaw from the terrace of the Royal Castle. Visible, among other sights, the Copper-Roof Palace and the Powiśle district. Painting by Bernardo Bellotto, known as Canaletto. Bottom: The adoption by ther Polish Sejm of the 3rd of May Constitution. Painting by Kazimierz Wojniakowski from 1806.

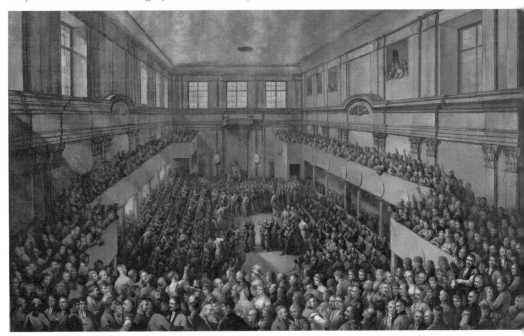

and prepare for the showdown with the Commonwealth, during which of course, certain pre-primed Commonwealth elements would 'invite' in the Tsarina's armies to 'restore order and freedom' on the Vistula and Niemen Rivers. This was the key role of Targowica and the natural continuation of this was, after a period of armed resilience, the penultimate act of the liquidation of the Commonwealth. The invasion by the Russian army began in 1792, followed by a heroic, though unequal struggle and, finally, the Second Partition. Those who distinguished themselves most in defense of Polish freedom at this time were Tadeusz Kościuszko (1746–1817) in the Battle of Dubienka and Prince Józef Poniatowski (1763–1813), commander-in-chief of the crown army, victorious in the Battle of Zieleniec. Immediately after this battle, the Order of *Virtuti Militari* was established, of which Prince Józef became the first recipient.

However, courage was not enough; allies were lacking. The army of Prussia was readied but readied in fact to deal Poland a stab in the back. The King seeing the danger tried to beg Catherine's pardon by offering to hand the throne in Poland to her younger grandson, Grand Duke Constantine. Catherine, however, wanted to bring the King and Poland to its knees. She ordered Stanisław Poniatowski to join the Targowica Confederation. Thus, making the King discredit himself and orphaning the great work that was the Constitution of 3 May. The King capitulated listening to Catherine's counsel while still hoping mistakenly that something could yet be saved. Outraged by this betrayal, Prince Józef Poniatowski returned his medals to the King.

By December 1792, Catherine was already set on another partition. She wanted to 'pay' Prussia with a piece of Poland in exchange for Prussian participation in the war against now-revolutionary France. At the same time, she succumbed to pressure from a powerful lobby in St Petersburg made up of senior officials and generals who simply wanted to again enrich themselves on the lands of the Commonwealth now annexed directly to Russia. With unprecedented cynicism, Catherine declared to the leaders of the Targowica that Russia must, after all, be compensated in some way for the aid it had given to Poland. The propaganda justification for the new Partition of the Commonwealth to be utilized in foreign courts was that it was an anti-revolutionary intervention. The French guillotine was already a feared symbol throughout Europe, presenting Poland and its Constitution as a second nest of violent untamed revolution on the continent together with France proved highly effective among the elites of Western Europe. Towards her subjects, Catherine also used the peculiar 'national' argumentation that she was only annexing 'lands that once rightfully belonged to her [i.e. Russia] and filled with people of one lineage and tribe and of course enlightened by one Orthodox faith'. In the pages of this book, we have already described just what this 'legitimate inheritance', a concept invented for the purposes of imperial propaganda of the Tsar, really was.

This time, the partition convention by Russia was concluded only with Prussia. The Russian court poet Vasily Petrov celebrated the act of the Second Partition with a particular poem: *Na prysoyednyenye polskikh oblastyey* (*On the occasion of the incorporation of the Polish provinces*). It is worth mentioning because he used an apt metaphor to formulate the new role that a powerless Poland was now to play. Poland was to be a bastion (literally: a breastplate – *napyerstnitsa*) of Russia. It was to protect Russia as a kind of filter against influences coming from the West. The last, ultimately also defunct, Sejm of the Commonwealth, sitting under the control of the Russian army in Grodno, was forced to approve the Second Partition. It closed its deliberations on 23 November 1793.

In the meantime, supporters of the now overthrown 3 May Constitution were conspiring in exile on a broader political and military plan of action that would, they thought allow Poland to regain her independence and further advance the work of reform. The culmination of these efforts became yet another Polish uprising (following those of 1733–1736 and the Bar Confederation) against Russian domination. This was the Kościuszko Uprising. On 24 March 1794, in Krakow, Kościuszko proclaimed its founding act: 'for the consolidation of the freedom and independence of the Commonwealth'. As part of a new strategy, he planned to also attract peasants to the cause of independence and, in this way to field an army of 100,000. These intentions symbolized Kościuszko's first tactical victory in a clash with a Russian force at Racławice on 4 April 1794. The head of the army, dressed in peasant's clothes not in an officer's uniform, and together with the Polish peasants taking part in the assault on the Russian cannons, armed with scythes – this was the image that would be permanently inscribed in Polish cultural memory associated with this battle, the common people rising.

In April of the same year, first in Warsaw and then in Vilnius, local uprisings led to the removal of the Russians from both capitals. In Warsaw, the shoemaker Jan Kiliński stood at the head of the townspeople attacking the Russian army. The uprising, led in the provinces by the nobility, broke out in most of the territories remaining after the Second Partition of the Polish-Lithuanian Commonwealth. Though ultimately defeated, this uprising left behind a critical political testament. It was not limited to symbols associated with the first attempt to attract peasants to participate in the fight for independence. The dynamics of the uprising's clashes in Warsaw and Vilnius led to the radicalization of moods. The events forced judgment on the representatives of the Targowica Confederation, who had been compromised by their collaboration with Russia. Among others, three hetmans and three bishops, considered to have been 'heroes of the Targowica', were hung on the gallows in a wave of reprisals against traitors to the Commonwealth. (TN Start) Such images had the unfortunate effect of re-enforcing Poland's image abroad as a replica of the more savage elements of the French Revolution. (TN End)

The fate of the insurrection was, however, a foregone conclusion. Prussian troops were advancing on Warsaw from the west, while several Russian corps were approaching from the east to be led in the final battle by Alexander Suvorov. Austria, which in February 1794 had accepted the Second Partition of Poland one in which it had itself received nothing now necessarily wanted its share. Catherine, on 22 July, officially invited Prussia and Austria for the 'final solution of the Polish question'. Kościuszko's attempt to face the Russian corps in the field at Maciejowice on 10 October ended in a Polish defeat and his own imprisonment.

On 4 November, Suvorov captured Praga, a Warsaw suburb on the Vistula River's east bank. He allowed his Cossacks to slaughter most of the prisoners and wounded but also to ravage the civilian population of the district. Probably no less than 20,000 inhabitants and defenders of Praga were slaughtered in a single day (among them General Jakub Jasiński and the commander of the Vilnius mass mobilization movement, Tadeusz Korsak). The Field Marshal then agreed to allow the remaining families of those so slaughtered to flee the right-bank Warsaw suburb so as they could convey firsthand the news of the crackdown on 'rebels' to the rest of

German Princess Sophie Auguste Friederike von Anhalt-Zerbst, better known as Catherine II Alexeevna the Great, Empress of All-Russia, became famous for her unparalleled ruthlessness, talent for political intrigue, and her irrepressible erotic temperament.

Frederick William II of Prussia von Hohenzollern, nephew and the successor in 1786 to Frederick II the Great. Neither his royal uncle nor Empress Catherine II held him in particularly high esteem, but this did not prevent him from completing his uncle's earlier work and participating in the Second and Third Partitions of Poland.

the capital's population on the other side of the river. Paralyzed with fear, Warsaw capitulated, the insurrection was heading for defeat, and the losses were to be significant. Several thousand insurgents were killed in battle, and a similar number were now exiled to Siberia.

A sign of the sacrifices made in this struggle was the thousands of identical gravestone crosses and the emptiness caused by the looting of cultural possessions by Russia from the Poles. For the first time on such a large and organized scale. As early as December 1794, on Catherine's orders, Suvorov began expropriating the collections of the first and most extensive public library ever founded in Europe: The Załuski Library in Warsaw. Four hundred thousand priceless volumes made their way by *kibitka* carriages to St Petersburg, where they were to launch the Russian Imperial Library (today, the library of St Petersburg State University). Of forty-three thousand volumes, less than an eighth were returned to Poland as part of the reparations agreed to in the Peace of Riga in 1921. This was a sign of the persecution that was to await Polish culture under its new "patron" partitioners.

(TN Start) Meanwhile Prussian forces, no doubt conscious of the legacy warning of Polish resilience left to them by their Great Elector Fredrich William, made their way to Krakow. There in a pre-meditated fashion they took from the royal seat at Wawel the coronation jewels and relics of the Polish Kings disassembled them confiscated the jewels and melted down the precious metals to make Prussian coinage. Only the famed coronation sword the Szczerbiec survived. Poland it was intended, would never arise again. (TN End)

In her last political gestures toward the now liquidated Polish-Lithuanian Commonwealth, Catherine II, the only Tsar Emperor of direct German origin, also illustrated clearly to the Poles and her subjects the true significance of her achievement. She has a medal minted one that can still be admired today in the State Historical Museum of Russia on Red Square in Moscow. Where it is displayed in a place of honor. The engraving on it reads *ottorzhenya vozvratich* – 'what was taken away, I restored'. Thus, a clear interpretation emerges here: in the three partitions, the Empress took away only what had always been Rus', that is, belonging to Moscow. She was merely the instrument through which historical justice was realized. Poland must be reduced to zero or to some Vistula River fiefdom because these lands, historically, traditionally, and geopolitically belong to the sphere of influence of Russia. The empire's civilizational status merited it. Furthermore, this idea has been successfully instrumentally inculcated into the minds of successive generations of Russians and by now, unfortunately, many influential Western academics and political minds. Partners, often trading partners, of the Russian Empire.

There was also a second argument that Catherine made quite explicit in the act introducing the Third and final Partition. We are liquidating the Polish-Lithuanian Commonwealth because it has become a hotbed of dangerous anarchy, a source of the 'French disease' that has now spread from Paris to Central and Eastern Europe. A disease that may yet infect its neighbors. Such a disease can threaten the tranquility not just of the inhabitants of the former Commonwealth but also the innocents of neighboring countries. Poland must therefore be eradicated as a source of ferment, and disorder. Both arguments should be remembered as the guiding lines of Russian policy toward the Commonwealth towards Poland, towards any nation with the temerity to resist Russian will.

The Polish "plague "of freedom and liberty, the Polish connection as a bridge to the dangerous West, was thus the second reason why the *Commonwealth* had to be wiped off the face of the map. Which necessitated the handover of responsibility for introducing order in the area to St Petersburg or Moscow. This mode of argumentation remains, unfortunately, common parlance for many still today, with similar statements emanating from the Kremlin shortly before the full-scale invasion of Ukraine in February 2022.

The Russo-Prussian treaty was concluded on 24 October 1795 and demarcated the new border between the two states after the final division of Poland (the Third Partition). A month later, King Stanisław August Poniatowski, already taken under guard by the Russian ambassador to Grodno in January, signed the act of abdication put before him. Already an ex-king, he was now brought as a special trophy to St Petersburg. Poland was finally completely erased from the political map of Europe. Austria received the lands of Lesser Poland together with Krakow, southern Mazovia and the Lublin Voivodeship up to the Bug River in the north. Prussia took most of Mazovia including Warsaw and also Podlasie. Russia, the rest: from Vol-

Top: Thaddeus Kościuszko takes an oath to the Polish nation on the Market Square in Krakow. Painting by Michał Stachowicz. Bottom: Wojciech Bartosz (Głowacki) captures a Russian cannon. From a fragment of the 'Racławice Panorama' view by Wojciech Kossak and Jan Styka.

hynia in the south to the Lithuanian lands, with Vilnius and up to Courland. In total, during the three partitions, Russia seized 436,000 km² (an area almost the size of Spain) with a population of almost 6 million, sizeable for the Europe of that time. Austria received 129,000 km² with over 4 million inhabitants, Prussia 141,000 km² (almost doubling the total surface area of the Kingdom of Prussia by means of these 3 Partitions) gathering with it over 2.6 million inhabitants.

On 26 January 1797, after Catherine's death, her son and successor, Paul I of Russia, signed a secret convention with Austria and Prussia in St Petersburg. According to its contents, the three partitioning empires agreed not mention the name of the 'former Kingdom of Poland' in any documents to destroy the memory of it once and for all.

The significance of the Commonwealth's partitioning, not only for the history of Poland itself but also the history of Europe, was huge. Not just because the Commonwealth was such a large state, the second-largest in Europe at the outset. It was its geopolitical significance that weighed. This was evidenced by its location and the fact that it was occupied by three of the five major European powers of the time. This already made the 'Polish problem' unique from all other 'national problems' that would come to light in the 19th century. The question of for example Ireland's quest for independence would clash with England only; the question of Hungary, or of Bohemia, with the Habsburg Empire only; the unification movement of Italy, also with the Haspburgs; the Greeks, with the Ottoman Empire only; the secessionist movement of the Belgians, with the Netherlands; the national movement of the Finns, with Russia only. In each case just one major power would be directly engaged, its interests directly at risk.

Poland, in contrast, was divided by as many as three of the five major powers in Europe at the time, powers that would decide the shape of European politics over the next hundred years: By Russia, Prussia and Austria (the Habsburg Empire). Two of these: Russia and Prussia (around which the Second and Third German Reichs would later be formed), would represent from 1870 onwards, perhaps even to the present day, the most important centers of economic and geopolitical ambition on the European continent. It would be the legacy of the Commonwealth to be the no man's land lying between them.

Hanging of the Targowica confederation traitors. An act which included the symbolic hanging of portraits of members of the Targowica from a gallows erected in the the Old Town Square in Warsaw as well as the very tangible execution of several actual members of the Targowica such as Field Hetman of Lithuania Józef Zabiełło seized and judged within a few short hours in Maj 1793 events which for many in Europe were reminiscent of the reign of terror taking place in Paris at that time.

For Russia's imperial aspirations, the incorporation of the provinces of the former Polish-Lithuanian Commonwealth was of great strategic importance, for it was through these lands that led the shortest route to Europe the envied center of civilized models of life, envied at least since the time of Tsar Peter I. It was also an area where the Russian Empire would confront other powers several times militarily. Thanks to the Partitions of the Polish-Lithuanian Commonwealth, Russia moved its border 600–800 kilometers westwards in 23 years (1772–1795), shortening the distance it had to cover to strike at or indeed collaborate with the centers of European politics. It is worth noting that soon, as early as 1799, Russian troops were able to intervene effectively against revolutionary France. Commanded by Suvorov (the same one who had captured Warsaw five years earlier), the Russian army would soon reach Verona, Milan and Turin via Switzerland incursions virtually inconceivable just 30 or 40 years earlier.

Imagine, on the other hand, what would have happened if the Commonwealth had remained intact within its pre-1772 borders and later Napoleon had been able to use it as a base from which to attack Russia in 1812? The Grand Army would then not have had a thousand, but less than 400 kilometers to cover on its way to Moscow. The Empire of the Tsars had, through the Partitions, now entered the center of Europe while also gaining a huge buffer of security. Prussia and Austria, actually lost their buffer in the security sense, with the liquidation of the Commonwealth, Russian power and ambition was now on their doorstep.

In a certain sense, the most accurate summation of the geopolitical significance of the Partitions and their eventual future repeal, i.e. the rebuilding of an independent Commonwealth, was given in the 19th century by none other than Karl Marx: 'The rebuilding of Poland means annihilating (Imperial) Russia, the cancellation of the Russian bid to rule the world'. Marx was formulating this opinion when another great Polish uprising against Russia was already underway the January Uprising of 1863–1864. For the Partitions marked the Age of Uprisings. And they would ultimately, contribute greatly to the fall of the Tsarist Empire.

Under Tsarist Rule –
the 'Colonialization'
of the Slavs (1795–1917)

L iteracy is a key element for considering the significance of the
    Polish-Lithuanian Commonwealth's three Partitions from the per-
    spective of Russian policy. We must realize that from 1795 onwards,
more people in this expanded Russian Empire could read and write in Polish
than Russian. (TN Start) For most in the Orthodox cities that once belonged
to the Commonwealth including Kyiv the language of the educated was
rather Polish and not Russian, Belarussian or Ukrainian. (TN End) This
situation came about largely due to the operation of modern schools in the
partitioned territories of the Commonwealth. This was not just a result of
Father Stanisław Konarski's educational reforms in the 18th century. Another
factor was the strength and persistence of the Polish cultural tradition
throughout the preceding centuries. In Russia, it was not until the reign
of Alexander I (1777–1825), grandson of Catherine II, that a network of
school districts with a modern education system finally began to emerge.
This inevitably resulted in a sense of conflict between the ambitions and
fundamental interests of the Russian noble elite in the Empire and those
elites located in the newly acquired Polish territories. This was structurally
an unavoidable problem. The old Russian elite viewed the Poles disdainfully.
Many of these Polish elites had not yet formally seen their rank or titles
degraded by any mass discriminatory decision on the part of the Tsarina.
They had not yet become second-class subjects. Moreover, the Polish nobility, having sworn an oath of allegiance to Catherine II, now had formally
the same rights as the Russian nobility and most importantly they were
far more numerous and often far better educated than their Russian peers.

Could Russia assimilate such a considerable mass of Polish nobility so
well established, educated and, if one may say, mature in the national sense?
For centuries, the Russian imperial elite had developed through the constant
assimilation of peripheral (often hostile) elites flowing into it due to the

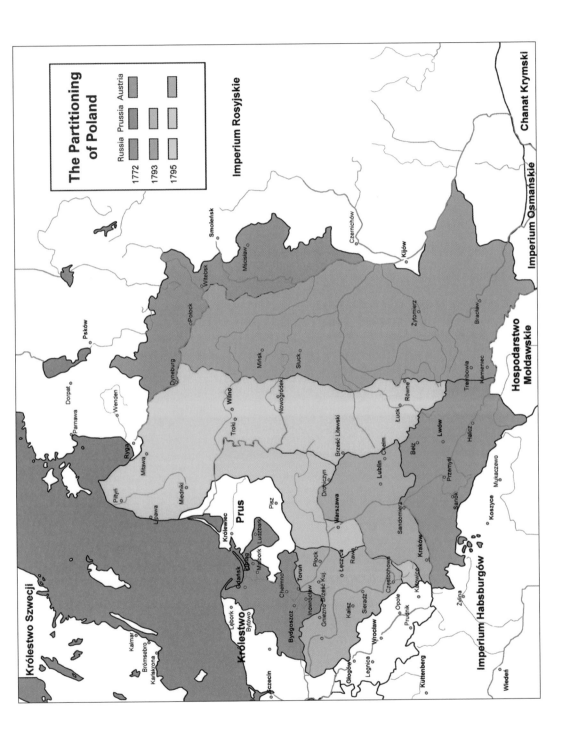

The Partitioning of Poland

	Russia	Prussia	Austria
1772			
1793			
1795			

Imperium Rosyjskie

Chanat Krymski

Imperium Osmańskie

Hospodarstwo Moldawskie

Imperium Habsburgów

Królestwo Szwecji

Prus

Królestwo

Smoleńsk

Mścisław

Czernichów

Kijów

Witebsk

Żytomierz

Bracław

Połock

Psków

Dyneburg

Mińsk

Słuck

Dorpat

Wenden

Kamieniec

Trembowla

Parnawa

Ryga

Wilno

Nowogródek

Równe

Łuck

Lwów

Halicz

Mitawa

Troki

Brześć Litewski

Bełz

Przemyśl

Mukaczewo

Płynia

Miedniki

Chełm

Drohiczyn

Lublin

Sanok

Koszyce

Libawa

Pisz

Warszawa

Sandomierz

Królewiec

Malbork Lidzbark

Płock

Żylina

Elbląg

Gdańsk

Chełmno

Toruń

Łęczyca

Rawa

Kraków

Lębork

Bytowo

Inowrocław Brześć Kuj.

Częstochowa

Kłobucko

Bydgoszcz

Gniezno

Kalisz

Sieradz

Opole

Prudnik

Szczecin

Głogów

Legnica

Wrocław

Kuttenberg

Wiedeń

centuries-long policy of expansion through conquest. One trace of this is that among the surnames of the Russian nobility at the end of the 19th century, 10 percent were of Tatar origin: the Tatar *murzas* had become, over generations, a cadre of the loyal Russian noble elite. Meanwhile, after the Third Partition of the Polish-Lithuanian Commonwealth, more than half of the Empire's elite now consisted of Polish noblemen, the overwhelming majority of which were still not unreconciled to the ultimate collapse of their own state.

Catherine II, a German by birth was, in fact the committed 'founding mother' of Great Russian nationalism, or Russian chauvinism. She was eager to give privilege to the Russian nobility, still in an informal manner through various incentives. She also intended to gradually eliminate any trace of the centuries-old presence of Polish culture in the lands taken by Russia in the "Partitions". Concerning the lands seized in the first two Partitions (the territories of today's eastern Belarus in 1772 and central Ukraine and Belarus in 1793), this intention was clearly formulated in the acts introducing Russian rule. The situation was somewhat different with the lands of the Third Partition, covering the area of Lithuania proper, western Belarus and Volhynia, most of which formed the core of the historical Grand Duchy of Lithuania, lands for centuries united by the Union with the Kingdom of Poland. The population in this area was more Catholic in composition than in the territories absorbed by Russia in the two previous partitions. Moreover, the cultural strength of the Polish elite, especially in cities such as Vilnius, with its university, was difficult to dispute. In Catherine's manifesto to annex the area to Russia, the argument of 'restoring the Ruthenian lands' to the homeland via the 3rd partition no longer appeared as such a plausible argument on the ground. The Empress addresses herself formally to the 'subjects of the Grand Duchy of Lithuania', thus emphasizing that she was not conquering those territories as Russian dominion in the strictest sense of the word through her creation of the new subservient Kingdom of Poland, but at the same time as if recognizing a separate political tradition in this area, different from the Russian identity.

The Vice-Chancellor and head of foreign policy of the Russian Empire, Alexander Bezborodko, made several remarks characteristic of this dilemma in his instructions to those entrusted with the management of these newly annexed lands. He stated that experience showed how attempts to make

Russia's Poles (Polish nobility) friends of Russia were doomed to failure. That is why it was necessary to abolish their state as a buffer because Russia could not really rely on them. How, then, to govern these people as subjects of the Russian Empire? While the territories previously annexed such as Malorussia (or Little Russia, i.e. a section of central and eastern Ukraine) could be subjected more readily to effective *obrusyenyu* (assimilation into the 'Russian nation'), the lands annexed in the Third Partition had to be recognized as distinctive, in part due to their strong historical and legal traditions. These could be changed by violently introducing the Russian political legal and cultural order into the new area: a culture of lies legal ambiguity, terror and denunciation, all in the name of 'order'.

This situation is best expressed in the words of a manifesto issued in December 1794 to the 'Lithuanian citizens' by Prince Nikolai Repnin, appointed military governor of this land by Empress Catherine II after the suppression of the Kościuszko Uprising:

'The invincible forces of Her Most Imperial Majesty of All-Russia confided to my central government, having defeated and exterminated everywhere the internal enemies of the Grand Duchy of Lithuania, and has fortified this country from fear and confusion, where the spirit of debauchery prevailed over all consideration, where traitors to the Fatherland, having appropriated the prerogatives of power, ruined civil and political rights, spilt the blood of fellow citizens in tyrannical cruelty, deprived them of their property, forced the God-fearing and peaceful to participate with themselves through threats and oppression [...]. The cunning of these outcasts, having dared to rise against the security and tranquility of their homeland, committed all kinds of tyrannical acts and took up arms against the Russian army, despite all laws and all national statutes, compelled my Most Gracious Empress against her will to take up the sword to protect the borders of her Empire and to quell the rebellion in the adjacent lying lands....'.

(You will note this is largely the same 'argumentation' used by Vladimir Putin and his propaganda machine to justify the Kremlin's aggression against Ukraine!).

And so it went on for the next 120 years for Catherine ultimately decided that Lithuania would no longer become an 'adjacent situated' land but simply a part of the Tsarist empire. Just three years after the Kościuszko

Uprising, there would be another group of 'outcasts', i.e. the 'rebels' unreconciled to the loss of their state that needed to be crushed. That conspiracy of Father Faustin Ciecierski (1761–1832) in 1797 opened a long list of rebels born in the Lithuanian lands that would culminate victoriously 120 years later, with Józef Piłsudski. It is worth quoting the reaction of the imperial authorities to the first symptoms of this rebellion. The participants in the pro-independence conspiracy were deemed 'no longer worthy not only of their birth and surname, but even of being called human beings'.

So, the generations of 'loyal subjects' of the former Commonwealth continued to grow under the control of Repnin's successors. Yet there also rose against this coercive control, generations of so-called 'abominable violators' of imperial servitude. These included conspirators and insurgents, from the Ciecierski brothers, through to the Philomaths (a note on them later), then insurgents from the Lithuanian-Ruthenian lands of 1831, Szymon Konarski's grand conspiracy, down to the participants of the last Commonwealth uprising in the years 1863–1864. They were all guided by the words of a song composed for Polish soldiers in Italy in July 1797, just six short months after the final act of the 3rd partitioning of the Commonwealth. A song authored by Józef Wybicki called the 'Dąbrowski Mazurka'. It would become the anthem of the future Polish state, a call for independence and liberty. Indeed, when Poland regained its independence in the 20th century – it became and would remain the official national anthem (as of 1927).

Let us draw attention to a few excerpts from its original text:

'Poland has not yet perished
From Italy to Poland
Under your command
We shall rejoin the nation

[...] The German, the Muscovite will not settle,/when he has taken up the cudgel,/the motto of all will be harmony/and our Homeland'. The starting point of the composition is the loss of national independence, which is then countered by the will to regain it. For as long as there are Poles who want to fight to regain independence, Poland exists, even if not currently on the map. The formula of political community presented in the 'Dąbrowski

Top: General Jan Henryk Dąbrowski, commander of the Polish Legions, enters Rome. Bottom: Polish students sent into Siberian exile, spend the night "in stages". ("Stages" were the names given to the primitive buildings used for holding people condemned to Siberian exile, here they would spend the night in unimaginably cramped conditions, without any essential facilities). A great map of the Russian Empire towers above these tormented young men…

Mazurka' is done so in a highly modern form, for the late 18th century at least. It is based on the assumption of active participation in the community by society at large, a struggle, an armed struggle, for its very existence. Moreover, this community, supra-state, is called a nation. Furthermore, it also identifies not the names of individual rulers but actually the other opposing national communities – 'German' and 'Muscovite' (i.e. Russian) as adversaries. The struggles against these other nations should be factors to mobilize its own people to unite in this quest to regain the 'Homeland'.

The adjutant of Tadeusz Kościuszko, who had been released from a Russian prison, one Józef Pawlikowski, wrote down the Commander-in-Chief's vision of the struggle for independence and presented them in 1800 in an anonymously published pamphlet: *Can Poles Break Out for Independence?* The question contained in this title brings a positive but also a conditional answer. Yes, Poles can regain their independence, *if* and only if they create a modern nation, reject state divisions and draw the liberated peasant masses into the struggle. The preparation of a people's uprising, taking the shape of a guerrilla war led by masses armed with scythes. This was a vision that contrasted with the road to independence based on the legion the idea commonly present in Napoleonic France at the time. Simultaneously, this vision envisaged stimulating a similar struggle by all the peoples of the various nations located in all three empires that had divided Poland. Poland was not just to be independent in its own right. It would also be the foundation stone of freedom for all the peoples of the Romanov, Habsburg, and Hohenzollern Empires, stimulating the peoples' struggle against authoritarian rule.

In the Russian Empire, the addressee of Poland's freedom propaganda was to be the four-million-strong 'element of Malorussia' (i.e. Ukraine) in particular, though not only. Indeed, it was to be the 'Russian people' themselves, who should take up arms against the oppressive Tsarist regime. This was a political line leading in two directions. Firstly, a project to split Russia along its ethnic seams (a reference to an independent Ukraine) or secondly the slogan 'for our freedom and yours' directed in hope towards the Russian subjects of the Tsar. Pawlikowski adopted the former direction, providing to Napoleon in 1807 a first detailed blueprint for the partition of the Russian Empire, breaking up what was portrayed as the Tsar's prison of nations.

220

There was however, more fantasy than truth in such nationalistic projects. Catherine and her successors conducted the *real* policy. Towards part of the seized lands ('the eternally Ruthenian'), the imperial authorities attempted at once to implement, as we have already pointed out, *obrusyenya*, a policy of gradual cultural assimilation. Towards the other part (the western part, with a more substantial presence of Polish and Catholic traditions) 'only' a policy of pacification of sorts. The most conspicuous manifestation of the former trend was Catherine II's campaign to introduce the Orthodox rite, regarded as the religious determinant of 'Russianness', in place of the by then now well-established Uniate rite [in the future, the term Greek Catholic will become common to describe this Uniate branch of Orthodoxy editor's note], that was subordinate to the Pope. This was the dominant form of Orthodoxy in the 18th-century eastern provinces of the Polish-Lithuanian Commonwealth. In the territories of today's Ukraine and Belarus that were incorporated into Russia, as many as 9,300 parishes and 150 monasteries were now forcibly converted from Uniate (or Greek Catholic) to Russian Orthodoxy. At the same time, during Catherine's lifetime and often with the help of the military, there was a resultant brutal persecution of those who tried to defend the Uniate rite. Nearly 1.7 million people (mainly in Ukrainian lands) thus 'converted' to the Orthodox or Russian rite.

Catherine's successors, the briefly governing Paul I of Russia (1796–1801), (a man assassinated with his own son's consent, that of Catherine's grandson, Alexander I) had to constantly grapple with the policy dilemmas arising from this Polish conquest. A conquest that somehow could not be fully digested. Paul I managed to make a gesture, releasing Kościuszko from prison in Shlisselburg and giving a ceremonial funeral to the unfortunate ex-King Stanisław August Poniatowski, who died in a golden cage in St Petersburg. Alexander I (1777–1825) in contrast had far broader plans: he wanted to increase Russia's influence in Europe by strengthening the Polish factor or bridgehead, gathering all the Polish lands under the Russian scepter and extending his rule to other lost Polish lands in the west... *de facto* by now snatching "lost" Polish holdings from Prussia and Austria. This indeed was the plan suggested to him by his long-time friend from the years preceding his accession to the throne, a man who had previously been Catherine II's hostage, the Polish Prince Adam Jerzy Czartoryski.

221

Prince Adam entered the four-member Secret Committee within which the Tsar discussed his reform projects. One of these became the great reform of the educational system. Czartoryski presented such a plan to the Secret Committee in 1802, and the Russian Empire was already in the following year divided into six great school districts. Their centers were to be universities, including three newly established ones: St Petersburg, Kharkiv and Kazan. Czartoryski was appointed superintendent of the school district, the heart of which was to be symbolically the reformed Polish university in Vilnius. The Vilnius district encompassed all eight *gubernyas* (governorates) that Russia had organized in the territories seized from the former Commonwealth. The new district thus guaranteed the educational congruency, so to speak, of the "Partioned" to Russia area. Moreover, educational issues in this zone would actually continue the work of the Polish Commission of National Education for the next 20 years (through to the end of 1823, when Czartoryski was then forced to resign from his position as superintendent). The second pillar of the Vilnius district, besides the university, was the Gymnasium, and later the Lyceum, in Kremenets (Pol.: *Krzemieniec*) in Volhynia, established in 1805 at the initiative of Tadeusz Czacki (1765–1813), a co-author of the 3 May Constitution.

However, the hopes pinned by a section of the Polish elite on Alexander I aimed at even loftier heights than mere matters of education and culture. Appointed by the Tsar first as Vice-Minister and then from 1804 as Minister of Foreign Affairs of the Empire, Czartoryski intended to avail of the ruler's trust in a way that would reconcile Polish patriotism with the expansion of Russian influence into half of Europe. Transforming the entire political map of the continent in the spirit of the national idea. He articulated this concept to the Tsar in the treatise *On the political system to be followed by Russia*, drafted in 1803. Interestingly, and rarely noted by researchers, this memorial combines Kant's ideas (Czartoryski was a diligent reader of this German philosopher) with the heritage of the Polish Enlightenment school regarding the rights of nations. To the ideas of Kant's treatise on *Perpetual Peace*, the Polish Minister of the Russian Empire added a new element: the need to introduce just relations between not only states but between nations. Here he pointed out the most essential condition for achieving lasting peace in Europe:

Prince Adam Jerzy Czartoryski (1770–1861) was an eminent diplomat strongly committed to the Polish cause. He wanted to see a rebuilt Poland and originally based this vision on cooperation with his then close friend Tsar Alexander I.

'Each nation has its own language, customs, habits, ways of seeing and feeling. They cannot understand or know each other well; foreign rule cannot suit any nation. Each strives to be master of his own home [...] Let us note here that the division into nations corresponds more or less to a geographical division, for in settling down, people followed instinctively the boundaries which nature indicated to them'.

Prince Czartoryski was hoping to play to the "enlightened" instincts the idealized "father of the Slaves" vanities of Tsar Alexander and in doing so convince his long-time friend to this initiative to rebuild Poland. A reconstruction to be carried out under the scepter of his Tsarist brother, Grand Duke Konstantin Pavlovich, while simultaneously taking up patronage for the aspirations of the peoples from the southern Slavic lands and emancipation for them from Turkish rule all the while furthering the expansion of Russian influence and dominion. However, plans to rebuild the Commonwealth alongside Russia would have required a confrontation between the Tsarist Empire and the German states, which, after all, held most of the historical Crown lands of Poland at this point. The Tsar recognizing this dilemma retreated from such a prospect at the last moment – and renewed his friendship with Prussia, abruptly abandoning Czartoryski's designs in 1805. This was an important lesson: the Russian ruler, given a choice between the risky plan of placing the Commonwealth at the side of his own empire, ultimately always prefers the safer option, that of a pact with a German partner: over the heads or indeed, if necessary, the corpses of the Poles.

Czartoryski was ultimately dismissed from his post but in the meantime, a new voice for Polish statehood was being reborn at Napoleon's side. This was a continuation of the path taken by General Jan Henryk Dąbrowski's legionnaires from Italian soil to Polish soil, at the side of a Western power, and in defiance of the partitioning powers. The substitute state created by Napoleon after his crushing victories over Poland's partitioners, the Duchy of Warsaw was very modest in size but it was essential in nature. It restored the conviction that Poland could be reborn and had not been irrevocably destroyed. The very existence of the Polish state in any form was meaningful, as it overturned at least in part, the Partitioners' verdict against the Republic. Its continued existence or development depended primarily on the relations between the two superpowers that now divided Europe between them: Napoleon's France and Alexander's Russia. Napoleon tried to avoid a decisive clash with Alexander for dominion over the continent. In 1810, Napoleon thus asked the Tsar for permission to marry his sister. However, in the secret political convention that accompanied this effort, Alexander proposed introducing the condition that the Kingdom of Poland would never be reconstituted as the first point on his agenda. The Tsar's concern, was of course, that a Polish state independent of Russia should never be established. A Poland next to Russia, totally dependent on it, was within the scope of his plans as far as he was concerned. Napoleon however, did not agree either to this or to the other conditions proposed by the Tsar. Another war was becoming inevitable.

The Tsar then resumed his 'Polish policy' to win over the Polish elites before the impending decisive clash. Inspired by the Tsar, representatives of the aristocracy of the former Grand Duchy of Lithuania, (specifically Prince Michał Kleofas Ogiński and the young Prince Ksawery Drucki-Lubecki), prepared a project at the end of 1811 for the autonomous separation of the Grand Duchy of Lithuania from the Russian Empire, and its then further reconstruction under Alexander's rule of the Commonwealth within the 1772 borders. More significant results from these surveys, however, were not forthcoming. The existence of the Napoleon sponsored Duchy of Warsaw as a "temporary" substitute for a robust new Polish state meant that fighting against it by recreating a competing Lithuanian Duchy allied to the Tsar was increasingly regarded as an unpatriotic endeavor among Poles in Russia. A fight unworthy of a 'good Pole'. It was of course a fact that thousands of representatives of the Polish nobility partitioned to Russia would nevertheless still serve the Tsar as officers in his army during the Great War of 1812. Still, hopes for the restoration of Poland, the Commonwealth in the coming clash were linked far more closely with Napoleon and the expansion of the Duchy of Warsaw, and not to a Russian victory and further expansion of that empire.

Colonel Jan Nepomucen Umiński's 'golden hussars' a Polish cavalry detachment so admired by the French Marshall Murat, was the first detachment to enter Moscow in 1812 some two centuries after Poles first occupied the Kremlin. They now did so at the side of the French. Polish cavalry detachments were also the last to leave this city just a few months later. Napoleon's Grand Army, so faithfully accompanied by the Polish contingent but logistically hopelessly overstretched, would lose the great war that decided the fate of Europe for the next hundred years at least. Alexander I and Russia's strategic depth, triumphed again. The Tsar's armies continued to 'liberate' all of Europe right up to their conquest of Paris. In the hard-fought diplomatic battle at the subsequent Congress of Vienna, he would stand his ground, including on matters concerning the Polish issue.

The decisions made at the Congress of Vienna (1815) brought about significant changes to the "Polish arrangements" in place until that time between the 3 partitioning powers. These new lines on the map would thereafter last for a century, until the First World War. The Russian ruler was to now additionally gain dominion over some of the Polish Crown lands previously seized by Prussia and part of the Third Austrian Partition, i.e. central Poland, including the capital Warsaw. As we have already mentioned, this had significant implications for strategic relations with other powers. The most important consequences of this change would be for Polish-Russian relations. In addition to the 463,000 square kilometers of Polish-Lithuanian territory with a population of 5.5 million that Russia had gained due to the three partitions, Alexander now captured a further close on 130,000 square kilometers, with a dense population of around 3.3 million. Prussia as compensation strengthened its German character by exchanging the lands of central Poland for Saxon possessions. Only 7 percent of the territory of the former Commonwealth now remained under the rule of the King of Prussia but this including the key strategic stretches of the Baltic coast. Under the control of the Emperor of Austria, in 'old' Galicia, about 11%. Under the rule of Tsar Alexander and his successors was now 82% of what had been the old Commonwealth.

Two radically opposite conclusions could be drawn from this for those interested in Poland's future political existence. The Commonwealth could from now on, only be rebuilt by pinning its hopes on Russia, either through an accord with it or by that Empire's future decline or defeat. Russia was the keystone in any project to re-unite the lands of the former Poland and Lithuania in a new Union. However, if such a hope for accommodation with Russia as embodied by Prince Czartoryski, had proved unsuccessful, then Russia and its rulers now had to become and endure in the roles of the ultimate enemy. Without who's defeat, it was impossible to dream of

Napoleon grants the Duchy of Warsaw a Constitution. First from the right stands Józef Wybicki; the Emperor awarded him the gold cross of the Order of the Legion of Honor during the ceremony. Copy of a lost painting by Marcello Bacciarelli.

regaining independence. A revolt against Prussia or Austria could, even if successful, only bring about the liberation of the periphery of the former Commonwealth. Poland's future as a political entity had to be decided by its relations with Russia.

But: what did Russia mean in 1815? And what did 'Poland' now represent? The project of extending its sovereignty to the territory of the former Duchy of Warsaw was pushed through by Tsar Alexander I himself. He also decided to give this territory, which had been ceded to him by treaties with Prussia and Austria – the new status of the Kingdom of Poland. The proud name was admittedly limited to an area of just under 130,000 square kilometers carved out from Napoleon's previous entity the Duchy of Warsaw. Since the existence of this new, minor Kingdom of Poland was, as it were, sanctioned by a major international congress and would come into diplomatic use within such reduced boundaries for the next hundred years, a new mental map started to be drawn in the minds of the Western elite. Poland came to be synonymous with this limited notion of the Kingdom of Poland. This minor vassal state, a mere appendage to Russia with no true voice of its own in European affairs would unfortunately gradually replace, in the consciousness and memory of Europe's political elites, the former notion of the great Commonwealth its borders and its traditions.

This new (renewed) Kingdom was immediately given a coat of arms, one adequate to its status, defining its specifics. This coat of arms depicted a great double-headed black Russian Eagle, on whose breast the Polish White Eagle was depicted. This was the Kingdom of Poland within Russia and it was to be, according to the treaties of 3 May 1815, 'forever united with the Russian Empire'. Its King was to be the Tsar of Russia together with his legitimate successors. At the same time, however, this Kingdom received a Constitution, the most liberal of all such documents that remained on the European continent after the fall of Napoleon, as well as a system of government, administration and law that was separate from those existing in Russia, in addition to its own treasury and currency even, a separate army. The King (or, at the same time, Emperor of Russia) was to be crowned in Warsaw and be sworn in by the Polish Constitution he had granted to the new Kingdom.

Many historians believe, probably rightly so, that the Tsar treated his new Polish conquest not only as a bridgehead of imperial influence in the center of Europe but also now as a kind of testing ground on which he wanted to try out the possibility of reconciling liberal institutions with autocracy. Indeed, the Tsar's advisor, Nikolai Novosilcov, acting as unofficial overseer of the Kingdom of Poland, wrote a secret draft of the 'Constitutional Charter of the Russian Empire' at the behest of his sovereign, envisaging the establishment in the Kingdom of Poland, and also in Russia, of a 'state parliament' consisting of a Chamber of Deputies and a Senate.

Soon, however, these bold projects were hampered by changes in the situation in Europe in 1819–1821 (terrorist attacks in Germany and France, political disturbances in Spain and Naples), as well as revolts in the settlements of Russian military landholders near Kharkiv were then accompanied by a revolt in the guards' regiment in St Petersburg itself. Alexander shocked by the immediacy of this threat to his family and his rule, was to depart from his previous reformist intentions. However, let me put forward the thesis that the key to this change should really be sought in the actual dynamics of Polish-Russian relations. It is the dynamics of national emotions and their political mobilization that would be of fundamental importance for the further history of Poland and the Russian Empire's intertwined fate.

The representatives of the Polish social elite in the Kingdom were certainly exhausted, materially and emotionally, after their participation in the epic Napoleonic wars. Hence their orientation towards stability and genuine gratitude to Alexander I for the exceptionally favorable conditions offered to a former ally of Napoleon. For this stabilization embodied in the sanctioning of the new Kingdom of Poland. A lasting symbol of this gratitude was a song published in the *Gazeta Warszawska* to mark the first anniversary of the Kingdom's establishment. A song modelled on the English anthem 'God save the King' and praising Alexander. The words of this song, written by Alojzy Feliński, would later be amended over the decades, taking on the character of one of the most popular patriotic and religious songs (*Boże, coś Polskę…*). The words are sung eagerly to this day. Initially, however, it was an expression of hope for the permanence of the work undertaken by the Russian Tsar in restoring the Kingdom of Poland.

Poles rejoiced at the possibility of building a new university in 1816 in Warsaw and much-needed technical schools: The Mining Academy in Kielce, a school of forestry, road and bridgebuilding engineering or the

Tsar Alexander I hands over the foundational document for the University of Warsaw. The Russian emperor was able to create a convincing appearance of friendliness towards the Poles, though in reality, he pursued a policy of extensive Russification throughout the lands seized from Poland during the partitions.

Preparatory School for the Polytechnic Institute – the forerunner of a first Polish polytechnic – established at Warsaw University in 1826. There was much satisfaction with the economic development of the small Kingdom, ensured by the wise investment and financial policy of Minister Ksawery Drucki-Lubecki. They could praise the cultural developments, best symbolized by the Music School in Warsaw and its most famous graduate, Frederic Chopin. However, the question that continued to trouble the Polish elite was the following. "What about our brothers from across the Bug River", from the territories seized by Russia? Should we say goodbye to them forever?

When Alexander I opened the session of the Sejm in Warsaw in April 1818, he made a solemn speech in which he alluded both to the possibility of uniting the lands of the former Commonwealth in a single Kingdom and to the granting of a constitution and the introduction of a parliament

Participants in the Congress of Vienna, who decided on the future shape of the political map of Europe following the fall of Napoleon's empire. Unfortunately, none of the European powers cared much for the restoration of the Polish-Lithuanian Republic… An illustration by Jean-Baptiste Isabey.

in Russia itself. Provided of course that the Polish political elites showed that they were still prepared to accept the merging of parliamentarism with autocracy and not with liberty. This would be a Poland with a Russian face. The Kingdom of Poland was supposed to be a bridge connecting Russia with Western models of freedom and political modernization. At the same time, a filter for more dangerous liberal phenomena that might have penetrated the borders of the Tsar's Empire along with these models.

But there were political elites in Russia, too, after all. Their point of view on Alexander's 'Polish idea' proved decisive. Opposition to the Tsar's reformist plans was formed around the traditional power elements the empress-dowager of Paul I and Admiral Alexander Shishkov. On the other hand, the voice of the younger generation, stunned and emboldened by the successes of the Russian armed forces, which had led Russian officers all the way to the cafes

231

of Paris, was now gaining strength. Both these groupings were unanimous in that they were highly critical of Alexander I's plans. The former considered any idea of changing the autocratic system in Russia extremely dangerous, both to the system's stability and to its historical identity, founded precisely on the idea of autocratic rule. For the latter grouping of young officers, it was outrageous to treat the Polish provinces, conquered once again by the Russian army, as being better suited for parliamentarism and liberty. Meriting of the western freedoms in the lands of France that these young officers had recently experienced during their occupation there. New ideas that many of these young men now wished to see installed, but in Russia not in Poland.

Both the reformer movement supported by Alexander at the time and, even more so the traditional and patriotic elements in the Tsar's entourage, viewed the Poles around the Tsar (especially Prince Czartoryski) as potential traitors, agents of the West, of anti-Russian Europe. These sentiments were further reinforced by the experience of the real empire threatening confrontation with Napoleonic Europe in 1812 and the very clear often decisive presence of Poles within it. All this underlined their continued threat as dangerous opponents. All these factors made the plans, and later Alexander's decisions, to rebuild the Kingdom of Poland more disconcerting in Russian circles. Circles we could surmise as being the intellectual inheritors of the national idea in Catherine II's times. Even more outrageous was the alleged rumored possibility that other lands annexed by Catherine's partition and regarded in these circles as 'eternally Russian' often lands being under the direct ownership of these circles, that these lands might also be added to the new Polish Kingdom. This, combined with the sense of humiliation felt by many when seeing the defeated traitorous Poles now being presented with their own constitution and parliament. Institutions that the Tsar was still refusing to introduce in Russia. These were the principal reasons for the formation of a conspiracy of young Russian officers, in which the idea of assassinating the Tsar now emerged. Put forward by a later participant in the Dekabrist movement, Ivan Yakushkin. The first conspiratorial union the Order of Russian Knights put at the top of its program 'the unconditional and perpetual extermination of the name of Poland and the Kingdom of Poland, and the turning of all Poland, including the Prussian and Austrian held lands, into Russian *gubernyas* (governorates).

232

Information about these sentiments reached Aleksander, and he could not be indifferent to them. However, he must have also fallen under the impression of the speeches made by one of his court appointees. A man who enjoyed exceptional authority in the "enlightened" Russian society of the time: the court historiographer and famous writer Nikolay Karamzin. In his fundamental *History of the Russian State*, widely read by subsequent generations, Karamzin consolidated in the consciousness of the Russian elite the vision of the Poles as the foremost, eternal enemies of Russia.

Earlier, in 1811, the historian had spoken directly to the Tsar with an extensive and open criticism of his liberal reforms, to which he added a warning against any concessions to the Poles. In October 1819, in a direct conversation with Tsar Alexander, Karamzin, showing great courage, again delivered a crushing criticism of the Tsar's policy towards Poland. In the name of cold political realism, he regarded any moral sentiment (redressing the wrongs of the Partitions) as a fatal misunderstanding of Russia's *raison d'etat*. The sword conquered Poland – just as the sword was the origin of all the greatness and conquest of Russia. If Alexander would grant even a modicum of freedom to the Poles, then the same could soon be demanded by all the other peoples previous conquered by the Moscow Tsars. Then the whole Empire would crumble.

Karamzin had one thing to offer the Poles as subjects of Tsarist Autocracy; that they will finally enjoy order because this Polish will to fight for independence and liberty brings them, in his opinion, only misfortune. It is in fact according to the "enlightened historian" a symptom of 'primitive savagery'. The historian expressed for the first time so definitely the vision of a clash between two political centers, Russia and Poland, for domination over the areas of the former Kyivan Rus (Ukraine and Belarus) and the whole of Eastern Europe. 'Either-or' there is no place in one Empire for two powerful political elites with different governing methodologies, with different foundations of historical and cultural identity. Either the Poles or the Russians will ultimately triumph. The Russian Tsar must take this into account and not strengthen the Poles. He should instead strive to liquidate any form of their political existence, to liquidate the autonomy of the Kingdom.

Karamzin's opinion, so boldly formulated, was a self-fulfilling prophecy. Alexander I, who subjugated not only, as we already know, the Kingdom

The Russian writer and advisor to the Tsar Nikolay Mikhailovich Karamzin (1776–1826), author of, among other works, the "History of the Russian State" and "Letters of a Russian Traveler". He was known for his highly virulent anti-Polish views. Portrait by Vasily Tropinin.

of Poland but also Finland, Bessarabia, Georgia, Armenia and Azerbaijan, attempted to create a model for the modernization of his Empire that would maintain its unity regardless of the ethnocultural divides between the elites of the center and those of the new peripheries. The Russian elites, however fortified by the historical memory of the centuries-long conflict with Poland, and further stimulated by the experience of the victorious war with Napoleon, threw a resounding veto in the way of their Tsar via the speeches and writings of the enlightened Karamzin. The clash with the 'Polish problem' began, or at any rate, revealed for the first time so dramatically the issue of nationalism in political relations within the Russian Empire. As we shall see, this problem would later prove to be fatal for the Romanov Empire, as it may also soon prove to be for Mr Putin's Russian Federation.

In 1819 Alexander moved back from his policy towards the Kingdom of Poland and the related new initiatives for Russia. He abandoned his attempts at reform. The vision of a Polish-Russian concord, quite popular with the Polish noble elites in the Kingdom after 1815, would begin to unravel. A harbinger of this new course was the affair unleashed or uncovered by Senator Novosiltsev of an alleged grand political conspiracy by the students of Vilnius University: the so-called "Philomath" affair of 1823. This was already a turning point, and it is vividly recalled by one of those men persecuted at the time, the poet Adam Mickiewicz, in his work *Dziady Part III*. It was again open conflict at least east of the Bug River against 'unreasonable Polish nationality', as Novosiltsev put it. Czartoryski, as superintendent of the Vilnius school district, was forced to resign as a result of this academic conspiracy. The systematic destruction of his educational work would now begin with a new wave of Russification.

The death of Alexander I in 1825 and the accession to power of his younger brother, Nicholas I (who reigned 1825–1855), finally extinguished any hope of some form of 'cohabitation' with the Russian Empire in keeping with Polish national interests and the traditions of the Commonwealth. Unlike his late elder brother Alexander I, the new Tsar Nicholas I reverted to his grandmother Catherine II's program for the partition of the Commonwealth and subjugation of its people. It was a program that reflected Karamzin's position discussed above. The lands incorporated by Catherine were to be treated as part of Russia, and any institutional or cultural distinctiveness that they had

235

inherited from or referred to during the time of the Commonwealth was to be obliterated. However, Nicholas I was also aware of his international legal obligations under the Vienna Congress and had no intention of liquidating the Kingdom. In May 1829, he arrived in Warsaw to hold his formal coronation as King of Poland. In his discussions with representatives of the Polish aristocracy, he dismissed local complaints against the actions of Novosiltsev and Grand Duke Konstantin. He also stated that he would not uphold any previous promises made by Alexander to the Poles (concerning the proposed unification of the Polish Kingdom with the "Russian" lands of the former Commonwealth) indeed that he considered them to be erroneous.

Nicholas I would formulate Karamzin's doctrine of force even more clearly: wherever the Russian flag had been, it must never again be lowered from the mast. This doctrine, we should add, is still in force, upheld in Putin's Russia, even in its most far-reaching pronouncements. Such as the opinion of Alexander Prokhanov (b. 1938), president of the nationalist Izborsky Club. A man who declared on the threshold of the latest assault on Ukraine, that Russia should return to the rule over Paris. After all, it had already been captured by Russian soldiers in 1814.

The consequences of the disastrous Polish-Russian conflict are very much to be deplored because we Poles have in fact longed for an accord with our Slavic brothers, with whom we can communicate and identify with often on an individual basis. Communication being far more straightforward than with our German neighbors to the west. We can communicate with our Slavic brothers in a half sentence; their culture is still in some respects familiar to us and even admired by us in many ways. This is why so many of us regret that this dispute persists and is so difficult to overcome. Yet what could we do when Imperial Russia was not prepared to make any real compromise with Poland? Neither in 1829, nor in in 2010. In 2022 who would even try.

This kind of opinion was expressed most clearly in the Kingdom of Poland by the young Maurycy Mochnacki in a letter entitled: *The Voice of a Citizen from the Poznań Area*. The letter was penned already after the 'Philomath affair' and following Nicholas I's violation of the Kingdom's rights. It circulated at the time of the Sejm Court, which, under pressure from Nicholas I, was to try Polish conspirators from the Patriotic Society.

Mochnacki was attacking the program of bringing Poland closer to the Russian state. He aimed to raise up the romantic and somewhat elitist concept of the Motherland, to remind us that 'it is not the sandy-soil expanse of Mazovia, nor the Vistula cutting across our immense plains, nor the capital city, nor the magnificent seats of government authorities there that constituted it. Instead, the Polish Motherland was in fact the great idea of liberty and political independence. The hope that one day, with God's guidance and assistance, we shall be united into one inseparable whole, that we shall be again a fortress of Europe, a stronghold against evil neighbors, become the chosen people from among the Slavic nations'.

Maurycy Mochnacki exposed the fundamental contradiction between the partitionist policy of the Russian state and the concept of rebuilding a whole and independent Poland at its side: 'We are a province of a neighboring power, conquered, ruled by proconsuls, oppressed severely. A place where these harmful actions against the principles of political life directed towards the annihilation of our family and our name are constantly taking place. From this viewpoint, the axis of the conflict is the struggle for the Lithuanian-Rus lands. A struggle which excludes any notion of an accord with Russia. Without these lands, Poland could not be truly independent, and without them, the imperial policy of Russia would also be paralyzed. The equation was and is binary in nature it is either-or. Just as it was outlined in Karamzin's writings.

And what was the natural progression of this train of thought? Next was the vague but firm conviction that Poland deserved complete independence and that Poles would follow those who dared to act. That such a nation fighting for its own liberation from the rule of a foreign empire will not be stopped by anything. These concepts encapsulated the most important rationale for the national uprising of November 1830 that was then brewing. It was a combination of the ideas expressed in the texts of Mochnacki (a man who, incidentally, belonged to the civilian part, formed in 1829, of the anti-Russian cadet conspiracy) and the patriotic emotions aroused by the publicly debated judgment on members of the Patriotic Society or the earlier Philomaths. It also arose from the skillfully cultivated memory of the Commonwealth and the ever-renewed tradition, of the struggle for independence. This, rather than any external inspiration, was the rationale

The Battle of Olszynka Grochowska ended in a strategic victory for the Poles, who prevented the Russians from seizing Warsaw. The painting by Bogdan Willewalde shows exploding Polish congreve rockets (a prototype form of rocket weaponry), which stopped the Russian cavalry attack.

for the uprising. It was a combination of a sense of strength and fear, the strength of conviction in the importance perhaps for many the superiority of one's own Polish culture and identity, and at the same time, fear for the future of that identity in the face of autocracy.

The Tsar had clearly declared that Polish autonomy could be preserved only within the territory of a small kingdom, covering less than one-fifth of the former land mass of the Commonwealth. It thus excluded other brother Poles. Moreover, the very continuation of this limited autonomy depended in practice only on the Tsar's ongoing will and whim. The fear among Poles arising from such a tenuous foundation did not seem absurd. That fear proved to be contagious. Added to this was the Romantic breakthrough, which took place in Polish culture between 1822 and 1830, playing an unquestionable role in spreading and expressing these emotions. Its most important symbols became Adam Mickiewicz's successive works: from the poetry published in 1822 to the novel *Konrad Wallenrod*, published, paradoxically, during the poet's (relatively mild) exile, in St Petersburg, where

Józef Chłopicki and his military staff arrive on the battlefield at Olszynka Gro-chowska; the Polish general was severely wounded in the final phase of the clash with the Russians. Painting by Wojciech Kossak.

censorship proved to be less strict than in his native, repressed Novosiltsev's Vilnius. Indeed, the young poet's genius even attracted admiration as well as many admirers…

Thus, opened another bloody chapter in this struggle against Russia an uprising for Polish independence and a return to the previous borders of the Commonwealth. Following in the history of the 1733–1736, Bar Confedera-tion, and the Kościuszko Insurrection, still alive in the historical memory of older Poles. This uprising which had so many willing 'parents' would be named after the month in which it broke out it would be the November Uprising. This is not the place to recall its full history and the mistakes made during it, both political and military. We will not settle the dispute as to whether victory could have been achieved. We know that attempts to negotiate with the Tsar, were begun by Prince Lubecki almost immediately after the initial outbreak of fighting in Warsaw. That such attempts were rejected by St. Petersburg. The Tsar instead called on his generals to 'avenge the honor of Russia'. The subsequent dethronement of the Tsar as "King of Poland" by the Sejm of that Kingdom cut short with finality any hope for the peaceful coexistence of a truncated state with Poland's name within the great Empire of the Tsars.

An all-out war between Russia's then 50 million population and the four million-strong Polish Kingdom began. It lasted less than ten months. It registered several heroic episodes, the battle for Olszynka Grochowska at Stoczek, the expedition against the Russian guards, and the defense of Warsaw (Sowiński in the trenches of Wola, the Ordon Redoubt). There were also regrettably some embarrassing military episodes on both sides. The slogan 'for our freedom and yours' was born at this time. It was with this wording that the Poles addressed themselves to Russian soldiers drawn from the innumerable ranks of Russian serfdom. This rallying cry initiated by the circle of the democratic youth loyal to Joachim Lelewel, did not however, gain much traction. The West, from where Poland hoped aid would come, in particular from France and to some extent, from London, in the end neither provided any assistance. The uprising was doomed to failure.

Summing up his many years of research on this particular uprising, the Warsaw historian Tadeusz Łepkowski put its significance in these words: 'it opened a new period in our history, expressing firm opposition to the system of dependence that would (have us) bow down to spiritual enslavement and adaptation to slavery. […] It was a "no" said to the process of belittling and trivialization of national goals, reducing them to "realistic" half-goals, the "bearable vegetating" of Poles in a half-kneeling position. The November Revolution did not overthrow dependence but indicated that one must not give up on the greatest and most important goal, that of the struggle for Poland's full independence and sovereignty, even if that great, supreme goal seemed at the time utopian'.

It cannot be overlooked that, by its outbreak and course, in Russian opinion the uprising had the impact of strengthening the image of Poland as Russia's most dangerous enemy. The association of Poland's futile yet heroic struggle for independence and the related elaboration of an anti-Russian stereotype in Western public and elite opinion, triggered an absolute explosion of anti-Polish sentiment in the views of the educated elites of Moscow and St Petersburg. The interpretation of the Polish-Russian conflict earlier elaborated by Karamzin now came to triumph in 1831 also in cultural terms. In the poetry of, among others, Alexander Pushkin. His poems, published that year in the form of a propaganda pamphlet intended to strengthen the fighting spirit of the Russians against the 'Polish rebellion', would form a kind of canon for the Russian vision of the deadly existential conflict not only with Poland but also with the West (Western liberalism) that dared to support the treacherous Poles in their fight for liberty. In particular, Puszkin's poem *"To the Slanderers of Russia"*, repeated to this day in popular Russian culture and media, has huge significance.

In the first place, the failure of the uprising meant repressions. The Supreme Criminal Court established by Tsar Nicholas sentenced ten leaders of the uprising to death in absentia by beheading with an axe, including Prince Adam Czartoryski and Joachim Lelewel. More than 200 others were to be sentenced to death by hanging. The Tsar commuted this sentence to hard labor in chains. Most of those convicted were by then already in exile, beyond the Tsar's reach. The repression, however, would have an effect on their remaining estates. This effect would be considerable. In the Kingdom of Poland alone, more than 720 landed estates of more than 150,000 hectares were now confiscated. Similar confiscations took place in the estates of noblemen sympathetic to the uprising in the Lithuanian and Ukrainian governorates. In keeping with past practices many confiscated estates were then handed over to Russian generals meritoriously for their role in suppressing the uprising.

Here, the logic of repression took on a peculiarly national character: the new lords were to strengthen the Russian character of the defeated periphery or, at any rate, weaken its Polish identity. This logic can be seen even more clearly in other decisions by Tsar Nicholas taken after the uprising. Like Catherine after the Third Partition, Nicholas now ordered the removal from the reconquered Warsaw all that, which had constituted its cultural strength: the library and archive collections, which the populace had struggled to reconstruct for over three decades. The University of Warsaw and the Society of Friends of Science were also liquidated, and in turn their library and art collections were confiscated. More than 150,000 books, nearly 100,000 prints and paintings, collections of medals and antique weapons were taken from Warsaw to Russian museums and libraries in St Petersburg. Events repeated by the Kremlin's soldiers in Kherson Ukraine in late 2022. The Polytechnic Institute in Warsaw and Vilnius University (still among the most prominent universities operating in the Russian Empire in 1830) and the Krzemieniec Lyceum were also liquidated. In this way, Polish culture and science were deprived of virtually all the institutions that had sustained them allowing them to develop under the Russian partition during the first three decades of the 19th century.

The planned liquidation of this state of perceived Polish cultural supremacy in the lands of the former Commonwealth, a liquidation process that had already begun at the end of 1823 under Senator Novosiltsev, now definitely accelerated. On the western borderlands of the Empire, the imperial centers began a new phase of its Russian *Kulturkampf*. The aim of Russian policy in the lands of the former Commonwealth became a kind of 'acculturation' of the local nobility and Catholic clergy through violence: this was expected to naturally lead to the final abandonment of resistance to Russian rule in these lands the political and cultural traditions of these lands associated with the Commonwealth would now fade from memory forever.

The eradication of more than 300 Catholic monasteries and religious congregations in the lands of the former Commonwealth, carried out after 1830, was combined with a planned reduction in the influence of the Catholic church on the local population (read: Polish) education, previously conducted in the monastic schools. Educational instruction in these lands should no longer serve the purpose of sustaining a Polish identity.

Two massive social engineering actions were now on the table to be carried out by the Russian administration in these lands with the aim to overcome all remaining traces of the former Commonwealth. The first was the forced liquidation of the Uniate Church in 1839. Since in the lands of Ukraine, Volhynia and Podolia, the actual liquidation of the Uniate Church had already been brought about by Catherine II, the new action extended primarily to the lands of today's Belarus, where adherents of Christianity under the Uniate rite were subordinate to the Pope and were still in a clear majority. From 1839 onwards, nearly 1.5 million Uniate Church members in Belarus became part of the Orthodox Church along with the entire ecclesiastical infrastructure required to strengthen their 'spiritual unity' with Russia.

One of the initiators of this action, Archbishop Antoni Zubko, went even further in his ideas. He proposed the following year that all Roman

The protagonist of Juliusz Słowacki's poem – Anhelli, the story of a young man who traveled through the 'white hell of Siberia'. Painting by Witold Pruszkowski.

Catholics – subjects of the Tsar – should now also be made subordinated to the Orthodox Church. This was to be something like a 'reverse union', aimed at eliminating the importance of Catholicism as the core of a foreign identity, potentially hostile to Russia. One certainly identified by the Tsarist administration as an element of Polishness. 'Very interesting, important, but premature. To be kept secret until its time' this was what Nicholas I himself wrote about the project. He was consciously not only looking for ways to guarantee the loyalty of the Polish elites in the western borderlands of the Empire in the Kingdom. He was beginning to consider taking up the struggle for the identity of the Polish 'folk'.

Alongside religion, the other recognized vehicle of this initiative was language. Nicholas I, therefore, decided to personally engineer the 'Cyrillisation' of the Polish language, i.e. the replacement of the Latin alphabet, in all printed matter, with the Cyrillic ('Russian') alphabet now taking its place. This was stopped by the Tsar's Minister of Enlightenment, Sergey Uvarov, who understood that such radical measures in the 'struggle for culture' would ultimately undermine the possibility of loyal cooperation between the old elites of the Polish periphery and the imperial center.

A third determinant of this Polish identity, besides religion and language, was, from the point of view of the imperial center, the nobility. This notion had an important socio-cultural sense, historically encompassing not only the holders of landed estates but also hundreds of thousands of petty, landless nobles, nevertheless proud of their rights as free men and cherishing the memory of the traditions present in the old Commonwealth. After the uprising, two methods were used against this group. The first was the mass resettlement of the petty nobility from the lands of the former Commonwealth to the governorates of southern Russia and the Caucasus. This action involved several thousand families.

Of incomparably greater scope was this the second significant piece of social engineering implemented by the Russian administration. An operation carried out on the territory of the 'western governorates' during the twenty years following the suppression of the November Uprising. This took the form of a kind of 'great purge' of the noble state. Special commissions, set up in 1831, were to investigate the validity of noble titles. Those who did not own landed property and could not produce the relevant documents confirming the conferment of nobility, were condemned to degradation. To the status of so-called *'odnodvortsy'*, similar, in fact, to the status of a free peasant. This operation was decisively accelerated by the new Kyiv governor-general, Dmitri Bibikov, beginning in 1838. He actually succeeded in inducing some of the wealthy nobility to collaborate with him in this program for the liquidation of the poorer nobility. In doing so, he took advantage of the atmosphere of terror that he had introduced following the discovery of yet another Polish independence conspiracy in his subordinate territory in 1837.

Eventually, in the Ukrainian *gubernyas* alone (Kyiv, Podolia, Volhynia), some 340,000 people lost their nobility rights. These we people who had previously formed the social basis for the continuation of the politically understood (civic, not ethnic, or religious-based) concept of Polishness. Having now been relegated to the status of *'odnodvortsy'*, most of them, within three generations, simply melted into the social sea of the local peasantry. As we shall see, although Polishness in the ethnic sense was thus significantly weakened, it was not Imperial Russia that would ultimately win out, but the new national movements that were only now forming in the second half of the 19th century: primarily Ukrainian and also Belarusian, which would now 'absorb' a large proportion of these disinherited descendants, these victims of Tsar Nicholas and Bibikov's social experiment and in doing so would be fortified by them.

The French historian Daniel Beauvois emphasized this fact in his analysis of collaboration by part of the wealthy Polish nobility with the Tsarist administrative apparatus in the process of depriving their 'younger brothers,' i.e. the poor nobility, of their social status. This collaboration allowed them to maintain their own estates and to prolong their rule over a total of hundreds of thousands of peasants. This was Bibikov's plan: since the Polish nobility was too numerous and too economically strong to be administratively liquidated in its entirety. Within the framework of a state such as Russia, it was necessary to divide it and draw some of it into collaboration. This collaborating part was supposed to be afforded the opportunity to survive and develop economically and to also modernize its estates. The price for this was to be precisely the breaking of national and state solidarity and, above all, the final erasure of any thoughts regarding the rebirth

245

of the Commonwealth. Wiping such concepts from the horizon of this group's expectations. The price of this collaboration was to be a conscious separation by these people from Poland and Polishness and a "reconciliation" with the Empire.

The Polish historian Jan Kieniewicz, analyzing this phenomenon, called it civilizational oppression. By this, he means the breaking down of the protective barrier defending the value system of a given society and the subsequent wresting of control over it by the dominant empire. A process performed especially with regard to the subjugated periphery's elites. A Pole a nobleman, wishing to hold on to his landed estate, or latterly an intelligentsia member desirous of making a career, was faced with a situation of conflict. Between the interests of the nation he perhaps still aspired to reforge and that of the Empire he was obliged to serve. Such a choice could or should lead to a betrayal of his inbred value system. A betrayal made consciously to facilitate the ongoing perspective of potential societal advance for both himself and his family. In other words, a choice to submit and accept the recognition of a foreign value system, by conceding to the superiority of the rulers and the life chances they could subsequently deign to offer.

In addition to the 'western *gubernyas*' [western governorates from Moscow's point of view, from the Polish point of view, these were eastern territories – *editor's note*], there was, however, still the actual Kingdom of Poland to deal with. The experience of 1815–1831 convinced the political elite of the Russian Empire that without breaking the attractive nostalgic force of memory associated with the Kingdom or the Commonwealth, the assimilation of the 'western *gubernyas*' could fully not succeed. The Tsar abolished the Constitution of 1815, the Sejm and Senate as well as the Kingdom's separate army and budget. Nicholas formally granted the Kingdom the so-called Organic Statute, which proclaimed that 'the Kingdom of Poland, forever annexed to the Russian State, is an inseparable part of that State'. In such a form it could of course no longer exist without connection to "the larger body". The Tsar no longer had to crown himself King of Poland in Warsaw from that moment onwards. The government (the Administrative Council), limited in its powers, would meet and deliberate under the leadership of the new governor, Ivan Paskevich. Nicholas would instruct him repeatedly and intensely:

Top: Peasants carry a wounded insurgent into a room. Painting by Stanisław Witkiewicz. Bottom: Similar dramas were unfortunately not uncommon: the arrest of an insurgent by Russian soldiers in a painting by Stanislaw Masłowski.

'As far as this country is concerned, although you assure us that in ten years it will reach the state we wish for, I insist on ninety-seven years, but I rely more on Russian bayonets and cartridges than on other means; only fear, in my opinion, affects the Poles' (3/15 July 1838). '[...] they are only held back by fear and the fear of losing all they have left to lose. As long as our strength is not only in military numbers but also in the inexorable means of uniting them with Russia, of depriving them of all the separateness which constitutes the remnant of their supposed nationality – we shall have the advantage over them, though only in some time and with full consistency. But if we only falter in applying these measures or allow ourselves any overconfidence in their effectiveness – all will be lost, and inevitable doom awaits us'. (6/18 April 1845).

A few years after the uprising, the internal administrative structure of the Kingdom was changed, replacing the provinces in 1837 with *gubernyas*, which were named and administered in the same way as in Russia. The Russian monetary system and the Russian system of measurements (the pood, fathom, *garniec* (ca. 4qt. measure, etc.)) were also introduced in the Kingdom. The control of political sentiment was to be supervised by the Third District of the Russian Gendarme Corps. The symbolic and real seal on all these changes was the construction of the Citadel, a building which dominated over the city of Warsaw. It was the headquarters of the Russian garrison and the site of the central political prison. It was built at the expense of the city itself. Receiving a city delegation in 1835, Nicholas threatened to demolish Warsaw in the event of any new revolt. In doing so, he uttered the following meaningful words to the Poles: 'If you persist in dreaming of a separate nationality, an independent Poland and all these chimaeras, you will only bring more misery upon yourselves'.

By 1915 more than 60,000 prisoners would have passed through just this one political prison in Warsaw– the 10th Pavilion of the Citadel. More than 20,000 would set off from there on a further cruel journey: a journey of exile deep into Russia. Several hundred – executed in the Citadel – would remain there forever. A further way of terrorizing the population of the Kingdom was also to extend conscription into the Russian army. As a result of the 1832 conscription, nearly 28,000 men from the Kingdom were taken into the military. More than 25 percent of this group was sent to serve in the Caucasus, where the Russian army had been suppressing a highland uprising led by Shāmil for some 30 years. Recruits from the Kingdom were also sent *en masse* to serve in the Orenburg Corps, fighting for the conquest of Central Asia and the Siberian Corps. Service in Nicholas I's army lasted for between 15 to 25 years. By 1855, nearly 200,000 men (or about 4% of the Kingdom's entire population) had been selected in this way, of whom about 150,000 died or perished, and at most 20,000 to 25,000 little more than 10% ever returned home.

It is worth recalling these figures when asking the question whether the struggle for independence from such Russian exploitation, from such a drain on the 'human resources' of the Polish nation, was truly 'unreasonable'. A mere a wasteful romantic endeavor, as some still claim. Certainly, it was not very romantic at all to die in service of the Tsar's army in Siberia. This question was not only answered by the great Romantic literature now created in exile after the November Uprising – by Mickiewicz, Juliusz Słowacki, Zygmunt Krasiński, and later by Cyprian Kamil Norwid. This question was also answered by the actions of successive conspiracies established in the Russian partition in the years following the defeat of the November Uprising. This question was also answered by Prince Adam Jerzy Czartoryski, who, in his new place of exile, centered around the Parisian Lambert Hotel, now set about creating an apparatus for the diplomatic and public or indeed propaganda-focused representation of the Polish nation. Framing his actions as a reaction to the threat posed by Russian imperialism to the whole of Europe. It was also within his circle that the concept of breaking up the Empire through the cooperation of all the nations and religious communities oppressed within its borders was developed. From the Finns, through the Latvians and Estonians, to the Ruthenians-Ukrainians-Cossacks, the Crimean and Volga Tatars and others. Poland, the Commonwealth, was to be obviously the centerpiece of this action. A centerpiece which could potentially prove effective when supported by one of the Western Powers (Great Britain or France). Prince Adam did not live to see this moment and experienced great disappointment during the Crimean War (1853–1856), when the Western powers did indeed clash with Russian imperialism but retreated from the prospect of pursuing it to the point of breaking up the Empire itself. Instead making peace, allowing Russia to regather its strength through modernization and thus increasing its potential for further aggression.

Hopes, revived after the Crimean War, that a temporarily weakened Russia, under the new reformist Tsar Alexander II (reigned 1855–1881), would change its policy towards Poles. This was quickly cooled though by the Tsar himself during his visit to Warsaw, on 22 May 1856. In his memorable words to the humble representatives of the Polish elites there to listen: 'No dreams, gentlemen. The prosperity of Poland depends on its complete fusion with the other nations of my empire… What my father [Nicholas I] did, he did well'.

Some tactical concessions were made by the Tsar to calm the turbulent Polish 'periphery' at a time of internal upheaval in the center of the Empire. This was the period of the enfranchisement of the peasantry (freedom of the Serfs) Alexander's great reform. Moreover, open discussion of reforms, had their limit in Poland and in Russia. The aforementioned tactical concessions were often forced on the Tsar by mass protests on the streets of Warsaw (and not only) during the so-called moral revolution of 1859–1861. The resultant terror alone, with hundreds of demonstrators killed, the churches closed, the Citadel filled with prisoners, all this was not enough to bring calm. Because some Poles would consciously choose to protest, risking their lives and livelihoods. Alexander instead tried to keep his focus on those who, having no popular support depended solely on the grace of the Tsar. People through which he could pursue a policy of 'pacifying' the Kingdom via certain concessions, concessions that could of course be revoked at any time.

This was the time of the implementation of several reforms, important and valuable certainly from the point of view of the emancipation of the Jews, somewhat less effective as far as the emancipation of the peasants in Poland was concerned. The Warsaw Main School (Głowna Szkoła) very important in developing Polish thought, was established as part of these reforms and tactical concessions. The administration began to be 're-Polonised'. However, for the Tsar and his political advisers, all decisions were exclusively related to Russia's interests, which at this point, merited just a temporary softening of the course towards Poland. The long-term goal did not change even one iota; it was determined by the Tsar's statements and the ideas we have outlined above. The Lithuanian-Ruthenian lands were

Another rendering of Polish Siberia-bound deportees' during their overnight stay 'in stages'. 'Stages' ('na etapie')… Painting by Jacek Malczewski.

Siberian paintings by Jacek Malczewski. Top: January Insurgents Siberian exiles forced to work in a mine, during a rest period. Bottom: deportees 'at a stage'. In the foreground – Polish insurgents.

to become entirely Russian in cultural terms: no trace of Polishness could remain there. The Kingdom of Poland could continue based on a certain autonomy, which would gradually be reduced so that it would not become a dangerous magnet for the Lithuanian-Ruthenian lands. Such was the logic and principle; such was the foundation of Russian policy towards Poland in the 19ᵗʰ century.

An experienced keeper of the Tsarist peace, Count Nikolai Orlov, advised in 1861 to give enterprising Poles 'as much prosperity as possible' (just how much – this would be decided in St Petersburg), but not power, nor even a guarantee of distinctive legal rights or a constitution based on their own traditions. A new, wealth-oriented middle class (*sryednyeye soslovye*), that, unlike the old nobility or priests burdened by the historical memory of Polishness, could be viewed as a chance to calm down tensions in society, and stabilize the situation in the Congress Kingdom, reconcile its inhabitants to their fate. This was to be achieved by replacing historical, largely patriotic elites with new economic ones. An elite that would develop under Russian rule, the rule of the 'liberal' empire on the Vistula, offering the perspective of upward social mobility. Giving instructions to the new Viceroy of Poland, his brother, Grand Duke Konstantin Nikolayevich, the Tsar added a warning: 'there can be no question of any deeper concessions, especially no talk of a constitution or a separate army, which could threaten Russia's control over Warsaw, to agree to this would mean giving up Poland and recognizing her independence with all the disastrous consequences for Russia, that would entail. Precisely the potential detachment from Russia of all that Poland had once in turn laid claim as Commonwealth lands, lands which Polish patriots would continue to see as their historical homeland.

Fulfilling their forebodings Polish patriots reacted to the program of Tsar Alexander II and Wielopolski in just such a way. If someone wants to take Poland away from us, truncate it, or deprive the country of its historical identity, then we must fight for it. This was the most straightforward reason for every uprising. Including what would now be the biggest most widespread uprising that encompassed all the lands of the old Commonwealth it would also be the most tragic of the uprisings: The January Uprising, the last uprising in defense of the joint Polish-Lithuanian Commonwealth. The one with the tricolor of the Polish Eagle, the Lithuanian Pahonia and the Ruthenian (Ukrainian) Michael the Archangel on its coat of arms.

Again, in this case, we will not delve fully into the history of this January Uprising, having broken out on 22 January 1863. As an actual uninterrupted armed action, the uprising lasted 'only' a few months, from January 1863 till April 1864, afterwards it was sporadic guerrilla fighting that prevailed, for a prolonged period of time. Statistically, it can be summarized by the number of battles and skirmishes fought by its partisans against Russian troops. On the territory of the Kingdom of Poland, there were 764 in 1863 and 191 more in 1864; on the territory of Lithuania with Belarus – 227 in 1863 and 10 in 1864, and finally in Ruthenia (i.e. right-bank Ukraine and Volhynia) – 32 in 1863 and 3 in 1864. According to traditional Polish historiography, in total between 150,000 to 200,000 insurgents took part in these various battles and skirmishes (though an estimate of between 100,000 and 150,000 seems more likely), although never more than 30,000 would take to the field simultaneously. Opposite the uprising was the rapidly expanding Russian army now reformed after the Crimean War. In the military district encompassing the Kingdom of Poland from January 1863 to January 1864, its presence grew from 93,000 to 170,000 soldiers: in the Vilnius district, encompassing Lithuania and Belarus, from 66,000 to 145,000, respectively. Suppose one were to add to this the additional Russian troops guarding the imperial order on the territory of right-bank Ukraine, then in that case, one might conclude, in 1864, that Russia needed more than 400,000 soldiers in the field not to mention a massive advantage in armaments, to contain and control by force the situation in the lands of the former Commonwealth.

Let us note here that this enormous effort, which lasted several months, also had its financial implications for Russia, which overlapped with the costs of the peasant reform that the tsarist government had to bear in 1864–1865. Together with the indebtedness of the budget resulting from the construction of railways over huge distances and with costs in materiel only comparable to what was taking place in the US at that time. The costs of pacifying the uprising and securing the borders of the Empire against the war emergency of the summer of 1863 undoubtedly exacerbated the already existing crisis of Russian debt during Mikhail Reutern's first years as Finance Minister. Reutern himself emphasized this very strongly in his secret report to the Tsar on the state of Russia's finances in 1866. In it, he pointed out that 'since January 1863, the Polish uprising and the European war threatening Russia' had essentially eroded the confidence [of Western European banking houses – *AN*] in Russia's credit standing; with the 'Polish rebellion' interest payments on Russian sovereign debt soared. The uprising also entailed huge direct costs in maintaining armies in the field and the decline in economic activity in the regions affected (in 1862, the Russian Empire's expenditure amounted to 328 million roubles; by 1864, it was already 447 million!) and they needed to take out huge loans to cover the rapidly growing deficit.

The resultant financial crisis resulted in the decision to sell Alaska to the United States, a transaction finalized in 1867. The second reason for this decision, besides the financial one, so fraught with geopolitical consequences, was also that of strategic considerations in 1863: the conviction that the Russian state was incapable of effectively defending the far eastern coast of the Empire against a possible attack by the British fleet. Geopolitical security concerns in this part of the empire would later be accentuated by the rise of Japan. The sale of Alaska to the United States, with which (specifically the Union North, fighting against the Confederates in the Civil War) Russia had established a near-allied relationship at the time, was seen by St Petersburg as a move that would nip in the bud the possibility of any British strategic pressure from this American side. Thus, perhaps, it is worth considering the aftermath of the Polish uprising of 1863–1864 from this unexpected side: the sale and acquisition of Alaska.

Indeed, the immediately visible consequence of the uprising, and especially its impact on relations with the Western powers' attempting to apply diplomatic pressure on Russia, was a sharp turnaround in the political mood of the Russian elite. Just as during the earlier November Polish uprising, only this time on a much larger scale. This was a turn towards extreme Russian nationalism. The influence upon Russian public opinion previously enjoyed by the liberal émigré Alexander Herzen, a man courageously sympathetic to the Polish cause, collapsed sharply. Mikhail Katkov became the editor of the daily *Moskovskiye Vedomosti* and 'director' of opinion in 1863. He renewed the legend of a 'Polish conspiracy' that had almost taken over the whole of

Russia and was now also manipulating Russian 'nihilists' (i.e. radicals). He called on all the patriotic forces of Russia to wage a mortal battle against Poland, along with the Catholic priests and nobility representing them. Like Karamzin, Katkov now preached a hard alternative: either the 'Polish conspiracy' would destroy Russia, or Russia would finally kill the 'Polish vampire'. (TN Start) This turn in the public mood finds its echo in many of the great works of literature produced in Russia in the years following the January uprising. (TN End)

Just as before, the vision of a great, inevitable confrontation between Russia and the West, with Europe, was renewed with the outbreak of the Polish uprising. The Empire must defend its Russian identity by finally Russifying its western provinces for good and all. Almost the entirety of Russian opinion, from liberals to conservatives, agreed with this, applauding even the most brutal of methods employed by Mikhail Muravyov in Lithuania. Concerning the Kingdom of Poland, the idea of establishing effective Russian rule on this territory by attempting to attract Polish social elites was finally abandoned. The program promoted by a group of radical pan-Slavists (Nikolai Milutin, Yuri Samarin, Alexander Hilferding, Vladimir Cherkassky) now prevailed. According to this program, the main support for Russian policy in the Kingdom should be the common people not the elites, the peasants. Their acquiescence garnered by the radical enfranchisement reform that would be as favorable to them as possible. The peasants were to be gradually educated and raised by learning to read the Cyrillic alphabet into 'good Slavs', the first step in their true incorporation into the great Russian nation. The pre-condition for the success of this action was to turn the peasants against their 'lords and priests' as the perpetrators of their historical poverty and the only true 'fermenters' of Polishness. Men who had to be countered if not stamped out by any means. This program was to be implemented not only in the name of the Russian Empire and its interests but also in the name of social progress, in the way of this program stood that the 'old' Polish historical-cultural identity and Polish Catholicism.

The participants in the Uprising of 1863–1864, Poles, Lithuanians, nascent Belarusians and Ukrainians, all fought to rebuild the type of political community the Commonwealth represented in its territorial shape

A peaceful demonstration by 200,000 workers in St. Petersburg led by the Orthodox clergyman Georgy Gapon was crushed by tsarist troops. One thousand people were killed and 2,000 wounded. 'Bloody Sunday' on 22 January 1905 gave rise to the 1905 Revolution. Drawing by Ludwik Samosiewicz.

257

from before the partitions some 90 years hence. They yearned to achieve something akin to the liberty and tolerance that they, or at least some of their forefathers, had experienced or could have aspired to in that bygone era. They lost in that fight and the sense of defeat was acute. It was created first and foremost by the enormous losses in life and material suffered in the Uprising and in the repressions that followed. Some 20,000 partisans died in the fighting alone. More than 700 insurgents were executed (about 500 just in the lands of the Kingdom). Between 35,000 to 40,000 were sent into exile or forced settlement far into the depths of Russia. Nearly 60 percent of these were insurgents from the Lithuanian-Belarusian governorates and more than 35 percent from the Kingdom. We know with precision that between 1863 and mid-1866, the Warsaw-Petersburg railway transported 34,000 political prisoners from the insurgency areas to the east.

According to the Russian Ministry of the Interior estimates, in 1872, there were still approx. 40,000 Polish exiles, of whom about 20,000 were in Siberia. For comparison: between 1861 and 1870, an average of just 3 to 20 people were sent from the lands of European Russia (non-partition lands) to Siberia annually for political offences, So the ratio of Polish exiles after the January Uprising to repressed Russian revolutionaries was several hundred to one. Some 3,500 landed estates (of which 1,660 were in the Kingdom, 1,794 in Lithuania, and more than 100 in right-bank Ukraine) most historically belonging to the Polish nobility were also confiscated in the years between 1863 and 1867. Alternatively, their owners, sentenced to be deported, were forced to sell their land. The confiscated land was usually handed over to Russian officers and officials who had "earned it" through their services in suppressing the uprising.

In addition to the repressions directed at participants of the uprising, the Russian authorities also reinforced their policy of complete Russification of the 'Western Country'. On 22 December 1865, Tsar Alexander II issued a decree that forbade all persons of 'Polish descent' in the nine governorates of the 'Western Country' to buy land. This was unprecedented in the Russian Empire, as it explicitly identified a specific national origin as the only criterion for legal discrimination. Until that time, it had been the 'confessional' measure that had been the litmus test: A Catholic equaled a Pole. Now, however, recognizing the possibility of insincere conversions to Orthodoxy, Russian governors were to decide who was Polish and who was not.

Muravyov had already ordered that all police offices as well as middle and senior administrative positions should be held only by Russians. The first test of 'Russianness' for the authorities was membership in the Orthodox Church. The desire to keep one's post in the administration, to keep one's land or even (as far as the peasants were concerned) to gain 5 roubles for changing one's religion – these were the motives that prompted more than 70,000 Catholics to convert to Orthodoxy within just a few years. Because the Russian authorities still saw Catholicism as the basis of Polish identity, they ordered the closure of 30 more monasteries in the 'Western lands' and the conversion of 160 Roman Catholic churches into Orthodox ones. There was also a ban on building new Catholic churches and the renovation of old ones. Muravyov even tried to introduce the Russian language into the Catholic liturgy.

The second criterion of Polishness was language. The governor-general of Vilnius decided not only to Russify all levels of education completely but even introduced extremely high financial penalties for secretly teaching the Polish language. A total ban was imposed on the use of the Polish language in public places in offices, courts, but also on the street, in shops, theatres or cafés. All Polish periodicals were now closed down, Polish signposts were abolished, and the keeping of parish books in Polish was also banned. Repression also hit against the Lithuanian language. Lithuanians were banned from using the Latin alphabet, instead the Russian Cyrillic alphabet was imposed. The Ukrainian language was also treated as an instrument of 'Polish intrigue'. Thus, as early as July 1863, the Minister of the Interior, Pyotr Valuyev, banned the publication of any educational or religious periodicals in Ukrainian. (TN Start) Kyiv, a city where the Polish language was still considered to be that of the educated and where the elite would now undergo a more comprehensive process of Russification (TN End).

Also, in the lands of the Kingdom of Poland, the institution of the Catholic Church was hit, along with education and public rights for use of the Polish language. Immediately after the uprising, nearly 1,500 priests were put in detention centers and prisons, and 550 were sentenced to exile. More

259

than 200 were sent to Siberia (roughly half of this number came from the Kingdom, half from the 'Western Country'). After the Archbishop of Warsaw, other Catholic bishops, 12 in all, were also deported deep into Russia. More than 150 monasteries in the Kingdom were abrogated. Catholic priests were treated as functionaries of the state, moreover, functionaries under suspicion and therefore subject to constant police surveillance. An attempt was even considered, not for the first time, to detach the Church in the Kingdom of Poland out from under the supremacy of the Pope and establish a 'Slavic Catholic Church'. 1875 saw the final quashing of the Uniate Church (still in union with the Pope) the remnants of which existed in the eastern part of the Kingdom. Any resistance by the faithful of this Church against forced conversion to Orthodoxy was liquidated with the army's intervention. Twenty-six Uniates defending their faith were killed, and more than 600 were exiled deep into Russia.

The Polish language was gradually rooted out from education, and government offices and Russian was introduced in its place. From 1866, Russian was taught compulsorily in all secondary schools in the Kingdom, and only in this language were geography and history allowed to be taught. Two years later, Russian became the language of the Kingdom's administration. Polish officials were gradually removed from it, starting with the higher positions now reserved exclusively for Russians. In 1869, the Main School (Szkoła Główna) was abolished, and henceforth no Polish university in the Kingdom would exist. The new superintendent of the Warsaw School District, Aleksander Apuchtin, appointed in 1879 and exceptionally zealous in suppressing all manifestations of Polish identity, became a symbol of this drive towards the complete Russification of education.

In a very oft-repeated interpretative schema, the January Uprising was a manifestation of Polish pathology, of the 'romantic madness' of an active part of the social elite which had failed to see (unlike Wielopolski, who was alone or at any rate remained in the minority) the opportunity for modernization that was opening up by the reforms in Russia following the Crimean War. Polish 'romantic nationalism', which lacked 'rational self-control', was readily contrasted with the Czech national movement, which acted differently, i.e. rationally. While 'emotional and heroic' Poland was seemingly sacrificing its chance of a better future at least in the material sense.

260

The road to modernization led through the struggle for independence. And it was not only the bureaucracy of the Habsburg Empire, weakened after its defeats in the war with Prussia as in the aforementioned Czech case, that stood in the way, but the conscious policy of the Russian elites, to which we should add, those of Bismarck, now Chancellor of Prussia. These two powers, Russia and Prussia, unlike Austria (the Habsburg monarchy) treated the question of Poland's potential reconstruction as a mortal threat to the stability of their state structures and their developing national programs: be they pan-Russian or pan-German.

Indeed, without a struggle, the Russian Empire was not prepared to give the Poles any form of independence, even within the separate, limited territory of a Polish Kingdom. It was only by fighting for the freedom that of the 'whole nation' that the Polish landed gentry could reorientate themselves and go beyond the constraints imposed on it by its historical social imperative to perpetuate their domination over the peasantry and control of the land.

In the lands partitioned to the Hapsburg's the 1848 limited local uprising prepared by the Polish nobility forced the Austrian governor of Galicia to implement its program for the freeing and enfranchisement of the peasants; a similar phenomenon, only on a larger scale, was repeated in the Russian partitioned lands as a result of the January Uprising. The program of radical enfranchisement of the peasants, announced in the manifesto of the short-lived insurgent Polish government on 22 January 1863, now had to be as it were, followed through upon by the Russian authorities. A policy which became the Tsarist Act of 2 March 1864. In both cases, the long-term effect was to free the most numerous social group, the peasantry, from feudal dependence and a slave mentality. Contrary to Russian hopes, however, the peasants did not become grateful subjects of the Tsar. Instead in an expression of their freedom either in the second or third generation after that enfranchisement, in 1914, 1918, and 1920 – these former slaves would choose Polishness and they would be ready to fight for it.

Although the Belarusian-speaking Orthodox peasantry benefited analogously from the response of the Russian authorities to the Polish uprising, they were subjected to more substantial assimilation pressure to subsume themselves into the 'great Russian nation'. This would impede the development of their distinct cultural identity. However, in the political project of

the Belarusian nation, relaunched at the beginning of the 20th century, the
memory of the January Uprising as a struggle for liberation by the Belarusian peasantry and its symbol, Konstantin Kalinovsky, will prove to be very
important. In right-bank Ukraine, where the uprising struggles were much
more ephemeral and were in some cases suppressed with the assistance of
local peasants, the Russian authorities – as in the Lithuanian-Belarusian
lands – gave the enfranchisement reform implementation a more favorable shape for the peasants than in Russia 'proper'. This accelerated social
emancipation also in these three governorates (Kyiv, Podolia, Volhynia).
And over this area, it did not so much support the project of a 'great Russian nation', but it did instead strengthened the tendency to build a separate
Ukrainian nation in the future.

The January Uprising did not defend the historical, pre-modern era form
of the Commonwealth. For this was not what its initiators were fighting for.
They cast the dice, seeing in it the last chance to rebuild the Commonwealth
within its historical borders of 1772. Yet this was to have been a Commonwealth renewed altered, socially transformed. This was completely different
to the other uprisings of the age. The Confederates of the southern states
of North America, who were waging their struggle (1861–1865), rebelling
against the US federal government in an effort to defend the status quo of
slavery, instead the Polish insurgents fought for the final liberation of all
the peasants throughout the territory of the Commonwealth. The battle to
restore the borders of the Commonwealth was of course lost. However, in
the longer-term struggle for social modernization and enfranchisement of
the wider population the uprising would prove to be a victory despite its
cost in human lives and human hardship.

The ultimate result of this struggle with at least a partial genesis in
January 1863 was an acceleration of the underlying social crisis that would
ultimately lead to the disintegration of the Russian Empire itself. The first
dimension of the future break-up was evident; it would take place along
the national seams, just as many Polish conspirators planned the scenario
of a breakup of the Russian Empire. This was also what the late Polish
concept of 'Prometheanism' ultimately amounted to, as envisaged by Józef
Piłsudski, [in political terms, a concept aimed at gaining independence
by means of the power of multiple nations. All the nations conquered by

Bolshevik poster celebrating the 1917 Revolution. At the bottom is the inscription: 'The year of the dictatorship by the proletariat'.

the Russian Empire or the USSR, rejecting the forced Russification or latterly sovietization in those conquered countries that Russia would seek to impose – *editor's note*]. Making the empire entirely Russian was, of course, impossible because it was in essence, multinational.

The only reliable population census, conducted in the Tsarist Empire in 1897, showed that the Great Russians, or Russians proper, numbered just 44% of the population at the time, and the 'Malorussians' (Little Russians) and White Russians actually the Ukrainians and Belarusians were the second largest component, with a 22% figure. Without the absorption of these latter two still emerging and strengthening in identity East Slavic nationalities, descendent nations at least some extent, from the Commonwealth, the Russians were only the largest minority in their multiethnic empire. That is why they strived at all costs on the threshold of the 20th century (and still now in the 21st) to incorporate fully the Belarusians and Ukrainians into the *'Russkiy mir'* ('Russian world'). It seems they will ultimately fail in this attempt. Yet the example of the Polish struggle for independence, undertaken so many times in the 18th and 19th centuries, even when it seemed and indeed was, a hopeless endeavor, this had an extremely contagious effect on other nations. Often increasing ever more with each successive uprising. It made them aware of the need to fight for their rights, and sometimes in the case of Ukrainians or Lithuanians it would regrettably also to lead to conflict with the Poles and Polishness.

However, the internal disintegration of the Empire took place not only along these national seams but also out of the increasingly odious ethnically intolerant nature of the centers of power in Moscow and St Petersburg for the non-Russian peoples of the periphery the un-redeemable. These centers even began to close themselves off to the influx of other nations. Already in the second half of the 19th century, no Pole could even dream of serving as a governmental minister. After 1900 the *numerus nullus* rule applied to Poles in the Corps of Gendarmes, which meant that no single Pole could find a place for himself there. Also, from 1880–1890 a regulation was adopted in the Russian army that no Pole could ever advance to a rank higher than a colonel regardless of merit. Though during the First World War dozens of Polish colonels were swiftly promoted to the rank of general, but war conditions forced this.

Alexander II's successor, Alexander III (reigned 1881–1894), went on to issue hundreds of edicts restricting Poles' access to various offices of importance to the Empire. His son, the last Tsar of Russia, Nicholas II (reigned 1894–1917), faithfully continued this tradition dating back to Catherine II. Some representatives of 'maturing' non-Russian peoples (including Jews, Latvians, previously loyal Tatars, Lithuanians, and Ukrainians were also now treated with particular suspicion by the Empire's 'defenders of purity') and prevented from pursuing intra-imperial careers. They would themselves out of frustration turn against the Russian center of power.

(TN Start) The Jews of the old Commonwealth were a case in point. A realm to which they had fled from Western Europe taking shelter under the Polish Crown's pledge of religious tolerance. A Commonwealth in which they had flourished though not without tensions or difficulties. The Jews were not spared in the religious massacres that took place after the 1648 uprising nor the *Koliivshchyna* that followed it some 120 years later during the Bar uprising. Yet now after the partitions and under the rule of the Tsars Jews throughout the commonwealth would find themselves victims to frequent systematic and savage pogroms by Russian authorities and their local enablers. These became especially brutal after the assassination of Tsar Alexander II in 1881 reports of savage these programs crossed the Atlantic in the waves of migration that followed as Jews now fled the land of the pogrom for a new distant land of tolerance perhaps a new Commonwealth across the great ocean. Among the Jewish population that remained behind the resultant fear and resentment would later be cleverly instrumentalized by among others the Soviets in their tactics of population control and recruitment to their security apparatus of such brutalized minorities, the oppressed, the marginalized the "friendless". Many would thus become captured instruments in the exercise of Soviet power. (TN End).

Steadily all these increasingly educated and emancipated masses would naturally move towards a more robust identification with their own peoples and also towards a common hatred of the Tsarist system, this would be offered to them by the most influential ideology of resentment in history, the doctrine of hate, precisely: the twisted Bolshevik version of Marxism, especially in its later Soviet version. Of course, the core of the Bolshevik movement was Russian. Still, there were activists in leading positions in the movement, such as the Ossetian Dzhugashwili (Stalin), or an offspring of the Polish borderlands Feliks Dzierżyński, even Vladimir Ilyich Ulyanov – half-Kalmuk, quarter-Jew, quarter-German, or also exiles from Jewish historical-religious identity, such as Leon Trotsky, Lev Kamenev and Grigory Zinoviev.

Bolshevism grew and 'swelled' in this way, not least because the Empire eventually undertook to persecute all non-Russian national identities in the multi-ethnic state. A policy which began with the deadly struggle against Polishness from the 18th century onwards. The most radical elements were able to merge in this situation into one terrible, destructive, nihilistic current. They no longer identified with their nations with any constructive program – be it the building or preservation of Polishness, Georgian identity, seeking a national solution for the Jews, as the Zionist movement eventually did, or seeking a state of their own for Ukrainians or Lithuanians. These broken, nihilistic elements instead concentrated on a hostile program of demolishing, destroying everything this was largely how, the foundations upon which, the strength out of which the Bolsheviks would grow.

These symptoms were already discernible at the time of the first revolution in Russia, in 1905–1907. However, after the tactical concessions forced by this revolution, Tsar Nicholas II and the most talented Russian politician of his era, Prime Minister Pyotr Stolypin, quickly returned by default to the persecution of non-Russian peoples and the systematic weakening of the beginnings of parliamentarianism (the *Duma*, or Russian Parliament, established in 1905). A symbol of the renewal of the Tsarist Empire's post 1905 became again the traditional, vigorously anti-Polish policy, especially in 1912, with the administrative detachment from, the now tiny Kingdom of Poland of its eastern lands (Siedlce and the Lublin area) and the incorporation of them, as the renamed Chełm *gubernya*, directly into Russia 'proper'.

Despite this consistency of action by Tsarist Russia, a part of the Polish economic and social elite still found their way into its system, building careers for themselves where it was allowed, as in business and the engineering professions. There were no obstacles in this sphere. The flowering of Russian culture during the 'silver age', that is, the early 20th century, with the dramas of Anton Chekhov, the ballets of Igor Stravinsky, the poetry of Alexander Blok, and earlier, the admiration for the genius of Tolstoy or Dos-

266

Józef Piłsudski as a young PPS (Polish Socialist Party) activist. A portrait photograph from the year 1899.

toevsky, Tchaikovsky or Mussorgsky. All this had tamed, as it were, at least part of these elites. Imbued by these Russian successes with the conviction that it was wonderful after all to belong to the Russian Empire, that this was perhaps indeed the empire of the future populated with towering cultural figures and achievements, that it was no longer worthwhile recalling the old grievances. Especially as there was an active and aggressive enemy in the west: the Second Reich, pursuing a genuine and clearly ruthless policy of Germanisation of which rumor and reports had spread. A Reich very similar in aims and methods to the struggle against Polishness seen in the days of Catherine II.

Thus, at the dawn of the twentieth century, there will be an argument in favor of reconciliation with Russia as the mistress of Poland – a mistress that will eventually show herself to be kind, open to liberalization, finally putting down the sword and allowing reconciliation to take place based on modernity. This path will be followed by some liberals, such as the eminent lawyers Włodzimierz Spasowicz and Aleksander Lednicki. Others, such as Józef Mackiewicz, who would recall these times from the perspective of a child enthralled by St Petersburg. They would recall that it was familiar, somehow cozy and safe under the wing of Russia and it perhaps was only the communists who posed the real significant threat. They did not understand the connection between the growing success of Bolshevism in Russia and the specific substratum for this success engendered by the Tsarist system of ethnic and religious intolerance, including especially the methods of Tsarist repression.

However, the most important program of agreement, at least tactically speaking, with Tsarist Russia was built by the prominent 20th century Polish politician Roman Dmowski. A program based on a geopolitical-national vision of a Poland shifted westwards, though the power of modernization, a Poland renouncing the heritage and eastern lands of the former Commonwealth. The main, intransigent enemy for Dmowski lay in the west it was none other than Germany.

As an interesting aside to the modern day. Before the Smolensk tragedy of 2010, the famed publicist and founder of Gazeta Wyborcza Adam Michnik in an interview with the most famous historical magazine in Russia (published by the administration office of the Russian president), unexpectedly praised the historical choices favored by Roman Dmowski, at least in one aspect. Stating he was a wise and realistic politician who always sought an agreement with Russia not like the romantic fervor of Józef Piłsudski, who only led to the spoiling and destruction of potential for good relations with Moscow. 'Roman Dmowski is a model of wise Polish realism', Michnik admittedly addressed these words only to Russian readers, but perhaps he would have been ready to repeat this to a Polish audience as well.

Undoubtedly, Roman Dmowski possessed an outstanding agile and astute political mind and was great advocate of Poland patriotism, although, like so many politicians of the time, he made mistakes and was known for his antisemitic views, being generally mistrustful of Poland's multi-ethnic demographic composition at that time. He was certainly by no means a Russophile. Quite the contrary. His mistake concerning Russia was his *de facto* contempt for Russian political tradition and disregard for the power of 'Russian influence on the Polish soul'. This Dmowski clearly underestimated, believing that only Germany (and the Jews – according to his obsession) were a threat.

Dmowski believed that Imperial Russia would accept the rebuilding of a strong Poland on its western periphery as a bulwark against Germany. He hoped that he would eventually succeed in bringing about such a 'calming' of independence emotions in the Polish lands under the Russian partition and that the Russians would finally come to terms with a Polish presence, limited in its ambitions. That the Tsar would finally break with the legacy of the Potsdam treaty signed between St Petersburg with Berlin some two centuries earlier. This did indeed happen but only in 1914. When after much personal hand wringing on the part of the two cousins Kaiser Wilhelm II and Nicolas II. Russia finally made the decision to mobilize against Germany heralding the Great War, in which these two historical partners in partition would now stand on the opposite sides: Germany and Austria. This was immediately visible to many as the crack in the great geopolitical dam that once breached would allow Poland to regain its independence in the wave of independence movements that followed.

But Imperial Russia, including the later Soviet version, never came to terms with this Polish independence. Dmowski died in January 1939, he did not live to see the renewal of the Postdam partition treaty between Moscow and Berlin, its worst embodiment and with its most criminal repercussions: the Molotov-Ribbentrop Pact. This pact was concluded barely seven months after Dmowski's death. But behind this pact stood the whole history of the Empire, the entire history of the 'long XIXth century', the time of the Polish partitions: Russia regardless of who ruled it was always ready to agree with a Germanic partner to divide Central Europe and control Eastern Europe. A tendency that would persist for as long as it remains a Russia in the "Imperial Russian" tradition.

Dmowski's rival, Józef Piłsudski (1867–1935), he'd grown up in an ethnically mixed environment with a strong Jewish presence and was no antisemite. He had a different vision for Central Europe and a broader understanding of the ongoing struggle for control 'over Polish souls' or souls of the old Commonwealth. This was evident in the Polish political movement he represented at the dawn of the 20th century. Born in Lithuania just after the January Uprising and brought up in the cult of that struggle, he was a conscious heir to the tradition of the Confederates and Insurgents. To the Czartoriski Hotel Lambert concept of cooperation between non-Russian nations against an enslaving empire emanating out of Paris since the 1830s. He was an heir to the Romantic tradition of Słowacki and Mochnacki. He did not exclude the possibility of finding an accommodation with Russia, as a country but never as an Empire. For Pilsudski accommodation could only be achieved after the Empire of the Tsars had been broken up and the reconstruction of that Empire was rendered impossible. This was his goal.

Somewhat paradoxically, and somehow working together Dmowski and Piłsudski, pursuing their different paths, jointly brought about Poland's independence during the time of the First World War, during which the Petersburg Empire collapsed. However, a new form of empire was immediately established in the east to fill this vast vacuum and perpetuate, at least for some, the benefits arising from empire and its colonial nature: this would be the Soviet Empire. Its leader and creator, Lenin, moved the capital back (from St Petersburg/Petrograd) to Moscow. To communism's renewed Third Rome – now the Third International.

Poland Defends Itself, the Soviet Shroud and an Unrealized 'Third Russia' (1918–1939)

P olish sovereignty was restored in November 1918. The Russian Empire lay in ruins. However, a new formation was already rising from the apparent chaos. Soviet Russia, a new entity with a double agenda one old and one new. Firstly, to re 'collect the lands' of the recent empire and then, secondly and as soon as possible, to conquer the whole of Europe and eventually the whole world and impose the ideology of communism across the globe.

Poland did not yet have any of its borders firmly established in November 1918 it was a nebulous state in the making that would have to forge these borders largely through the ongoing sacrifice of its people. A civil war was just beginning in the east within Russia between the Bolsheviks, controlling most of the Moscow-Petrograd core now facing off against the emerging centers of resistance of 'White' Russia or the defenders of the Russian Republic (which existed from March to November 1917 and was overthrown by Lenin), as well as supporters who simply wanted the restoration of the earlier Tsarist rule. Was a reborn Poland doomed to fight this Russia to fully assert its new independence? If so which one 'red', 'white' or both? These were exceedingly practical questions, but they had to be answered and soon. They could no longer be elaborated upon in leisure at a café table in Warsaw. There was also another question, was this 'Red' Russia, even Russia at all? Or rather was it in fact the future oppressor of Russia?

Let us recall that shortly after gaining power in Petrograd and Moscow, the Bolsheviks, still lacking offensive capabilities, signed the Brest Agreement with Germany in March 1918, in which they largely relinquished the (European) imperial legacy of Tsarist Russia covering the territories of the Polish Commonwealth in favor of the Second Reich of Germany. With allowance for the creation of among others new dependent (largely on Germany) states, specifically Ukrainian and Polish "states". However, Lenin assumed, in line with his strategy, that he only had to wait out this difficult geopolitical moment. A moment when he did not yet have an effective army (the Red Army did not exist yet). It was a moment when one German division, could secure the occupation of Moscow or Petrograd; one decision taken in Berlin in the spring of 1918 and there would have been no Bolsheviks. Lenin thus decided in this situation to trade land (not his own) between the Black Sea and the Baltic Sea "selling" it to Kaiser Wilhelm II's generals in exchange for the time required by the Bolsheviks to entrench themselves in power. Above all, to organize a military strike force loyal to them, one built from scratch: the Red Army. Lenin was confident and was, generally accurate in his predictions, that soon the moment would come when Germany would lose the war on the Western Front. That would be the moment when the Red Army would spring forward towards the Vistula, and then onwards towards Berlin where the banner with the hammer and sickle would soon be hung.

On 17 November 1918, six days after Germany signed the armistice, which would prove to be, its de facto surrender on the Western Front, the head of the then-nearly one million-strong Red Army, Leon Trotsky, at a briefing in Voronezh just North East of the current Ukrainian border, announced the sovietization of Poland, Ukraine and Finland, referring to them as the links between Soviet Russia and a future Soviet Germany. This showed the most critical geopolitical direction of the Bolsheviks, for which Poland itself was unimportant it was merely "transit" territory. The most important thing for them was to reach Berlin, to reach the proletariat of Germany.

This resulted from the principles of Marxist doctrine, for which the economic base was the key element, and Germany was clearly the most economically powerful country in continental Europe. The social facts on the ground were also the result of this economic base. Germany had as a result the largest working class in Europe. It also had the most significant number of conscious, informed workers, affiliated with social democratic organizations, which the Bolsheviks believed would inevitably move to join the communist side. Since the largest workers' movement existed precisely in Germany, it was, therefore, necessary to reach that location so that in the struggle of the revolution against the capitalist world, now reinforced with German economic and military might the scales would tip in favor of the revolutionary side.

Leon Trotsky (1879–1940), one of Lenin's closest associates. Co-founder and one of the leaders of the RFSSR, the USSR and the Red Army. An advocate of the theory of 'permanent revolution'. He was assassinated on Stalin's orders in 1940 in Mexico.

This conviction was deeply engraved in the consciousness of all the leaders of the Bolshevik party, people who were culturally fascinated by Germany, its military power, as well as its technical and organizational prowess. Lenin despised Russia, just as he despised the whole of 'sprawling Slavism', including Poland, as we can read in his letters from the many years spent living in Krakow, and the smaller Southern Polish towns of Poronin and Biały Dunajec. The German library and the Swiss post office were cultural models for him. He spoke German no worse than Russian (although I do not know whether he also swore in German as colorfully as he did in Russian, as we can read in his *Collected Works*...). Similarly, two other members of the Politburo of the Central Committee of the Bolshevik party, Lev Kamenev and Leon Trotsky (the Politburo was at that time composed of four members), were both of Jewish origin and were people culturally oriented toward the language of Karl Marx, i.e. towards Germany. They also despised Russia and it is important to realize this, as many Polish political actors of the time did. However, it so happened that the Bolsheviks won the revolution in Russia and so they had to deal with Russia's interests, in the geopolitical sense. It was the starting point for the implementation of their plans the keystone of which was Germany. With Germany conquered the advantage would be on the side of the Bolsheviks across the entire continent. Then together, they would prevail over France and England.

How could Germany be reached from Russia? Only through the corpse of 'white' Poland that was the Bolsheviks' reasoning. Moreover, this is the reason for the perhaps less famous metaphor coined by another man. One who like Trotsky, would prove to be a direct protagonist of Polish-Russian history, Joseph Stalin-Dzhugashvili. He was the fourth member of the then Politburo, not particularly fluent in German, a speaker of Russian though with a heavy Ossetian accent for all his life. He headed the People's Commissariat for Nationalities, i.e. he was in charge of preparing all nationalities that inhabited the Russian Empire for 'liberation' by the Bolsheviks. On 17th November 1918, when Trotsky announced the sovietization of the Polish Republic and other countries, Stalin penned and published an article entitled *'The Partition wall'*, dealing with Poland and other 'dwarf little countries' which separate the mighty *kulak* of the proletarian revolution born in Russia from the equally strong hand of the German proletarian. These *kulaks* must break through

275

the thin divide, the thin (Polish) partition wall of these little countries, to at last shake the fraternal German hand of the proletariat in Berlin. The entire Bolshevik leadership agreed that this was the most important goal. Ideology was conveniently combined here with geopolitics and the matter did not end with mere ideological dreams; after all, Trotsky's statement above about the imminent sovietization of Poland was made at a briefing of the Red Army's higher command, this was to be the new reality in the neighborhood.

On 11–12 November 1918, when the armistice ending World War I was being signed in Compiègne, a meeting of Polish communists led by Julian Marchlewski (among others, the co-founder of the Comintern) was taking place in Moscow. As early as 11 November, exactly the date when we Poles celebrate the beginning of Poland's reborn independence, these Polish communists began to prepare the task set before them by the Kremlin. The task of conquering and sovietizing Poland. A month later, on 12 December, the Western Army, part of the Red Army, received operational orders to now preemptively seize Vilnius, and the towns of Lida, Baranowicze and Pinsk. An offensive was thus launched from the east, which soon occupied large parts of Lithuania and Belarus.

On 25 December, the newspaper *Izvestia*, the organ of the Lenin-led government of Soviet Russia, published an article entitled *'The Enemy'* by Yuri Nakhamkes-Steklov (who, we should add, was harrowingly described in the last moments of his life in Alexander Wat's memoir *My Century*). Steklov's article outlined that the 'counter-revolutionary center' in Vilnius was about to be smashed and announced that a socialist Lithuanian government was being formed in its place. Thus, *Izvestia was already* reporting what *was about to* happen, and the Red Army then simply would bring this "news" to its natural realization. The same Moscow daily, on 7 January 1919, conveyed the following thought in an article under the telling title *Revolutionary prospects in Poland*: 'The forthcoming period in Poland will be a time of disappearance at lightning speed of the ideology of the nation-state present in the broad masses of peasants and workers'.

Izvestia somewhat exaggerated this lightning speed, for it took more than 90 years for the Marxists, the Red Army and today's neo-Marxists, to truly spread by force and by stealth their influence all the way to the West including several opinion-forming political institutions of Western Europe and

Another Bolshevik propaganda poster; this time showing the enthusiastic welcome of the Bolshevik 'militants' by working people of all nations.

North America. Though it appears they may not have fully succeeded in this endeavor, yet. At that time, in 1919, they certainly had not yet succeeded in any envisaged field of activity in the west. The Red Army, however, sacrificially it tried and bled to meet the timetable set. The very next day, 8 January, *Izvestia* announced the establishment of the Revolutionary War Council of Poland, that is, the first Soviet government for Poland, something almost no one in Poland remembers today. We do remember the later Provisional Revolutionary Committee of Poland from Białystok that of Marchlewski and Dzerzhinsky, but we have wrongly forgotten that already in January 1919, a Soviet government for Poland was ready and waiting. It was to be headed by: Samuel Łazowert, Adam Śliwiński-Kaczorowski and Stefan Brodowski-Bratman. We do not remember these names, for, the plan failed, and they played no lasting role. This was not because the Red Army simply stopped its advance westwards after capturing Vilnius on 1 January 1919. It happened because it *was* stopped, halted by the determined resistance of the nascent new Polish Army, which came out to meet it head on. The Red wave clashed with it in the area of what is now western Belarus, near Bereza Kartuska. There, in the subsequent stalemate the unmoving front of the Polish-Soviet War was established for more than a year. Having advanced 400 kilometers westwards, having taken Vilnius, Pinsk, Baranovichi, Lida all those towns and cities mentioned in Trotsky's earlier order, the Red Army was halted. The rapidly resurgent Polish Army blocked its way further west towards Warsaw and Berlin.

The Committee of Communists, with its composition determined in Moscow, did not reach the Vistula River and did not replace the legitimate government of Ignacy Paderewski. A Government performing its duties based on a political compromise between Piłsudski's Warsaw centrist movement and the National Committee (of Dmowski) in Paris. A government it should be noted approved by a democratic verdict of the elected. Universal franchise (for men and women), the new democratic Polish Sejm. In the following months, the danger arising from the plans Lenin, Trotsky and Stalin had set in motion was postponed, it seemed possibly forever by the violent and irregular dynamics of the Russian civil war. The Red Army now had more urgent concerns focused on eliminating the threat from the internal enemy, the 'Whites', than with implementing its plan to sovietize Poland

and break through further towards Berlin. The bitter and bloody Russian civil war, in which the 'Reds' eventually defeated the 'Whites', continued throughout almost all of 1919.

It is regarding this period, the time leading up to and that subsequent to the Red victory in the civil war, that the most serious accusations and criticisms directed towards Polish leaders of the time, still relate. Accusations and criticisms that have riven and divided Polish historical debate and politics for the last 100 years. Most if not all of them were in fact put forward by Russian or Russian leaning publicists since 1920, being later repeated by, among others, eminent figures such as the author Aleksandr Solzhenitsyn. Today they continue to be commonly raised by contemporary Russian publicists and their more naïve, foolish or indeed perhaps complicit followers in Poland. One of the accusations is that we the Poles did not help the 'Whites' in the fight against the 'Red plague' when there was still a chance stop it, to avoid so many of the later misfortunes. The eminent *émigré* writer Józef Mackiewicz also repeated this accusation in his journalism. He also writes about it in a particularly interesting way in his correspondence with the National Democracy ideologue Jędrzej Giertych (I had the opportunity to read these letters in Mackiewicz's archive in Rapperswil). Mackiewicz, an anti-communist and anti-nationalist, and Giertych, a firm nationalist, both agreed on one point, that Piłsudski could have helped to destroy the 'Red Hydra' and did not do so because of his hatred for Russia. Mackiewicz was outraged that the interest of the nation-state, the interest of Poland, could have prevailed over a clear anti-communist imperative. Giertych in turn condemned most everything Piłsudski would do. Both agreed that it had been imperative to help the 'White' generals, even though these men of the Tsar would clearly not have agreed to the rebirth of a Polish Republic of the kind most Poles envisaged after any such White victory. At most, they would have accepted something like a truncated Congress Kingdom, under no circumstances recognizing the rebirth of a sovereign Poland, certainly not a Poland with borders extending eastwards beyond the Bug River.

Let us, therefore, take a closer look at whether the allegation made by the publicists mentioned above is indeed tenable. In October 1919, the army of 'white' Russia, above all its southern section commanded by Anton Denikin (the Polish-born son of a Polish dressmaker and a Russian officer),

Lenin and his diligent disciple Stalin at a meeting in a country house in Gorki. Photo taken by Lenin's sister, Maria.

was advancing from the south, closing to a distance of 300 km or so from Moscow. Denikin had already taken Kursk and Oryol, important cities in central Russia. Some considered that the Bolsheviks were at risk at this point. Simultaneously, the second round of secret Polish-Soviet negotiations was already underway, conducted with Piłsudski's knowledge on the one hand and Lenin's consent on the other. Poland was not at the time actively fighting against Bolshevik Russia there was a stalemate in the lands of western Belarus. As of 1 September 1919, Poland suspended all active hostilities, allowing for the withdrawal of 40,000 Red Army soldiers from the anti-Polish front, who could then be turned against Denikin.

280

The Red Army, however, at that point in time already totaled 3.5 million soldiers. The three of the scattered centers of the 'White' armies that existed at the time, Admiral Kolchak's already shattered army in Siberia, General Yudenich's tiny but strategically crucial Baltic bridgehead, and finally, Denikin's third and largest, together had only 656,000 troops. Now let us try to calculate even if this provides limited proof, (history is not an experimental science) can we prove anything by projecting backwards with alternative scenarios. Let us calculate if those 40,000 Red Army soldiers had not been withdrawn from the anti-Polish front, could the 656,000 have won against 3.5 million? It would be intellectually precarious to make such an assumption. Mathematically undoubtedly incorrect, but is it historically a realistic possibility? I leave the speculative answer to this question to you the reader...

Why then instead did Piłsudski's active assistance to Denikin not materialize. Though there were attempts to establish political contacts between the two? I have devoted an extensive scholarly book to just these matters, *Poland and the Three Russias* (White, Red and the Third). For which I endeavored to examine all possible archives from Moscow, via London, to New York. The archival traces leave no doubt, the representatives of 'White' Russia were exceptionally foolish spokesmen for the interests of their state. In this deadly struggle, in which the help of other nations was fundamental for the defeat of Bolshevism, simply essential, these men did not want to negotiate. Not only with Poland but any other nation that was fighting for its independence in the territories of the former Tsarist Empire. Denikin did not want to give up anything east of the Bug River to Poland. He made it clear that Poles had the right to install a Polish administration only up to the line of the Bug River and that what came next would be decided by the Russian Constituency when the 'Whites' reached Moscow. No one in Poland would have accepted such a compromise at the time, and no party could have accepted such an offer and hoped to legitimately remain in power. Had Piłsudski, the Head of State accepted it, he would have been considered a traitor to Poland's nascent new democratic state.

Piłsudski was however pondering should he make a deal with Denikin, accept the role (then covertly) assigned to Poland by the Western powers, to then at the most favorable moment strike to try and suppress Bolshevism? Or, on the other hand, should he hold back the offensive in the east, wait

281

for the civil war in Russia to be resolved, and for both sides to be weakened? Perhaps only then should Poland finally fight to irrevocably change the geopolitical map of Eastern Europe diminishing the Russian Empire creating a neighborhood where alongside a strong Poland room would be found for a Lithuanian-Belarusian state federated with Warsaw and also for a sovereign Ukraine? This latter option was undoubtedly Piłsudski's goal (something for which his opponents of the time and even contemporary critics continue to criticize him).

What was Piłsudski's thinking at that moment? This was best captured in a beautiful quote from a conversation he had with Count Michał Kossakowski at the Belvedere Presidential Palace on 31 July 1919, a man who had just been delegated to secret talks with Lenin's envoys, first in Białowieża and then in Mikaszewicze. Kossakowski noted down the words of the Supreme Commander on that same day, so this should represent a faithful account not clouded by the fog of distant memory. Here are then the cited words of Poland's then Head of State:

'We have such invaluable moments, such a wonderful opportunity to do great things in the east, to take the place of Russia only with different slogans, and we hesitate; we are afraid to perform bold deeds even against the coalition. I am not afraid of the power of Russia. If I wanted to now, I would even go to Moscow, and no one would be able to oppose my strength. However, you must know clearly what you want and are aiming for. Awaiting a change of mood overseas [this refers to the position of the Entente states – AN], we would not achieve anything. I would rather die than despair later in life that I lacked the courage to seize perhaps the only opportunity to resurrect a great and powerful Poland. We need more faith in our strengths and courage; otherwise, we will perish and fail to fulfil our task and separate Poland from its enemies so that it can write its greatness not through revolution and the terrible experiments of the east but by evolution. The stigma of enslavement lingers in our souls. Despite the thousandfold proof of how robust the power of Polish culture is and how much it has done in recent years – during which Poland as a state no longer existed – we are afraid to give it too great a task – now that the power of culture has been supported by statehood. And what of the fact that our generation is rotted through, debased in the cradle of slavery. New generations will come along and claim better conditions of existence than some of our current cowards seem to find sufficient'.

We may agree or disagree with Józef Piłsudski's way of thinking. Still, it was undoubtably a way of thinking about a great and fully sovereign Poland that was not afraid to take on significant tasks yet fearful of the impact or interference of those with modest foresight and bereft of the ability see and seize the moment, people who through hesitation would ultimately drive Poland into oblivion. We must also remember that the decision to hold talks at Białowieża on a temporary, informal ceasefire on the anti-Soviet front was taken up by Piłsudski at a moment of extreme difficulty for Poland. In August 1919, the Polish Army numbered, on paper at least less than 600,000 men. Most of these were conscripts without experience, only just 'drafted'. With such an army, indeed with only a fraction of it truly capable of frontline combat, it was challenging, indeed fanciful to think of a 'Moscow expedition'. All the more so since the Treaty of Versailles had not yet been ratified. At any moment, there was a threat of renewed war in the west with the Germans not yet fully disarmed or reconciled to the loss of Pomerania or even Greater Poland (the area around Poznan) and the fate of Silesia with its heavy industries, rich natural resources and mixed ethnic composition also hung in the balance. It was necessary to have an army ready for such a situation in the West.

On 24 September 1919, the Polish high command, i.e. Piłsudski, decided to send a delegation to a second meeting with representatives of the Soviet side in Mikaszewicze. Piłsudski's personal envoy was Captain Ignacy Boerner, and Lenin's envoy was Julian Marchlewski. The two most important conditions dictated by the Polish Supreme Commander for a possible tactical agreement with the Bolsheviks boiled down to the following: 1. That Bolshevik Russia renounced completely the ideological struggle and the export of the revolution (this was like asking a wolf to give up its nature and not hunt sheep); 2. That the 'Red' Moscow would recognize Ukrainian independence and that the Red Army would not attack Poland's strategic ally, Ukraine. That state was still struggling in its first fight for independence of the modern era with the Ataman Symon Petliura, representing Ukraine. The earlier Ukrainian People's Republic had firstly been driven back from Kyiv by Soviet Russia and then additionally attacked by Denikin's forces.

Ukraine was fighting with the remnants of its strength to maintain its new statehood, having by now been virtually confined to the vicinity of Kamieniec Podolski.

Leon Trotsky communicated Pilsudski's conditions presented to Marchlewski at a Politburo meeting on 14 November. On the issue of exporting the revolution, the Soviet leaders could, of course, promise not to export anything, they wouldn't keep their word anyway. On the other hand, there was a more significant problem with the second condition, Ukraine. For here, the demand was very specific, and it would be a quick test of the Bolsheviks' credibility. So, they answered unequivocally that they would not give up Ukraine. It was and must be Soviet because the power of the Kremlin, of any Kremlin, including the 'Red' Kremlin, depended on Ukraine. Denikin and the Whites knew it too. It was the bridgehead, for the revolution; White and Red both knew that without Ukraine, they could not achieve anything in Europe.

It is worth remembering that Piłsudski had earlier given a conditional approval to a project to help 'White' Russia. Still, this would have had to be also supported by the West. Poland could not afford an expedition to Moscow on its own (especially in terms of finance and equipment). He, therefore, asked his Prime Minister Ignacy Paderewski to request of the Entente Supreme Council, i.e. primarily British Prime Minister David Lloyd George and French Prime Minister Georges Clemenceau, whether they would politically and economically give their endorsement and support for such a Polish offensive on Moscow to augment Denikin's efforts. This was on 14 September 1919, i.e. just before the talks began with Mikaszewicze. It is not, therefore, that Piłsudski immediately and wholly ruled out the possibility of aiding 'White' Russia. However, to pursue such a campaign against the will of the Polish people (who were primarily reluctant, certainly all the so-called People's Parties, as well as the PPS-Polish Socialist Party) to do so additionally without backing from the West? Such an action would have been madness. On 15 September, Prime Minister Ignacy Paderewski received an unequivocal answer from the Western powers: the Poles must not go to Moscow, the Entente would not support it.

Someone who holds a grudge against Piłsudski for not deciding to help Denikin under these circumstances is perhaps expressing the noblest of

General Antoni Listowski (left) commander of the Polish 2nd Army, in conversation with the Ukrainian Ataman Symon Petlura. Berdyczów, Kyiv expedition, April 1920.

intentions arising from knowledge of what Bolshevism would become in the following years and how many millions of victims it claimed. However, such criticisms and critics, would it seem, have wanted the Commander-in-Chief to perform political harakiri and not on just on himself, but also on the Polish state.

In a letter addressed to Józef Mackiewicz, who continued to raise the accusation that it was Piłsudski who 'saved Soviet power from collapse', the essence of that situation in the autumn of 1919 was perfectly articulated by the *émigré* historian Zbigniew S. Siemaszko:

'That Piłsudski did not want to support the "Whites" is hardly surprising. In the fight against the Bolsheviks, he could at least count on material help from the West, while in (any potential subsequent) fight against the victorious "Whites", the West would be entirely on the side of the "Whites". On the other hand, the demand that, for the sake of humanity, Piłsudski should cooperate with the "Whites" regardless of the consequences to himself is excessive; it would be hard to find a politician willing to sacrifice his interests in the cause of humanity. And besides, humanity, as we know from other examples, would never appreciate it. And, by the way, the "Whites" did not lose in principle because Piłsudski did not actively support them, but because they fought to restore a system that had finally come apart during the (great) war during which it demonstrated its incapacity to endure".

The Mikaszewicze talks were finally broken off at the end of November 1919, when it was already known that the Soviet side would reject the Polish conditions, and Piłsudski knew that he would have to reckon with a new offensive by the Red Army. A Red army that had already pushed Denikin into a deep defensive position. Then as a paradox, a sudden counter accusation against Piłsudski now emerged. It is in fact the same accusation simply inverted and now repeated about Poland's attitude towards Soviet Russia. In this case, it takes the form of a hypothetical thesis that it was still possible to compromise with Lenin. That Poland did not have to fight a war with the Red Army in 1920, and that just as in the previous case 'everything was Poland's fault'. This accusation we can even find repeated in (some) high school textbooks in Poland (a legacy of the Polish People's Republic) and even more strongly in the works of Western historians who unthinkingly (and sometimes perhaps even deliberately) adopt the pattern of Bolshevik propaganda or viewpoints according to which the war with Soviet Russia was actually initiated by Piłsudski, that it was Poland which was the aggressor in this war that 'started' only in April 1920 with the rash Polish 'expedition to Kyiv'.

Let us emphasize that the war had begun earlier, back in November 1918, with Soviet aggression, with the Red Army's expedition and conquest of Vilnius and of Pinsk (birthplace of the celebrated Polish journalist Ryszard Kapuściński). An advance halted only in February of the following year by the Polish Army. After a break in the fighting, in the late summer and autumn, on the threshold of the following year (January 1920), the Kremlin ordered a seminar paper by the Chief of the Operational Department of the Red Army General Staff, Boris Shaposhnikov, later Marshal of the Soviet Union (the actual commander leading the Soviet aggression against Poland in September 1939). The paper was a detailed plan for a general offensive against Poland. I found this plan in the military archives in Moscow in 1995 and published it as an argument against those who say that the 1920 war was the exclusive result of Piłsudski's 'imprudent decision'. This minutely detailed plan of the offensive against Poland was submitted at a briefing by the Supreme Commander of the Red Army, Sergei Kamenev, to the Chairman of the Military-Revolutionary Council of the Russian Federation, Leon Trotsky. Who, in turn, presented it to Lenin on 27 January. The project was approved for implementation by the highest Soviet authorities.

Shaposhnikov clearly stated in his paper that Poland remained the central strategic problem for the Soviet state in the west: 'On the western border, the Soviet is faced with a compact barrier of small states set up by the Entente against Bolshevism, ready to continue the struggle. The characteristics of Poland as the central link in this chain left no doubt that there could be only one solution, a military one. Poland is the largest territorially and the strongest in spirit of the reborn nations, already striving to secure its existence through the creation of an army of considerable size. Boosted by the Entente, with its inherent Polish 'honor' and developing chauvinism, thanks to its easy victories over our numerically weak troops, Poland is apparently eager to take on the role of 'messiah' in the East. The military-political situation definitively places Poland in the ranks of our open enemies, the Entente's most faithful and righteous agent, a country intoxicated by its own successes while at the same time striving to be at the forefront of the eastern policy of the destroyers of European culture'.

Staff officer Shaposhnikov further outlined what specific forces and means and at what sections of the front, they were to be developed to achieve the military objectives. The offensive's first phase meant retaking Vilnius, Lida, Minsk, and all of Belarus. It was at this point that the further plan for the offensive broke down at the Bug River, where its continuation required political decisions. Where was the Red Army's assault on the Polish front to lead to, exactly? This could not be decided by military specialists but only by the top political leadership. We can learn about this, for example, from Lenin's correspondence with Trotsky and from the slogans published on 28 February 1920 in *Pravda* [the official publication of the Central Committee of the Bolshevik party – *editor's note*]: 'The Polish imperialists are shamelessly reaching out for a huge part of the Soviet republics. Comrades, we shall be as together as a clenched fist. Proletarians, we will stand firm with hammer and rifle in hand'. Deeds followed these words; on 1 March 1920, the Military-Revolutionary Council, the highest military authority in Soviet Russia, decided to accelerate conscription by six weeks for the next mobilization. It was also now when the transfer of entire divisions and brigades from Siberia and central Russia to the Polish front accelerated. Russia was mobilizing for war against Poland just as she had done against Germany in the prelude to the outbreak of WWI.

These preparations included an offensive plan approved by the highest Soviet authorities from 10 March onwards. In Smolensk (once again Smolensk as a strategic point on the map!), where the Red Army's Western Front staff was based, a meeting was held with the Army's Supreme Commander, Sergei Kamenev. It confirmed that the main blow would be inflicted in the direction of Minsk and then further on towards Warsaw. The supporting strike of Semyon Budyonny's 1st Horse Army was to go towards Berdychev, Rivne, Kaunas and Brest. These two strikes from the south and north were to meet at Brest, continuing together towards Warsaw.

Piłsudski however preempted the strike which had been scheduled for early May. As we know, he commenced his own offensive on 25 April directly at Kyiv and with Ukrainian support. He struck there for political reasons. He believed that, with the help of the Polish Army, he would be able to shield

Top: Lenin addressing Red 'militants' on Sverdlovsk Square in Moscow on 5 May 1920, shortly before the all-out assault against Poland. Bottom: Representatives of the 'Polrevkom' who were to form a government in Warsaw on Bolshevik orders. After the Polish victory at the battle of Warsaw, they fled eastwards in panic.

the Ukrainian state that was then fighting for survival. He had to make great efforts to explain the actual sense of the whole undertaking to a considerable part of political opinion in Poland that was reluctant to prolong the war. Even more so to those reluctant in particular to support the independence aspirations of Ukrainians, (TN Start) Ukrainian nationalist had tried to seize Lwów/Lviv only a year earlier leading to bloodshed between the two nations as they struggled towards their often, geographically conflicting visions, of independence (TN End). So, gathering to his side the army generals and officers politically unconnected with his camp, who were to provide a large part of the military basis for the project Piłsudski explained the gambit in highly literal terms. Ukraine was to be a dam holding back Russian imperialism, be it 'White' or 'Red'.

The political communiqué of the Volhynian Front Command of 1 March 1920 proclaimed bluntly that: 'The Head of State and the Polish Government support the absolute weakening of Russia to reduce the danger threatening Poland from both Bolshevik and monarchical Russia'. Sometimes, as in Piłsudski's conversation with the Apostolic Nuncio, Archbishop Achille Ratti, but also the political journalism published in preparation for the adoption of an alliance with the Ukrainian leader Symon Petliura, there were notes and references deepening the vision of the conflict to the rank of a clash of civilizations and cultures. This was Poland returning to its role of a shield and sword for the West in its eternal struggle with the onslaught from the East. As Poland's Head of State submitted to the later Pope Pius XI, Ukraine was to be a kind of extension a continuation of Poland's mission in this domain.

At the same time, while preparing the Ukrainian card with the maturing Petliura alliance, Piłsudski was also preparing his additional Russian card, the card of a new non-imperial Russia a Third Russia. In January 1920, that idea was revealed in talks he held at the Belvedere with Boris Savinkov and Nikolai Tchaikovsky, representatives of this 'Third Russia', i.e. a republican one that was anti-Bolshevik, but also crucially not oriented towards a restoration of the Tsarist Empire. It was here that the most secret and ambitious dimension of Piłsudski's strategic concept was revealed. Years later, its significance was most succinctly recalled by Józef Czapski. The young Czapski was a friend to a group of Russian *émigrés* now seeking the last viable foothold for their national hopes paradoxically in Warsaw.

He enthusiastically supported their search for a political accommodation with the Polish Head of State. 'In short, they wanted to create a kind of political unity (at least in a cultural sense) between Russia, Ukraine, and Poland. From Poland's point of view, it was vital that the game was three sided and not two sided. It is a well-known thesis in politics that you can play sides only when there are two potential partners, not only one. So, for Poland, these two sides were going to be Russia and Ukraine.

Piłsudski was indeed playing both with Russia and Ukraine. In his 'maximum' plan, he was looking to replace the Russia of Lenin and Trotsky but also the White the Russia of Kolchak and Denikin with a 'Third Russia', personified by Savinkov. This was to be a partner that would, as it were, aid and abet in the divesting of Russian statehood from its imperial heritage. A Russia that would come to terms with the loss of Ukraine. For even the successful placing of Ukrainian statehood in an alliance with Poland was still no guarantee for the long-term viability of a new political order in Eastern Europe. After all, a Russia bent of revenge and reconquest, with its vast natural and geopolitical reserves, would always be capable of destroying or at least seriously imperiling any such order based on a Warsaw-Kyiv axis. The ideal solution would therefore be to extend this new axis all the way to Moscow.

The road to such an ideal was naturally a long one. It required first to break the Bolsheviks in military confrontation followed by the successful launch of a revived Ukrainian statehood on the Dnieper. The Russians chosen as partners, Savinkov and a group of his political associates – had to be induced to accept that most challenging condition for any Russian: to part not with Warsaw but with Kyiv. The capital of Rus with all the religious and founding heritage associated correctly or incorrectly with that city for the history of the Russian state. At the starting point of the talks, in January 1920, Savinkov was still being persuaded by Piłsudski that the latter did not identify his planned action solely with Petliura and Ukraine. The border issue was also naturally relegated to a topic for the future. It was overshadowed by the vision of 'creating a testing ground for Russian democracy under the cover of Polish bayonets', as Savinkov himself put it. He and the volunteer formation of General Stanisław Bułak-Bałachowicz, which could be used to both renew the idea of a federation in the North, involving Belarus and

291

also serve as a striking force one the 'Third Russia', was to play a role in the last act of the strategic scenario. A scenario that Piłsudski began to put in motion in April 1920. It first though had to be preceded by complete success in the initial 'Ukrainian' act. Otherwise, the scenario written for the 'Third Russia' did not stand the slightest chance of even being played out.

The Kyiv offensive was intended to give Petliura a chance to stabilize the shaky foundations of Ukrainian statehood. The political sense of this action, without revealing his most secret plans for Russia itself, was most clearly explained by Piłsudski to General Anton Listowski, who was to succeed him in command of the Ukrainian Front: 'By going deep into Ukraine, but only to the [17]72 borders, by the same token illustrating we do not recognize the partition and by then proclaiming 'independence' in these lands we were as if correcting the mistakes of our ancestors. We want to give [Ukraine] the possibility of self-determination and rule by its own people. I've taken a gamble, and I'm playing my last gamble to do something for Poland in the future if only to weaken the possibility of a future powerful Russia and, if successful, to help create a Ukraine [...] But the question is whether this Ukraine will come into being and has (it) enough strength in its people to create and organize itself, as we cannot sit here (there in Kyiv) forever. I can't create [17]72 borders, as I once wanted to; Poland doesn't want these borderlands, Poland doesn't want to make sacrifices, and all parties have clearly stated that we don't want to bear the costs or give anything and without exertion, sacrifices, nothing can be created! So there is no other way out – but to try to create an "independent" Ukraine. Petliura plays no role here; he is a tool, nothing more. And if nothing can be done, we will leave this chaos to its own fate. [...] And what happens further... the future will show!'.

Piłsudski only envisaged Polish military support for Ukraine until autumn at the most. Was this the root of the plan's failure? Perhaps instead his own military mistakes? The strength of the Soviet thrust in the north? Perhaps above all, it was the lack of significant organized support from the Ukrainian population for yet another attempt at building anew their statehood, even though this time it was supported by foreign Polish bayonets. All these factors combined with the absence of real determination (or perhaps even strength) on the part of Polish society to engage in this semi-conspiratorially prepared plan for realization of the Chief of State's great eastern policy. Yes,

The Polish Army entered Kyiv on 7 May 1920 as part of Piłsudski's pre-emptive strike against the Red Army; the photo shows Khreshchatyk Street, the city's main artery. In the upper photo, Gen. Edward Rydz-Śmigly reviews the parade of Polish troops.

the plan's failure had multiple sources. In July, Piłsudski irritably stated that the Ukrainians themselves had to make a *fait accomplis* being cognizant of the fact that contrary to the opinion of Europe, Poland could no longer engage in military support of Petliura. On the other hand, Piłsudski also knew that he could not allow Petliura to draw on the strength of Ukraine in Eastern Galicia (an area of territorial dispute between Polish and Uranian nationalists) in spite of the apparent acceptance for this in Polish public opinion. Earlier in the campaign, during a conversation at the Belvedere in May with Roman Dmowski, who was naturally expressing his reservations about a move to create an independent Ukraine. A state that according to him, was bound to eventually turn against Poland. Piłsudski finally gave vent to his exasperation at the weakness of the tools offered to him by history: 'if Poles are such fools that they cannot master it [Ukraine], then they are not worthy of a better fate [than that which would await Ukraine]'.

The Polish-Ukrainian Kyiv operation in late April and May 1920, did however, weaken and delay the momentum of the prepared Soviet assault on the Vistula, an assault which had been in preparation since the beginning of the year. On the threshold of July, however, the great offensive of the Red Army was launched and strengthened by reinforcements from all over 'Red' Russia. An order from the Commander-in-Chief of the Western Front directed at Warsaw, Mikhail Tukhachevsky, dated 2 July 1920, read: 'Red soldiers! The hour of retaliation has struck. The armies of the Red Banner and the armies of the rotting White Eagle face a deadly clash'. Here is the additional content of Tukhachevsky's orders: 'Before the offensive, fill your hearts with anger and cruelty. Drown Piłsudski's criminal government in the blood of the crushed Polish Army. An iron-clad infantry, brave cavalry, and menacing artillery must sweep away the white trash like an unstoppable avalanche. Let the cities destroyed by imperialist war witness the revolution's bloody retaliation against the whole world and its minions. Soldiers of the workers' revolution! Turn your gaze to the West. In the West, the fate of the world revolution is being decided. Treading over the corpse of 'white' Poland leads the way to the world on fire. On our bayonets, we will carry happiness and peace to working humanity. Onwards to the West! To decisive battles, to resounding victories! Prepare the battle columns. The hour of the attack has come. To Vilnius, Minsk, Warsaw – march!'.

This order, dated in Smolensk, was signed by Tukhachevsky and two political commissars – Józef Unszlicht, who was to oversee the sovietization of Poland, and Ivars Smilga. It is difficult to accuse them of lacking sincerity in this lecture on the aims of the great offensive, the 'rotting white eagle' was to be beaten back by the 'red banner'. The offensive was launched on 4 July. 'Over the corpse of "white" Poland', the Red Army was to go further west. Its rapid success caused what can be called, in the words of Lenin, from a pamphlet he published, a 'dizziness of success'. What this head spin looked like can be seen from the exchanges of correspondence in the second half of July 1920 between members of the Politburo. Of course, the most important voice was that of Lenin, Trotsky in second place, Lev Kamenev in third and Stalin in fourth. Zinoviev and Bukharin were at the time only deputy Politburo members.

Lenin wrote this to Stalin on 23 July: '...I, too, believe that it is necessary at this time to stimulate the revolution in Italy. I think that Hungary should be sovietized for this purpose, and perhaps also Czechoslovakia and Romania'. Why was this suggestion addressed to Stalin? Well, he was at that moment the commissar, or political overseer, of the South-Western Front, which was going not towards Warsaw, i.e. Berlin, but now instead to the south, to Lviv and onwards. That is why Lenin spoke to Stalin about Italy, Romania and Hungary. These were to be Stalin's next destinations after taking Lviv and Krakow. Germany was to be dealt with by Tukhachevsky and Unschlicht. Stalin, who had promised to take Lviv within a week, answered Lenin the next day: 'Now that we have the Comintern and a defeated Poland, and a more or less decent Red Army, it would be a sin not to stimulate a revolution in Italy. The question of organizing an insurrection in Italy and in such unconquered countries as Hungary, and Czechoslovakia, must be posed. Romania will have to be smashed. In short: it is necessary to hoist up the anchor and set sail before imperialist forces have had time to repair their crumbling wreck'. Comrade Stalin also had colorful language, although not as much as Lenin. (TN Start) One can only imagine the impact such words and sentiments could have had on Italian political activists both communist and especially fascist in the subsequent years (TN End)

The aim, therefore, was to sovietize what was essentially the whole of continental Europe. The road to London was still perhaps a little too far, but the rest of Europe appeared within reach, if only Warsaw could be sovietized. Yet Warsaw did not fall. That is the significance of the Battle of Warsaw for Europe, something we here in Poland often forget. This battle did not only save the independence of the country for 20 years. Not just allow the culture of a newly independent Poland to flourish and mature; above all, it also allowed the nation to bring forth a magnificent generation of Poles, the greatest of our country's 20th-century history, the generation of Krzysztof Kamil Baczyński, Tadeusz Gajcy, the future Pope JP II Karol Wojtyła. It allowed these men to survive and thrive, to mold their character in those 20 precious years of liberty. This victory also allowed at least part of Central and Eastern Europe to survive for 20 years without the destructive influence of totalitarian imperialism out of Moscow. Without it, there would have most likely been no Czechoslovakia, no Romania, no Lithuania, no Latvia, no Estonia, no Finland, perhaps even no Austria, and perhaps no more countries further afield. Britain at the time decided to accept the perceived facts on the ground and the impending sovietization of Poland. France did not like it, but it could not effectively help Poland by itself. France and Britain would not have agreed so quickly to the sovietization of Germany, and some new continental war would inevitably have started. It isn't easy to say whether there would have been any compromise as a result though if one had emerged it would have certainly involved some new measure of Polish sacrifice and enslavement. For the sovietization of Poland was openly and unreservedly agreed to by the most important state in Western Europe, of the Entente, i.e. Great Britain. Such was the declaration made by the British Prime Minister to Lev Kamenev a member of the Politburo of the Bolshevik party, person number 3 in the hierarchy of Soviet power. A delegate who was received with honors in London on 10 August 1920 as the Soviet armies closed in on Warsaw. We should of course add that the Minister of War in Lloyd George's Cabinet at that time, Winston Churchill, was opposed to such a shameful policy, but was also powerless to stop it.

Poland, as we know, won the Battle of Warsaw and then the subsequent September Battle of the Niemen, achieving peace with the treaty of Riga. It won because the 960,000 recruits in the Polish Army were aware of the stakes in this battle and prepared to fight, to the end. Some historians and columnists seemingly possessed of the curious specialization to find every fault and flaw in of historical Poland often emphasize today that there were mass desertions from the army and protests against this war. Of course, there were desertions (though not mass ones); there are desertions from every army and always there are those who protest against the war. Yet in August 1920 these were protests by negligible minorities. If the majority had deserted, as they did from the Tsarist army in 1917, as they did from the Ukrainian military in 1917, Poland would not, could not have survived. The majority of Poles instead bore witness in 1920 to their will to fight for an independent Homeland. Most of them were people who only became conscious Poles over the previous two or three generations. These were the descendants of the old Polish peasantry previously more tied to the land and locality than any notion of a nation who formed the core of that army. They decided who would win the Battle of Warsaw. After all, it was also to them that the Bolshevik propaganda machine was constantly addressing its message. Encouraging them to desert turn in their bayonets, just as their Russian, Ukrainian and Belarusian Slavic brethren had done. These Polish peasant-soldiers instead defended their homeland, they defended Poland.

After the miracle on the Vistula in Polish leadership there was a return to the 'minimum' variant plan, that is, to the defense of that space separating Bolshevik Russia from the centers of Polish national life. The pursuit of the 'Russian' act, i.e. expelling the Bolsheviks from the Kremlin and installing representatives of the 'Third' option, non-imperial Russia in its place, was firmly out of the question. Its proponents Savinkov and Bulak-Balakhovich could only act as a kind of helpful diversion, supporting the Polish military effort against the Red Army in its final phase and also as an asset in the truce and peace negotiations now beginning in Riga. The only symbolic though short-lived result of Piłsudski's undertaking a grand strategic game simultaneously with his chosen Ukrainian and Russian partners came from "White" Russia. Whose last representatives, still fighting the Bolsheviks finally recognized Ukrainian independence. Drawn into Pilsudski's game by Savinkov, the last chance to prolong the real struggle and overthrow the rule of Lenin and Trotsky, the defending General Wrangel in Crimea agreed to this condition through his Foreign Minister, Peter Struve, on 1 November 1920.

Struve's modest formulation of the political principles of a possible alliance with Petlura under the aegis of Piłsudski's actions was expressed most clearly by the first point: 'The Supreme Command and the Government of the South of Russia agree that a freely elected Ukrainian Constituent Assembly will determine the future fate of Ukraine and its state system'. Unfortunately, it was only a White Russia taken to the edge of defeat that could accept some concept of Ukraine's right to independence. Just a few days later, Wrangel, his government and his army were pushed into the Black Sea by the Bolsheviks.

Savinkov, who remained hosted in a wing of the Belvedere in Warsaw, was able to continue to elaborate increasingly desperate, increasingly unrealistic plans, to which the Ukrainian People's Republic government, which also remained in exile in Poland, became his main partner. Indeed, the fact that on the day the Riga Treaty was signed, bereft of representation by either a 'Third Russia' or an independent Ukraine in the form of Petlura, the representatives of Savinkov's Russian Political Committee and the Government of the Ukrainian People's Republic adopted a draft agreement on the creation of a 'Union of States' around these two centers (Kyiv and Moscow) of the post-1917 former Russian Empire. This political line would be referred to later, after Piłsudski regained power in Poland in 1926, as the 'Promethean' initiative: organizing the cooperation and sustainment of anti-Bolshevik movements, especially among the non-Russian nations of the former Empire, under the patronage of Warsaw activity that would of course attract the ire of the new Soviet government and add to its desire for vengeance.

Poland stopped the 'Red Moscow' empire, nullifying the idea of the revolutionizing or, rather, a sovietizing of Europe. However, Piłsudski, like Lenin, failed in his grand project in 1920. In a clash with the mood of general fatigue after the great turmoil of war and revolution that had already exhausted the forces of Eastern Europe for more than six long years. A clash with the heritage of the history in this part of the continent. Yet it should be acknowledged that the very conceptualization of such a grand plan and the practical if ultimately unsuccessful attempt at realizing it, all this would become part of this common regional history. Influencing the future shape of things to come and showing perhaps the chance of some future accord

Marshal Józef Piłsudski portrayed by Aleksander Krawczyk.

Roman Dmowski (1864–1939), Polish independence activist and Polish delegate to the 1919 Paris Peace Conference. One of the signatories of the Treaty of Versailles.

in the region. How much suffering the Ukrainians, Poles and other peoples of Eastern and Central Europe including (perhaps first and foremost) the Russians themselves had to endure as a result of the political (as opposed to military) failure of 1920 was most painfully seen from the perspective of the subsequent years of communism's existence and expansion.

The accusation is sometimes made that when the armistice was concluded in October 1920, that the Poles did not go further east, and the chance of a full or a more complete victory was wasted. Here, too, historical reality must be defended against the fantasies of café strategists. Soviet Russia had at its disposal at that moment a Red Army that numbered, at least on paper, more than 4 million soldiers. Even if the actual force at Lenin's disposal was much smaller, it still exceeded Poland's mobilization capacity several times over. Moreover, no political party in Poland was in favor of further war and the Second Republic was undoubtedly a democratic country at the time. One where the conduct of war depended on parliamentary support representing the will of society. We also know that Piłsudski saw the hopelessness of further attempts to break Bolshevism at that point. He repeated to his adjutant, Major Kazimierz Świtalski, that everything had already been done and that we might reach Kyiv again and have to leave it again. When the whole of Polish society did not want any further fighting. When Ukrainian society did not want it, should the Polish army alone try to create a new order for Poland and Ukraine? Would that be democracy in action? Piłsudski realized that this would not, could not succeed in 1920. That the Polish state needed a period of stabilization, a pause, so to speak, as soon as possible. Let us not forget Poland's western borders were still fluid especially in Silesia where the border dispute with Germany would remain unresolved up until 1922.

The Riga Peace Treaty (1921), which ended the war with the Bolsheviks, is sometimes also subject to resentment, particularly acutely felt towards an influential member of the Polish peace delegation, Stanisław Grabski. Criticized for making too many concessions. However, it was not Grabski's error that led to Poland failing to obtain the whole of Belarus, allegedly offered to it at the time by the Bolshevik delegates headed by their chairman, Adolf Joffe. In fact, as we learned recently, thanks to Jerzy Borzęcki's incredibly insightful monograph on the Treaty of Riga, the Soviet side did not want to give up eastern and central Belarus even for a moment. What

301

the Polish delegation achieved in Riga was the realization of Piłsudski's minimum demand.

The Commander-in-Chief renounced pressure for Poland to obtain Minsk and instead wanted to acquire the so-called Grabski Corridor, i.e. a strip of Belarusian land that separated Soviet Russia from Lithuania. For Lithuania at the time was an existing recognized state. One regrettably now unequivocally hostile to Poland due to a tragic and violent dispute over Vilnius. This Lithuania even allied for a time with Soviet Russia against Warsaw at the most challenging moment for Poland during Tukhachevsky's offensive on the Vistula River. Yet Piłsudski, like any other Polish general, realized that if Soviet Russia maintained a direct link with Lithuania after the war, it would automatically also have a direct link with Germany, as Lithuania bordered with East Prussia. This would create an axis in which Lithuania, dominated by either Soviet or German influence or indeed both at once, would become a corridor and conduit for destroying Poland's strategic security and increasing the possibility of an attack on it. At that point, Piłsudski, like all the parties in the Sejm, wanted only to secure independence and to stabilize it.

In the autumn of 1920, it became apparent that Poland, after more than a century of partitions and six years of war unparalleled in its destructive power sweeping across its territory, simply did not have enough strength to fight on alone for the entire legacy of the Commonwealth. So, it came to a division of that heritage, with tragic consequences for Ukraine and Belarus and the nearly one million ethnic Poles left behind east of the border agreed at Riga. We will speak more on this further on. Yet Poland survived the first onslaught of Soviet Russia, which was the most important thing for its citizens and their heirs. Moreover, within the borders of this Second Polish Republic, at least part of the Ukrainian elite was also able to survive, albeit largely in conflict with the Polish state, but not destroyed by the programmatic genocide that Stalin would inflict on the Soviet part of Ukraine. The same was true of a divided Belarus. What was preserved, in this sense, was the starting point for a future renewal of other Eastern European nations, the region would not be just a Soviet empire.

From the view of 'Red' Moscow, the significance of stopping its march near Warsaw looked quite the opposite. Lenin's delegate to the 1920 alliance talks with Germany, Viktor Kopp, wrote with some melancholy to

The Russian General Anton Ivanovich Denikin (1872–1947) became one of the most important 'White' commanders opposing the Bolshevik movement after the October Revolution (1917). He did not recognize Polish aspirations for freedom.

Moscow on 4 November: 'The Peace of Riga has finally shattered the hopes of National-Bolshevik circles in Germany for a rematch in alliance with us'. Just before the final peace was signed in March 1921, he called the consequences of the 'disgraceful' – as he put it – treaty, formally confirming Moscow's acceptance of a strong, independent Polish state, with these words: 'There is no reason to make a boon out of necessity, to close our eyes to the fact that, separated now by a double wall from Western Europe, as a revolutionary factor we are losing, at the present moment, a great part of our influence'. He did not, of course, wring his hands but kept up his talks as best he could with German industrialists (including Krupp) and *Reichswehr* officers representing the secret 'R' Group, which had been set up in late 1920 by General Hans von Seeckt to prepare the groundwork for secret collaboration with the Red Army to circumvent the Versailles treaty.

And what did Lenin, the primary recipient of these remarks, think? In public speeches in October 1920, he, like Kopp, assessed Poland as 'a buffer separating Germany from Russia' and 'a battering ram [of Western 'imperialists', specifically France – *AN*] against the Soviet Republic'. He reiterated that 'it appeared that the peace of Versailles was holding on to Poland' and lamented that 'we did not have enough strength to see the war through'. After all, we have at our disposal another document, not introduced in Vladimir Ilyich's collected works, but a fascinating record of his reflections at the time on the possibility of a tactical alliance with Berlin. This record was made in the second half of September 1920. It conveyed the content of the strikingly frank and penetrating remarks Lenin made in a conversation with the Swiss delegate to the Second Congress of the Third International, Jules Humbert-Droz. The party leader and Chairman of the Council of People's Commissars seemed to be responding to Kopp's complaints: Nothing that bad had really happened, what goes around, comes around seemed to be the mood. The agreement with Germany is only temporarily delayed, once Poland is stabilized within the 'Riga-Versailles' borders those borders may even be guaranteed but it will be up to the Kremlin's hosts to decide freely when to 'consummate' the earlier agreement with the revanchist Germans. Lenin said it outright in the following words:

'Poland, we will possess it regardless when the hour strikes, and anyway, the projects for creating a 'Great Poland' are grist for our mill because as long as Poland claims it, Germany will be on our side. The stronger Poland becomes, the more the Germans will hate her, and we can use this indestructible hatred of theirs. [...] The Germans are our helpers and natural allies, for their bitterness at the defeat they have suffered leads them to riot and disorder, by which they hope to break the iron shackles that the Peace of Versailles is for them. They want revanchism, and we want a revolution. For the moment, our interests are shared. They will split eventually, and Germany will become our enemy on the day we want to see whether a new Germanic hegemony or a Communist European Union will emerge from the ruins of old Europe'.

This scenario as envisaged by Lenin, as we know later came to pass: via Stalin's pact with Hitler on 23 August 1939, followed by a great war between them ending, ultimately with the hanging of the red banner over Berlin. However, as Lenin put it, Soviet authorities failed to fulfil this project 'from the first blow' directed towards the Versailles system in 1920. The defeat of the Red Army at Warsaw pushed back by one generation the realization of the 'red' Kremlin's dream of reaching Berlin, the sovietization of all of Europe.

Let us note here that, paradoxically, in a similar way the Polish victory could be portrayed as a salvation, a chance a boon for the future for Russia itself! This is the assessment of the significance of the Treaty of Riga. A treaty that resulted in the forced severing of direct links between the Soviet state and Germany. An Assessment formulated by the original Moscow intellectual, Nikolai Trubetzkoy, creator of a new geopolitical concept in 1920, influential in Russia still to this day, that of Eurasianism. This idea, which I have analyzed at length in another study (*Metamorphoses of the Russian Empire, 1917–1921*), was taking shape within a group of young Russian émigrés in Sofia. For the Eurasianists, precisely with Nikolai Trubetzkoy at the head, the most important thing was the juxtaposition of Russia and Europe, i.e. the 'Romano-Germanic world'. The strength to persevere in such a perennial confrontation with the West was to be sought by Russia in its separate, not European, but Eurasian identity. The summer of 1920 was a particularly lively moment of discussion around the political significance of this identity: when first the Bolsheviks acted as defenders of the 'Ruthenian land' against the invasion of Kyiv by the 'Polish masters'

305

and then developed a great offensive westward, which 'over the corpse of "white" Poland' was to lead the new, 'red' Russia deep into Europe.

Fascinating remarks on the relationship between the Bolshevik movement and the West were put forth by Nikolai Trubetzkoy in a letter to a friend in Prague, a sympathizer of Eurasianism. A man who was also the founder of structuralism in linguistics, Roman Jakobson. Trubetzkoy wrote this letter from the perspective of the end of the Soviet-Polish War and the Riga negotiations that were already concluding. He was therefore proposing to embrace its totality and to consider the blood-chilling consequences for the Eurasianist arising out of the hypothetical success of the Bolshevik assault on Warsaw and the Red Army's arrival in Berlin. If Lenin had indeed succeeded in his plan and bolshevized Germany 'the axis of the world would have instantly shifted from Moscow to Berlin'. Trubetzkoy was aware that the ideological basis of Bolshevism communism, was by no means Russian but an efflorescence of the 'Romano-Germanic civilization'. The Germans would have built an ideal of a communist state in line with these Western sources, but in Russia as a result of its cultural difference this would be impossible to realize. After the fall of Poland and Tukhachevsky's arrival in the center of Germany, Berlin would become 'the capital of a pan European, or perhaps even an all-world Soviet republic'. Trubetzkoy had no doubts: 'Masters and slaves have always existed, are and will always be. They also exist in the Soviet system with us in Russia. In the universal republic, the masters will be the Germans, generally the Romano-Germans, and the slaves will be us, that is, everyone else. The degree of slavery will be directly proportional to the 'cultural level', that is, the remoteness from the 'Romano-Germanic pattern'. Trubetzkoy, resolutely anti-communist, did not see the Bolsheviks as any 'saviors' of Russia. Instead, it was rather the effect of their defeat in the Battle of Warsaw, the arresting of their march westwards, that would allow them to play the role of a formational element that would sustain the separateness and even the opposition of Russia towards the 'Romano-Germanic' world. The Eurasianists' assessment of the geopolitical consequences of 1920 can ultimately be summarized in one sentence: The Poles saved not only Europe from sovietization but also (Bolshevik) Russia from being subjected again to the yoke of the West that this time would have been focused in a Soviet Berlin.

306

The signing of the Treaty of Rapallo between the German Reich and Soviet Russia on 16 April 1922. From left: Reich Chancellor Joseph Wirth, German Foreign Minister Walther Rathenau and the Soviet delegation: Leonid Krasin, Georgy Chicherin and Adolf Joffe.

In a sense, Trubetzkoy was not wrong in this assessment regarding the consequences of Polish victory in 1920. Although Lenin was very keen to realize in one leap his world project or at least a European revolution, exploiting Russia only as the first base for this leap, he knew at the end of 1920 that, for at least a dozen years, Russia would remain alone as the power base of communism. In such an arrangement, Russia's traditional geo-strategic interests again took on fundamental importance for the current 'red' Kremlin leadership. There was a return to the strategy already known from the Treaty of Brest, at the beginning of 1918, based on the assumption that the Soviet state would survive and strengthen itself gradually, taking advantage

307

of the divisions in the camp of its 'imperialist' opponents. It was now possible to count on an economic and strategic partnership with Germany, defeated in the Great War and unreconciled to its outcome especially its new border with Poland. Moreover, it was possible at the same time to blackmail the Western powers with this agreement between Moscow and Berlin, treating it as leverage for the importance of Soviet Russia in international relations. This was how the way was opened for the not-too-distant Treaty of Rapallo, when, in April 1922, the People's Commissar of Foreign Affairs Georgy Chicherin and German Foreign Minister Walther Rathenau signed a treaty of close anti-Polish cooperation between Moscow and Berlin.

A broader, global horizon of possibilities was revealed in pitting 'red' Moscow against Europe, the West, of which Poland was again considered to be the bulwark, or rather even a hostile spearhead pointed at Russia. Here, Soviet Russia was entering a rut already gouged in intellectual and political history, at least from the time of the old formula of 'Moscow as the Third Rome', opposed to the Latin 'First Rome', on through the 19th-century variants of Slavophilism and Panslavism, to the Eurasianism just recently mentioned, the latest variant of building the same axis of conflict between Russia (non-Europe) and Europe proper.

Russia, or rather the Russians, would suffer unimaginable torment under Bolshevik rule, as did other subject peoples. Yet on the very threshold of the 1930s, having finally consolidated his power, Lenin's successor, Stalin, decided to openly identify the Soviet state with the Russian anti-Western tradition. On 19 July 1934, he addressed a letter to his Politburo colleagues entitled '*On Engels article: The Foreign Policy of the Russian Tsar*'. Frederick Engels, the co-founding father of communist ideology, was exposed by Stalin as a German nationalist, denigrating Russian history and politics in the name of the eternal hatred of the Western powers competing with Russia. Although the letter from the leader of the Communist Party of the Soviet Union (CPSU) was not published until seven years later, a dozen days before the outbreak of the German-Soviet war, a breakthrough in the Soviet system's approach to Russian history began as soon as he sent it.

At a Politburo meeting devoted to history textbooks at the time, Stalin expressed the meaning of this breakthrough in a concise formula: *russkiy narod, vsjegda prisoyediniawshyy drugiye narody, pristupil k etomu i seychas* (the Russian people, always appending other nations, has also joined in now). The policy of '*koryenisation*' (i.e. strengthening of cultural identity/roots) of the non-Russian republics came to an abrupt end. A top-down Russification policy replacement is now dominant, under Moscow's centralization, a synthesis of what was imperial, of what had served to expand the size of the state and its military-political power in the history of pre-revolutionary Russia – with a new Soviet identity. The historical synthesis of the new ideology was now being built around the Russian center, surrounded once again in this construction by the hostile world. The Western powers and their 'agents'. The Russian past, in previous years generally treated by the Bolsheviks like the Russian present, as terrain of brutal conquest, was transformed from 1934 onwards into a treasury of models of Soviet patriotism. Figures such as Prince Alexander Nevsky, the butcher of Warsaw's Praga district, Field Marshal Suvorov, and finally, immortalized in Sergei Eisenstein's propaganda film masterpiece, Ivan IV the Terrible himself served as Stalin's prototype or doppelganger (we mentioned this earlier), struggling against the state's internal and external enemies.

Stalin sketched the central tenets of his policy in subsequent military plans. We have an excellent monograph by the candid, wise, late Russian historian Oleg Ken (1960–2007), who analyzed the Soviet Union's military plans between the two world wars. His findings confirm that Poland was always mentioned first among the enemies to be attached. It was either Poland in combination with Romania, supported from afar by Britain, or, after 1933, Poland in combination with Germany, this is how it was imagined in Soviet strategic planning.

Stalin was preparing his country for war, for confrontation with the outside world. Still, an essential part of this preparation was internal transformation: industrialization and a huge, top-down social revolution, far bloodier than the Bolshevik Revolution of 1917. While the first phase of the Bolshevik revolution claimed more than 2 million victims, Stalin's top-down revolution of 1929–1938, roughly how long it took to remake Soviet society according to the Father of Nation's designs, claimed nearly ten times as many victims.

In embarking on this great economic and social operation, or rather this great crime, Stalin was afraid that his opponents should exploit the resulting temporary weakening of the Soviet Union. He, therefore, advocated a tactical improvement in relations with Poland at this time. It is fascinating to see how Stalin persuaded the leadership of the People's Commissariat for Foreign Affairs, systematically and steadily persistent in its hatred of Poland, to do so. Stalin was simply more calculating. In a letter to Deputy Foreign Commissioner Maxim Litvinov, a Vilnius-born Russian Jew with the family name Meir Wallach-Finkelstein, Stalin persuaded him not to get carried away with his hatred of Poland at that moment because, in 1931, the Soviet Union was facing a difficult situation, experiencing extremely deep, dramatic internal transformations. It is necessary at such a moment to grit one's teeth and conclude a non-aggression treaty with Poland. It was subsequently signed on 25 July 1932. And, of course, it was later trampled underfoot by Stalin, although it is not uncommon today to see it presented as another unrealized opportunity to arrange lasting, permanent relations between Warsaw and Moscow.

It is worth noting that, in addition to this pact (which later in 1934 was extended in duration until 1945), by invading Poland in partnership with Hitler, Stalin would break not only the Riga Treaty, of course, but several other bilateral agreements with Poland and international agreements that the Soviet Union had signed, such as the so-called Briand-Kellogg Pact (Pact of Paris) on the renunciation of war as a means of resolving political conflicts, signed in 1928.

For the Kremlin's host, agreements with 'Western enemies' had no lasting significance. After waging a great internal upheaval with violence, once he had begun to have an increasingly powerful industry at his disposal, Stalin also began to set increasingly ambitious military tasks. As early as the mid-1930s, he was already drawing up plans that called for the Soviet Union to have more aircraft and armored weapons than all the other countries combined. In quantitative terms, this plan was largely realized by 1939; Stalin had, in any case, more tanks and aircraft than all the European countries combined.

During the preparations for war, measured not only by the number of aircraft and other weapons produced, Stalin also paid particular attention to preparing society for it as well. For this reason, he based his new state ideology on the traditions of the Russian Empire. And it was also for this reason that he treated the non-Russian peoples of the empire, especially those who had their homeland beyond the reach of his power, as a potential 'fifth column' to be pre-emptively eliminated. No other nationality in the Soviet Union was thus affected by Stalinist terror to the same extent as the Poles. We must recall here Order no. 00485 of 11 August 1937, issued by the head of the NKVD, Nikolai Yezhov, based on a decision taken two days earlier by the Politburo of the All-Russian Communist Party (Bolsheviks). This order was in practice Stalin's decision. It was an order for the genocide of Poles living in the USSR. There had never been a single document published before that entailed the deliberate liquidation of such a large number of people based purely on ethnicity. Yezhov announced the fight against the 'fascist-insurgent, spying, sabotage, defeatist and terrorist activities of Polish intelligence services in the USSR'. Allegedly carried out by the huge network of the Polish Military Organization (acronym: POW – already broken up entirely within the Soviet state in 1921). He also set a clear task for subordinate NKVD services throughout the state for: 'the complete liquidation of the hitherto untouched broad, diversionary and insurgent hinterland of the POW and the basic human reserves [*osnovny lyudsky kontyngyntov*] of the Polish intelligence services in the USSR'.

This 'hinterland' and 'basic reserves' could have been formed by anyone with the entry of 'Polish nationality' in their internal passports. According to the 1926 census in the USSR, there were 782,000 such people. According to the next census, in 1939, the number of Poles in the USSR decreased to 626,000. This was precisely the effect of the system of unprecedented persecution to which Poles were subjected in Stalin's state. More than 150,000 were shot (not only in 1937–1938), died during deportations or were starved to death in 1932–1933. No less than every second adult male was deprived of life in this Polish community of fate.

The first book about this crime (*The First Punished Nation: Poles in the Soviet Union 1921–1939*, Warsaw 1991), written still without access to primary Soviet sources, was devoted to a Russian by birth, a professor at Opole University, Nikolay Ivanov. The work of Russian Memorial researchers Nikita Petrov and Arseniy Roginsky (1993 and 1997), who presented official NKVD data, was a breakthrough in understanding the scale of this operation. Those who are mistrustful of the Polish tendency to overemphasize 'suffering' should at least trust the NKVD's internal reporting. These are its figures: in the 'Polish operation', between September 1937 and September 1938, 143,810 people were arrested. Of these, 111,091 were executed. Not all were ethnic Poles; the number of indigenous Poles among those executed in this one operation is estimated at between 85,000 to 95,000.

The aforementioned order no. 00485, originally intended to last three months, was extended for nearly two years. Its deadly effects, let us recall more than 111,000 executed under a single order, that is, more than five times as many as in the entire Katyń operation of 1940 were complemented by another order from Yezhov, issued four days later. It bore the number 00486 and concerned the families of 'traitors to the fatherland' (not only Poles). Only those who had betrayed their loved ones could avoid arrest. Children over the age of 15 were subject to 'adult' repressions. The younger children were to be sent to orphanages or to work.

Harvard University Professor Terry Martin pointed out the unprecedented scale of the repression directed by the Soviet state against the Poles. Based on a list of names of victims shot in Leningrad in 1937–1938, he calculated that Poles were 31 times more prevalent than other populations of the city. In other words: a Pole in and around Leningrad was 31 times less likely to survive during the height of the Great Terror than the average resident of this city, most affected by Stalin's crimes.

Yale University professor Timothy Snyder calculated such a statistic for the entire Soviet Union at the time of the Great Terror: the Poles were, unfortunately, a chosen people within it. Stalin's choice determined that they were 40 times more likely to be shot than the average for all nations of the USSR. Poles accounted for 0.4% of the total population in the USSR but made up 13–14% of the 681,000 victims shot between 1937 and 1938. So much for dry statistics based on NKVD data. But, as Snyder rightly wrote in his book *Bloodlands* (2010), we must, above all, remember that each victim had a name and an individual biography and deserves human remembrance.

With poignant empathy, the fate of Poles murdered as part of NKVD operations in Ukraine from 1937–1938 was portrayed by perhaps the most eminent contemporary scholar of the Stalinist system, Professor Hiroaki Kuromiya of Indiana University. In his book *The Voices of the Dead: Stalin's*

The Second Polish Republic. The shape of its borders were fought over by the Poles with guns in hand, since at the Versailles talks, Poland was in fact originally granted territory covering a smaller area than the historical Duchy of Warsaw.

Great Terror in the 1930s (Polish edition 2008), we can see this great crime through the prism of the individual fates of people executed simply for saying 'Poland is a good country' (which constituted in itself 'fascist agitation') or for refusing to renounce a Polish husband or wife. Another authority on the study of Soviet totalitarianism, Professor Norman Naimark of Stanford University, in his book *Stalin's Genocides* (2011), does not hesitate to compare

313

the situation of Poles under Soviet rule from September 1937 up until July 1941 when the 'amnesty' from the Sikorski-Mayski agreement came into force, to that of the Jews during the Holocaust.

The American historian of Polish origin Marek Jan Chodakiewicz, as well as Nikita Petrov, draw attention to an essential aspect of remembering the crimes of the Soviet empire against the Poles – chosen as victims, not for any 'class' reasons, but precisely because they belonged to the Polish nation, hated in the tradition of that empire and always 'suspect': 'In remembering the victims, we honor them and simultaneously condemn the executioners. By passing on the story of the victims, we help others come to terms with their past. Coming to terms with the past is a challenge for post-Soviet people, mostly the descendants of the victims of communism, but they do not know this or do not want to know. [...] By raising the history of the extermination of Poles in the USSR, we are creating an alternative paradigm to the official [Putin's – *AN*] version of how to remember the victims. This official version is based on the Russification and Orthodoxisation of the victims. It is worth remembering these words as we watch the Orthodox Church begin to exert dominate over the Katyń massacre of imprisoned Polish officers in 1940. It is also worth hearing the voice of Nikita Petrov, an honest historian from the Putin-banned human rights organization 'Memorial', who lamented during Donald Tusks political rapprochement with Vladimir Putin that the current 'Russian authorities are acting in the role of those covering up Stalinist crimes'.

The dream of a 'Third', non-imperial Russia failed to materialize after Poland regained independence after the victorious repulsion of the Soviet invasion. However, if we want to preserve this hope for the future, regardless of how difficult that is to imagine in the present day, we must remember. We are indeed obliged to remember this history, as it actually was and not a version of it. We cannot allow ourselves to be told that for the sake of historical or contemporary 'non-aggression pacts' or the facilitation of economic collaboration, that we should simply forget about it.

'Liberation', i.e. Stalin Conquers Poland and Eviscerates the Commonwealth (1939–1945)

'The name Stalin is inextricably linked with the twofold liberation of the Polish nation' – this was the slogan that the Central Committee of the Polish United Workers' Party (PZPR), the ruling party under the authority of Stalin, issued as obligatory for all subjects, i.e. all inhabitants of Poland under Moscow's rule. It was formulated on the 70th birthday of the 'Father of Nations' in 1949. On this particular occasion, 3,376,000 copies of special color magazine supplements were printed, as well as 955,000 portraits, sheet music and books celebrating the 'Liberator'. This slogan of double 'liberation' was to be set firmly in the minds of all Poles and indeed it was. Although perhaps not in the way the creators of the slogan had initially imagined. However, the question remains: which past events and actions of Stalin were to be encompassed by this slogan this twofold expression of gratitude?

In 1920, Stalin marched as the political head of the South-Western Front on Lviv and Krakow – but at that time the policy of 'liberation' failed. Instead, Stalin's political legacy fits more closely within the context of the slogan describing Soviet aggression against Poland on 17 September 1939. A campaign 'liberated' just over half the territory of the Second Polish Republic together with several million of its inhabitants. The vast majority of this territory would be cut off from Poland once again, this time with finality after Moscow's "cooperation" with Berlin had been broken off and the Soviet Red Army rolled back the Nazi tide in 1944. This further partition of our country of Poland would then be recognized as politically expedient by Stalin's new allies Roosevelt and Churchill. Men who were latterly eagerly joined in this cynical geopolitical gesture by General de Gaulle of France. A 'proper' Poland, according to Stalin, i.e. the kind of Poland that even some Tsars would graciously agree to – a Poland pushed west of the Bug and the San Rivers was fully 'liberated' by the Red Army only in 1944–1945 (with south eastern borders broadly along the lines of the Piast dynasty and Rus border lands dispute of some 7 centuries earlier). After that, it was solely the process of liberation, or the 'de-fascisation', or de-nazification that was deepened. Under the supervision of NKVD divisions, Soviet 'advisors' in the security and defense ministries of Moscow's puppet government on the Vistula. Perhaps it was these two stages of 'liberation' that the PZPR referred to in this slogan: one carried out while the war was still going on, and then the other afterwards and continuing long after Stalin's death, until the Soviet Union itself collapsed and disappeared from the map?

In this chapter, we will look at the implementation of Stalin's plan in its first stage. It was a plan of geopolitical expansion, guided by the objectives set from the same hegemonic perspective that the previous non-Communist hosts in the Kremlin had held over the past centuries: securing the Empire on its crucial western flank. Here, the 'Polish question' inevitably had to be 'solved'. Let us first ask whether the so-called 'Father of Nations' had any personal motives for his attitude towards Poland other than simple imperial geopolitics (written it should be noted into the Communist plan). Some believed that Yosif Dzhugashvili might have been a Pole, or at any rate, the son of a Tsarist officer of Polish origin. In support of this thesis, one recalls the claimed visit of General Nikolay Przhevalsky (Pol. spelling – *Przewalski*) to the Caucasus near Gori, where Stalin was born. It so happens that this Russified Pole, Nikolay Przhevalsky (1839–1888), a general in Russian service, a great traveler, geographer and discoverer of very many previously undocumented places in Central Asia and Siberia, was a virtual visual copy of Stalin (or rather the other way around: Stalin resembled him 'from head to toe'). When we look at the bust of General Przhevalsky in the Museum of the Geographical Society in St Petersburg – we see a striking resemblance to Stalin. Many seekers of historical sensationalism have sought to highlight this resemblance as an opportunity to speculate about an affair between the general and a simple peasant woman from Gori, Stalin's mother, during General Przhevalsky's geographical exploration of the Caucasus.

In reality, however, Przhevalsky had never been to the Caucasus. He was primarily in Mongolia and Tibet where he was the first to describe the uncommon species of horse he encountered there, named in his honor, i.e. the Przewalski horse. He did not have an affair with Keke, Stalin's mother;

in fact, he was a representative of a different sexual orientation altogether and did not have relations with women. So, where did this passionate search for Stalin's 'Polish roots' come from, and why is it even worth mentioning in this book? Well, this theme is interwoven into the historical Russian-Polish accounts often as yet another reproach against Poles. From the Russian side the accusation reads as such. See you Poles the man who murdered the most Russians in history was your criminal, not ours, yet another '*Wallenrod*' (a mythical historical figure being the subject of another work by Mickiewicz and symbolizing a man who uses disguise and deceit to realize his patriotic goal against the enemy). Of course, this reproach is more often linked to another undoubted murderer of hundreds of thousands of Russians, who was unquestionably of Polish origin – Feliks Dzerzhinsky, founder of the Soviet crime machine: the ChK, later the GPU, OGPU, NKVD, MGB, KGB, now in its most modern form the FSB. There is a paradox here. Often, the same people who praise Stalin as the creator of the greatest empire in the history of Russian statehood, also at the same time, blame him and his alleged Polish origin claiming that this empire could have been built with a little less spilt Russian blood...

So, let us repeat: did Stalin, indeed a Georgian by descent, or perhaps as the people of South Ossetia claim the greatest Ossetian in history, have any personal, unique relationship with Poland? We know that he was in Poland. Between the second half of November 1912 and the second half of January 1913, he stayed in Krakow in a house at 237 Królowa Jadwiga Street, where Lenin also lived. He stayed in the shared quarters of Vladimir Ilyich, his wife Nadezhda Krupskaya and his mistress Inessa Armand for more than two months while on his way to Vienna, where he planned to study the national question as Lenin's designated party specialist.

Reflecting more broadly on whether the 'Father of Nations' had any nationalistic prejudices, several historians who have studied the matter (including Hiroaki Kuromiya, mentioned in the previous chapter) conclude that if so, they likely did not play a significant role in his actions. He is known to have pursued genocidal policies against various nations and was sometimes accused of anti-Semitism in connection with the anti-Semitic campaign he undertook in the last months of his life. However, Stalin approached all the mass crimes he organized calmly and pragmatically.

'Lenin in Poronin'. The stay of the revolutionary leader on the Vistula River and his frequent visits to the Polish mountains in 1913–1914 became an important element of communist propaganda after 1945.

Above all, he was guided by the principle of political interest, which he understood, as encapsulated by Alexander Wat the principle of concentrating maximum power or authority over a broad area. Added to this principle was the maxima of ruthless elimination of all potential opponents and rivals, provided they could be reached and eliminated. This was Stalin's uncomplicated political philosophy, acutely in line with the tradition of some Tsars, only implemented with incomparable brutality and on a far greater scale.

Not only was Ivan the Terrible Stalin's forerunner in this, but also, it must be admitted, Niccolò Machiavelli and his book *The Prince*. He first came into possession of this book during his Siberian exile from a fellow exile, Lev Kamenev, later Lenin's successor as Prime Minister of the government

319

of Soviet Russia. He left many interesting remarks in the margins of this copy. He refined Machiavelli's thoughts on the ways of exercising power by terror and deception, leaving out the republican part of the Florentine's legacy. He was not at all the dark or uneducated man some portray him to be. Stalin knew the basics of Latin and Greek (Greek better than Latin), knowledge he had acquired while attending the Tbilisi seminary; he is said to have read Plato in its original language version. He also knew some German. In general, he read a great deal, especially history books. To the end of his life, he was a passionate devourer of books – not just people. Characteristically combining these two passions, he added a real life postscript to his reading of that copy of *The Prince* he received. On 25 August 1936 in accordance with the orders of the then Kremlin 'prince', Kamenev was executed. Stalin ordered to have the bullet that went through Kamenev's skull brought to him. It was later retained as a trophy by the then head of the NKVD, Yezhov, who was carrying out the 'Great Purge' operation and who himself was also eventually executed on the orders of the Commander-in-Chief. Yezhov was accused of anti-Soviet activity due to his recent record of "unfounded arrests". With Yezov's death, Stalin could now keep this memento of Kamenev for himself. A shiver runs down one's spine at the thought of the inhuman, icy cruelty emanating from Joseph Stalin.

But was it only cold political calculation that determined Stalin's attitude toward Poland? I think some personal reckoning may have occurred in connection with the 1920 war. The defeat of the Stalin-led attack on Lviv and the further dashing of his dreams of onward crusade to Budapest, Vienna, and even Rome, hurt him deeply. In addition, he was saddled with the political responsibility for the failure of the entire conquest of Poland because he had long delayed carrying out the order approved by Lenin and Trotsky that he re-enforce the attack on Warsaw by transferring Budyonny's Cavalry Army to Tukhachevsky's section. Stalin would have to listen to numerous bitter remarks in September 1920 at the Ninth Conference of the Russian Communist Party (Bolsheviks), accounting for the war's failure. Of course, he remembered this as a profound humiliation, for no member of the leadership had been criticized as harshly as he had been for the failure. Unsurprisingly years later, none of those who so denounced Stalin survived the 'Great Purge'. However, the main culprit for this annoyance

Top: Forced laborers on the frozen Gulf of Varnek on their way to the mines at Cape Razdzielnyy, USSR, 1930s. Bottom: Prisoners on their way from the Murmansk Railway station to the Solovki Special Significance Transit Camp at Kem on the Solovetsky Islands.

in the ambitious Georgian's life was the Polish Army, which stopped his advance already close to Lviv. It is with the memory of this very humiliation that some scholars associate the thought of revenge against the Poles, which Stalin was to finally consummate at Katyń (altogether, in the whole Katyń operation, a dozen Polish generals and several hundred senior officers many participants in the 1920 war were murdered).

However, I believe that Stalin's primary motive for acting against Poland was not a desire for personal revenge. Instead, it was an icy, predatory political calculation in line with a peculiarly Russian imperial *raison d'état*. I deliberately write 'Russian' because geopolitics is determinant, in this case, the continuity between Russia and the Soviet Union and then again from the 1990s between the Soviet Union and Russia. Irrespective of what the country is currently called, imperial geopolitics dictate the treatment of Poland as a barrier (a 'partitioning screen', as per Stalin's terminology) to further expansion towards the center of the continent, towards Germany, on the way to dominating all of Eastern and Central Europe. This is the primary, though obviously not the only, rationale behind Stalin's policy towards Poland. There were also ideological and Marxist considerations. After all, Stalin did not take ideology lightly, indeed further strengthening his exterminatory policy towards Poland and giving it a particular profile.

In keeping with the tradition of Russia's imperial geopolitics, Stalin eagerly took up the idea already hinted at by his master, Lenin: of cooperation with Berlin in the joint work of destroying the Polish 'partitioning screen'. Hitler's rise to power of course complicated such a scenario, for the Führer did not initially betray any desire to cooperate with the Communist dictator. Hence, Stalin's almost panicky fear that Hitler might even come to an accord with Poland and jointly strike at Moscow. This fear created the specter of the non-existent and reheated to this day by Putin's propagandists (and his 'useful idiots' in Poland and elsewhere), the so-called 'Beck-Hitler Pact'. Beck being the Foreign Minister of Poland in the 1930s. As is well known, no such anti-Soviet pact was ever concluded by Warsaw with Nazi Berlin, despite the especially fervent urgings for such an accord by Hitler and Ribbentrop in late 1938. Only a non-aggression pact, bereft of any secret protocols, was signed in January 1934. This was, nonetheless, undoubtedly a difficult time for Stalin's strategic plans.

At the end of September 1938, the Munich Conference was organized, which sealed the fate of Czechoslovakia. The Soviet Union was not invited to this conference, which Stalin saw as an attempt to exclude it from great power politics. The Soviet Union earlier had possessed an alliance treaty with Czechoslovakia and an alliance treaty with France since 1935, yet neither of these treaties had a tangible impact in the event of the German diplomatic aggression against Czechoslovakia. After the Munich Conference, as if to indicate his readiness for revenge, the USSR's Deputy Foreign Minister, bearing the historic name Potemkin (just as the initiator of the final partition of the Commonwealth, though this time he was not a Grigory instead a Vladimir), met with the French Ambassador in Moscow, Robert Coulondre in October, at Stalin's behest. During the meeting, he bluntly stated that the failure of the Western powers to invite the Soviet Union to the Munich decision meant that now Russia would have to move closer to Germany and partition Poland.

The problem, however, was that Hitler had to also want such a rapprochement. So, Stalin awaited his moment though not passively, to strengthen the Poles' determination to resist Hitler, he organized a new (post-1932) 'love campaign' toward Poland in October and November of 1938. He submitted a declaration upholding all the obligations of peaceful cooperation between the Soviet Union and Poland so Warsaw would not align themselves behind Hitler's war chariot under any circumstance.

However, this was not the reason why Poland did not accept Hitler's offer. It was because as Poland's Foreign Minister Józef Beck put it, if it had accepted, Poland would have only one future role to play, that of the complicit and compliant herders of German cattle in the Urals. For this was the role envisaged for Poles by Adolf Hitler's ideology, an ideology which treated all Slavs as 'sub-humans'. The situation changed in March 1939, when Hitler launched his second and final aggression against a truncated Czechoslovakia. This significantly changed British policy, concerned now in earnest by the swiftness of Hitler's successes, and prompted a definitive London response.

At the 18th Congress of the CPSU in March 1939, Stalin indicated his openness to the possibility of talks with Germany and set conditions. The first was that Germany would renounce playing the Ukrainian card. For Germany had agreed in October 1938, much to Stalin's dismay, to create

'There is only one thing in the lives of people, nations and states that is priceless, and that is honor.' Stating these words on 5 May 1939, Polish Foreign Minister Józef Beck a protégé of the then deceased Pilsudski, already knew that war with the Third Reich was a foregone conclusion…

an autonomous government of the so-called Transcarpathian Rus from the eastern part of a truncated Czechoslovakia. An entity which could have also become a bridgehead for the Ukrainians' independence ambitions to free themselves from under Soviet rule. Germany, reading Stalin's intentions ideally after the liquidation of Czechoslovakia on 15 March 1939, now allowed the incorporation of this 'Carpathian Ukraine' (as this state was called) into Hungary. The Poles then experienced a moment of short-lived triumph, regrettably rejoicing that Poland had regained a common border with a historical ally Hungary. In fact, it was Hitler's gesture toward Stalin.

The guarantees given to Poland by British Prime Minister Neville Chamberlain in response to Hitler's annexation of Czechoslovakia finally put Stalin in the coveted position of the one who could now play the decisive role in European policy. Stalin could now await offers from the British and their allies the French on the one hand, and Hitler, on the other. It was known that an inevitable confrontation was imminent. Stalin played the timing masterfully. He delayed the deal with Hitler as long as possible, until the very last moment, so that Hitler could not just use it as a tool to discourage the Western countries from supporting Poland, even politically. For Stalin cared only about ensuring Hitler's war with the west, and to avoid getting embroiled in any conflict with Germany straight away. He wanted to remain the arbiter, the Fortinbras, who victoriously enters the (European) stage full of corpses in Act V of *Hamlet*. When, on 21 August Third Reich Foreign Minister Ribbentrop approached the ambassador in Moscow with an almost pleading request that Stalin receive him as a matter of urgency (Hitler was already preparing direct aggression against Poland), he was, in turn, invited for 27 August. From the point of view of German military planning, this was obviously too late, so Hitler decided to send a personal letter to Comrade Stalin, asking him earnestly to receive his envoy immediately. After two hours, Stalin replied to Hitler's letter with an invitation to Ribbentrop. He already knew that he had reached the end of his negotiating powers, that it was already well and truly over, that Hitler was on the brink of war and that it was probably too late for the British and French to withdraw their support from Poland. On the other hand, Hitler knew that he had a deal ready in his pocket, but the details remained to be agreed upon. These were the details of the partition of Eastern Europe: more than half of Poland, Latvia, Estonia, Finland and Bessarabia for Moscow, the western part of Poland and Lithuania – for Hitler.

The mainstream historical politics of contemporary Russia interprets the Molotov-Ribbentrop Pact concluded on 23 August 1939, exclusively as a non-aggression pact by means of which Stalin farsightedly pushed the perspective of war away from the Soviet Union. It was as if this agreement had nothing to do with the military onslaught on Poland as if it was a typical bilateral treaty between states to ensure the peace and protect populations, a treaty like hundreds of others. It may be astonishing to many that, as part of the 'warming' of relations with Putin's Russia, just such a Stalinist interpretation of the Ribbentrop-Molotov Pact was presented by the Polish daily newspaper *Gazeta Wyborcza* (anyone who does not believe it, let him/ her check the article by Rafał Zasuń, *Jak Polacy i Rosjanie młócą historii*, in: *Gazeta Wyborcza* 27 August 2009 – it was a true gift for Putin on his arrival at the Westerplatte WWII commemoration in Gdansk).

As it happened, Hitler appreciated more than anyone this act's significance when he met senior Wehrmacht officers at a briefing on 22 August. He knew that Ribbentrop was going to Moscow, and the treaty would be signed. Hitler then said that if Stalin had not replied to his letter, he would have had to withdraw from the war policy and instead make a big *"Parteitag"* at Nuremberg, which would have been held under the slogans of peace. Hitler would then simply have backed down. This was recorded in his diary under the date 22 August by General Franz Halder, Chief of Staff of the Land Army, who was present at this meeting. Hitler made it clear that if Stalin had not given him the green light by accepting Ribbentrop, then Berlin, at least temporarily, would have had to withdraw from war, as he was uncertain whether Stalin would not ally himself with the Western states. Hitler, however, got the guarantees he wanted from Stalin. Therein lies the crucial role of Moscow in the decision to launch the Second World War. Of course, Hitler was the initiator of it, Hitler wanted war, but without Stalin's approval, the war certainly would not have begun on 1 September 1939. This war, of which Poland was the first victim and also the first state to offer armed resistance to the German Third Reich.

Let us recall the facts that show how much the Soviet Union was focused on Poland's destruction at that moment. On 3 September 1939, when France and Britain declared war on Germany, the Soviet deputy in Berlin, Shkvortsov, went immediately to Adolf Hitler to assure him that the Soviet authorities were highly pleased with the Wehrmacht's military successes in Poland. Stalin's representative was an ardent supporter of the German state in the war against Poland and the Western states. On 7 September 1939, Stalin met with the Red Army's supreme command to present him with the assumptions of a policy whose realization was to be the Fourth Partition of Poland. On 8 September 1939, Lavrenty Beria, who had replaced the 'Bloody Dwarf' Yezhov as head of the NKVD in 1938, gave the order to prepare nine special NKVD operational units, each consisting of around 70 Chekists (each also having 300 NKVD soldiers at their disposal), which were to deal with the preparations for the invasion of Poland – capturing politically dangerous individuals, intelligence surveillance and the elimination of the main enemies of the Soviet state on Polish territory. On 9 September 1939, which is also very characteristic, Vyacheslav Molotov, formally Prime Minister of the Soviet Government, sent a heartfelt congratulatory message to Adolf Hitler on the capture of Warsaw. On that day, German tanks had just reached the capital's outskirts, but the news had mistakenly spread that Warsaw had already been captured on 9 September. Molotov, therefore, hastened to congratulate Berlin that the entire Soviet nation was rejoicing on the occasion of this great victory of the brotherly German nation. Let us emphasize after all, Moscow was not yet at war or even in active conflict with Poland still being subject to the non-aggression treaty it had signed and then extended with Poland, binding till 1945.

That changed on 17 September 1939, just before dawn, Soviet aggression against Poland began but without any declaration of war. Vyacheslav Molotov announced over the radio that the Polish state had ceased to exist and was bankrupt. Therefore, Soviet troops were entering its territory to secure the fate of the Belarusian and Ukrainian proletariat. Of course, throughout the period from 1 to 17 September, the Soviet military infrastructure supported the Wehrmacht. The trajectory of the air raids on Warsaw was done with the assistance of a radio station in Minsk. The Soviet fleet, which was a significant force, especially in 1940 and 1941, made its naval base on the Kola Peninsula available to *Kriegsmarine* submarines, which were already waging a fierce naval war against Britain. Examples of strictly military

Soviet-German cooperation from this time can, of course, be multiplied. From September 1939 onwards, Stalin turned his country into a supply base of raw materials and military logistics for Hitler's war effort. Fifty-two percent of exports from the Soviet Union went to the needs of the Third Reich. This was a truly massive effort to support Adolf Hitler in this war. A WWII which by no means began the Kremlin's propaganda claimed and still continues to claim, on 22 June 1941. The day of Germany's attack on the Soviet Union. This war clearly raged from 1 September 1939, when for 22 months it was Moscow that was Hitler's most important ally.

What is particularly important and tragic for us Poles were the auxiliary, enabling crimes that began on Polish soil from the very first day of the aggression on 17 September for example the on-the-spot liquidation of Polish officers. In the military archives in Moscow, I came across documentation containing claims by the NKVD against the army in September 1939 that Polish officers were being executed *en masse* without any order yet there must be an order: first, the captured prisoners of war especially officers must be interrogated. Their usefulness was examined from the point of view of Soviet intelligence. And only then the 'useless' ones were to be shot. On 20 September 1939, the 6th Ukrainian Front Army commander, Filip Golikov, issued a directive ordering the shooting of surrendering Polish officers without any trial. Similar instructions for a 'simplified form of struggle against the bandits' (this category included, in addition to Polish officers, gendarmes and 'Polish bourgeois nationalists') were also issued by other senior commanders of the Red Army, which occupied the eastern territories of Poland.

One of the greatest Soviet slaughters occurred after the Red Army captured Grodno. A town heroically defended by both the Polish army and the local youth. Everyone captured was shot soldiers, schoolchildren, and civilians randomly encountered on the street.

On 28 September 1939, the second and more critical Molotov-Ribbentrop Pact, formally called the 'German-Soviet Boundary and Friendship Treaty' between the Third Reich and the Soviet Union, was signed in Moscow. It was concluded because the situation had changed. Stalin had not anticipated that the war would proceed the way it did that the Western states would take no military action and that Hitler would therefore retain the option of

The foreign ministers of the Third Reich and the USSR, Joachim von Ribbentrop and Vyacheslav Molotov sign the Soviet-German Non-aggression Pact in the presence of Stalin. The treaty's secret protocol provided for Poland's division between the two totalitarian powers. Moscow, 23 August 1939.

329

making peace with them since he had not yet become embroiled in a 'hot' war with them. Paris and London had only formally declared war for the time being. This worried Stalin and prompted him to change his original plans. In August, he assumed that Germany would struggle for a long time against the Western states and that in this situation, it would be worthwhile to have a toehold of ethnic Poland in his hand at once – for a future offensive against the soon to be war-exhausted German ally via Polish lands. That is why, according to the first Molotov-Ribbentrop Pact, the line of division of the Polish lands was especially drawn in such a way that a large part of Białystok, Podlasie and part of Mazovia was left on the Soviet side. Stalin wanted a bridgehead to be able to create the Soviet-Polish Republic relatively soon. But on 28 September, he knew this future plan was slipping further and further away from him.

The Kremlin's host was anxious that Hitler should not consider the conclusion of terms with the Western powers. For this purpose, it was necessary to convince his partner in Berlin of his absolute loyalty and the absence of any issues of dispute. There were to be no disputes over Polish territories, only a final, perfect, consensual partition. So, Stalin exchanged ethnically Polish regions (the Lublin Voivodeship and part of the Mazovian Voivodeship) for Lithuania, which, according to the first Ribbentrop-Molotov Pact, was to originally be granted to Germany. The second secret protocol stipulated that both sides would not tolerate any Polish conspiratorial activity in the areas they controlled. This was how cooperation was initiated and then consummated in fighting the common enemy the Polish underground. A fight to which, among other things, four future conferences between the Gestapo and the NKVD were devoted, the most famous of which were held in Zakopane and Krakow (in the officers' mess on Zyblikiewicz Street). The NKVD played the role of instructors at these conferences. They were incomparably more experienced and successful in eradicating Poles than their German peers in 1940. In the eastern territories of the Second Republic occupied by the Red Army the leadership of the first Polish underground, the Service for Poland's Victory and the Union of Armed Struggle were infiltrated, mostly arrested and later liquidated by the savvy NKVD.

Once the lands of the Second Polish Republic were under military occupation, the Soviet Union used the same methods of 'assimilation' that the Tsarist empire had successfully practiced for centuries. Firstly, and incessantly, terror. Then the pretense of legalizing the partition. Just as the nobility in the territories annexed by Russia's successive partitions had to swear allegiance to Catherine II (and report on the 'misfits' who rebelled against it), so the 'democratic' Soviet Union, just a few dozen hours after crushing the armed resistance of the last regular Polish troops, set up 'election committees' on 7 October 1939. This would be for votes to be held for the People's Assemblies of Western Ukraine and Western Belarus in the occupied territories. This was to be the official name of the territories conquered by the Red Army in accordance with Hitler. The propaganda campaign preparing for the 'elections' was conducted under the slogans of confiscation of huge bourgeois-owned land areas and church property, the nationalization of banks and industry, and the incorporation of the eastern lands of the Second Republic into the USSR. At the same time, in the wake of officers and NCOs of the Polish Army being sent to camps – including those at Kozelsk, Starobyelsk and Ostashkov – the terror operatives of the NKVD (the name of the Soviet 'security forces in this period) now additionally seized policemen, priests, Polish political, social and cultural activists as well as scientists. On 22 October 1939, when the bodies of these defenders of the Second Polish Republic's borders, murdered 'out of spite' by the Red Army and the NKVD agents, had not yet cooled, 'free elections' were held. Each ballot paper had just one name on it; there was no alternative this was autocracy with a democratic face.

According to the results fabricated under the control of the NKVD, 92.83% of eligible voters in 'Western Ukraine' took part in the vote, of which 90.93% voted for the designated candidates (political candidates completely unknown to the local population), and in 'Western Belarus' – 96.71% and 90.97% respectively. This new pattern of 'democracy' would be repeated later, after the war, in all the satellite states of the Soviet Union. The new 'representatives' of the inhabitants of the lands of the Second Republic 'requested' that these fruits of Stalin's pact with Hitler be voluntarily incorporated into the Soviet Empire. On 1–2 November, the Supreme Soviet of the USSR acceded to this 'request'. The annexation thus sanctioned, four weeks later, the same Supreme Council issued a decree on the forcible granting of Soviet citizenship to the 'former Polish citizens who were on

Propaganda poster 'Dear Stalin – the happiness of nations!'.

the territory of the western districts of Ukraine and Belarus when they became part of the USSR'. Much of this activity will resonate ominously with readers mindful of the recent democratic referendums organized in Ukraine in late 2022. However, this tragi-farce for locals proved very useful for Stalin when he explained facts on the ground to his new allied partners, after 1941, Prime Minister Churchill and President Roosevelt. Partners conveniently distanced from these lands were now presented with the alternative facts backed by elections. The narrative that the seizure of 201,000 square kilometers of Polish state territory with a population of several million was in no way a violation of the principles enshrined in the so-called Atlantic Charter. A charter that was to be binding on the members of the anti-Hitler coalition and made clear the non-recognition of any annexations made during the war. There was no violation there had

NKVD shooting exercises.

been no invasion but merely a protective Soviet umbrella for the oppressed. Everything was fine because the people of these lands had 'freely expressed their will to join the "brotherhood"' of the USSR. Thusly clarified Stalin all concerns around self-determination, and the Western partners duly nodded their heads in agreement.

The next stage, and a tool at the same time of imperial conquest, was the deportation of the 'uncertain elements', which in this case meant, above all, the destruction of Polishness and, more broadly – the traditions of the Polish-Lithuanian Commonwealth, in those lands seized. Four large deportations: on 10 February, 13 April, 20 to 30 June 1940, and again in June 1941 – according to the lowest NKVD estimates – seized no fewer than 340,000 people. However, the total number of deportees was much higher throughout this period. According to reports submitted to Stalin in December 1940 by Beria, almost 300,000 people had already been deported by that time, while in a report submitted to Stalin in 1941, Andrey Vyshinsky, Prosecutor General of the Soviet state, stated that just over 400,000 people had been deported from the eastern lands of the Second Polish Republic. Exiled to Siberia, the steppes of northern Kazakhstan and the Vorkuta or Kolyma mines, the deportees often did not live to see their destination, dying along the way in overheated (in summer) or frozen (in winter) cattle cars. Those who made it to their destination died from the devastating work (especially for children and women), illnesses, or an NKVD bullet. Of the deportees, several tens of thousands died. To the cities thus emptied – Lviv, Grodno, Stanisławów, Baranovichi, Ternopil and hundreds of other sites new 'colonists', i.e. officials, military officers and their families were brought in from the depths of Stalin's empire.

This is precisely what Ivan the Terrible did to Veliky Novgorod, Kazan or Astrakhan; events we've made reference to in earlier chapters.

And what of those who remained on the ground? Terrorize still further and after a time elicit collaboration. This is another example of conquest by means of the same Moscow 'technique'. In his report of 12 December 1940, Beria stated that, in addition to those deported, 407,000 people had been arrested in the lands of the Second Republic occupied by the USSR (and there were still more than six months of further arrests to be carried out in the area). Thousands died in executions that had already been preordained 'ordered'. During the evacuation of prisons from the areas invaded by Hitler's armies on 22 June 1941, thousands more Polish prisoners were hurriedly killed with machine guns and grenades. In Lviv alone, no less than 4,000 people were hastily murdered in this way in the so-called Brygidki and in Zamarstynów prisons. The NKVD also carried out mass shootings of prisoners in Lithuania, Oshmyanya, Minsk, Smolensk, Kharkiv, Boryslav, Stryj, Lutsk, Rivne, Berdychiv, and Kyiv in the last days of June 1941 as the Germans invaded. How many people were killed then 20, maybe 40,000? We will probably never know this with complete accuracy.

Relatively speaking, we know the most about a crime that came to symbolize the macabre policy of 'liberation' by Stalin's empire. It was a decision taken coldly to liquidate the Polish intelligentsia and elite: doctors, lawyers, teachers, university professors, landowners, industrialists, priests, and archi-

Wehrmacht and Red Army soldiers in Brest-on-the-Bug. On 22 September 1939, a joint parade took place there with the armies of the two aggressor states which had invaded Poland. The parade was reviewed by General Heinz Guderian and Kombrig Semyon Krivoshein.

tects. Men who had been taken prisoner by the Soviets as officers in the Polish Army in 1939. On 5 March 1940, just such a decision was taken by the Soviet Politburo, headed by Joseph Stalin. Beria, in the report preparing this decision, wrote explicitly about the outcome of this operation to Moscow: 'A total of 14,736 former officers, clerks, landowners, policemen, gendarmes, prison service, settlers and intelligence agents were being held in camps for prisoners of war, not including privates and non-commissioned officers. By nationality, more than 97 percent were Poles'. The idea was to hit the Poles hard, to cut off the Polish head. In the end, a single order from the Politburo, forwarded to the head of the NKVD, Lavrenty Beria, sentenced to death 25,700 Polish citizens held in POW camps and prisons. The order concerned principally the prisoners of war from the camps at Kozelsk, Ostashkov and Starobilsk, and the symbol of this crime would become Katyń near Smolensk, where prisoners from the Kozelsk camp were killed by a shot in the back of the head.

A crime this horrific in scale was clearly not just about terrorizing. It was about winning over collaborators by utilizing this fear factor. As early as 18 September 1939, on the second day after the Red Army's aggression against Poland, the Political Department of the Ukrainian Front advancing on Lviv began to publish the Polish-language newspaper *Słowo Żołnierza* (Soldier's Word). Ten days later, it was renamed *Czerwony Sztandar* (Red Banner). The paper became, under the latter name, the central organ of sovietization propaganda utilized against the Polish population. It attracted some of the left-wing intelligentsia of the Lviv milieu to collaborate – among the contributors to *Czerwony Sztandar* in 1939–41 were: Julian Stryjkowski, Stanisław Jerzy Lec, Adam Ważyk, Tadeusz Boy-Żeleński, Jerzy Putrament, Aleksander Wat. They wrote terrible, disgraceful things. And that's just what Stalin had in mind. These men would be the grotesque 'new head' sewn onto conquered Poland instead of the old one, cut off in the Katyń Forest Massacre.

The Polish intelligentsia, that part which was not executed now had as the governor-general of Vilnius had said after the January Uprising a choice. That of complete pauperisation, destitution (it can 'sell soap and long coats'), or it had a 'chance' to – serve the Empire. The latter path will soon be paved (as of February 1941) by the more ambitious magazine of Moscow's collaborators: the literary monthly *Nowe Widnokręgi* (New Horizons). Wanda Wasilewska, the author of political novels esteemed by Stalin, would become the magazine's editor-in-chief, and her closest collaborators would be, in addition to those already mentioned, Zofia Dzierżyńska (Felik's widow), Julian Przyboś, Mieczysław Jastrun, Janina Broniewska, Julia Brystygier, Karol Kuryluk, Zofia Bystrzycka. The magazine's consistently pro-Soviet propaganda line guided the later manipulation of Polish culture by communists after the war's conclusion in the People's Republic of Poland.

As early as mid-October 1940, the NKVD authorities began probing talks with a group of Polish officers selected from among those who had survived the spring slaughter and those who had been interned after the annexation of the Baltic States (including from Lithuania and Polish held Vilnius) in the summer of that year. In these talks, the NKVD put forward the thesis that the legal Polish government, operating in exile in London under the direction of General Władysław Sikorski, was 'self-proclaimed' and did not represent the Polish nation and that the only prospect for Poland was its merger with the USSR. The group of Polish Army officers selected for the talks, headed by Lt. Col. Zygmunt Berling, accepted this perspective and the possibility of participating in the formation of a Polish army under the total control of the USSR. After these talks, the group of 'Berling' officers, numbering a dozen or so, was transferred to a villa in Malakhovka near Moscow, known as the 'pleasure villa', where, under NKVD control in the winter and spring of 1941, they developed plans for collaboration.

It was a new Targowica, a hundred times worse than in 1792 because it was built on the pyramid of thousands of Polish officers just recently murdered, the additional misery of hundreds of thousands of Poles already deported to Siberia or suffering in NKVD prisons. It must be stated that the limits of collaboration, or rather the moral price to be paid for it, were raised by Stalin to a level higher than they had ever been in the history of the Moscow Empire's relations with the Polish 'periphery'.

The appetite of the Kremlin's overlord was not only limited to the territories gained under the Ribbentrop-Molotov Pact. On 4 June 1941, the Politburo decided to reform the 238th Rifle Division of the Red Army stationed in Central Asia into a division composed of Polish speakers. This unit was to be the spearhead of Poland's new 'liberation' and was linked to Stalin's planned strike against Hitler's Germany. Hitler, however, struck earlier. Stalin had to postpone his envisaged march west once again though only as it turned out for 3 short years. After all, in a war that was only just developing, he wanted to play the Polish card so that the rest of Poland, now shifted westwards, would become a new advanced Soviet foreground. This has been the geopolitical interest of the Russian Empire for centuries, and this is how Stalin saw it – Poland is to be transformed through its western transplantation (in territorial terms), into a strategic bridgehead for yet further imperial expansion into Western Europe.

This process was laid out in stages. In the first, Moscow, surprised by the strength and progression of the attack by its recent Berlin ally, had to reckon and align with its new Western partners, firstly London and then the Polish government in exile functioning there. Following Stalin's instructions, in his first conversation with the Prime Minister of the Polish Government in London, General Sikorski, on 5 July 1941, Soviet Ambassador Ivan Maisky was to state that his master was graciously withdrawing from the idea of making Poland into another Soviet republic, but that he did not intend, however, to give back the lands that had been seized from the Polish Republic in September 1939. He would only recognize a Poland shifted westwards, a slightly enlarged 'Congress Poland' (the one of 1815). The lands of the first three annexations by Catherine were to remain with Russia, supplemented by the annexation of Lviv and all of eastern Galicia. Against the resistance of the Polish Foreign Minister August Zaleski and President Władysław Raczkiewicz, General Sikorski allowed himself to be drawn into such a game and, in a treaty signed on 30 July with the Soviet Ambassador to Great Britain Ivan Maisky, he failed to force the Soviet side to make an explicit renunciation of its claims to the eastern lands of the Republic and to recognize a return to the pre-1 September 1939 border. The agreement did, however, achieve some important immediate objectives. It made it possible to rescue hundreds of thousands of Polish citizens still held in camps in Siberia and Kazakhstan. It also temporarily postponed the project of Stalin to set up a puppet 'Polish National Committee' completely subordinated to Moscow.

For its collaborators, however, the Kremlin already had a new or instead renewed, even ancient, in fact a traditional argument ready for just such

The shocking sight of bodies of the Polish officers murdered by Soviet thugs in the Katyń forest. Photo from 1943 after the discovery of the mass graves by the Germans.

Corpses of victims of the NKVD prison massacres who were murdered on the orders of Lavrenty Beria following the commencement of Operation Barbarossa. Lviv, the courtyard of the prison on Łącki Street, 1941. Among those shot were Poles, as well as Ukrainians and Jews.

subordination. It was no longer 'merely' the ideology of the communist brotherhood of proletarians but a classic tool of Moscow's imperial policy. This was the slogan of pan-Slavic brotherhood, with Russia in the role of the elder sister or brother of all Slavs (including the Poles, those problematic Poles, forever straying towards the West). On 11 August, at a huge 'Slavic rally' in Moscow, the All-Slavic Anti-Fascist Committee was formed. Within it, a Polish section was set up, and the aforementioned publicist Wanda Wasilewska was appointed vice-chair of the Committee. The Poles, however, were to be segregated under this policy from the Slavs who were 'closer' to Moscow, i.e. the Belarusians and Ukrainians living in the Polish territories occupied by the Red Army in 1939. On 1 December, the Soviet government issued a note stating that all inhabitants of the eastern areas of Poland occupied by the USSR and located there on 1 November 1939 had now acquired Soviet citizenship and that only 'ethnic' Poles', and no longer Ukrainians, Belarusians or Jews (whom Stalin also sought to separate and set in opposition to 'proper' Poles), could now be possibly considered Polish citizens.

When General Sikorski went to Stalin for talks on 3–4 December, he was placed there in the role of a supplicant who had to plead for Poles still being held in prisons and gulags and to inquire fruitlessly about the fate of the 'missing' officers. In response, the Kremlin host 'joked' that perhaps the Polish officers who had not yet been found had escaped to Manchuria. He was also pushing hard for sufficient food rations for the Polish army now being formed in Russia under the command of General Władysław Anders. Stalin was 'teasing' and procrastinating, while at the same time, he was already sending his agents to Poland to prepare the nucleus of his power and authority over the country. These were the communists parachuted in at the end of December 1941 who founded the so-called Polish Workers' Party (PPR). Its main aim was to fight not Germans but the Union of Armed Struggle (what would later be called the Polish Home Army – the *AK*) and the representatives of the Government Delegation (General Sikorski) for Poland. Subsequent First Secretaries of the PPR (Marceli Nowotko and Paweł Finder) oversaw the organization of a special cell to collect data on the Polish underground state, which was then handed over to the Gestapo in accordance with instructions from Moscow.

Stalin did not need an army loyal to the legal Polish government in London. He also wanted his own Polish army to serve the empire, not Poland. By restricting supplies to Anders' army, he prompted its evacuation in 1942 across the Caspian Sea to Iran. On the threshold of 1943, when the scales of war on the eastern front had already begun to tilt towards the Soviet Union, Stalin was able to proceed, or rather return, to the long-planned second stage of expansion and total subjugation of the whole of Poland – that is, of course it's 'liberation'. On 4 January, his agents Wanda Wasilewska and Alfred Lampe, sent a letter to the Soviet government on behalf of a group of communists gathered around the journal *Nowe Widnokręgi* (New Horizons) in Kuybyshev, asking for permission to create (around their group) a political representation of Poles remaining in the USSR after the departure of General Anders' army. On 1 March, the Soviet press agency TASS published an official statement accusing the Polish government of refusing to recognize 'the historical rights of the Ukrainian and Belarusian peoples to be united within their national borders'. The statement also claimed that the government in London 'does not reflect the true opinion of the Polish people', which virtually amounted to an outright announcement that the diplomatic recognition of the highest authorities of the Republic would be withdrawn. Stalin would create his own 'Polish government'.

On that very same day, the Communist-led Union of Polish Patriots (*Związek Patriotów Polskich* (ZPP) – a name personally invented by Joseph Stalin) was officially established in Moscow. In the first issue of its press organ, the weekly *Wolna Polska* (Free Poland), the ZPP announced the creation of a 'truly' free Poland, united with the USSR by 'fraternal relations' and a fight against the Polish government in London, which it accused of ideological commonality with Hitlerism. The new organization, which included Wanda Wasilewska, Alfred Lampe, Włodzimierz Sokorski and Zygmunt Berling, immediately set about seizing the offices and property of the Polish embassy delegates. Berling prepared a memorandum to the NKVD outlining a plan to organize Polish troops attached to the Red Army. Lampe (1900–1943), a pre-war Jewish activist and publicist, the somewhat forgotten creator of the new program of Soviet Poland, set out the principles of Moscow's new imperial rule over the Vistula in an exceptionally clear, if somewhat broken Polish redacted, memorandum for Stalin: 'the old Poland cannot reorient itself [geopolitically – *AN*] to a pro-Soviet position, without a łomki [breaking down] of the social structures of the *vsyeryoz* […] and *na dolgo*'. The old Poland cannot be geopolitically pro-Russian because Poles have historical memory. This memory causes a deep distrust of imperialism, the center of which is perceived in Moscow, whether red, white or any other color. So, for Poland to become truly geopolitically pro-Russian, this old head of Polish society must be cut off, and social structures broken up, in a word, the country needed to be 'de-fascisized'. The name of Poland can and even must be left as the program of conquest will be carried out under the banner of the Union of Polish Patriots, and it will invoke the name of Adam Mickiewicz now as Pushkin's greatest friend and supporter of the 'Polish-Russian revolutionary brotherhood', likewise instrumentalized would be the name of Tadeusz Kościuszko (a name familiar to Stalin's WWII ally the USA) as in the Moscow radio station or as in the name of the 1st Division of the 'Polish People's Army' created per Stalin's orders.

For the final ''breakdown' of relations, however, the discovery of Katyń was needed. On 13 April 1943, Berlin radio reported the discovery of Polish officers in mass graves near Smolensk, accusing the Soviet authorities of committing the crime. When the Polish government-in-exile officially asked the International Red Cross in Geneva to send a delegation to investigate the graves of Polish officers discovered by the Germans at Katyń, the Soviet Information Office immediately issued a communiqué attributing the Katyń crime to the Germans, who had allegedly murdered Polish officers in the summer of 1941. Stalin, with unparalleled cynicism, it must be said here, in the entire history of Russian imperialism, used his own unimaginable crime as a pretext for a moral outrage against the victims, or more precisely, against their relatives, who only wanted to pursue the truth about the fate of these victims. On 21 April, he sent dispatches to Churchill and Roosevelt, describing the Polish government's behavior on Katyń as 'completely abnormal'. Stalin declared that the Soviet side had decided to break off relations with the present Polish government, which had 'stooped to the path of collusion with the Nazi government'.

One must stop here and take in just what a tragic moment this was for Poland for the perspective of any future narrative truth about Poland and its experience during WWII. At the same time, the Germans, with the help of auxiliary formations, including some collaborators of Ukrainian, Latvian and Lithuanian descent perhaps even some Poles, were liquidating the remnants of the Warsaw Ghetto, ruthlessly destroying the heroic resistance of the Jewish insurgents there and executing any Poles caught trying to offer them shelter or assistance. Almost simultaneously, a new and terrible wave of systematic ethnic driven slaughters of the Polish population began Volhynia, carried out by hard-line Ukrainian nationalists in (including among others the villages of Janowa Dolina – about 600 people murdered, Zabara, Baszkowce and Chołbutow). Horror now pilled upon horror all facilitating the seemingly irrevocable progression towards the realization of Stalin's ultimate objective. The final destruction of the multi-ethnic multi denominational heritage of the Second Republic and the Commonwealth. On 26 April, Vyacheslav Molotov (the same man who, shortly after the Ribbentrop Pact, called the Polish Republic 'a mangled bastard of the Treaty of Versailles') read out to the Polish Ambassador Tadeusz Romer in Moscow a note dictated personally by Stalin, which informed him that the Soviet Government had 'broken off' diplomatic relations with the Polish Government. Stalin had finally opened the way for creating a new, Moscow-subordinated center of power over Poland, which would not only accept the annexation of the eastern lands of the Second Republic by the USSR but would also guarantee the Kremlin's complete future domination over Poland in every sphere of life including how this future Polish "state" would recollect its Sovietized WWII history.

Less than two weeks later, on 8 May, the Soviet press and the organ of the ZPP, published under the derisive name of *Wolna Polska* (Free Poland), announced that the Soviet government had agreed to form a Polish infantry division named after Tadeusz Kościuszko. The Soviet authorities appointed Berling as commander and Włodzimierz Sokorski as his deputy for political affairs. All that was missing were officers (those who had 'escaped to Manchuria'). In this situation, nearly 70% of the division's officers instead came from the Red Army. A month later, a triumphant congress of the Union of Polish Patriots, chaired by Wanda Wasilewska, was held in Moscow (it suited Stalin that his creature was the daughter of the first Foreign Minister of the Second Republic, Leon Wasilewski, and the goddaughter of Józef Piłsudski himself. This all created a much better appearance than

Stalin:

    „Ich frage hiermit die Vertreter von Finnland, Estland, Litauen, Polen und Rumänien: Ist einer gegen meinen Vorschlag?"

Stalin:

    „Zapytuję się niniejszym przedstawicieli Finlandii, Estonii, Litwy, Polski i Rumunii: Czy ktoś sprzeciwia się mojej propozycji?"

Stalin portrayed pointedly and accurately as a bloody oppressor of nations.

the composition of the first Soviet government for Poland, planned back in January 1919, which I wrote about in the previous chapter. The adopted 'Ideological Declaration of the ZPP in the USSR' announced the recognition of the annexation of the eastern lands of the Second Republic, the alliance of the future Poland with the Soviet Union, and the introduction of a system free of 'landowners and capitalists'.

Stalin's Western allies of course initially demanded that Moscow restore relations with General Sikorski's government. The general, however, quickly fell victim to an air disaster in Gibraltar as early as the beginning of July 1943. A disaster of great convenience for many of those shaping Poland's future fate. His successor as Prime Minister of the Polish Government, Stanisław Mikołajczyk, could not, of course, enjoy the same recognition as Sikorski among the members of the anti-Hitler coalition. Everything was to be decided anyway by events at the front, or more precisely, by a political decision as to just where the Red Army was to reach and where the Western states would form a second front. That issue itself was already decided by the end of August 1943 at the Allied Staff Conference in Quebec. It was agreed at this conference that the sphere of action of the Allied Commander-in-Chief (i.e. in practical terms, the armies of the USA and the UK) would include in Europe France, the Benelux countries, Norway and the part of German territory agreed by the governments of the three powers (the USA, UK and the USSR). The decisions adopted already in Quebec meant leaving the whole of central and eastern Europe as a zone of operations for the Red Army. Stalin's empire thus had a designated 'zone' of, first military operations and subsequently political domination, all with the consent of its Western partners. This sanctioned sphere of operations or influence is the same one to which Putin lays claim today.

The meaning of the new situation was laid out with great satisfaction to his Western partners at the time by Maxim Litvinov, then Moscow's ambassador in Washington: 'The Poles will have to learn to live within ethnographic boundaries as a small nation, abandoning the idea that they were once a great power. They were a haughty nation that did not have enough ability and strength to realize their exuberant nationalism'. This did not sound like the message of a communist ideologue of the brotherhood of the proletarians but more like the open declaration of a proud heir to the earlier work of Catherine II. Further negotiations between Soviet diplomats and their Anglo-Saxon partners on the subject of Poland proceeded along the same lines and with a similar attitude. At the conference of the 'Big Three' foreign ministers in Moscow in October 1943, only the resulting conclusions from this attitude were being prepared for the meeting of Roosevelt and Churchill with Stalin, the real winner of this game, in Teheran. There, between 28 November and 1 December, Roosevelt and Churchill accepted without any resistance the concept presented by Stalin of moving Poland westwards. 'The Big Three', under the dictates of their Kremlin host and without the participation of representatives from the Polish government, agreed that Poland's eastern border after the war would run more or less along the line earlier drawn by the Molotov-Ribbentrop Pact while the western border was to be based on the Oder and Neisse Rivers. It was also agreed that Warsaw would have to maintain 'friendly relations' with the USSR, which, in practice, meant that the Western states agreed to Soviet domination over Poland.

Stalin now prepared two complementary centers of his influence over the Vistula, a customary diplomatic initiative for the Tsars in the 18th century, from the time of Peter I to Catherine II. While at the same time to some extent, playing them off against one another other. He had already treated the legitimate government (in London) as eliminated from the game. He was now only playing with "his" Poles. On 9 November, Wanda Wasilewska presented him with a proposal for the makeup of the Polish National Committee. A pro-Soviet Polish government to be formed in Moscow, in opposition of course, to the Polish government-in-exile. Two days earlier, the Central Committee of the Polish Workers' Party had decided to set up the Homeland National Council (KRN) for just a similar purpose this time under the leadership of a proven agent, Bolesław Bierut. Which "agent" center would be more useful and how to exploit the personal rivalry between them, this was to be decided by Stalin himself, based on an ongoing analysis of the needs of his empire.

His army was already re-entering the Second Republic. Again, of course, as a 'liberator'. This time it was indeed removing the nightmarish, criminal German occupation from the occupied area. Yet just what kind of 'liberation' did this Red Army bring to the inhabitants of the first regions occupied by

Stalin's minions, what did they bear witness to? A question of particular relevance to the soldiers of the great, certainly the largest underground army in Nazi-occupied Europe – the Polish Home Army (AK Armia Krajowa). [In the summer of 1944, it was estimated to number 400,000 soldiers – *editor's note*], all loyal to the Second Republic. They were the first to be "enlightened" by the nature of Stalin's liberation. They attempted, following the politically unwise, though emotionally understandable, orders of Operation *'Burza'* (Tempest), to act openly as hosts in the areas into which Soviet divisions were entering. By engaging in large-scale combat against the retreating German criminals, they naively entered into agreements on localized combat cooperation with Red Army commanders. It ended the same way everywhere: after the removal of the Germans, there then followed the disarmament of the Poles, and later the deceitful arrests of AK officers by Soviet 'partners', followed by imprisonment and deportation to camps for those soldiers who refused to lay down their arms or continue their service now under orders from Moscow.

This was the case in Volhynia, Lviv, Lublin and Rzeszów, and in the region around Vilnius, among others. In this later example, after the temporary liberation of Vilnius itself and the subsequent capture by the NKVD of almost all AK soldiers participating in these battles (nearly 5,000 were sent to camps deep inside the USSR), the symbolic *Operation* 'Burza' ended at Surkonty. On 21 August 1944, an AK unit under the command of Colonel Maciej Kalenkiewicz *nom de guerre* 'Kotwic" (in 1939, he had been the deputy to Major Henryk Dobrzański *nom de guerre* 'Hubal') managed to escape from the encirclement near Vilnius but was later cornered by the Soviet army on his way to the Białystok forests. The entire unit, including the commander, were killed in the battle; even the wounded Home Army soldiers were killed all the Soviets.

The Home Army had to be presented as a 'spit-stained dwarf of reactionary forces'. It was to be necessarily destroyed, to achieve success in the operation to 'liberate' Poland from the 'fascists', i.e. the true patriots, invariably loyal to the sovereign Second Republic. The newly created Polish Army in the USSR, now from July onwards on Stalin's orders proudly calling itself the Polish People's Army (LWP), under the command of Michal Żymierski, an NKVD agent since 1932, was to play an essential role in this operation.

Top: Signing of the Sikorski-Mayski Agreement in London, 30 July 1941. Restoring diplomatic relations between the USSR and Poland. From the left: Władysław Sikorski, Anthony Eden, Winston Churchill and Ivan Mayski. Bottom: Participants in the top-secret military conference in Quebec (codenamed: 'QUADRANT'), 17–24 August 1943. Seated from the left are: Mackenzie King, Franklin Delano Roosevelt and Winston Churchill.

Not only was it to fight the Germans (many soldiers of the LWP did indeed undertake this duty in good faith and with the utmost heroism) but above all, it was to serve as a counterpoint to the 'bad', 'fascist' Poland – the 'new', 'good', 'progressive', 'realistic' Poland. This was the binary categorization system to be used in Poland, those subjected to Stalin's empire were to be called by such epithets, chosen to suit the circumstances. At the end of May, Stalin decided to recognize Bierut's KRN as the sole 'representation of the Polish nation' and forced his second tool, the Moscow ZPP, to accept this decision. In return the KRN now dutifully expressed gratitude to the ZPP for its merit in creating a Polish army in the USSR and 'uniting the forces of all patriots at home and abroad'.

On 21 July, Stalin's "legitimate representatives", now taken from both the KRN and the ZPP, established the Polish Committee of National Liberation (PKWN) in Moscow. In Stalin's plans, the new creation was to play the role of a subordinate government for central and western Poland, occupied now by the Red Army. The PKWN was headed by Edward Osóbka-Morawski, an activist of the pro-Moscow socialist group in the country. His deputies were Wanda Wasilewska and Andrzej Witos, representing the Polish communists from Moscow. The Ministry of National Defense was taken over by General Michał Żymierski, while Stanisław Radkiewicz in turn took over the Ministry of Public Security (so crucial in the communist system).

The Red Army was already crossing the Bug River by this time. A PKWN 'government' was to be installed west of that river. It was expected to put on a good show of pretending to be a Polish government. That is why, as early as 23 July, it published a periodical under the proud title *Rzeczpospolita* (the Republic; editor – Jerzy Borejsza) as its official organ. Quietly, however, as early as three days later, the PKWN, in a special document, assured supreme, unlimited power on Polish territory to Stalin as Commander-in-Chief of the Soviet army. Article 7 of this document established that, in the war zone, the Polish population was now subject to the jurisdiction of Soviet military courts. Based on this article, Soviet field courts then commenced a "legalized" crackdown on the "criminal elements" of the Polish independent underground, both military and civilian, on a massive scale.

A day later, PKWN Chairman Edward Osóbka-Morawski and Vyacheslav Molotov signed a secret agreement on the Polish-Soviet state border. The

PKWN formally accepted the so-called Curzon Line as the eastern border of the Polish state, i.e. it gave up, among other things, such historical and symbolic cities of the old Commonwealth as Grodno, Wilno/Vilnius and Lwów/Lviv. One day later on 28 July, a decree was issued, already officially, by Stanisław Radkiewicz, head of the PKWN's Ministry of Public Security, ordering the punishment of all those who would not surrender their weapons or submit to a mobilization order from Stalin's puppet government. So, potentially all those loyal to the Polish independence underground 'with the full severity of the laws of war'.

It was already clear that Moscow was effectively pursuing not only the age-old project of territorially truncating the Polish-Lithuanian Commonwealth to the shape first depicted in Tsar Aleksey Mikhailovich's plans of 1656. Or indeed those of Nicholas II's Foreign Ministry during the First World War. This was a plan to vassalize, or rather internally and institutionally rape, this truncated remnant of Poland. Prime Minister Mikołajczyk decided in this situation, pushed by London and Washington, to fly to meet Stalin in the hope of saving the country from this second and perhaps worst stage of imperial enslavement. Stalin received Mikołajczyk as part of a game still being played with Churchill and Roosevelt to win their approval for his creation – the PKWN. Mikołajczyk heard the demand that the re-formed government should include 14 members of the PKWN and only four ministers from the London government. It was the beginning of August 1944. The (Warsaw) Uprising against the German occupying forces was now already underway in the capital city. It was intended to strengthen the position of the legal government against these 'liberators' from the east. Stalin exploited the situation with his usual flair as the best student of Machiavelli's advice and Catherine II's legacy. Although his troops were just reaching the eastern banks of the Vistula River near Warsaw, he not only stopped their offensive to cross to the west bank of the great river but actually prevented the Western Allies from providing even air support and supplies to the Polish insurgents. He only sustained Warsaw's heroic struggle for just as long as the Germans could (and wanted to) carry out the dirtiest job for him the further slaughter of the Polish elite, *de facto* a second Katyń. This time focused in the Capital Warsaw. It should be added that this bloody 'job' was carried out by German overseers partly with the hands of

Russian collaborators from the RONA formation (the Russian Liberation People's Army, already "distinguishing" themselves in the slaughter of the inhabitants of the Polish capital as the *Waffen SS 'RONA' Sturm- Brigade*).

This all 'freed up' additional political room for Stalin's collaborators from the PKWN and KRN it is how the imperial strategy of conquest and subjugation works. On 31 August, a month into the heroic fighting by the insurgents, the PKWN issued a decree on penalties against 'fascist-Hitlerian criminals' and 'traitors to the Polish nation'. This decree later made it possible to convict tens of thousands of soldiers from the Polish patriotic underground, including those Warsaw insurgents who survived (General Emil Fieldorf 'Nil', organizer and head of the Kedyw of the *AK* (Home Army) Headquarters, was sentenced to death based on this decree in 1952. Three days later, specialists in the more delicate work of implanting a new intellectual consciousness in Poland, headed by Jerzy Borejsza, a man already been tried and tested in this capacity, began publishing a weekly under the symbolic title of *Odrodzenie* ('Rebirth'). This literary and social periodical was to become the instrument of a more 'gentle revolution' in culture and pave the way for the new communist team to reach out to the minds of the remaining Polish intelligentsia. Among the magazine's editors and contributors were Karol Kuryluk, Jerzy Putrament, Ryszard Matuszewski, Stefan Żółkiewski and Zygmunt Kałużyński. The fight for the control of culture by communist ideology was to be fought by the *Związek Zawodowy Literatów Polskich* (Trade Union of Polish Writers), which had been reactivated two days earlier in Lublin, with a temporary board including Julian Przyboś (chairman), Adam Ważyk, Mieczysław Jastrun and Jerzy Putrament. This was the new elite, or rather part of it.

The second elite – sometimes mixed in with the first, 'cultural' elite, would consist of 'comrades from the security services'.

On 7 October, Stalin's PKWN formally established the 'Security Service formations'. Under the leadership of the head of the PKWN's Ministry of Security, Stanisław Radkiewicz. A police terror apparatus of the new government was created with provincial and district Security Offices (UB) and Civic Militia (MO) headquarters. The cadres of the newly established organizations were made up of Żymierski's soldiers, trained for their new tasks under the supervision of the NKVD. In its initial phase, the UB num-

Top: Red Square in Moscow; Red Army units advance to the front against the German invaders, 1941. Bottom: Victory Parade in Moscow, 24 June 1945. NKVD formations with captured German banners.

bered about 500 officers, and the MO had about 14,000 people. The more experienced executives were, of course, sent from courses undertaken in the center of the empire. The first security service school specifically geared towards operations in the Polish lands was established in Smolensk as early as September 1940. Already at that time, after all, Stalin had assumed that it would be necessary to 'reclaim' these lands. A task for which he needed cadres who would be able to infiltrate this new Poland to organize it in such a way that it would be easier for comrades in the army to conquer it, and then to hold it, forever. The school in Smolensk, active for several months, produced 200 graduates. In June 1941, after the outbreak of the Soviet-German War, it was replaced by a new course organized at a training center for Polish NKVD adherents in Kuybyshev.

This course proved particularly fruitful in preparing cadres for the security services in Kremlin-subjugated Poland. Among those to emerge from there were Aleksander Kokoszyn – chief of military information of the LWP, Władysław Spychaj vel Sobczyński, head of the Security Office (UB) in Rzeszów and a specialist in post-1945 Jewish pogroms, Mieczysław Moczar, Konrad Świetlik, commander of the Internal Security Corps (KBW), and many others. All later meritorious functionaries in consolidating Moscow's influence in Poland. As early as 20 October, based on the new cadres, the 1st Brigade of Internal Troops was called into service (rather: for elimination purposes) under the command of Henryk Toruńczyk, formerly the head of the Security Corps' Assault Battalion. The brigade, with the help and guidance of advisors from the NKVD, was to deal primarily with the 'liquidation of outlaws', i.e. the physical extermination of members and collaborators of the Polish independent underground movement.

Of course, the efforts of such new Polish 'elites" were accompanied by constant assistance from the imperial center. Even before the end of October, the NKVD had sent three regiments (4,500 soldiers) to the tough and highly resistant area of Białystok to fight against Polish partisans. These people had risked their lives almost daily throughout the war without hesitation in the battle against the German occupying forces. In the following months, whole divisions of the NKVD would provide such 'brotherly assistance'. The 'legal' foundations for the terror paving the way for the new authoritative power over Poland were established by the PKWN decree of 30 October 1944. 'On the protection of the security of the state'. It provided for punishment by imprisonment or death in the event of a whole list of "crimes", among other things, keeping radios without permission, failing to report a crime to the authorities or the conveniently vague concept of preparing a political crime.

The new decree, signed by Bolesław Bierut, Edward Osóbka-Morawski, Michał Żymierski and Stanisław Radkiewicz, gave the terror apparatus organized by the PKWN almost unlimited possibilities for action. The decree did not enter into force on the day of its promulgation. Instead, according to its own Article 18, its effect would be retroactive, from 15 August 1944. This was a new norm from Moscow, contrary to the Latin legal tradition: the law could now act retroactively, i.e. as soon as the Kremlin so wished. In the same spirit, another decree of the PKWN was issued before the end of December, introducing censorship of correspondence, mail, telegrams, radio telegrams, as well as telephone and radio calls. To reinforce the gratitude to friends from Moscow for these and other innovations, the Polish-Soviet Friendship Society (TPPR) was founded on 22 November, which was to grow to a 7-million-strong organization in the future. Whole schools were enrolled in the TPPR, of course without asking anyone's prior permission.

This was the moment when Stalin could declare that Poland was all his. On 31 December, the PKWN changed its name to the Provisional Government of the Republic of Poland. Edward Osóbka-Morawski became Prime Minister, and Władysław Gomułka (1st Secretary of the PPR) became the First Deputy Prime Minister. Formally, the decision to form a government competing with the London Govt in exile was made by the communist National Council, 'acceding to the general demands of Polish society' the principles of self-determination, were it appeared, respected. In fact, the Kremlin's host and overlord, Stalin, made the decision despite increasing objections from the Western Allies, he was thus emphasizing his complete control over Poland's political future. He could now proceed to 'liberate' Warsaw and the rest of Poland.

On 1 February 1945, the 'Provisional Government…' moved its headquarters from Lublin to a now devastated Warsaw. Some of the PPR and PKWN leadership thought that, given the scale of destruction in Warsaw, the capital would have to be moved to Łódź or Krakow. The doubts were settled by Stalin (in a conversation with Władysław Gomułka). He stated

The Teheran Conference, or alternatively the new partition of Poland. Winston Churchill (seated first on the right) and Franklin Delano Roosevelt (in the middle) agreed to all of Stalin's demands. 28 November – 1 December 1943.

that without restoring the capital in Warsaw and rebuilding it, the new communist team would have no chance of winning the people's confidence. Stalin also ensured that his overzealous *holuys* (that's Russian for 'servants', 'lapdogs') did not replace the *Dąbrowski Mazurka* with some revolutionary song as the new Polish anthem. '*Mazurka khoroshaya pyesnya, ostavit' poka*' ('the Mazurka is a good song, leave it for now'). Raped and territorially mutilated in the east, Poland was to be brand new, 'fascist free', but at the same time, it should still retain a semblance of continuity.

This pretense was also needed in Stalin's final negotiations with his Western partners. Between 4 and 11 February 1945, he acted as host of the Yalta Conference. Already on the first day of the meeting, the controversy between Stalin and Roosevelt and Churchill over the approach to the fate of the central and eastern European nations, of course again unrepresented

Polish Gen. Leopold Okulicki *nom de guerre 'Niedźwiadek/the Bear'*, the last commander-in-chief of the Home Army (AK), during the "trial of the sixteen" in Moscow resolutely defended the good name of the Home Army and the Polish Underground State.

at the Yalta Conference, was marked. Stalin firmly rejected the right of such nations to have a say in the post-war order ('We three should decide how to preserve world peace'). The Polish case was discussed at the conference every day from 6 to 10 February 1945. Representatives of the United States and the United Kingdom had already tried to agree on their position with regard to the question of Poland's borders before the conference in the east. They had decided to adopt the Curzon Line with a possible request to Stalin to agree to let Poland keep Lviv and the oil basin around Boryslav. Stalin, however, rejected the proposals put forward by Churchill and Roosevelt, firmly insisting on his decision to seize all those eastern lands of the Second Republic. Lands which he had previously obtained under the Molotov-Ribbentrop Pact. He only confirmed the adjustment to the line of that pact already agreed in Tehran, now leaving Białystok and Łomża on the Polish side while firmly refusing to return Lviv. Churchill and Roosevelt quickly abandoned the Lviv proposal, accepted Stalin's position on the eastern border, and turned their attention to the future of the Polish government.

The aging Roosevelt's attitude, in particular, was characterized in this matter by uninformed perhaps willing ignorance, skillfully exploited by Stalin. Its glaring proof was the American President's characteristic remark that the Polish question 'has already given the world a headache for five centuries'. Roosevelt with other strategic priorities in mind, wanted to get rid of this pain as quickly and efficiently as possible, not fully accepting that at stake in the game imposed by Stalin was as history would prove not just the independence of Poland but also of half of Europe. Both Roosevelt and especially Churchill were opposed to recognizing the Communist Provisional Government as the legitimate authority of Poland. Still, they were not going to defend the rights of the London Government. It was therefore agreed that 'the Provisional Government now in place in Poland should be reorganized on a more democratic basis, with the inclusion of democratic leaders from Poland itself and from among Poles abroad'. This reorganization was to be undertaken in Moscow by a 'good offices commission' composed of Molotov and the ambassadors of Great Britain and the United States. The 'provisional government of national unity' under their control was to prepare and conduct 'free and unfettered elections based on universal and secret ballot voting'. 'All democratic and anti-racist parties' were to be admitted to the elections. However, it was not established precisely just in whose hands the power to define which parties were 'democratic' and 'anti-racist'. This power to define and judge was to be in the hands of Stalin and his communist representatives in Poland.

Moscow was able to proceed with the 'de-fascisizing' or, as Putin puts it today, the 'denazification' of Polish society. The society that had been the "first to fight" which had first, single-handedly resisted Nazi Germany and also its Moscow ally. Resisted if only for a time in the field but then subsequently for 6 long years (for many even longer) through stealth, organization and simple human heroism. From now on however according to the new equation of political mathematics: Poland's independence + the traditions of the Republic or the Commonwealth = Fascism, extremism, terrorism even antisemitism. Exactly on the day the Yalta Conference ended, 10 February, the Ministry of Public Security of Stalin's puppet government issued an instruction to subordinate provincial bodies, according to which the AK self-dissolution was to be 'treated as fictitious', and the AK itself as a 'resistance and anti-democratic movement'. In the *Political Dictionary* published then, the UB and Polish Army officers read that 'the AK had moved to *de facto* collaboration with the Germans'. Posters were reading 'AK – the spit-stained dwarf of the reaction' appeared on city streets and in offices. Mass deportations of arrested Home-Army men/women subsequently filtered through special concentration camps in Poland (including Rembertów, Skrobów and Krześlin near Siedlce) later to labor camps deep inside the USSR continued.

Officially appointed by Beria as a 'counselor to the Polish Ministry of Public Security', NKVD General Ivan Serov deceitfully 'invited' the leaders of parties loyal to the Polish government in London for talks in Poland. They were all kidnapped on 27–28 March and taken to Moscow. Just as Ivan III's executioners had done 470 years earlier with the elite of the Novgorod Republic: kidnap, deport to Moscow – and a subsequent show trial. Among those seized was the last commander of the Home Army, General Leopold Okulicki, Deputy Prime Minister of the Government – Delegate for Poland Jan Stanisław Jankowski, Chairman of the Council of National Unity Kazimierz Pużak of the PPS, as well as leaders of the National Party, the People's Party, the Labour Party and the Democratic Union. When all these representatives of free Poland were already sitting in the NKVD headquarters at Lubyanka, on 21 April, Stalin manifestly signed a 'treaty of friendship, mutual assistance and post-war cooperation' between the USSR and Poland. The other signatory was the 'Prime Minister of the Provisional Government' – Osóbka-Morawski – a political nemesis exchanged by the Kremlin, just like the leaders of the Targowica once after the conquest of Poland by Catherine's armies. There was also an excellent candidate for the role of the hetman. So, on 3 May, in a clear mockery of the traditions of the 1791 Constitution of that same day, an NKVD agent, Michał Żymierski, was by Stalin's grace appointed Marshal of Poland, now succeeding Piłsudski in the role. One of the first decrees of the new 'Marshal' was an order issued on 24 May 'on the liquidation of the armed underground in the eastern territories of the Republic'. It designated four infantry divisions (the 1ˢᵗ, 3ʳᵈ, 8ᵗʰ and 9ᵗʰ), as well as the 1ˢᵗ Warsaw Armoured Brigade, to deal with the post-AK partisan fascists and NSZ units, concentrated in the Mazovia, Podlasie and Suwałki regions.

Furthermore, a resolution of the Provisional Government established the Internal Security Corps (*Korpus Bezpieczeństwa Wewnętrznego – (KBW)*), a new formation designed mainly to combat the independence underground. At this point, according to a report submitted to Stalin by the USSR People's Commissar of the Interior, Lavrenty Beria, 25,000 Polish citizens (soldiers and activists of the Polish patriotic underground) were in NKVD camps and prisons. In addition, the NKVD held 33,000 Poles in prisoner-of-war camps and 7,000 Poles from Silesia in 'labour battalions' in Ukraine. Seven NKVD regiments took part in operations against the Polish underground; the 'Polish authorities' asked for an additional three cavalry regiments from Moscow to assist.

The war against Germany was over. Victoriously – for Stalin's Empire. Poland had been conquered. Deprived of half its territory and independence and forcibly moved westwards as Moscow's "eternal" geopolitical hostage. It was now to be subjected to further 'processing' by combining the ideology of Marx and Lenin with the legacies of Ivan III and IV, Peter I and Catherine II, Suvorov and Muravyov the ‚Hangman' of the January uprising.

Poland's Reluctant Return to the Fold. A New Soviet Empire of the Pacified (1945–1989)

P oland became part of a camp subordinated directly, formally and explicitly to a center of power that geopolitically was unchanged in its viewpoint from that which existed prior to communism. However, it had of course changed its ideological essence to one far more dangerous than all previous forms of subordination to the Russian Empire. Józef Mackiewicz, in an article published in the *London News* in May 1947, accurately captured the essence of this operation that the Soviet system now undertook not only on the Polish people but also on others who, along with Poles, became part of that system. He wrote: 'What constitutes the method of Soviet action on a conquered nation? This method could be compared to a surgical operation to take out the patient's brain and the national heart'.

This operation was carried out systematically over the 45 years this system formally existed in Poland, and its acute traces are certainly still felt today. As a second motto for this part of Poland's historical struggle against imperialism from the east, I would like to quote a translated passage from Czesław Miłosz's poem, *Trwoga-sen* (The Anxious Dream). It reflects accurately the situation of intimidation that the shadow of this Empire in its new, Soviet form, would cast on Poland, including on Czesław Miłosz himself. This poem is rarely recalled, which is a pity, as it is one of the Nobel Prize winner's most outstanding works. It comes from the 1987 volume *Chronicles*, translated into English:

> *The little child trembles before the pain. Before the Empire.*
> *Which moves and moves westward, armed with bows, ropes, 'papasha'*
> *submachine guns,*
> *Riding a carriage, striking the rider across his back,*
> *Or by jeep, wearing a papakha, with a file of conquered lands,*

And I have been running away for a hundred or three hundred years
Over ice and swimming, by day, by night, further away,
Leaving at my river-anchored home a hole-pocked armor and a chest of
the king's gifts,
Across the Dnieper, then across the Niemen, across the Bug, and across
the Vistula.

This is a poetic abridgement of the dramatic historical experience of the Republic in 1945. It was the end, as it seemed at the time. The end for the Republic that after 20 brief years of national revival had ultimately lost, shattered reduced to ashes like its capital Warsaw under the blows of the empires of Berlin and Moscow in their most brutal embodiments. A Poland that had now lost, any influence over the area of Lithuania, Ukraine, and Belarus. A region who's political and national culture it had co-created for more than four centuries from Krakow Vilnius and Warsaw. A culture it had helped to preserve for a further century as a resilient legacy for those under Tsarist occupation. All this had now been left behind, smashed by the totalitarian road roller of Stalin's state. The 'Great Famine' in Ukraine, then the NKVD's 'Polish operation' of 1937–1938, the annihilation through hundreds of summary executions of the nascent Belarusian intelligentsia and the remnants of Polish enclave settlements in Belarus all before 1939; then in 1940 and again after 1945. The mass deportations of Lithuanians fighting for freedom to Soviet gulags; similarly, the mass deportations of Ukrainians (not only those from the Ukrainian Insurgent Army) from the land of the former Polish-Lithuanian Commonwealth annexed by the Molotov-Ribbentrop Pact and the additional resettlement of those Poles from this area who had still managed to escape (to the west, to Wrocław, Toruń, to the new 'reservation' granted to them by the 'Father of Nations' for Poles west of the Bug River). These were further twists and turns of the Stalinist steamroller under whose weight millions of people quite literally, perished. (TN Start) Of course not only Slavs were on the move. Tens of thousands of Germans many of them from families' that had been residents of these lands for centuries, were now being raped killed and brutalized just as they were later, in their millions, driven west by the advancing red tide (TN End).

363

Warsaw, a symbol of Polish heroism, fell victim to a premeditated and pre-planned destructive action carried out by specially designated German sapper units. This is what the once elegant streets of the city once referred to as "the Paris of the North" looked like in 1945.

This picture was completed by the brutal liquidation of the last bastion of union between the Greek Catholic Church and the Catholic Church, precisely in western Ukraine, where nearly four million believers still lived in the tradition of this rite. A rite from the end of the 16th century, intended to bring the eastern Slavs closer to Rome and Latin culture. All the bishops, led by Metropolitan Josyf Slipyj, now ended up in concentration camps. Yet, another 'initiative group' of collaborators at the so-called Council of Lviv in March 1946 now annulled (illegally, of course) the Union of Brest and 'asked' the faithful to join the Russian Orthodox Church. The latter, we should add, was restored, after a period of persecution by Stalin. From 1943 onwards, as in Tsarist times, it was to be one of the pillars of Russia's imperial identity and an instrument of expansion of Moscow's strength

Major Franciszek Szabunia, inspector of the Suwałki Inspectorate of the AKO, among his soldiers (seated in the middle), 1945. Many former soldiers of the Home Army decided to continue their armed struggle against the new, Soviet occupying forces...

into neighboring territories. The Catholic Church within the new USSR's expanded post 1945 borders, was, now persecuted with particular ferocity by the Kremlin. Not so much as a source of 'religious superstition' but as a 'potential agent' of influence, the still enduring specter of historical Poland allied with the 'Vatican'.

There was no longer a Republic; there was instead a population scarred by 6 years of ferocious conflict and oppression in these lands. Conflict that was now culminating in an unprecedented Stalinist terror. For them the priority was the daily struggle to survive. In what seemed a hopeless situation, some collaborated with the oppressor. There were, of course, those who still tried to fight the *Żołnierze Niezłomni* (the 'Unbroken Soldiers'). They perished, nameless at the time and were mocked by the later propagandists out of ubiquitous fear (unfortunately, here the denouncers included Miłosz, who mocked the 'stupidity' of the Unbroken Soldiers in his columns in *Dziennik Polski* in 1945).

In the reservations left by Stalin for ethnic Poles, the People's Republic of Poland (now renamed the *'Polska Rzeczpospolita Ludowa'* as of 1952), a subjugation operation was being carried out, not only materially but also spiritually. The subordination to an imperial system based on Soviet ideology. This history is probably well-known, so I will not recall its exact chronicle here. Let us just identify the characteristic nature of the 'prelude'.

Between 17 and 21 June 1945, talks were held in Moscow, under the watchful eye of Vyacheslav Molotov, on transforming the so-called Pro-visional Government appointed by Stalin into a government formally recognized by Western partners. It would now derisively be called the Gov-ernment of National Unity. Stalin's somewhat ridiculous puppet, Edward Osóbka-Morawski, was officially left in charge. Added to him as Deputy Prime Minister was the fig leaf of this operation Stanisław Mikołajczyk, who still believed that he could save something for Poland in this way. The second deputy prime minister appointed alongside Mikołajczyk was to have incomparably more power. This was Comrade *'Wiesław'*, head of the PPR Władysław Gomułka. Communists sent from Moscow or approved by it were to take over all the key ministries, including Public Security (here, the already proven comrade Stanisław Radkiewicz would continue his 'mission').

No one doubted that full authority over this government and Poland rested with the Kremlin. Yet if anyone had such a doubt, Stalin staged, at the exact moment when a new government for Poland was being formed, the trial of the members of the previous legal government. The govern-ment ministers and heads of parties of the Underground State who had, as we mentioned previously, been kidnapped from the country in March 1945. Soviet prosecutors accused the Polish underground of anti-Soviet conspiracies, diversions, acts of terror and conducting hostile propaganda. Unlawfully brought before a Soviet court, the Polish leaders were convicted and deprived of any chance of defense. Among others, the last commander of the Home Army, General Leopold Okulicki, was sentenced to ten years in prison, and Deputy Prime Minister Jan Stanisław Jankowski to eight

Pervasive Soviet propaganda would become an unbearable part of the bleak communist reality. The inscription on the poster proclaims that 'Only Soviet power leads the workers to light and enlightenment'.

years. Both never left the Soviet prison system alive. The sentence was announced in Moscow and on the same day, 21 June, when the communiqué on the agreement on the Provisional Government of National Unity was released. This new government would be born cloaked in this new Soviet-imposed truth. The truth about the former government's "criminals" and their righteous judgment.

The first to recognize this government was General Charles de Gaulle, then seeking the favor of the Kremlin at all costs (preferably Polish). The Anglo-Saxon allies would follow suit. The Western world recognized that Poland belonged to Stalin, part of Moscow's well-deserved sphere of influence given its role in securing victory over the Nazis.

The new communist government immediately concluded a formal border agreement with the USSR, in practice, a mere validation of the current state of affairs created initially by the agreement of the Molotov-Ribbentrop Pact of 23 August 1939. Later endorsed during Stalin's talks with Roosevelt and Churchill at Tehran and Yalta. At the same time, this 'Government of National Unity' signed an agreement 'to compensate for the damage caused by the German occupation'. In return for the 'small change' granted from the Soviet pool of war reparations from Germany, Poland was now forced to supply the USSR with 52 million tons of coal over five years and, after that, 12 million tons every year 'at a special contractual price', a price ten times lower than the world prices, something which could only be regarded as a spectacular form of exploitation on Moscow's part. The exploitation was compounded by the plundering of economic resources and machine plants by the USSR administration in the Western Territories, bringing additional difficult-to-estimate losses and hobbling the task of rebuilding Poland.

In 1945, the main burden of the fight against the Polish independence underground was still borne by the NKVD, such as in the great manhunt for Polish partisans carried out in mid-July in the Suwałki and Augustów region by NKVD forces and SMERSH units (Soviet military counterintelligence). The order for committing this crime was given personally by Stalin, who wanted in this way to 'secure' the area surrounding the planned passage of his train to the last of the 'Big Three' conferences this time in Potsdam. (TN Start) A town that would once again be a place associated with the denouement of Polish sovereignty (TN End).

More than 2,000 inhabitants of the surrounding villages where the NKVD and SMERSH conducted their searches were detained in the so-called *Obława augustowska* (Augustów Manhunt). About 600 were taken away in an unknown direction, probably transported to the Grodno area and murdered there. No trace of these deportees has been found to this day. However, Natalia Lebedeva, the most reliable Russian researcher of the history of Stalinist repression against the Poles, has assumed that those kidnapped in this manhunt might have been taken to a secret camp, where they may have been subjected to experiments with chemical or biological weapons.

The tragic fate of these victims of the Augustów Manhunt is commemorated by a cross erected in Giby. The 530 known names of those irretrievably lost or murdered in just this one crime are found on it. The soldiers of the 1st Infantry Division of the Polish (People's) Army, the one that started its military history at the battle of Lenino in Belarus just 2 years earlier, it was these men who now disgraced their uniform in carrying out this mass crime. Its detachment supported the Russian agents in the pursuit and killing of Polish patriots near Augustów, was under the command of Maksymilian Sznepf. Moreover, his son Ryszard would become, a well-known diplomat of the Third Republic of Poland, an open supporter of Poland's potential participation in the construction of Putin's Nord Stream gas pipeline and, on the nomination of President Komorowski, was Poland's ambassador to the US in Washington.

Gradually, the role of the NKVD division in conquered Poland was taken over by the 'domestic' terror apparatus formed on its model. It is characteristic to compare its two most important institutions: the civilian special services, i.e. the Ministry of Public Security (MBP), and the Main Board of Information (GZI), i.e. the special military services. In the MBP, Soviet officers made up about 10 to 12% of the managerial elite, meaning they occupied all the key positions; the cadre was always functionally a Soviet officer, not a Polish one. As for the GZI, or special military services, the situation was the other way around; there, Poles formally constituted an extreme minority of 10%, and the remaining 90% were Soviets, mainly Russians. In addition to the special services were other 'advisors' from Moscow, whom I do not include in these previously mentioned percentages. These

369

May Day parades with obligatory slogans celebrating the 'one and only political system' with portraits of flagship revolutionary figures, in other words, the enforced celebration of the Sovietisation of Poland.

were people functioning, as it were, formally outside of Polish institutions, or more precisely, above them. From this imperial position, they taught or consulted on how to organize a system of violence, agents, control, and manipulation of society according to the best, or rather the worst, models that the Soviet security apparatus had managed to develop.

These were not only the models of Dzerzhinsky's *Cheka* but also harked back to the time of Ivan the Terrible's *oprichniki*. Their proud imitators, the 'soviets', overseeing the activities of the 'Polish' Ministry of Public Security, were commended for their activities in Russian, of course (successively, the key function of MBP councilors was held until 1953 by General Ivan Serov, Nikolai Selivanovsky, Colonels Semyon Davydov and Mikhail Biezboro-

Security services (UB) thugs carried out bestial murders of the Unbroken Soldiers. Lying dead: Stanisław Torbicz *nom de guerre 'Kazik'"*(left) and Edward Taraszkiewicz *nom de guerre 'Żelazny'* (right). Sitting in the middle is Stanisław Marciniak *nom de guerre 'Niewinny';* he was murdered two years later. Włodawa, 6 October 1951.

dov). They developed and oversaw an office predicated upon total violence that was impressive in size and intimidating in its effects. In 1953, some 265,000 officers of various special services were subordinate to it. The number of secret collaborators (spies in society) exceeded 85,000, and the MBP managed to encompass more than five million citizens with its persecution and surveillance. Fortunately, the story of their victims, among the bravest of Polish patriots, is now slowly being recalled today (TN Start) in a process that often results in social tensions as not just the victims but also the perpetrators and their descendants are being unmasked (TN End). Thanks to the actions of others the memory of these tragic fighters for Polish freedom has not been trampled into the ground along with their bodies, buried in nameless pits. That is why we will not even attempt to recall the names from this tragically long list of victims of the enslavement imposed by Stalin.

The first institution working on the 'reshaping' (*perekovka*) of Polish identity in the Moscow-inspired spirit, became the Slavic Committee (1945–1953). It was, in fact, a branch of the All-Slavic Committee, established in Moscow in August 1941. The Polish-Soviet Friendship Society (TPPR), also referred to earlier, grew rapidly as a form of distortion or humiliation of Polish memory. Not only the deep memory, dating back to the Soviet invasion of 1920 but also the most recent one the memory of the rapes and robberies carried out by Soviet soldiers in 1945, of entire cities blown to pieces by the Red Army's artillery, only to be later repopulated by Poles (as in the case of Gdańsk, Koszalin and dozens of cities in Silesia). As the organization's statute stated, the TPPR was to 'disseminate to the masses of Polish society information about the experiences and achievements of the first socialist state in history, about the role of the USSR in the struggle for the liberation of nations and lasting peace'. By 1954, it had 7 million members (every third adult citizen of the People's Republic of Poland). With 7,000 people (as early as 1950), the Speakers' Circle conducted lecture/reading campaigns, just one form of the TPPR's large-scale 'political-educational' operation. Two 'Months of Polish-Soviet Cultural Exchange' (15 September – 15 October 1947 and 1948) were followed further by the 'Months of Deepening Polish-Soviet Friendship' (celebrated from 1949 between 7 October and 7 November).

From 22 June 1946, the cause of this friendship was served by the publication *Przyjaźń* ('Friendship'), first as a monthly, and from 1948 as a weekly. With a circulation of over 300,000 copies, it popularized the heroes of 'progressive' Russian history and 'Polish-Soviet revolutionary brotherhood'. Tens of thousands of agitators pointed out the superiority of the Soviet Union that is, the 'older brothers' Russians and Russia over the rest of the world, including Poland, in every field. They argued that Mendeleyev was far ahead of Lavoisier in chemistry, Popov and Polzunov, rather than Edison and Marconi, were the first radio designers, and that the wheel and bow were invented near Moscow. Ivan Mikhurin refuted Western genetics into the dust. He proved in practice that the will of a brilliant Russian could 'force any form of animal or plant to change much more rapidly, in the direction desired by man'. Articles of this content filled the press on the Vistula from 1946 onwards.

The Red Army was obviously bringing liberation to Poland, along the same lines as in Suvorov's time, just like Catherine's army they sought to bring order and peace. This military liberation from Nazi Germany was of course achieved at the cost of great sacrifice, symbolized by the numerous monuments of gratitude to Soviet soldiers erected all over the country. There were also other expressions of gratitude: for the return of Polish monuments and works of culture that had somehow 'found themselves' on Soviet territory due to the war effort and territorial changes associated with the Second World War. There was no public mention at all of the facts that a large part of the plundered Polish collections (e.g. those evacuated from Warsaw in September 1939 to Poland's eastern territories and the archives of Poland's central state offices subsequently 'captured' by the Red Army) have not been revindicated at all (at least up until today, anyway). Just as the mass rapes and robberies carried out on Polish soil by the 'soldiers-liberators' couldn't be mentioned.

Witnesses to symbolically the most important crime Katyń, and those prepared to uphold the truth about its authors were simply physically eliminated. Methods ranged from the Chief Military Prosecutor's Office's investigation of witnesses Józef Mackiewicz, Ferdynand Goetel and Jan Emil Skiwski (their trial did not take place due to the suspects' fortunate escape abroad) to prison sentences meted out to students repeating the truth about Katyń in conversations or writing down messages from 'banned books' on the subject. The propaganda machine portrayed Katyń as a German crime, and th version of Soviet guilt was US slander aimed at undermining Polish-Soviet friendship. 'Political history' conducted on this issue by the Polish People's Republic was unambiguously staunch.

In the academic historical arena, there were specific instructions on how history, particularly the history of Polish-Soviet friendship, should be understood. Crucially selected Polish historians went directly to Moscow for instructions and then passed these instructions on to their colleagues at home. In a process crucial for the evolution of future academic study in Poland, those who did not want to submit to the new 'methodology' and did not want to approve this vision of Polish-Russian or Polish-Soviet relations ordained by Moscow, were simply removed from academic life. These included Władysław Konopczyński, the most eminent Polish historian alive at the time, a researcher on the policy of Russian imperialism towards Poland in the 18th century, or Henryk Wereszycki, who dealt with similar 'improper' topics concerning the 19th century. Others, in contrast, dealt with the promotion of 'proper' Polish-Soviet history in institutions specially set up for this purpose, such as the Polish-Soviet Institute opened in January 1952.

These versions were transferred to school level in textbooks for children such as the official school text book for "Contemporary History" (1864–1945), this was a "model" textbook edited by Zhanna Kormanova, within which the Second Polish Republic (the Inter-war Poland of Piłsudski) was referred to as a 'fascist state' 42 times and the Warsaw Uprising of Polish patriots against the Nazi Germany was decried as a 'criminal sabotage', a manifestation of 'class hatred'. Both cases backed up by the lack of agreement with the 'incoming liberating Soviet Army', and even a 'secret agreement with the Nazis, concluded at the behest of the Anglo-American counter reaction against the Soviet Army'.

This caused, let us note at once, a certain difficulty in the interpretative schema of the history of Poland's relations with its eastern neighbor. For was the Second Republic truly independent, especially from international imperialism? Or rather was bourgeois independence indeed even a value in itself? After all, that form of independence had manifested itself in such 'criminal' ways as armed resistance to the 'progressive' empire from the east, Poland's war with Soviet Russia in 1919–1920. The victorious defense of Warsaw turned out, in this perspective, to be universally stigmatized both in the press, political pamphlets and school textbooks, as a 'disgraceful brawl', 'conducted against the nation and its best interests'.

Polish Catholicism, the Catholic Church just as it had been in Tsarist times, was the most obstructive element to be overcome in this fight to dominate society and the public consciousness. A wave of persecution, therefore, turned against it. I have described them in another book *Kościół na straży polskiej wolności. Czas walki z Bogiem*, (Eng.: The Church in defense of Polish freedom. Time of battling with God) so here I will only recall the trial of

Top: Second Congress of the Polish Workers' Party, Warsaw, 14 December 1948. During which the PPR and PPS merged into a single workers' party. Bottom: The trial based on trumped-up charges conducted against the Bishop of Kielce, Czesław Kaczmarek.

May Day parade near the new Palace of Culture and Science in Warsaw.

Bishop Kaczmarek of Kielce, accused, obviously according to the Moscow method tried centuries ago against Novgorod and Kazan of "collaboration with the enemy", in this case, with Nazi Germany. A similar provocation was being prepared against the Archbishop Metropolitan of Krakow, Prince Adam Sapieha (1867–1951). Since it was not ultimately carried out during the life of that elderly cardinal, it was pursued posthumously after his death.)

In November 1952, twenty Security Service officers entered the Bishop's Palacec in Krakow. The search aimed to find the documentation stored in the palace on the Katyń Massacre and any material that would help fabricate charges that could disgrace the Krakow curia: unauthorized trade in foreign currency and works of art, espionage, etc. Archbishop Eugeniusz Baziak and Auxiliary Bishop Stanisław Rospond were soon arrested. In

376

January 1953, a show trial of a group of priests and civilian employees of the curia was brought before a military court. The trial of Father Lelita and other "agents of US intelligence" resulted in three death sentences and one life imprisonment. This was soon followed by the arrest and internment for three years, of the head of Poland's Catholic Church, Primate Stefan Wyszyński on 26 September 1953. The disintegration of the Church from within was to be ensured by 'patriot priests' recruited by the UB and 'Catholic lay intellectuals', supporting with their texts the slogans of 'realism', i.e. the subordination of Catholic patriotic Poland to 'progressive' Moscow.

The Church, however, was not broken. The aspiration of Poles for freedom was not broken either. It was heard loudly in the Polish workers' protest during June 1956 in Poznan. This was not just a social protest against a new unilateral demand by authorities to increase production standards coupled with low wages. The workers of the Poznan based in the Stalin Works (the former Hipolit Cegielski Works) gathered for a march on 28 June. A march that ultimately drew 100,000 workers out on the streets under national banners and with slogans such as 'Down with Bolshevism', 'Down with the Muscovites', 'We demand a truly free Poland'. They marched on to the buildings of the local party authorities, the provincial UB building and the prison. Poland's communist rulers did not hesitate for a moment. They threw 10,000 soldiers, 359 tanks and 30 armored personnel carriers into the city under the command of a Russian general in a Polish uniform with a second "Polonised name. Sergei Gorokhov (aka Stanisław Popławski). All these men and hardware were unleashed onto the streets of Poznan to suppress this spontaneous patriotic demonstration of the workers and to protect the buildings, symbols of totalitarian violence, from their wrath.

Uneven fighting continued until the evening of 29 June. At least 73 people were killed and around 800 wounded. The symbol of this sacrifice became thirteen-year-old Romek Strzałkowski, shot dead in front of the UB building. Today, all the victims of the June '56 uprising in Poznań are commemorated by a monument unveiled in 1981: two large crosses – symbols of death and resurrection, entwined together, next the head of a Polish eagle.

Under the cross of June '56, the eagle from Poland's national emblem was able to stretch its wings for a moment after this Stalinist violence. Gomułka, who had fallen into Stalin's disfavor, being perceived as an unreliable element (i.e. unlike Bierut, who had proven himself by his cadre collaboration with the NKVD), was now pulled out of house arrest. His new task, to save the credibility of the Communist Party in Poland in this moment of crisis. He was then, in October 1956, welcomed by the masses as a symbol of independence from the Kremlin, or at any rate, a loosening of the leash.

Circumstances seemed to confirm this role of Gomułka and the interpretation of this crisis as part of the Polish-Russian historical struggle. On 19 October 1956, Soviet troops stationed in Poland were put on standby to suppress another Polish uprising. A special delegation from the USSR suddenly arrived in Warsaw, with the entire renewed set of Kremlin masters in attendance: the now well-known Vyacheslav Molotov, Lazar Kaganovich and numerous military officers, including Marshal Ivan Konev. This delegation was headed by a new 'leader' Nikita Khrushchev (who in 1939 and 1944–1945 in Ukraine oversaw actions against the Poles in the territories then annexed to Ukraine, being the local party administrator). After Stalin's death in March 1953 and a year-long internal struggle for his inheritance was complete, such a powerful delegation to Poland shortly after the succession was a unique event for the time. Ultimately, the movements of USSR troops towards occupying Poland and its capital Warsaw were stopped at the last moment. As a result of complex negotiations, the new leadership of the PZPR, headed by Gomułka (now formally elected First Secretary at the Central Committee plenum on 19–21 October), convinced Khrushchev of its intention to maintain its previous 'policy of alliance and friendship' there would be no breakdown in Polish Russian fraternal relations.

Millions of Poles breathed a collective sigh of relief, there was also to be no further armed intervention by the Russian center in the Polish periphery, at least for now. On the contrary, such a prospect seemed to be henceforth relegated to a safe distance away, though this was not to be the case that year for Poland's traditional Hungarian ally in the south. The symbol of Soviet (interpreted as Russian) domination over Poland, the head of the Polish People's Army, Marshal Konstantin Rokossovsky, was now recalled to Moscow, followed by hundreds of other supervisors from the army and 'sovietniks' from the security services' structures. On 28 October, Primate Stefan Wyszyński returned to Warsaw after his three-year internment.

The Archbishop of Wrocław Bolesław Kominek, the Archbishop of Cracow Karol Wojtyła, Cardinal Stefan Wyszyński, the Primate of Poland, and the Archbishop of Poznań Antoni Baraniak bless the faithful with the relics of St. Jacek Odrowąż. Krakow, Church of the Dominican Fathers, during the Millennium celebrations of the Baptism of Poland, 7 May 1966.

The worst Stalinist period of 'red' Moscow's sovereignty over Poland was coming to an end. But the Soviet supremacy itself was by no means over. Gomułka, as he had promised Khrushchev and Molotov, maintained

379

the 'friendship and alliance'. He just did not want Moscow to humiliate Poland openly. Instead, the Poles were to remain silent and happy to be alive, to have survived under the umbrella of Soviet geostrategic 'protection'. However, this was still to be a Poland with a new head sewn onto it, a post-Katyń Poland. Without any memory of the free Republic, without a deeper civilizational identity, and especially without any Catholic foundation. For, Gomułka now sought to destroy this religious foundation with a ferocity that elected high praise in the Kremlin. A time of open 'dueling' for the Polish soul began, between First Secretary Gomułka and Primate Wyszyński, between the communist state, still a vassal of Moscow and the Polish Church as the repository of the Polish national and cultural tradition that Moscow had wanted to destroy for centuries.

In 1958, Gomułka inaugurated this renewed fight against the Christian face of Polishness with his intrusion upon the Institute of the Primate's Vows of the Nation at Jasna Góra. The struggle intensified with each passing year to reach its climax in the year of the Polish Millennium Jubilee celebrating the one thousand years that had passed since the first Baptism of a Polish ruler, Mieszko I. The Primate now further endangered himself by making a great gesture of moral magnanimity preceding these celebrations. He wrote a groundbreaking letter to the German Episcopate with an offer of reconciliation after the terrible experience of the German crimes against the Poles. This opened up of the prospect of a relative normalization of relations with the Federal Republic of Germany, and the weakening of the real or perceived threat of future German territorial revisionism subliminally imbedded in the minds of many Poles post Yalta. This was to prove a particularly sharp blow to the geopolitical argumentation for maintaining Poland's vassal-like attitude towards Moscow. Gomułka and the 'realists' who supported him (including so-called progressive Catholics) had all been particularly keen to appeal to this anti-German argumentation or fear. The Soviet Union/Russia, even if its 'protection' was a burden, was nevertheless the only guarantor for the security of Poland's western border.

The Primate together with the archbishops of Wrocław (Bolesław Kominek) and Krakow (a young Karol Wojtyła) showed by the example of their bold letter, that it was possible to think responsibly and courageously about Poland's position on the map of Europe. One could abandon the servile mentality rooted in fear, one did not need to be afraid. They also gave testimony to this effect to millions of their faithful with their consistent and constant efforts to educate the nation. Recalling its great historical traditions of liberty, citizens' rights and actively defending its freedom.

No one expressed the essence of this upbringing more emphatically than Primate Stefan Wyszyński doing so through dozens of sermons and occasional public speeches. He argued, one might say, openly, about the sense and significance of Polish history and identity. About the importance of national uprisings, about September 1939, about the Warsaw Uprising. This was a dispute not only with the official interpretation of communist propaganda on such matters but also with that intelligentsia, calling itself 'Catholic', which like the communists wanted to 'reform' the nation to combat the 'stupidity' or lack of "normality" inherent in Polish history in any celebration of it or any honest recollection of it. All in the name of compromise with the stronger brother, with the Empire.

The 100th anniversary of the 19th century January Uprising was to be a moment of particularly sharp clash in this regard. That 1863 Uprising was not, as the well-known 'realist' Stanisław Stomma of the *Tygodnik Powszechny* newspaper described it, the 'reflex of a mindless anti-Russian complex'. Stomma had gathered the applause of the communist authorities for this statement. It was something altogether different. To best encapsulate it, let us repeat just two sentences from the subsequent answer given by Primate Wyszyński during a sermon in the Świętokrzyskie region commemorating the centenary of the uprising: 'When a person or a nation feels bound and fettered in any sphere when he/she feels that there is no longer freedom of expression and opinion, freedom of culture and work, but everything is restrained by some chains and manacles, everything fettered like in steel corsets, then there is no need to have complexes. All one needs, is to simply be a decent human being, to have a sense of honor and one's personal dignity, in order to rise up against such bondage, seeking the means and ways to escape it.' In this speech, as on other 'anniversary' occasions, the Primate invariably defended Poland's 'failed' history, the successive unsuccessful uprisings, battles for honor alone with no chance of victory. Yet if that was to be the only route left to freedom, to preserve dignity and honor, to awaken the conscience of the nation, then so be it.

However, this was not just a defense of heroism and sacrifice. There was something more to this consequence: a note of a kind of messianism, of sacrifice and national resurrection inscribed in the vision of Polish history. Its positive goal would be 'to win the whole of the East for the Church in Poland', as the Primate wrote about it in his last word to the Episcopate, and, on the other hand, a sense of Poland's unique responsibility 'for this group of nations which are part of the Slavic tribe' a feeling apparently shared by another of the great fathers of the Polish Church: the Metropolitan of Krakow Karol Wojtyła, as of October 1978 Pope John Paul II, now Saint John Paul II.

With their subsequent policy of repression, the state authorities only strengthened resistance. This was the case when the Citizens' Militia (MO) and the Motorized Reserves of the Citizens' Militia (ZOMO) disrupted the most important millennium celebrations those in Gniezno (17 April), in Krakow (8 May), in Gdańsk (28–29 May), and in Warsaw (26 June), where a massive march of young people calling for freedom of speech and defending the dignity of the Primate under attack by the authorities. They were blasted with ZOMO water cannons. Several 'arrests' followed directed against pilgrimages those holding images of Our Lady of Częstochowa (a reference to the resistance against the Swedish army 300 years earlier) throughout the country, as well as large clashes in the town of Brzeg near Wrocław, connected with the eviction of priests from their homes and their defense by crowds of the faithful (26 May), such images served to complete the picture of a struggle for the soul of.

March 1968 in Poland was, in fact, a continuation of this struggle: in defense of freedom and the traditions of Polish culture, obstructed directly on Moscow's orders. Let us recall that the reason for the mass protests that year was not only actions by students but also workers and 'ordinary citizens' in a dozen or so cities (including Warsaw, Łódź, Krakow, Wrocław, Poznań, Gdańsk, Szczecin, Katowice, Radom, Tarnów, Legnica) it was a protest against the removal of Mickiewicz's play *Dziady* (The Forefathers' Eve), in a version directed by Kazimierz Dejmek, from the stage of the National Theatre in Warsaw. This was done at the request of the Soviet Embassy in Warsaw, the performance was halted due to 'anti-Russian themes' found in the national bard's arch-drama. Themes that were vividly picked up on

The Nowa Huta Lenin statue designed by Marian Konieczny, with a queue of comrades below him. A tribute to the leader of the revolution is a 'must be!' This applied even in the Socialist Realist decorations erected in his honor (bottom photo) which obscured the great beauty of Krakow's Main Square.

by the audience. After the last performance, on 30 January 1968, there was a demonstration in front of Mickiewicz's monument with the slogans 'Free art! Free theatre!'.

This was the beginning of March 1968. These events did not begin with any anti-Semitic emotions and intolerance as was often portrayed overseas, but with a patriotic reaction to the ostentatious rule of the 'Moscow ambassador'. Just as in the time of Catherine II, seeking to exert control over all areas of life even in matters of Polish culture. These true origins of 1968 must necessarily be recalled, lest this critical moment in history, a moment in which so many times Moscow tried to find justification for its rule over Poland. Due to the need to 'tame Polish anti-Semitism', in a word, to 'de-Nazify' Polishness. Yet this was and is a (largely) false premise. In fact, at the time, it was Moscow's agents in the party who, on the Kremlin's direct orders, carried out the anti-Semitic purge in the power elite. Led by among others Wojciech Jaruzelski, then head of the Ministry of Defense. A man who would 13 years later introduce Martial Law to Poland and would also be its future President. A man who was always towed the Moscow line. The youth speeches in defense of Mickiewicz and Polish culture were exploited and used as a cover for a factional fight among the communists themselves, with the aim of overthrowing Gomułka, the tool availed of, was state sponsored anti-Semitic rhetoric.

Yet Polish society continued to fight, ever more boldly, for freedom. The next stage of this struggle was to be the workers' protests on the Baltic Coast in December 1970. Once again suppressed by the authorities. They nevertheless led like those during the June 1956 events in Poznań, like the 1966 millennium celebrations, like March 1968, all towards a regaining or a reassertion of subjectivity by the nation. A nation finding its historical traditions in rebellion against a policy of enslavement by the Kremlin. In addition to the role of the Church in this process of grassroots self-liberation, the influence of culture was also significant. It constantly emerged as a factor imbued with its legacy of freedom even in new artistic works. The poetry of Zbigniew Herbert and his message on the dignity of man rebelling against baseness, against the violence of empires; the brilliant satirical poems of Janusz Szpotański, such as *Towarzysz Szmaciak* (Comrade Szmaciak) or *Caryca i zwierciadło* (The Tsarina and the Mirror), written in 1974 (with its depiction of the then Kremlin host, Brezhnev, as an incarnation of the spirit of Catherine II), or popular songs (such as the beautiful hymn written by Jan Pietrzak in 1976 – *Żeby Polska była Polską* (Let Poland be Poland) or later songs by Jacek Kaczmarski and Przemysław Gintrowski, all these cultural phenomena contributed to the collective spiritual uprising.

Naturally, the culture of the *émigré* community played a significant role in this process, where, in addition to works of independent art and thought could also take shape. It was especially important for the London milieu to stand steadfast with the banners of fidelity to the tradition of the free Republic. Also important was the search for new geopolitical ideas, an escape from imperial subordination conducted in the circle of the Paris-based *Kultura initiative* led by the erudite Jerzy Giedroyć. Together with his closest political associate, Juliusz Mieroszewski, Giedroyć sought to adapt the old Jagiellonian, 1920s Promethean and Federalist policies. Amending them to the new situation on the ground created by Soviet expansion during World War II, with the hope that this could gradually evolve into something different.

The Giedroyć-Mieroszewski program combined two assumptions: (1) support for the independence of Poland's immediate eastern neighbors: Lithuania, Belarus and Ukraine (LBU), recognition of the strategic importance of the independence of these countries' and agreement with them on the post-1945 borders, and: (2) a desire to improve relations with Russia –to the extent that the latter would be able to come to terms with the irrevocable separation of the LBU countries from the Russia Empire.

In 1976, for the third time, after the Poznań June 1956 protests and December 1970 protests on the Baltic Coast, Polish workers once again rose up. That same year, the so-called June events took place, a protest by workers from Radom and Ursus, among other places, against the authorities' attempt to introduce drastic increases in food prices (prices already high), this was subsequently suppressed by the police with brute force.

This protest coincided with amendments to the People's Republic of Poland's Constitution, which now emphasized Poland's dependence on Moscow even more emphatically. The principle of 'indissoluble Polish-Soviet friendship' was written into it, as a duty for all citizens. A greater debasement of the dignity of the Republic could hardly have been put in writing.

385

Understandably, protests were raised against this new act of degradation, leading to the birth of the phenomenon known as the democratic opposition. Its subsequent forms took on many embodiments, the Workers' Defence Committee (KOR), the Movement for the Defence of Human and Citizen's Rights (ROPCiO), the Polish Independence Alliance (PPN), the Confederation of Independent Poland (KPN), and finally the Free Trade Unions in Upper Silesia (founded by Kazimierz Świton in February 1978) and on the Baltic coast (two months later in April by Andrzej Gwiazda and Krzysztof Wyszkowski).

From the moment Cardinal Karol Wojtyła was elected pope on 16 October 1978, and especially from the spiritual awakening resulting from his pilgrimage to Poland in June 1979, this rising tide of public sentiment towards independence and freedom seemed unstoppable. It would later take the beautiful symbolic name of *Solidarność* (Solidarity) in August 1980. It is worth recalling from that historic first papal pilgrimage in June 1979 not only the Pope's appeal from Warsaw's Victory Square. The impassioned cry that the Holy Spirit would renew the face of the land, but also the meeting in Gniezno that immediately followed. There, John Paul II seemed to expand the horizon of influence for his pilgrimage, giving it an international dimension. He was not only concerned with the renewal of this Polish land. Here he also recalled the presence of Christianity in the life of the peoples of the whole of Eastern Europe. He addressed the Orthodox Rus with a message of reconciliation. He called on the three peoples who had inherited its traditions Russians, Ukrainians, and Belarusians, to recall their roots in Christianity on the threshold of a new millennium celebration, that of the baptism of Kyiv (in 988). At the same time, he emphasized the belonging of 'our Lithuanian brothers' to the tradition of the West. Nor did he forget the Czechs, Slovaks, Croats, Serbs, Bulgarians, and even the minority Sorbs living in the German Democratic Republic (GDR). To all of them, he called as a Slavic Pope, beckoning them to return 'back to the Cross and the Resurrection'. For the Soviet Union, then fighting against religion (including radical Muslim elements) in Afghanistan and other national 'centrifugal' movements, and doing so for the sake of the entire 'socialist camp', John Paul II's homily on the meadows of Gniezno was an open and potentially mortal challenge...

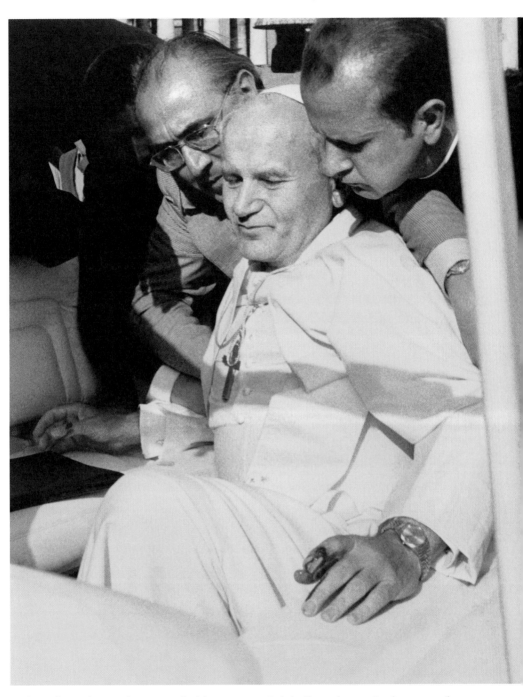

Holy Father John Paul II, wounded by an assassin's bullets, slumps in the arms of his secretary Fr Stanislaw Dziwisz. The attempted assassination on the Pope by Ali Agca on 13 May 1981 shocked the whole world.

The Kremlin watched the new Pope's successive gestures with ever greater disquiet. Taking note of features which testified emphatically to the fact that he did not intend to limit himself to raising his fellow Polish citizens from their knees. He wanted to awaken the faith and dignity of all the peoples of communist-subjugated Central and Eastern Europe. The KGB noted on the very second day after the inauguration of the pontificate that the Pope had instructed two priests from Krakow to take his cardinal's cap the *zucchetto*, as a votive offering in front of the picture of Our Lady of the Gate of Dawn in Vilnius, in Lithuania. The Kremlin was even more upset by John Paul II's decision to entrust the undersecretary's office in charge of relations with Eastern Europe at the Vatican's Secretariat of State to Father Audrys Bačkis, an *émigré* from Lithuania, son of the last ambassador of the independent Lithuanian Republic in Paris. The Polish Pope was manifesting his solidarity with the persecuted Catholic Church in, of all places, Lithuania. A month after his inauguration, he met with Cardinal Josyf Slipyj, the aged Metropolitan of the now completely outlawed Greek Catholic (Uniate) Church of the USSR. John Paul II saw to it that the underground Uniate Church was strengthened, soon appointing (in March 1980) Myroslav Lubachivsky as Cardinal Slipyj's aide and successor as Archbishop of Lviv.

In 1980–1981, inspired by the words and example of John Paul II, Poland experienced the challenging but hopeful months of yet another peaceful struggle for its dignity. One of the most important, or at any rate, the most symbolically significant events in this struggle, was the '*Message to the Workers of Eastern Europe*', addressed by the First National Congress of Delegates of the Solidarity Trade Union in Gdańsk. This statement adopted on 8 September 1981 on the initiative of one of the delegates, Henryk Siciński, was an open challenge by the Polish freedom movement to the rule of the Moscow Empire, not just in Poland, over other nations as well, this was Poland lighting the beacon. The leader of the Soviet Union, Leonid Brezhnev, stated plainly at that time, during a meeting with the Political Bureau of the Central Committee of the CPSU: 'This is a dangerous and provocative document. The words in it are few, but they all hit on one point. Its authors would like to sow confusion in the socialist countries, to incite groups of all sorts of dissenters.' Yes, that's what it was all about, sowing a freedom 'ferment' and finding brave 'renegades' in the other nations of Moscow's zone of domination who would dare to lead these nations out of the house of captivity.

However, the forces that sustained the reign of this communist system, this empire of human enslavement, were not passive. Fearful not just of the Pope's message but of his eloquence and panache in public settings, his ability to read his audience, all skills initially honed at theater classes in Krakow; the authorities now decided to construct their own macabre theatre. They made their presence felt on 13 May 1981 in St Peter's Square in Rome, when, on Moscow's orders, an assassin's bullets struck John Paul II. On 13 December, exactly seven months later, Brezhnev's nominee for the top post in Poland the aforementioned General Jaruzelski imposed martial law to crush Solidarity. Yet, the Pope survived the coup and now did all he could to ensure that Solidarity, outlawed by Moscow, would also survive.

Czesław Miłosz in his notebook from the autumn of 1987 could not but recognize the profound historical spell John Paul II and his message were casting over the people not just of Poland but throughout Eastern Europe for Orthodox and Catholic alike. 'Among the statesmen, monarchs, chiefs of the twentieth century, not a single figure corresponds to our image of royal majesty, except Karol Wojtyła. Only he could genuinely play Shake-speare's kings. [...] At the depth of its misery, Poland got a king and the kind of king it had dreamed of, from the Piast tribe, a judge of goodness, not entangled in the creaking reality of politics. [...] A king bearing a messianic faith, deeply convinced that there is a spiritual state where struggles and triumphs occur, right next to the other story, the living ones, but in close connection with it. [...] John Paul's travels to Poland can be understood as a battle waged in the hereafter for her soul. As if every joining of thousands of his listeners in brotherly love, even if only for a short time, moved the heavens, happened together both there and here on earth. Could it be that he knew in advance that he could raise people in a bloodless insurrection from collective humiliation?'.

This was the role of the Pope's successive pilgrimages to Poland after the imposition of martial law, traveling there in 1983 and 1987, reminding Polish youth of the example set by the small garrison defending Westerplatte in Gdansk in 1939. The Pope was breaking down the wall of hidden or obscured and misconstrued history, the wall separating Eastern Europe from Western Europe and, above all the walls limiting religious freedom and plurality of faith in other countries. The 1000th anniversary of Christianity in Rus (the old Kyivan Rus now largely the lands of Ukraine), was thus celebrated in 1988, John Paul II astutely harnessed its meaning as another opportunity to further his work. Through the Cardinal and Vatican Secretary of State Agostino Casaroli, the Pope handed Gorbachev a personal letter dated 7 June 1988. In a foresightful piece of diplomatic correspondence, he invited Soviet authorities to a serious discussion about the situation of the Catholic Church in the USSR while at the same time praising the initiatives made by Gorbachev in domestic and foreign policy. Initiative that eased tensions and helped to liberalize the system. Privately, in a conversation with Italian Catholic philosopher Rocco Buttiglione, John Paul II admitted things did not augur well for the success of Gorbachev in his mission: 'He is a good man, but he will lose because he wants to do the impossible. Communism cannot be reformed'.

The also Pope sought contact with other Russians who would allow him to better understand the situation in their great country, from which he by no means wished to separate himself and had no foreboding. He met with, among others, Irina Ilovayskaya-Alberti, editor of the prestigious *émigré* weekly 'Russkaya Mysl' and a close associate of Solzhenitsyn, then with Yelena Bonner – a prominent activist in the dissident movement, and finally (in February 1989) with her husband, the uncrowned 'king' of that movement, the physicist and human rights defender Andrei Sakharov. Together they openly discussed their hopes for a different, non-totalitarian Russia and the Slavic Pope.

We come here to the question of the historical meaning of this struggle. The struggle Poland waged under the leadership of St John Paul II. A Poland, faithful to its political and cultural tradition. Was its struggle, its stance, significant in stopping the Soviet empire, in setting in motion the process of its disintegration (or its dismantling)?

Some would argue that the system of Soviet domination based on communism (or if you prefer: the Soviet system) collapsed because it lost the battle of economic rivalry with capitalism. Others would put it somewhat differently: it lost out to modernity, failed to meet the demands or chal-

One of the most courageous activists of the Solidarity Trade Union, Anna Walentynowicz, a worker at the Gdańsk shipyard during the August 1980 strike. She later became a victim of the Smoleńsk catastrophe on 10 April 2010.

lenges of modernization, and proved to be a dead end for its people. Yet, let us note, that explaining the collapse of the Soviet system by means of inevitability alone, is not enough. It is instead, an excellent start to a historical interpretation, according to the classic triad of structure (though in this case, not fully sufficient), coincidence, and event. If we are not extreme determinists, we could also add to it an element of human will, of individual decision or initiative. Then we can say that communism would not have decayed on its own, or at least its process of decay would have lasted longer, much longer... Someone accelerated this process or interrupted it, leading to the system's dissolution at a pace and in a manner pre-empting its natural collapse.

Who? In addition to providence, another perspective besides the bottom-up revolution can be considered, that of a possible top-down revolution. Its initiators could have been, may have been those authors at the top. The top of the system was, of course, in Moscow. Russia has had a great tradition of top-down revolutions in its political culture facilitated by a highly centralized, hierarchical structure, from the great reforming Tsars Peter I and Alexander II to the Bolsheviks. In the second half of the 1980s, supporters of profound change in the Soviet system also began to make hopeful references to this tradition, including (for example, the eminent Soviet-Russian historian Natan Eidelman) and the actions of Mikhail Gorbachev also fit this paradigm of 'top-down revolutionaries'.

However, it is perhaps not so much in the weight of the Russian tradition but instead in the response of the various authorities of the Soviet Empire to the problems of that system they governed, where the sources of the real top-down revolution in the second half of the 1980s can be sought and found. Let us stress again: it is all about RESPONSES, so the questions, or rather the challenges that provoked these responses, must first be considered. This is where the phenomenon of Solidarity but that of 1980 can find a significant, perhaps even a crucial historical place. For it challenged the 'workers' based 'legitimacy' of the communist system and did so more effectively than any mass protest movement had done before. Communist ideology, which had been entering a phase of crisis since the death of Stalin, and certainly since 1956, would now finally collapse because it was no longer an acceptable idea for legitimizing rules. Clearly visible in August 1980 and again especially after December 1981, when the tanks of 'workers' power' stormed the new ideological fortress of 'workers Solidarity'.

The trouble with Poland, after all, had yet another ideological dimension for the Soviet system, although one also linked to the collapse. The system, now flushed from the inside out of its ideological content, could continue to maintain itself based on violence and coercion. Yet this had to be supplemented by the satisfaction of at least the elementary material needs of society, aroused by the ever more visible comparisons with the West. The maintenance of Poland within the system thus had to be paid for, and this was a drain on costs. It is such a conclusion that runs through the meeting minutes of the Political Bureau of the Central Committee of the Communist

Party of the Soviet Union available today, and also in the documentary testimonies of meetings between comrades from the Soviet headquarters and the administrators of the Polish periphery. However, since it is necessary to pay in order to keep Poland in the system and the Soviet comrades are beginning to wonder how to reduce these additional costs, another question may soon arise. That of the costs associated with maintaining the entire system (the entire empire) and the possibilities to reduce them.

These questions had, of course, not only just a 'Polish' or more broadly, intra-camp genesis. Likewise, the erosion of the ideological foundations of the system. The confrontation with the West revealed the material and ideological defeat of communism. Here, therefore, is the place to recall the role of those actors on the part of the West who consciously undertook this confrontation to win against communism. We have already spoken of the role of St John Paul II, which went beyond the political influence of the West. Now, however, we must necessarily mention the importance of the appeal to the evolving ideology of human rights and its formalization by the administration of President Jimmy Carter, followed, of course, by the propaganda crusade against communism undertaken by Ronald Reagan (1911–2004). The author of the memorable formula about the 'evil empire'. It was, of course, also crucial that they took up the Soviet Union's gauntlet in the arms race.

It was around 1977–1978 that the *détente* policy, which had lasted for nearly a decade, began to break down. The essence of this policy was a relaxation of USSR-USA relations on a 'realistic' basis by the US side's (Nixon and Ford administrations) respect for Soviet imperial interests in exchange for a reduction in the missile arms race. In any case, the *détente* policy unquestionably recognized the permanence of Soviet control over the countries of Eastern Europe, as confirmed by the Helmut Sonnenfeld doctrine (named after Henry Kissinger's deputy at the State Department), adopted in American politics as recently as December 1975. The content of this doctrine amounted to Washington's affirmation of the veracity of the inscriptions scattered throughout the squares in 1968 of a recently pacified Czechoslovakia: *S Sovětským svazem na věcně čásy a nikdy jinak* ('With the Soviet Union for all times and never different'). That same 'optimistic' slogan was deemed to be in force for all the countries of the 'camp'.

However, the Soviet Union had meanwhile reached out to Nicaragua, Ethiopia, Angola, the whole of Indochina, and finally, Afghanistan. The Sonnenfeld doctrine did not cover these regions these lands. Neither could the economic potential of the USSR, when trying to encompass this global scale of expansion. Moscow had imperceptibly crossed that boundary beyond which the twilight of any empire begins. This boundary has a succinct English term: *overextension*. Its crossing led to a response from the US one symbolized by the actions mentioned above, those of the Carter and Reagan administrations. However, it also led to a need to respond to the subsequent American reaction (i.e. above all, to a Washington now choosing to increase the pace of the arms race) to the dramatic question of the continued viability of a system now so burdened. Specifically, a response to the question of economic efficiency.

The specter of catastrophe began to loom over Soviet communism. Somewhere between 1977 and 1983, the temptation flashed through parts of the Soviet leadership elite to push back this specter by means of war: limited to Europe, yet war nonetheless. Strike while we still had a crushing advantage before the Americans installed their new missiles (Cruise and Pershing) on the Old Continent to level that advantage before they carried out their 'Star Wars' plan. This temptation was apparently expressed by the ambitious Chief of General Staff of the Soviet Army, Marshal Nikolai Ogarkov (1917–1994). However, the senior leaders of the Politburo were not eager to succumb to such a temptation, and anyway, after 1983 it was already too late.

This was precisely when the more important prerequisites for a top-down revolution at the system's center had already appeared. Mikhail Gorbachev became its symbol, and his election as General Secretary of the Central Committee of the CPSU in the spring of 1985 is often regarded as its beginning. By then, the American 'proposal' of an arms race of economic destruction, a race that America would inevitably win, already had to be put on hold. This is what the 1985 Geneva talks were about, followed in 1986 by Reykjavik. In their continuation, a change of status was also being negotiated for the countries of Eastern Europe, in which Poland of the now underground Solidarity and Pope John Paul II was still fermenting. The change in this status was becoming part of the Soviet strategy for escaping out of the economic dead end in which it had found itself.

394

The Round Table Talks in Warsaw resulted in the systemic transformation of the People's Republic of Poland. From 6 February–5 April 1989. Bottom: The Contractual elections of June 1989 as witnessed in Krakow.

For this change to be carried out smoothly, without significant damage to Soviet interests, it was necessary to recruit the executors or practitioners of the future potential top-down "revolutions" in each of the region's individual countries. After the experience of martial law and economic collapse, the power elite in Poland was exceptionally well prepared to undertake such a task. There was no need to explain its rationale: impending economic collapse was evident to many of the more astute elite members in Poland and was already parodied in popular film and television. Moreover, also for a part of the elite that we could nevertheless call the opposition (I mean, for the time being, the underground opposition), the same experiences and observations were a justifiable reason to adopt the possible and promising perspective of such a top-down revolution. What experiences? Firstly, the defeat of Solidarity in its clash with the state's apparatus of violence, founded, geopolitically, on Moscow backing. Secondly, the fundamental economic difficulties of the country.

The dream on the part of this section of the opposition elite was to reach out to Moscow itself. To become for it, perhaps not a partner, but a kind of subcontractor for at least the domestic part of the scenario envisaged by any future top-down revolution. This dream was most precisely expressed by Stefan Bratkowski, who tried to reach Moscow with his offer even during the unfavorable time of the first Solidarity period. In May 1982, in the Paris published based *Kultura,* he published these words: 'An act of long-term imagination is expected from a great power that has had semi-colonies: the conversion of a semi-colony into a controlled allied state. [...] I think that somewhere in Europe, there would be some quiet place, inaccessible to the press, radio and TV, where they could meet for confidential talks [...] the plenipotentiaries of the Western banks, the envoys of the governments concerned and the Vatican, all equipped with the appropriate prerogatives the representatives of the authorities in Poland and negotiators representing Polish society'.

The administrators of the People's Republic of Poland obviously did not want to lose control over the process of any possible negotiations; they did not want the representatives of the opposition elite ever to find a channel of direct contact with Moscow by going over their heads. They themselves were predictably looking for connections that would help them to roll back the most negative (including for the authorities themselves) consequences of the martial law they had been "forced" to implement in late 1981. Talks to share responsibility were becoming a pressing necessity when successive attempts at reforms to save the economy were clearly failing, and real reforms required serious social costs that could end in disaster also for those in power. The year 1988 turned out to be a watershed in this respect. The essence of the game undertaken at that time by the creators of martial law with selected representatives of the opposition, was most aptly expressed by General Wojciech Jaruzelski himself: 'The idea was to get the train moving, but to keep your hand on the brake'.

In the summer of 1988, direct preparations for the 'Round Table' talks began. Poland's top-down revolution, sometimes called the 'rationed revolution' by its historians, was entering a decisive phase. What was decisive at that moment was the impact of its mechanisms rather than the then meager and modest presence at the table of the original proponents of the 'Solidarity' revolution (despite all the courage and determination of its continuators). The strikes at the Gdańsk Shipyard and the Lenin Steelworks in 1988 were the effect of the top-down revolution rather than its cause. They certainly would not become a direct component of it.

The elections of 4 June 1989 proved to be the final, glorious chord of the grassroots revolution in Poland. Despite the election's organizational rules dictating that only some 50% of the mandates to the Sejm were contestable, the electorate voted with their conscience. The vast majority expressed themselves clearly against communism and the candidates that system put forward. They voted against the system, against the party elite, ruling on the orders of Moscow for 45 years. The electorate was also against, as it later turned out, the 'top-down revolution' arrangements. The compromises negotiated at the 'Round Table' were now visibly threatened for a moment. Voters completely rejected the national list, consisting of representatives of the party power elite. People whose ongoing mandate to continue governing after these first partially free elections, was guaranteed under the Round Table accords. The question arose as to whether the party would now maintain its hold on that brake of which General Jaruzelski spoke. Thankfully for him, the *Obywatelski Komitet Polityczny* (Civic Political Committee) immediately declared loyalty to the negotiated Round Table agreement. The logic of the top-down revolution would prevail even in the face of the people's clear lack of approval.

The question now became would Moscow manage somehow, to retain control over this 'hand-on-the-brake' experiment? Would it retain its influence in a new, indirect form, drawing on centuries of experience in mastering imperial techniques to control the periphery? Would Moscow itself succumb to these liberating forces so unleashed? The spirit of which now reigned irrepressibly in Poland. Moreover resonated out from it, from that nation's example, from the words and deeds of St John Paul II, from the symbol and spirit of Solidarity? These questions remained open in 1989. The Northern Group of Soviet Army Forces was still stationed on Polish soil, in the town of Legnica: tens of thousands of the Empire's trained soldiers, armed to the teeth, including with nuclear weapons. The 45 years since Stalin's puppet power had been installed had not passed without a trace. The influence of a peculiar anti-establishment, in the culture of first the bludgeon and then the nihilistic cabaret, both together pursuing the aims of Moscow's Empire, the spiritual enslavement of Poland. None of this had disappeared completely, not yet. The struggle to regain independence was not over. Poland was not yet entirely free after the elections of 4 June 1989. But it was an example for the sweeping changes that would now take place across Eastern Europe, through Kyiv, Vilnius, Riga, Tbilisi, and Baku and on towards Moscow. At least, so it seemed at the time.

The Disintegration and Malign Reconstruction of Colonial Relations with Moscow (1989–2002)

W e date the beginning of the Third Republic as of 29 December 1989. The date when the Sejm voted to return to the name of the pre-war Polish state, the Republic of Poland (Rzeczpospolita), and to restore its emblem in the form of the crowned eagle. For two more years, it was to exist side by side with a now limping Soviet Union, from which successive nation-states emerged during these turbulent times, starting with Lithuania, Latvia, Estonia and Ukraine. The decisive blow to the Empire, however, was dealt by a peculiar secession of its central component, Russia under Boris Yeltsin, following the failed putsch of August 1991 led by defenders of the old communist power structure in the USSR. Formally, the Soviet Union was dissolved on 26 December 1991. This dissolution resulted directly from a decision taken at a meeting on 8 December in the Viskuli hunting lodge, in the Białowieża Forest (*Belovezhskaya Pushcha*) just 10 or so kilometers from the Polish border. It was taken by the leaders of Ukraine and Belarus, Leonid Kravchuk and Stanislav Shushkevich, together with Russian President Boris Yeltsin. In place of the USSR, they established the Commonwealth of Independent States (CIS). Was this the disintegration of an empire or just another top-down driven transformation?

This last word 'transformation', which has entered the language of political scientists, and by extension, the language of expert commentators and journalism of the region and even common colloquial language. It seems to reflect well one interpretation of the changes the Poles were witnessing changes they were subject to. In using this term, we do not have to be immediate followers of the specific thesis. A thesis actually formulated and published in 1984 by none other than the former KGB Colonel Anatoly Golitsyn (1926–2008), a man who defected to the West in 1961. Golitsyn in his book, *New Lies to Replace Old Lies, the Communist Strategy of Deception and Disinformation*, presented a fascinating scenario for the top-down transformation of the USSR. Portraying it as a game of pretense initiated by KGB headquarters to confuse and divide an opponent that was proving to be simply too strong and too resolute in 1984, the West under the leadership of Ronald Reagan and Margaret Thatcher.

Referring back to General Jaruzelski's 'train and break' metaphor quoted in the previous chapter, let us state the banal truth that many politicians (both from Warsaw and Moscow, but also in Washington and Berlin) were eager during that heated time to keep their hand not only on the brake, but also on those levers which would allow the switches to be moved so that the peoples of the region would not be going where they wanted, but more where they were being sent. Among those who, at the end of 1988 and in 1989, wanted to take part in the race for control of this 'rolling train of history', to use this hackneyed metaphor, there were also representatives of the Polish opposition, people who until that time had remained of course underground. An interesting motif here is the letter from Bronisław Geremek (the future Foreign Minister of Poland who led its entry to NATO) addressed to Mikhail Gorbachev. A letter which Irena Lasota later found and was published by Professor Henryk Głębocki (*O 'politykę kontraktu społecznego'. Memoriał Bronisława Geremka z maja 1988 r.,* 'Biuletyn IPN', 5–6/2008). Here, as early as in the spring of 1988, one of the prominent intellectual leaders of the opposition proposed to the communist leadership in Moscow a peculiar settlement, 'the basis of which was to be economic reform', as Henryk Głębocki writes, 'and support for [communist party] reforms in exchange for partial democratization and legalization of the Union [Solidarity], with concurrent recognition of the dominant position of the PZPR'.

Equally informative, and probably even more fruitful, was the initiative to travel to Moscow that was taken by the leading Polish publicist and founder of Gazeta Wyborcza Adam Michnik a year later in July 1989. Michnik then leader of one of the ideological wings of the opposition sought to find a contact directly within the Kremlin with whom he could 'clarify' how much could be afforded or allowed for in Poland, i.e. how much freedom would be tolerated, regardless of what Gen. Jaruzelski declared or said. At that time, it was not yet known precisely what the composition of the future Polish government would be; Jaruzelski had planned to nominate

Top: Adam Michnik and Jacek Kuroń in Kuroń's Warsaw flat, September 1980. Bottom: Key participants of the Polish Round Table talks. From left: Tadeusz Mazowiecki (Polish Prime Minister from 1989–1991), General Czesław Kiszczak (Polish Interior Minister from 1981–1990), Lech Wałęsa, General Wojciech Jaruzelski (Head of Polish Armed Forces and later Polish President who introduced Marshall Law in 1982), Bronisław Geremek (Polish Foreign Minister 1997–2000) and Mieczysław Rakowski (Polish Prime Minister from 1988 to 1989).

Gen. Kiszczak (the imposer of Martial law in 1981) as Prime Minister. Michnik however returned from his reconnaissance in Moscow with happy news. News now openly referenced in Polish public and private media as he himself commented years later: 'They were busy with themselves there in Moscow, they said: do what you want. And if that's the case, I said: guys, we need to do a cash heist' (*chłopaki, skok na kasę trzeba robić*). However, Michnik immediately added that General Jaruzelski, remained the vital safety fuse for all the changes in Poland. The sluice gate on which Moscow's decision whether it liked what was happening in Poland or not would depend. Jaruzelski had just been elected President in July by the votes of the PZPR in the Sejm and Senate not by universal public suffrage. He'd also gained the support of some so-called Catholic MPs of the Civic Committee, actors always faithful to the attitude of 'realism'. Thus, as long as Gen. Jaruzelski was not only respected in Poland but was also recognized as a key element of the Soviet system, everything was fine from Moscow's side, the rest could be changed.

This was the time when, the slogan 'your President, our Prime Minister' appeared, and the right candidate for this 'our Prime Minister' was unambiguously identified as Tadeusz Mazowiecki (Jacek Kuroń and Bronisław Geremek also put themselves forward for contention). Gen. Jaruzelski commented on the choice of Tadeusz Mazowiecki in the most flattering terms: 'A serious, responsible, prudent man, he had experience from the Sejm of the People's Republic of Poland [he had indeed sat in the Sejm under both Gomułka and Gierek], and he knows the mechanisms of power and authority'. These were the best of recommendations from Jaruzelski, which, in addition were not to be disappointed.

The day after his appointment, Prime Minister Mazowiecki (I remember vividly the enthusiasm that many of us Poles felt on that day) quietly received the head of the KGB or State Security Committee, Vladimir Kryuchkov. He was as it turned out conveniently in Poland at the time. This was the first foreign guest, symbolically an important first guest, received by the Polish Prime Minister of the new Solidarity centered government. The first non-communist Prime Minister, as was emphasized at the time. Of course, we do not know what they discussed, and we probably will still not find out soon. In relation to this event however, it is worth recalling another coincidence. Just a week later, on 24 August 1989, the new Prime Minister Mazowiecki memorably said in the Sejm: 'We are drawing a thick line under the past (to separate ourselves from it)'. At the time, we referred to these words, and rightly so, primarily in terms of domestic matters. There would be no settlement or retribution for the crimes of the communist system, the economic ruin and destruction of the country, and the implementation of martial law. We Poles forget, however, that these words also had an external meaning.

Just the day before, 23 August, had been commemorated the 50th anniversary of the Molotov-Ribbentrop Pact the herald of 50 years of horror and hardship for Poland. On that same day, the populations of the three small (still oppressed) Baltic nations, Lithuania, Latvia and Estonia had come together quite literally as a symbolic reminder of the crimes of communism. They formed a human living chain of more than two million people stretching right across the 3 nations. Since the total population of these three Baltic republics was no more than 7.5 million, this meant that more than one in three and just slightly less than one out of every two inhabitants of these three small republics joined in this living chain stretching from Vilnius through to Riga and onward to Tallinn. All of Eastern Europe was shocked by the scale of this reminder aimed at underlining that great crime of Soviet imperialism, the Molotov-Ribbentrop Pact. In this context, the words spoken the very next day by Poland's first non-communist Prime Minister: 'We are drawing a thick line under the past'. also had their own symbolic meaning, which we sometimes, as I mentioned, wrongly forget. In Poland, the account of Soviet crimes against our country was somehow not to be a topic of particular emphasis at that moment. A policy of silence that the KGB's visiting head Kryuchkov no doubt enthusiastically approved of.

Indeed, Prime Minister Mazowiecki did not go to Moscow on his first foreign visit for perhaps that was no longer an immediate or urgent requirement, but he did go to the Vatican, and we Poles remember that. What we remember less well, however, is that on his second trip, his steps were indeed directed to the Empire's capital. There, instead of the previously obligatory visit by government guests from subjugated Warsaw to Lenin's Mausoleum, Mazowiecki as a form of compromise with his host, President Mikhail Gorbachev, paid his homage to the leader of the revolution in Lenin's office in the Kremlin. This visit did not, it seems, have any major significant political significance, but the order of these trips was symbolically important. The meeting with Pope John Paul II was undoubtedly an expression not only of the personal spiritual orientation of the Prime Minister himself but also that of most members of the society in which he grew up. The hasty visit to the Kremlin also grew out of his deeply rooted basis in that milieu, first of all via the PAX Association (founded with the NKVD's 'blessing') of agents and then with its more rebellious faction, from which *the publication 'Więź'* emerged. Its columnists, including the future Prime Minister, consistently emphasized in their 1960s texts that Poland must have a firm foothold in Moscow because only in this way would Poland be safe. This was 'realism', indeed solidly grounded in the traumatic experience of a Poland raped by Stalin, but was this realist maxim still in force at the threshold of the 1990s?

More significant was the visit to Moscow by President General Jaruzelski, the man whom Mikhail Gorbachev regarded as an essential partner. It was with Jaruzelski that he deposited some of the documents concerning the Katyń Massacre during an April 1990 visit. For the time being, it was only a fragment (roughly a quarter) of the truth about Katyń, but an important step forward to arrive at the whole truth about this painful wound in relations between Poland and the still-existing Soviet Union. The documents Gorbachev handed over spoke of the responsibility of the NKVD alone, as if it and not the Communist Party ruled the Soviet Union during these events. They contained no Politburo documents and spoke only of one crime scene, Katyń. Still unexplained was the question of the other locations where Polish officers and prisoners had died in the April 1940 operation.

When deciding to reveal this quarter-truth about Katyń, Gorbachev simultaneously did something that would cast a long shadow over other future Polish-Russian relations. Namely, he gave concurrent instructions to historians from the Academy of Sciences of the Soviet Union and employees of the secret services to search intensely and extensively in archival documentation for traces that would make it possible to create an 'anti-Katyń' narration. The idea was to show that the Poles also had on their conscience an equal or perhaps even a greater crime against Russian soldiers, against the Soviet Union a greater hurt than that which Katyń represented. The order was carried out and the search for an alternative historical narrative was soon crowned with success. The death due to disease and in some cases neglect of Soviet PoW's during Polish Soviet war 1919 to 1921. Since that time, that is, since 1990, thousands of texts have been published in Russia, implementing, in a sense, the historical research ordered by Gorbachev. They develop this one thesis: before there was ever Katyń, the Poles consciously, based on a cold decision, taken probably somewhere in Warsaw, had murdered Bolshevik POWs during the 1920 Bolshevik-Polish War. Indeed, POWs had died in prison from their wounds, disease, or exposure. Yet if a crime this was a crime of neglect in a time of war and foreign invasion, certainly not a premeditated event. We have to realize the fatal consequences for millions of ordinary Russians of this propagandistic, extremely cynical ploy by the first and last president of the USSR. In the years that followed, right up to the present day, they were and still are many convinced that the Poles were the murderers of the innocent Russians who formed the Red Army in 1920. That the Poles are murderers even worse perhaps than those rouge NKVD elements who had killed 'without sanction' the Polish officers with the White Eagle on their 'fascist' four-cornered military caps in 1940.

The change in Polish-Soviet relations was more visually reflected and associated at the time with the initiatives of Lech Wałęsa, then chairman of Solidarity. His first visit to Moscow took place in December 1989. At that time, he went to the funeral of Andrei Sakharov, the Russian human rights defender who had formerly been the developer of the hydrogen bomb for the Soviet Union. On that occasion, Wałęsa also met Boris Yeltsin, the man who had left the Communist Party and now was challenging Gorbachev for power over Russia. It was a critical moment because Wałęsa appeared to become embroiled in some personal dealings which appeared to evoke some form of gratitude from Yeltsin, a man who was just ascending in the Kremlin hierarchy. A few weeks later, in January 1990, Lech Wałęsa met with the Soviet ambassador to Poland. He did so, however, on a completely different footing to Prime Minister Mazowiecki's earlier meeting with the head of the KGB. Wałęsa received Ambassador Vladimir Brovikov, openly with the media in attendance, firmly demanding that the place of burial of the Polish officers murdered in 1940 be finally indicated. He also demanded clarification of all the historical issues involved, but above all, he ordered – and this was the most important – that Soviet troops be moved out of

The meeting between St John Paul II and Mikhail Gorbachev on 1 December 1989 was of momentous importance for the transformation of Europe.

Poland. This was a substantial public demand that changed the political atmosphere in Poland. At that same time the Prime Minister Mazowiecki, together with President/General Jaruzelski, was touring Poland's western garrisons and requesting an extension of the Warsaw Pact, which was supposed to guarantee Polish security from Germany and any future move by that nation to reclaim its lost lands.

Such behavior on the part of Wałęsa provided grounds for a different view of the future of Polish-Russian relations. This overly optimistic view may have come more sharply into focus in light of the internal struggle in Russia that took place after the failed putsch carried out in August 1991 by the defenders of the USSR. Wałęsa, already now president at the time, was very shaken by these events and decided to make a gesture of goodwill or indeed some might say fealty or obedience to the putschists: he placed an immediate phone call to them so they could accept his personal declaration of loyalty. However, the KGB ultimately resolved the putsch in Yeltsin's favor and to the detriment of the putschists themselves as well as Gorbachev. The intelligence services within the USSR evidently wanted to finally break free from the control of the already somewhat scabrous party and take informal ownership of the state. Work on this commenced immediately. Those curious to explore these events can read the best biography on Vladimir Putin, written by Masha Gessen. An author who may not be universally liked in all quarters but deserves the highest praise as the author of this portrait of Putin. Hardly anyone was aware at the time of the further impending consequences of the quiet takeover. The transfer of these 'brakes and levers' from the hands of the CPSU to the KGB. What was visible, however, were the immediate consequences: the actual disintegration of the USSR.

On the threshold of 1992, formally there was no longer an empire. Our eastern neighbors were now Lithuania, Belarus and Ukraine (and Russia – via the small Kaliningrad Oblast). At that time, the question of a polygonal game now arose: Poland-Russia and the LBU (Lithuania Belarus and Ukraine). This strategic game is still with us today. It is, of course, easier to play the geopolitical game for Poland's future in such a system than to have just one powerful, united empire all along the eastern border. That previous scenario inevitably condemned the smaller western neighbor to be coerced into the role of a western marching ground, or bridgehead, the role Poland had already occupied in history. In 1992, the Ukrainian President Leonid Kravchuk, who came from the Soviet *nomenklatura*, was already well entrenched in power in Kyiv. He was engaged in a genuine struggle to gain full sovereign control over a quite vast country, at that time a country with a population of nearly 52 million (today 30 years later, it has fallen to 37 million) and possessed of nuclear weapons (today it has none). Kravchuk wanted to enlist Poland's support as an ally, Poland had after all be the first to recognize the new Ukrainian State in 1991. The vague outlines began to appear of an opportunity to make a deal with a country that had not only possessed nuclear weapons but also the ability to produce them; only under pressure from the West did Ukraine agree to negotiate away its ultimate deterrence in return for security assurances. The events of 1992–1993 turned out to be crucial and, in a sense, reflect a pattern in Poland's relations with its eastern neighbors to this day.

To understand them, however, it is necessary to recall what had taken place a little earlier in this Eastern European polygon. The Minister of Foreign Affairs in Tadeusz Mazowiecki's government was Prof. Krzysztof Skubiszewski, the author of the concept of the so-called 'two-track policy'. On the one hand, this policy was intended to maintain the best possible relations with Moscow, headquarters of the then still existing Soviet Union, and on the other, to gently make it clear that we had nothing against independence movements in Ukraine, Belarus, Lithuania, Latvia and Estonia as they strove to emerge as actual states in their own right. The critical juncture for this policy was Moscow's military intervention in Vilnius in January 1991. An intervention intended to crush Lithuania's independence aspirations. The Polish state acted very cautiously, to say the least, unlike a large part of Polish society, which instinctively rushed to help the Lithuanians in distress. When Ukraine declared its independence a little later, the then-new Prime Minister, Jan Krzysztof Bielecki, quickly decided to move with Polish society and recognize it. This apt decision broke with Krzysztof Skubiszewski's conservative principle of always being one or two steps behind Western countries in declaring Poland's own policy towards our eastern neighbors.

However, further crucial decisions were made in 1992–1993. In May 1992, Leonid Kravchuk, while visiting Warsaw, proposed a treaty to Lech Wałęsa in which both countries would declare that they would in the future, undertake to have better relations with each other than with any other country from the former area of the Soviet Union, i.e. including the then Russian dominated CIS. Declaring this and seeking to go further in the direction of military cooperation and closer economic ties, especially energy cooperation between Poland and Ukraine. These were all steps that would have clearly weakened the possibility of renewing a post-Soviet Russia's imperial grip over Eastern Europe. However, just two days after Kravchuk's departure,

409

President Lech Wałęsa traveled to Moscow. With this subsequent (planned or unplanned) trip Wałęsa appears to have been making a clear choice, in line with the logic of that 'realism' previously represented by Prime Minister Mazowiecki or Adam Michnik in his political and journalistic endeavors. The latter himself bluntly expressed the sense of this logic: 'one must talk to the masters and not to the lackeys'. In 1989 or 1990, when the Soviet Union in all its menacing power still existed, this attitude, prescribing communication with Moscow regardless of domestic or PUWP deputies evolving preferences, was an attitude that could be justified even regarded as prudent. However, in 1992 and later years, it reflected a calculation made in a new, now altered geopolitical landscape a calculation that was fatal to Poland and prospects for freedom in the region: one must get along with the more potent 'partner', even on its dictated terms, even if this may be harmful in the long term. This choice was perceived preferable to efforts aimed at forming a coalition along the lines of a kind of self-defense or solidarity-based alliance of the weaker and threatened. This was the first installment of Poland's geopolitical pivot, a move that the government of Donald Tusk would from 2007 onwards repeat and maintain. It is simply summarized by the slogan of that eastern policy enunciated in January 2008, and subsequentially practically at all costs until early 2014 that of 'Moscow first'.

Again, it must be acknowledged that for Lech Wałęsa, when making this choice in May 1992, his country faced a less certain security situation than that of Donald Tusk and his advisors in 2008 with Poland already established in NATO and the EU by that time. Wałęsa in 1992 could have secured something tangible in return, not only for himself but for Poland. Specifically: the withdrawal of Soviet troops (already calling themselves Russian) from Poland because these troops now three years after the transformation of 1989 were still stationed within Polish borders. The principles of Russian policy remained the same, regardless of the incarnation of the Russia concerned: imperial, Soviet or republican. The principle was and remained: not to give up any asset or anything for no gain certainly not if you can keep it all. No moral or humanitarian issues must stand in the way. This is also how Russia played the subject of the presence of its military on Polish territory, delaying negotiations on its withdrawal and taking its time before making

Mieczysław Wachowski the former "Driver" of the leader of the Solidarity movement and later Head of the Presidential Ministerial Office here seated beside the no
former President of Poland Lech Wałęsa in the Polish Sejm, Warsaw 24 May 2001.

any decision. The new government and President Wałęsa, who was already in
power then, played the matter differently from Prime Minister Mazowiecki.
While insisting on withdrawing Soviet troops, he also agreed to a Russian
proposal to create some form of mixed Polish-Russian economic initiative
or business enterprises in the areas that were then to be handed back over
to Polish jurisdiction, the locations of the Soviet bases. These enterprises
or business interests were to 'manage' the assets left behind by the army.
The new government of Prime Minister Jan Olszewski was not willing to
include this point in the Polish-Russian agreement, concerned that such
'special economic zones' threatened to consolidate Russian influence. No

longer directly of a military nature yet exerting nevertheless a corruptive distortive impact on Poland's new emerging economic and business elite. There was a real threat that Poland's new economy could become entangled with the post-military Russian *nomenklatura*. This was undoubtedly a sensitive, critical moment, showing the way of the game from the Russian side: a game of sowing the seeds of division in the opponent's camp (and Poland was still treated as an opponent in the Kremlin, even at the time).

Simultaneously, the second aspect of this game was also revealed by Russia. It was related to using it growing energy exports, above all gas, as a tool of political influence and even blackmail. It was then that the possibility was offered to build the Yamal gas pipeline, running from the sources of gas extraction in western Siberia through Belarus and Poland, crucially bypassing Ukraine and Lithuania. So, Poland would receive in exchange a specific financial benefit this was the marriage of Russia's business and geopolitical strategic objectives. Yeltsin promised that the gas pipeline thus built would bring substantial financial revenues to the Polish side. Poland would of course collect transit fees for the billions of cubic meters of gas that would be pumped to the West, onwards to Germany, via Poland, and not through Ukraine or Lithuania. Russia's most important objective at this point was the destruction of the project known as the Third Republic, the geopolitical potential of which was still greatly feared in Moscow. The specter of a renewed political community or worse an actual alliance of the countries that once made up the Commonwealth, that is, Poland, Lithuania, Ukraine and Belarus, shutting off or limiting access to Europe for Moscow, this still haunted the corridors of Russian power. It was, therefore, primarily a matter of isolating the biggest 'players' from each other, Poland from Ukraine. What better way to interrupt any tentatively emerging cooperation on the Warsaw-Kyiv line floated by the Ukrainian President that summer of 1992? Wałęsa whatever his rational, clearly chose to play this particular game with Russia.

Wałęsa's hand was also guided by pragmatic reasons related to pressure from the West, which wanted Poland to play or at least get along with Russia and not with Ukraine. It was Moscow, and not the newly emerging states, even those with centuries of tradition of their own statehood, that had to be the guarantor of stability in the whole of Eastern Europe. This was the view in the eyes of the US State Department and in the eyes of a large part of Western European politicians. If you want to get closer to the West, Poland was instructed to first come to an understanding with Russia. Lech Wałęsa accepted this instruction, interpreting as best he saw fit. He did not choose to follow in the footsteps of Józef Piłsudski. Though, I do remember that at the beginning of 1991, when he visited the Józef Piłsudski Institute in New York (I was working on a monograph on Piłsudski's Eastern policy there at the time), he did his best to take on the pose of the Marshal but unfortunately, only by way of his haircut and moustache. He did not dare to try to reorganize the geopolitical space in our region in the face of pressure from the powers that be in the world. Wałęsa's options were of course not militarily in nature as Piłsudski's had been, but the possibility to engage in energetic political moves and geo-economic decisions existed. Decisions which could have over time, allowed Poland greater room for maneuver, afforded a greater space of freedom for Poland and its newly emerged eastern neighbors.

Wałęsa accepted this game in a situation when the short lived government of Jan Olszewski (1930–2019) and increasing circles of Polish public opinion were talking about the necessity of Poland's entry into NATO. This was notably advocated by the independence circles formerly associated with the Polish Independence Alliance. It became clear that Russian resistance to this would have to be overcome in order to enter the North Atlantic Pact. Lech Wałęsa concentrated on this and perhaps unwittingly obtained President Yeltsin's consent for Poland's entry into NATO. This happened during Yeltsin's visit to Warsaw in August 1993. The Russian Foreign Minister at the time Andrei Kozyrev was, of course, quick to deny any such consent, saying that this was not what Yeltsin had in mind when he spoke. That perhaps he had a bit of a slip of the tongue, or perhaps, as it was gently suggested, he had simply drunk too much during that visit to Warsaw. Either way, it could already be shown to the West that Boris Yeltsin had winked for just a moment and said: 'You can let them in'.

Yeltsin was by no means the naive or irresponsible politician concerning the interests of the Russian state, as he is sometimes perceived even by the Russians themselves or in Poland. He wanted to as far as possible hold the line, maintain Poland's dependence on Russia. He supported the introduction of the so-called 'Balladur Pact' in Poland and throughout Eastern

Europe. Édouard Balladur (born 1929), the highly influential French Prime Minister at the time, proposed on 9 June 1993 the conclusion of a treaty between the countries of Western Europe and the Russian Federation, called the 'Pact on Stability in Europe'. Under it, Russia would guarantee the validity of minority rights in all countries in our part of Europe. For Western Europe, Russia was to be a party to this treaty. This would, of course, give Moscow almost unlimited possibilities to interfere in the internal affairs of its recent Soviet 'colonies'. Just as the Grzymułtowski Treaty signed by King Jan Sobieski once gave it similar rights in the name of protecting Orthodox minorities in the Polish-Lithuanian Commonwealth, or the later treaties with Turkey, analogously did in the area of the Ottoman Empire allowing Russia to play the role of 'Protector of the Slaves'. This game's essence was to draw Western Europe's powers into it. Separate them from the US and invite them to jointly control or perhaps passively supervise the central part of the continent, the eastern part of which was, Moscow's 'natural zone of responsibility'.

At the time, this seemed of little threat to a near homogeneous Poland (homogenous thanks primarily to the barbaric exertions of Hitler and Stalin); the reasoning was that it could be about minorities such as the Kashubians an ethnic group based near Gdansk, for example, a group without any separatist aspirations (such ambitions on the part of any definable Silesian movement were still little heard of at the time). Moreover, sexual minorities were not at the time a common topic in European political discourse. In the case of other nations, however, e.g. Lithuania, Belarus, Ukraine, Latvia, here Russia could act as a judge and enforcer over the rights of its own actual or claimed (Russian speaking) minorities, i.e. the many Russians who had been sent to these countries during Stalin's conquests as their colonizers. Fortunately, Yeltsin was too weak at the time, engaged in an ongoing internal struggle with his own communist parliament. Western Europe was not united. France's ambitions as Russia's main partner, nourished since de Gaulle's time, indeed, since the era of Napoleon III, did not arouse the enthusiasm of Germany, which of course, would ideally have aspired to such a role for itself. Nor did the United States directly express support for this French project of bringing Eastern Europe under Russian control. The Balladur plan, therefore, did not come into effect.

414

On 25 August 1993, Boris Yeltsin, President of the Russian Federation, during his visit to Poland, laid flowers at the Katyń Cross at the Powązki Military Cemetery in Warsaw and asked Poles, on behalf of his nation, for forgiveness for the Katyń Massacre.

Yeltsin then launched a different path of Polish dependency. Already during his August 1993 visit to Warsaw, he directly inaugurated the issue of Poland's dependence on Russian gas. But before I come to that, I want to mention another significant positive symbolic act. In 1993, the Russian state unequivocally paid tribute to the victims of the Katyń massacre and condemned the crime unlike in the Gorbachev era and did so definitively, unlike later under Putin. It also pointed out Moscow's responsibility for these crimes in full. During his visit to Warsaw, Yeltsin paid tribute to those murdered in Katyń at the cross in the so-called Katyń Valley at Powązki Cemetery. Earlier, in Katyń itself, the Russian Vice-President, General Aleksandr Rutskoy (born 1947), paid tribute to those murdered. From the lips of the Russian President, a request for forgiveness was made to the Poles in Warsaw. At that time, Yeltsin also brought the files of the so-called Suslov Commission, which was established by the Political Bureau of the Central Committee of the Communist Party of the Soviet Union to deal with the so-called Polish crisis of 1980–1981. From these files, which have since become publicly available, we now know for sure that in December 1981, there was no actual real threat of a Soviet intervention in Poland. There had been such a threat in 1980, but for the martial law crime in 1981, judging from this new evidence the entire responsibility for it lies exclusively with General Wojciech Jaruzelski and his entourage. Of course, we must remember that he was of course acting as part of an imperial system whose center invariably remained in Moscow. However, despite being under limited direct military duress he certainly did not oppose this system, choosing instead to go to war against his own people.

Continuing rapprochement in the fields of memory and commemoration followed Yeltsin's visit to Warsaw, important documents were also brought to Poland by Rudolf Pichoya, the Russian state archives chief director. It was almost the complete documentation of the Katyń Massacre (it was not augmented in the following years: the so-called Belarusian list that is still missing, and there is no information regarding the priests who were deported from the three camps in December 1939 in an unknown direction). It unequivocally confirmed the full responsibility for the Katyń massacre not only on the part of the NKVD but of the entire Politburo of the Central Committee of the Communist Party of the Soviet Union, *de facto* the whole of the Soviet state, of which the Russian Federation still remains the legal and international successor. This is also how Boris Yeltsin presented it in 1993. One may wonder whether it was at this point in time if another opportunity for a genuine Polish-Russian understanding appeared, a reconciliation on the level of truth, at least when it came to history. As I have already mentioned, Boris Yeltsin was embroiled in an intense struggle with the internal opposition, represented by the communist parliament, the Duma, which he ultimately dispersed by force in October 1993. Yeltsin resorted to brute force against political opponents but unambiguously, at that moment he also represented an anti-communist option.

The chance of an agreement that was then in sight could only be realized via this anti-communist platform: a full condemnation of Soviet crimes, abandoning the slogan of 'writing off the past with a thick line'. This line needed to be scratched out so that it would not be scarred over by the membrane of further baseness and lies, to paraphrase the words of one of the masters of the Polish intelligentsia. Recalling the great crimes that resulted from the reign of communism, crimes whose victims included Russians, Poles and other nationalities, this could have been an opportunity for a moral cleansing and the construction of a bulwark against Russia's return to the worst of its historical mutations: imperial-Soviet. Unfortunately, what was lacking at the time among the political powers that be in Poland was the readiness to seize on such an opportunity and the determination to see it through. At the time, Lech Wałęsa supported the 'left leg' of the domestic political spectrum this was his new political slogan. In addition, contemporary Polish public opinion, including television news on most channels, was largely ruled by the front pages of *Gazeta Wyborcza*, which promoted a completely different, even opposite line, the line of historical oblivion. The alleged reconciliation of victims with their executioners? Why the topic simply no longer existed? It was precisely this line of thinking that hampered understanding of the potential for a historic Polish-Russian rapprochement. This is worth recalling and emphasizing.

Let us not forget, however, that in 1993 there was also a lack of that kind of 'social propellant' for such a reconciliation on the grounds of anti-communism; also, or perhaps above all, in Russia. This was sustained by the powerful instruments of power in the Russian state, the most important

417

President of the Republic of Poland Lech Kaczyński received by Georgian President Mikheil Saakashvili at the Georgian Parliament in Tbilisi, during the invasion on that country by the Russian Federation August 2008.

of which was the security agency – the former KGB. Yeltsin found himself becoming more and more dependent on them with each passing year. The symbol of this dependence eventually culminated with the appointment of Lt. Col. Vladimir Putin (born in 1952, an experienced staff officer of the Brezhnev and Andropov era security services, latterly under Yeltsin, head of the FSB, the successor to the KGB) as Boris Yeltsin's successor.

In the mid-1990s, the old pattern of political dependence on the Kremlin began to be renewed in Poland. Part of the political elite of the Third Republic still tied their hopes and careers to Moscow. Boris Yeltsin wanted to celebrate the 50th anniversary of the end of the Second World War in Moscow in 1995. At the time, President Wałesa was seeking re-election and was fighting against a now resurgent post-communist SLD camp, although he had previously tried to appease it. From here, a heated debate arose as

A rally in support of the Georgian authorities, with speeches by the presidents of five countries, Tbilisi, 12 August 2008. From left: Polish President Lech Kaczyński, Georgian President Mikheil Saakashvili, Ukrainian President Viktor Yushchenko and Lithuanian President Valdas Adamkus (in a dark suit).

to whether the new SLD prime minister, Józef Oleksy (1946–2015), should attend this celebration. Especially since a year earlier, the celebrations of the 50th anniversary of the Warsaw Uprising, had borne witness to a great lack of respect for the Polish side that not a single high-ranking representative of the Russian Federation attended. A fact widely noted. The chance of a Polish-Russian rapprochement on the playing field of anti-communist sentiment was rapidly melting away.

There was, however, a deeper rationale behind these historical and symbolic issues, it related to the material means by which Poland's dependence on Moscow would be maintained. Essential in this respect was the Falin-Kvitsynsky doctrine, formulated back in 1990. Its creators were Valentin Falin (1926–2018), the last Soviet ambassador to the Federal Republic

419

of Germany in Bonn, and Yuli Kvitsinsky, the first deputy foreign minister of the Soviet Union. Within this document the Foreign Department of the Central Committee of the CPSU formulated the Soviet Union's strategic concept toward the countries of Central and Eastern Europe. In it, they stated that the former role of the Red Army, as a stabilizer of Moscow's influence in the area (now clearly declining), that role should be henceforth entrusted to Russian companies supplying oil and gas. In this doctrine, formulated in the body responsible for the foreign policy of the Soviet Union, this was precisely how this envisaged 'EnergieWende' was expressed. The Falin-Kvitsynsky doctrine is, of course, still playing itself out today. When, on 8 August 2003, the government of the Russian Federation, already under President Vladimir Putin, approved Russia's strategy until 2020, it affirmed therein 'that the strategic objectives of developing the gas industry are to secure Russia's political interests in Europe and neighboring countries, as well as in the Asia-Pacific region'. Geopolitics was the primary driver and making money or reducing CO_2 emissions were merely it seems only ancillary benefits. This strategy does not change beyond 2020 either. The issue of the Pacific Ocean will not be dealt with here, but Europe, especially the neighboring countries, is the area where Polish interests are located. Russia used the gas tool as a weapon against Poland for the first time in the winter of January 1992, when the district heating system in Poland was cut off from the supply of Russian gas. This was a kind of preparation for the upcoming negotiations referred to above on whether Poland would be more politically aligned with Ukraine or Russia. Then, already in 1992, Poles were reminded by Moscow, just who was more important economically, and who it was that could cut off the gas.

On 25 August 1993, during Yeltsin's visit and during the time a 'yes' was given to Poland's entry into NATO (only to later be rescinded), an agreement was signed on the supply of gas and the construction of a 665 km-long section of the aforementioned Yamal gas pipeline through the territory of the Republic of Poland. A company, Europol-Gaz, was established to administer the resultant agreement between the Polish state-owned gas corporation, PGNiG and Gazprom on the use of the new pipeline. Under that agreement, Poland undertook to receive only 3 billion m³ of gas a year, even though the country required far more not just for power and heating but also for fertilizer production. That agreement was not a bad one from an economic point of view. It did not violate Polish interests as long as it backed Moscow's strategic goal of separating Poland from Ukraine and Lithuania. The acceptance of that particular offer differed fundamentally from the later concessions made towards Russia by Donald Tusk's governments. Lech Wałęsa, by giving up a chance for deeper cooperation with Ukraine, was getting a relatively favorable economic deal on gas in return and perhaps the associated accelerated withdrawal of Russian troops from Polish territory. Donald Tusk, in contrast, got virtually nothing from Russia in return for his policy of separating Poland from Ukraine. Quite the contrary, he made Poland more dependent than ever on long-term energy contracts that fulfilled all the principles of the Falin doctrine. Indeed, Poland paid a higher price for the gas than many other European nations proved themselves able to negotiate while also giving a free hand for gas blackmail by Russia towards the Ukrainian state.

Returning to our chronology, in 1999, the section of the Yamal gas pipeline running through Poland was finally completed, with a few years' delay. Poland then had the opportunity to renegotiate a comprehensive deal more favorably for itself, as Russia had not in fact honored the original terms of the agreement for constructing the second line of the pipeline. This ever-recurring issue and I am referring to the second line of the Yamal gas pipeline, was then used by Putin after 2000 to destabilize the Polish political scene. Although in many aspects, the AWS government (1997–2001) may be assessed critically, in terms of energy security, this government did try to pursue Polish political interests. In particular, Deputy Minister Piotr Naimski pushed this line and tried to diversify gas supplies to Poland. An agreement with Denmark and Norway for a new pipeline was pursued near to completion; literally, just a few signatures were missing to finalize it already in 2001. This deal was to provide Poland with a supply of 3 billion m^3 of Norwegian gas via a pipeline built jointly with Denmark. This pipeline would have made it much easier for Poland to face down further efforts at gas blackmail from a Russia now under Putin's stewardship. Unfortunately, the former communists of the Democratic Left Alliance (SLD) won the parliamentary elections that year, and the resultant Leszek Miller government was formed. Not only did Miller's government abandon the agreement with

421

Denmark and Norway but, in 2003, they concluded a new agreement with Russia, signed by Deputy Prime Minister Marek Pol. It essentially deprived Poland of the benefits of gas transit fees while strengthening its dependence on Russian supply. The so-called 'Orlengate' affair that followed proved to be a fascinating insight into the various maneuverings around the gas and oil issues in 2002–2003, during the time that Leszek Miller's SLD (ex-communist) government was negotiating Poland's EU entry.

Before we discuss it, let us recall that 2002 was a very important year in Polish-Russian relations the year the new Russian President visited Poland for the first time: Vladimir Putin, a representative of the elite of the totalitarian state's secret services. Putin's political metamorphose was not as unusual a carer transformation as it initially seemed to many in the West. To prove this fact the Scottish political scientist Steven White analyzed a thousand biographies of people who held key positions in the Russian state between 2003 and 2007. The result he obtained was unprecedented in the history of the world. In some periods, between 40% and 78%, and never less than 15–20%, of the power elite (i.e. government ministers, members of the *Duma* (parliament), ministers in the president's cabinet, governors of individual regions) boasted in their official data that they had been officers of the secret and special services: KGB, GRU (military service) or their successors after 1991: FSB and SWR. In no other country in the world is there such a second ruling elite, a percentage of people in positions of political power trained for so many years to deceive and manipulate others, and even, when so required to kill with impunity political opponents. Such an exceptional governing cadre is found in the largest country in the world, with which we Poles have the misfortune to be neighbors of. Vladimir Putin is a typical representative of this formation; one could say he is a KGB tsar.

All of this, unfortunately, was parked away temporarily by the good atmosphere in which this visit by President Putin to Poland took place the first and last since he ever came to Poland as a president only visiting in his later incarnation as Prime Minister. Then, at the beginning of 2002, Putin made symbolic gestures in Warsaw to the Polish memory of the deportations to the depths of the Soviet Union in 1939–1941. From this point of view, his visit could not be faulted. No parallel propaganda game was openly played at the time to weaken the significance of these gestures,

Top: Former Ukrainian Prime Minister Yulia Tymoshenko and Vitali Klitschko at the 2014 European People's Party summit in Dublin. Bottom: Foreign Minister Radoslaw Sikorski (left) and Russian Foreign Minister Sergey Lavrov during a press conference after a meeting in Moscow on 6 May 2009.

which recalled the Soviet state's guilt towards Polish citizens during World War II. However, the friendly atmosphere accompanying this visit was only a mere propaganda ploy for the fundamental true purpose behind Putin's stay in Poland. This boiled down to a specific business venture: the sale of a large part of the Polish domestic oil refining and distribution market to the powerful Russian oil company Lukoil including the sale of the refinery and Naftoport in Gdańsk. This was not only to ensure access to the Polish oil market from the Baltic but also to effectively have this market monopolized by Russia, and thus cut off the alternatives. Other sources which could have been used to supply energy-producing hydrocarbons by sea from other energy exporters than Russia

Talks on this issue were already well advanced, with Minister Janusz Kaczmarek participating from the SLD-government side. The prominent at the time businessman Dr Jan Kulczyk (and his business interests) was also very heavily involved and met twice on this matter, including in Vienna, with the famous not just in the business world agent, Colonel Vladimir Alganov. Perhaps Dr Kulczyk did not communicate optimally with Minister Kaczmarek; there was, in any case, a dispute between the two interest groups. While Kaczmarek seemed to be in favor of dividing the Polish oil market into two parts and only wanted to sell one of the pieces to Russia, Kulczyk was supposedly interested in gathering up all the assets and selling them in their entirety to Russia while gathering a large profit for himself, at least this is how we can interpret events from the official accounts given by the Office of State Protection (UOP) to the affair that subsequently unfolded, the earlier referred to 'Orlengate'.

Ultimately, in 2002, Putin left Poland completely empty-handed due to the domestic conflict within the circles of the various influential Polish SLD barons. To his mind he failed to settle a key economic and strategic interest in Poland: to make the Polish oil market entirely dependent on Russia. This caused Polish-Russian relations to go from seemingly normalized, to radically worse, overnight. It is not, therefore, that these relations only turned bad in 2004, with the outbreak of the so-called Orange Revolution on the Dnieper River in Ukraine and the resultant support given to this movement by Poland including in part by the former communist President Aleksander Kwaśniewski himself. A kind of negative reset had already taken place in

Moscow in 2002. Putin, of course, was not going to walk away from a strategic goal of the Russian state and did not give up on further strengthening Poland's dependence on Russia in the gas, oil and other sectors.

In 2004–2005, the situation changed abruptly due to a general change in the geopolitical scene. A prelude to this change was Poland's entry to NATO in 1999, and the later government of Leszek Miller then making certain moves that greatly annoyed Moscow. A cooperation commitment with the US was entered into, an attempt by Poland under the SLD government, specifically Leszek Miller, to play the role of an important ally of the United States in the game being then played out in the Middle East, in Iraq. This was a time when the US needed Poland. When the so-called 'Old Europe' (France and Germany), which was moving ever closer, ever more acquiescent towards Putin's Russia. This was contrasted with the 'New Europe', which now clung closer to the United States. It seemed that Poland had a chance for a greater role in Central and Eastern Europe based precisely on the USA. A breakthrough did indeed soon occur.

In November 2004, the Orange Revolution broke out, and 2005 saw a Law and Justice (PiS) victory in the parliamentary elections in Poland together with Lech Kaczyński winning the presidential elections that same year. Russia would now face a hawkish geopolitical stance from Warsaw, the doves had flown. So Russian influence in both Poland and Ukraine was now directly threatened in a couple of specific ways. Firstly, there was the liquidation of the WSI – the Polish Military's Information Services (espionage or spy services), which had been a continually important channel for consolidating and augmenting the covert influence of its former Moscow HQ over Poland ever since 1990. This was a crucial move on the part of the new PiS government, made at the personal intervention of President Lech Kaczyński. Secondly, there was an attempt to organize a system of energy security for Poland to get out of the gas dependence noose that Russia was systematically trying to tighten around Central Europe in various ways. One of Moscow's methods in this regard was to block the estuary or bay of the Vistula River east of Gdansk and, thus, the strategic inland port of Elbląg. Reaching this port by sea was only possible through Russia's territorial waters. The Law and Justice government then launched a program, unfortunately, abandoned by the next government, aimed at escaping from this trading trap left by Stalin's map drawers. It was envisaged to dig a short canal across the narrow Vistula land Spit in the section belonging to Poland. This canal would facilitate ships interested in calling at the inland port of Elbląg to enter the Vistula estuary without problems, i.e. without asking permission from the Russian Federation.

On the other hand, a direct way of defending Polish economic sovereignty was to organize an alternative network for transporting energy resources to Poland. President Lech Kaczyński energetically set to work and organized three successive energy summits precisely on this topic. Many Poles remember more the symbolic aspects of Mr Kaczynski's presidency, and yet this very tangible initiative is sometimes forgotten. It was developed based on an attempt to cooperate with Ukraine, Georgia and Azerbaijan, and further east on the other side of the Caspian Sea with Kazakhstan and Turkmenistan. Summit meetings between these countries led to the first concrete decisions: the Odesa-Brody section of a gas and oil transmission line project, which was then to continue by sea through on to Georgia to Azerbaijan, with that country's considerable oil and gas resources, even on through the Caspian Sea towards Kazakhstan and Turkmenistan. This agreement could have protected Poland and a large part of Europe from Russian gas blackmail. It was a potential antidote to the whole project of making Central and Eastern Europe, indeed Europe in general, dependent on Russian energy resources. And the project of this dependence was, after all, developed by Vladimir Putin, a man with a PhD in the gas sector. A salient fact worth recalling. For not only was Putin a lieutenant colonel in the KGB, but he also holds a doctorate in gas science, obtained before he became President, based on a thesis defended at the Gas Institute in St Petersburg and devoted strictly to this very topic – how to use the gas resources of the Russian Federation as a tool of influence and political advantage.

Putin's alternative strategy envisaged two great arms with which Europe was to be rendered dependent in a great hydrocarbon bear hug. In fact, these aims were all but realized with Nord Stream I and the Nord Stream II the Northern gas pipelines running along the bottom of the Baltic Sea, closely together and directly linking Russia to Germany and onward to other Western European countries with gas supplies from Russia. A second arm of the bear was to embrace Europe from the south, the so-called South

Stream, a project we talk less about, running across the Black Sea towards southern European countries, primarily Austria and Italy. These two arms were supposed to provide Russia, through economics, with a lasting, stable political influence in Western Europe and to give it the opportunity, if necessary, to blackmail any 'disobedient' countries that would for any reason seek to destabilize the system. This southern arm would have been effectively weakened by President Lech Kaczyński's initiative to build the alternative line referred to above connecting Poland via Ukraine with Georgia, Azerbaijan and the Caspian countries. The importance of this issue became doubly apparent when Putin decided to rebuke the independent Georgian President and provoke a war in August 2008, into which Mikheil Saakashvili unwisely allowed himself to be drawn. With Russian troops marching on Tbilisi, the diplomatic and personal intervention of President Lech Kaczyński, later applauded by the then US President, prevented the Russian plan to enter the Georgian capital and directly overthrow Saakashvili by force of arms.

Then, still in 2008, it seemed that Poland's gas dependence on Russia could be prevented. Unfortunately, the change of government in Poland that took place in late 2007 already began to undermine the trend toward rebuilding Polish sovereignty in its relations with Russia. The initiative to halt the march of Russian neo-imperialism, was swiftly rejected by Prime Minister Donald Tusk's new team through their political decisions. It is instructive that symbolically the first visitor Tusk received on the day he took office as Prime Minister was the Ambassador of the Russian Federation. An event with echoes of Tadeusz Mazowiecki's first visitor when he became PM of the 3rd Republic back in 1989. This was a clear sign: Moscow now comes first. On the surface, it is difficult to protest such an assumption because, after all, Russia is Poland's most important eastern neighbor from the point of view of geography, economic potential and, in some sense, cultural significance. However, this should not mean either domination or subordination these are perhaps some of the lessons I have tried to impart in this book.

And above all, it should not allow us to forget that Russia is governed by a unique power elite, unique in its aims and methods, things I will attempt to characterize for you with a few examples as we conclude our journey. The main opposition to the expansion of Gazprom's influence and the implementation of its projects in Bulgaria and Slovakia has been paralyzed by political murders. People who resisted Gazprom's expansion were simply liquidated.

If we talk openly about these methods, then we know who we are dealing with, and we can reflect on what happened in 2009 when Prime Minister Donald Tusk decided to hold direct talks with now Prime Minister Vladimir Putin. Moscow divided the representation of the Polish state into those with whom Putin wanted to talk and those with whom he did not wish to speak, namely in the latter category the serving President of the Republic of Poland, Lech Kaczyński. The sovereign Polish government of Donald Tusk and he himself, actually accepted, acquiesced in such a policy. The boycotting by a foreign power of his own Head of State. How is it possible, is it even permissible, for a representative of a sovereign country to decide with impunity on this kind of arrangement with a foreign power? Especially a foreign power with a decidedly malign geopolitical heritage, especially towards Poland? This tragic, let us call it in the most delicate terms, misunderstanding fully showed its consequences in April 2010. The humiliation of Poland, which is connected to everything concerning the catastrophe, the Smolensk Aircraft tragedy. The subsequent investigation into the matter, the systematic humiliation of Polish authorities by the Russian side, all reflected this state of political entanglement into which we have been led by the ill-advised, let us phrase it in the gentlest terms, policy of Donald Tusk's government. Let us recall that this government took power in Poland at the end of 2007.

Meanwhile, as early as February of that year, at the annual Security Conference in Munich, Putin personally announced to the entire Western world in so many words that he was declaring a new Cold War against it. It was a shocking and sobering statement for many previous supporters of a 'reset' in relations with Moscow. Yet it was at just such a moment that Tusk after his electoral victory over the Law and Justice party, decided to erase everything that his defeated domestic opponents represented, also in the field of foreign policy, a foreign policy that the then still serving President Lech Kaczyński embodied. In breaking with what had been a tradition in the 3rd Republic Tusk decided to make his first eastern trip, outside of the

European Union, not to Kyiv, as all previous Polish prime ministers had done since 1991, instead he went directly to Moscow.

Of course, this turn could have been seen as rational calculation, a return to 'realism'. This was certainly how it was presented by two politicians devoted flagbearers of the PO-PSL government. One was not even a minister at the time; it was Bartłomiej Sienkiewicz, who, as a publicist, made it his trademark to reject the Parisian 'Giedroyć's dogma' and to instead practice 'cool realism' in relations in particular with regard to Ukraine. The second figure the new Foreign Minister, Radosław Sikorski, who held the post of Foreign Minister for the duration of the PO government, he also consistently held the same view: one must talk to the stronger and shout at the weaker or simply ignore them. He even articulated this in one of his ministerial exposés to the Sejm (in March 2011) when he stated simply that the place of our partners in foreign policy should be determined simply by the level of their GDP: 'our GDP is one-third of the Russian economy, however, it exceeds Ukrainian GDP by two and a half times and Lithuanian GDP by thirteen times'. Hard realism indeed. It meant a straightforward and clearly not a 'values-based bet' on Moscow. The reasoning was: the Ukrainian Orange Revolution had burned itself out and was now compromised by internal conflicts. The United States (especially after Barack Obama's presidency) was withdrawing from active politics in Eastern Europe, pivoting towards Asia. Nobody in Europe wants a 'Russophobic' Poland especially with the Russian gas business booming, the first North Stream pipeline was already under construction. These were three critical arguments to support this pivot further. These arguments served to roll out the red carpet under the feet of only 'viable' partner in the East: Vladimir Putin. Such a choice, however, had its consequences.

Donald Tusk had only been in office a few months when Putin first put a gas pistol to the head of Ukrainian Prime Minister Yulia Tymoshenko, at the beginning of 2008. The new Minister of Foreign Affairs, Radosław Sikorski, demonstratively went to Moscow, not to Kyiv. *"Poland closer to Russia in the gas conflict with Ukraine"*, was the headline of the *Wall Street Journal* in its Polish edition when publishing a commentary on this visit (22 January 2008). Sergey Lavrov used the visit to convince Ukrainians that gas from Russia to customers in Germany or Austria did not have to flow through Ukraine but could instead be rooted through Poland. This is the blunt fact of the matter, Polish foreign policy benign, complicit or simply naïve (please choose your own adjective) facilitated this argumentation, serving the same role as Nord Stream I and II would in the following years. Of course, the Polish government was aware of this. Still, its foreign policy and even the Polish *raison d'état* were completely subordinated to it by the logic of internal tribal warfare. Actions reminiscent with the expectations and actions of Russia's imperial policy since the time of Catherine II's and the games with the anti-King opposition in the last years of the Commonwealth. What shocking results this has led to is evidenced not least by the well-known (in Poland) long-term gas deal signed by the deputy prime minister of Tusk's government, Waldemar Pawlak, with Gazprom. Let us recall that Sikorski was soon followed to Moscow by Tusk. During this joint visit, on 10 February 2008, Putin was said to have proposed to the Polish Prime Minister that they participate in the partition of Ukraine. This was how Sikorski later reported it: 'This was one of the first things Putin said to Prime Minister Donald Tusk during his visit to Moscow. He said that Ukraine is an artificial country and Lviv is a Polish city, and why not sort it out together'. Tusk did not respond. Crucially neither did he pass on any memo on this suggestion (clearly not an insignificant proposal by Putin) to his then serving Head of State President Kaczyński. Nor did he inform his counterparties in Kyiv of such suggestions. Instead, when Sikorski later disclosed these facts in a 2014 interview with *Politico*, an affair de facto discrediting Tusk as a serious politician loyal to his own country arrose. Tusk immediately forced Sikorski to 'retract' that inconvenient piece of information, prior to departing for his new EU role in Brussels.

What was the truth of the matter? It was evident that Tusk was striving with all his might to prove himself in the role of a statesman. That he would be able to invite Putin to Poland and show that he could achieve what the 'losers' and 'incompetents' of the Law and Justice (PiS) party had never been able to achieve: a reset with the Kremlin. To welcome Vladimir Putin on Polish soil, at Westerplatte, on a symbolic day 1 September 2009 in a symbolic place. That same day Minister Sikorski announced in a column in *Gazeta Wyborcza* what many would consider, I include myself, the most disgraceful text in the history of Polish diplomacy after 1991. A text in which

President of the Republic of Poland Lech Kaczyński at the ceremony marking the 70th anniversary of the outbreak of World War II at Westerplatte. In the top row: Prime Minister of Latvia Valdis Dombrovskis and Prime Minister of Croatia Jadranka Kosor. Seated in the bottom row from the left: Prime Minister of the Republic of Poland Donald Tusk, German Chancellor Angela Merkel and the then Prime Minister of the Russian Federation Vladimir Putin.

he stated that Russia had never honored more the principles of freedom and democracy and had never been on such good terms with Poland as at that precise moment in time.

Why should I take the liberty of describing this text to you the reader so emphatically? Because at the same time, at the end of August 2009, Magnitsky, one of the world's best-known victims of Putin's ruthless regime, was languishing in a Moscow prison (a little earlier, on Prime Minister Putin's birthday, Anna Politkovskaya that resolute investigative journalist had been murdered). On the streets of Moscow, representatives of national minorities were simultaneously being killed by the dozens by the militia-linked

'White Wolves' organization. Moreover, at the same time, the Russian army, during its 'Northern' maneuvers near the Polish border, was practicing the deployment and development of a military operation to be carried out, after the conceptualized event of a tactical nuclear attack, on Warsaw...

Flattering Putin with such a column at such a time was supposed to be justified by the fact that it had been possible to get him to attend the WWII celebrations to sit down with Poles in Poland during such an event. An event to remind us indeed the whole world of the fundamental historical fact that the Second World War began with the invasion of Poland. However, what did Putin say at Westerplatte? Something that shocked the world media (though the government-friendly media in Poland were almost completely silent on this, the most important aspect of Putin's speech that day): the Second World War was according to Putin the result of the 'unfair treatment' of the two great states, Russia and Germany, by the Western powers who had been victorious in the First World War. Germany and Russia thus had every right to agree and seek to rectify this injustice. So much for the historical success of this diplomacy.

The homage paid to Putin by Donald Tusk and Minister Sikorski at Westerplatte contrasted most starkly with the disregard shown by the Polish Prime Minister and the Foreign Minister to the Ukrainian Prime Minister, earlier blackmailed by Russian gas, Tymoshenko also present there that day. Minister Sikorski did not even mention Ukraine in his program article on the new eastern policy, it did not exist, geopolitically to the east of Poland there lay, only Russia.

Such a radical turning away from Ukraine by Poland certainly influenced the mood on the Dnieper River as well. Did it contribute to the then pro-Putin Yanukovych victory over Tymoshenko in the presidential election? In any case, it was most painfully perceived by pro-European-minded Ukrainians. *'The new Warsaw deal'* was the title of one of the issues of Kyiv's most prominent liberal (certainly not any 'Bandera' or neo-Nazi) weekly, *Ukrainskyj Tyzhdenh* [Ukrainian Weekly], publishing on its front page a large photo of Tusk and Putin shaking hands. The subtitle, also on the cover, further stated: 'Donald Tusk's government has fallen into a strange dependence on the Kremlin. This poses a threat to both Poland and Ukraine'.

In Poland, a lot of painful food for thought was given to this sentence by the demonstrative separation of visits the following year to Katyń. Prime Minister Tusk's in April 2010 (at the direct invitation of then Prime Minister Putin). A visit thus decisively separated by Putin from the previously planned visit of President Kaczyński. Whereas Warsaw had previously been looked upon as a place of hope, to gain a foothold, a foothold via Poland in Europe in the west in the face of growing pressure from a neo-imperial Moscow. This was the view that had been common not just in Kyiv, but also in Tbilisi or Vilnius. Capitals where no one doubted the extreme methods to which that 'Empire's' secret services were capable of resorting. In May 2010 after the Smolensk air disaster, several free-thinking Russians (including Vladimir Bukovsky and Natalia Gorbanevskaya) would address themselves to the Poles in an open letter. It is worth quoting the words from their letter: 'It is difficult to get rid of the impression that for the Polish government, rapprochement with the current Russian authorities is more important than establishing the truth in one of the greatest national tragedies'. There is no more straightforward and blunt statement of what happened between Poland and Russia regarding the Smolensk tragedy. The decision of Donald Tusk's government to forego the possibility of revealing the truth about the Smolensk catastrophe through an international investigation, with the support of NATO allies, their seeming reluctance to demand the most elementary decency in the conduct of the Russian side in this case, all convinced the other peoples of Eastern Europe that they could no longer count on Poland in their quest for more Europe, more of the West and less of the East.

When, back in November 2013, the PiS Party declared the need to provide effective diplomatic assistance to Ukraine, a country whose people were already again struggling for independence on the *Maydan*, Minister Sikorski immediately responded with the following tweet: 'I expect PiS politicians to declare how many Polish billions they want to pump into the corrupt Ukrainian economy'. In early December 2013, Minister Sikorski unexpectedly appeared at a parliamentary group meeting on Ukraine. He came to shine with another *bon mot*: 'The PiS party ceases to be able to think whenever they are confronted with relations with Russia. All you have to do is wave a red Russian sheet. These are the reflexes of an enslaved person who needs to show off to others that he even exists at all'.

From the very outset, the PO government of Donald Tusk was it seems set on a course of complete capitulation to the East. They pursued the fastest possible track for dismantling the system of agreements, political and economic contacts, this entire capital of trust that the successive governments of the Polish Third Republic had managed to build up in Poland's relations with Ukraine, Lithuania, Georgia, Azerbaijan, and also, for example, with the Czech Republic. The policy that President Lech Kaczyński was still trying to salvage concerning Georgia, Lithuania and Ukraine, one of creating a joint energy security program, proved to be ultimately still born. It was 10 April. Frightened by the sudden capitulation of the Polish government, by the open manifestation of its resignation from any attempt to at least defend its sovereignty, its dignity and elementary state interests in relation to the investigation ceded to Putin's Russia after the Smolensk plane disaster. Now the authorities and public opinion in other, 'weaker' countries, which had until then looked to Warsaw with hope, decided that this hope had to be abandoned. It was difficult to avoid this conclusion when looking at Warsaw after 10 April 2010. To see how the patron of the most brazen election rigging activities in Russia, a man criticized by the whole civilized world Vladimir Churov, was now officially invited by Warsaw to give instruction Poles to the State Election Commission in Poland (September 2012). This even though examples of his own electoral manipulations were multiple in his role as the head of the Russian Central Election Committee. Or to see the Russian Foreign Minister Lavrov invited to the Polish capital as a mentor to a gathering of the Polish ambassadors (September 2010); how the PO government agreed to hand over the investigation into Smolensk to the Russian prosecutor Yuri Chaika a man whose investigative powers were discredited, worldwide, though apparently not in Poland. A man who'd been criticized openly for his supervision of the investigations into, among others, the murder of Anna Politkovskaya and the poisoning of Alexander Litvinenko. Or finally to see how the Military Counterintelligence Service (SKW) in Warsaw would now accepts without a word of objection, a decree from President Putin (May 2013), officially informing them about the SKWs new cooperation with the FSB, the proud continuation of the KGB. If this was to be how Warsaw would act going forward, then one must accept the 'protection' of Vladimir Putin, and one must accept the return of the Empire. Poland is no foothold no beacon to the West.

Only the subsequent open aggression of Putin's Russia, after Georgia, against Ukraine in 2014 and then the change of government in Poland after the 2015 elections, would shake the Polish authorities out of their, let me put it this way, geohistorical slumber. This is recent history, I will no longer analyze it here. I will only point out that it is moments such as the civic, societal choice of the Ukrainians to stand against the Empire at the end of 2013, as well as the return of Polish politics to the tradition of expanding the zone of freedom, the belief that Europe can reach to the east of the continent, that allow us to believe again that the far-reaching plans of top-down 'transformation', of controlling peoples and nations with 'brakes' and 'levers' in the hands of imperial power are finally ultimately failing.

It was difficult not to see at that moment, however, at the threshold of 2014, just how far we had strayed from the message that John Paul II had so assiduously reminded us of, a message derived from the spirit of Polish history. Given the prophetic nature of the gesture, let us recall it as it happened. An event similar to those witnessed by so many Poles in Warsaw, Gniezno and Krakow in 1979. It was perhaps the last time the Polish Pope, heir to the great Romantics, tried to change the European East a moment that occurred during his pilgrimage to Ukraine in June 2001. The Kremlin-subordinate hierarchy of the Moscow Patriarchate reacted to this visit with open hostility. Patriarch Alexei II of the FSB was himself at that moment demonstratively visiting President Lukashenko's Belarus and the Russian-Ukrainian-Belarusian borderlands, as if to emphasize that the political unity of the Slavic republics of the former USSR is for him the highest good, which he defends against the specter of the 'Polish', 'Western' Pope. While John Paul II was again repeating his plea for forgiveness for the offences committed by Catholics against Orthodox believers on Ukrainian soil, while not even venturing to request any mutual recognition of faults by the other side, the Patriarch of Moscow was repeating the gestures of a defender not so much of the true faith more that of the Russian Empire. In Ukraine, millions of Orthodox believers could see first-hand during this visit that this Latin Pope was not a threat to them but, on the contrary, an opportunity for their entire homeland to overcome the legacy of communism and historical hatred.

The visit to Kyiv and, above all, the joyful meetings in Lviv where nearly one and a half million faithful attended Mass (overseen and conducted by the Pope) in the Uniate rite – showed the world the face of a Ukraine not poor and torn by political conflicts, but serene and spiritual. It was a great moment of consolidation for Ukraine's young statehood.

This Ukraine and the kind of Poland most beautifully represented by the words and deeds of John Paul II, these were the peoples who wanted to destroy the Kremlin empire. Why? Well now there is a whole book about it, which we are now closing. However, at the provisional finish line (because there is no real end to history), especially such a complicated and tragic history as this; let us look again at today's Russia. That we can understand how it is currently creating, under Putin's dictates, a kind of synthesis of the imperial-political heritage of Ivan I (Kalita), III and IV (*Groźny*/the Terrible), Peter I and Catherine II, that also of Lenin and Stalin.

As it were, the official seal on this synthesis was placed by President Putin himself in the succinct formula of his annual message, delivered on 25 April 2005. The day when he called the collapse of the Soviet Union 'the greatest geopolitical catastrophe of the century'. Few still remember the words of another message presented in print 14 years earlier as 'A Word to the People'. This rhetorical message was presented at the end of July 1991 in the pages of *Sovetskaya Rossiya*, words serving as an ideological inspiration for the attempted putsch to defend the Soviet Union a month later. The current Russian President has firmly and repeatedly declared that there is no return to the Soviet Union. There is no reason to question the credibility of these declarations. The communist ideology and the communist mono-party system that formed the core of the Soviet Union were rejected by Putin, just as the clear majority of Russian society has rejected them. If we compare excerpts from his official 2005 speech with the 1991 putschist ideology transcript, it is only to point out that the communist content was irrelevant in both cases. The predominant reference is to that heritage which constitutes the Great State in both cases. That state that attained the height of its power during the Soviet era but had previously been united by the forces of 'history', i.e. Russian history and the laws of 'nature'.

History and nature are intertwined in the foundation of the greatness and unity of this state, to which Joseph Stalin gave its most total shape. These

The Holy Father John Paul II during Mass in the Eastern Rite at Chayka Airport near Kyiv. First visible from the right is the Major Archbishop of the Ukrainian Greek Catholic Church, Lubomyr Huzar. This Apostolic Visit of St John Paul II to Ukraine took place on 25 June 2001.

are fundamental premises of that peculiar didacticism to which the last defenders of the Soviet Union were appealing. The same elements appear in the ideological construction of Putin's regime. They have their logical complement in one more point. Since the Great State was cemented together by history and nature, then it could only be shattered by sinister external forces. They are explicitly mentioned in the above-quoted 'A Word to the People' (Soviet) of 1991. One can also recall President Putin's first programmatic message to the Federation Council in 2000. In it, he essentially repeated what those behind the 1991 putsch had warned against: 'Russia has collided with a systemic challenge to state sovereignty and territorial integrity. It has come face to face with the forces seeking a geopolitical *perestroika* of the world. The evil forces are still out there and are still seeking to weaken our state the geopolitical heir to the USSR, deplete it territorially, to deprive it of its sovereignty and global importance. Starting his first term as President of the Russian Federation, Vladimir Putin made it clear that he recognized these forces and that he intended to confront them.

These motifs did not come out of the blue. They were consistently present in Russian public discourse after the collapse of the Soviet Union. They did not dominate it immediately but developed gradually. In the briefest of terms, it is worth recalling a few of their characteristic manifestations to help us understand better this historical consciousness that the Putin regime refers to and builds up simultaneously. Immediately after 1991, when Boris Yeltsin was building his political position on the explicit opposition of the new Russia now led by him towards the old communist system, favorable references to the Soviet Union were limited primarily to circles of the national-communist opposition. This current of opinion, represented by newspapers such as *Dien'*, *Zavtra*, as well as *Pravda* and *Nyezavisimaya Gazeta*, among others, was effectively marginalized by Yeltsin from mainstream political life. However, this opinion continued to steadily expand its argumentation and influence in intellectual circles. Representatives of the academic elite of recent Soviet times did not lose their scientific positions: members of the Academy of Sciences, directors of institutes, heads of departments, and university professors. Some of them went in the direction prompted by the new man in power. Some worked for purely scientific purposes. Some, however, did the intellectual work of adapting the old Soviet ideology to the situation in which the Russian Federation now found itself, treating it as an heir to the Soviet Union. Of course, an heir is obliged to fight for the entirety of the great inheritance.

'Scientific expertise' working in this vein rapidly produced astonishing results. Researchers at the Institute of General Genetics of the Russian Academy of Sciences 'discovered' the common genetic code of the inhabitants of the USSR, which *Pravda* cited in late 1992 as proof of the natural character of this unity. A unity which had been so extremely violated through the collapse of the Soviet Union. From another sphere of research, some Russian geologists pointed to the fact that the Russian (Eurasian) geological platform extends to the former western borders of the USSR as evidence of the same natural law governing the spatial dimensions of the Great State.

The upper echelons of Russian sociologists from the Academy of Sciences then presented a comprehensive study of the country's reforms and transformations. They were crowned by 'theses about the future', most of which involved a characteristic assessment of the country's past. The authors stated in the first thesis that 'the (Soviet) Empire-Union was not the product of the natural aggressiveness of the Moscow rulers, but the result of the natural-historical, political and economic integration of the interests of the people? Which people? The people who voluntarily and consciously combined their efforts and sought defense and protection in one of the most developed (in both material and cultural terms) civilizations on the planet – the Russo-Russian (*russkoy rossiyskoy*) civilization'. The seventh and final thesis expressed an almost messianic belief that Russia would not only reunite the peoples of the 'Empire-Union' but would in doing so create a new 'epicenter [*sic*] of world economic and spiritual life'. The new Eurasian Union will create a model for the whole world of the transition from an industrial society to a post-industrial society of stable development harmonized with nature. 'Time is working for Russia and the union of brotherly nations'. These words conclude not a journalistic manifesto of some original political party but a near 400-page volume of analyses published by the Institute of Social and Political Studies of the Russian Academy of Sciences.

We quote this study not because of the originality of its theses but because of how typical it is. The typicality of combining, in Russian intellectual practice after 1991, a 'stamp' of scientific analysis with an ideological project: the project of rebuilding the 'Empire-Union' in the name of the noblest slogans. Hundreds of such books, analyses, and studies, signed with academic titles from the most diverse fields, above all from the social sciences, can be referenced. Russia (as interpreted by its intellectual elites) once again felt cheated by the West, reasserting its essential civilizational distinctiveness. The 'Empire-Union' was its political foundation, undermined by attempts at further occidentalization. Many academic political sciences, sociology, and history authors followed the same path. From their disillusionment with the effects of Gorbachev's *perestroika* and the 'democratization' during Yeltsin's first years, towards a rehabilitation of the merits of the Soviet period. For others, a similar tendency aroused an increasingly visible nostalgia for the 'real' Russia, i.e. the former, pre-revolutionary, imperial, Tsarist Russia. Alexander Solzhenitsyn, the symbol of this orientation in his program publication of the mid-1990s: *The Russian Question at the End of the Twentieth Century*, gave striking examples of this kind of apologia for imperial Russia. Dressed in the guise of historical, scientific argumentation, the great writer's rhetoric served the purpose of several distinct theses, which would then be reproduced in an innumerable variety of other publications simultaneously. Let us list out these theses.

Firstly: the western political institutions and models adopted by or imposed on Russia by the West are harmful to Russia. (Strikingly, Solzhenitsyn dissects the thesis that the merchant republic of Veliky Novgorod could have been a systemic alternative to Moscow's authoritarian system. In the spirit of 19th-century Tsarist propaganda, he portrays the Novgorod republican model as, in fact, a 'rotten oligarchy', offering its subjects not a shred more freedom than the Moscow system did, instead exposing the state to pernicious anarchy. Like Karamzin before him, Solzhenitsyn pointed to the salvation that could be found in a strong Tsarist government genuinely supported by the masses of loyal subjects. The threat to this system comes from the West – and its symbol, recalled by Solzhenitsyn, is the *Great Smuta* (Time of Troubles), reduced almost exclusively to the crime of the 'Polish intervention'. Poland's temerity to propose a new Union with an equal role for Moscow a different form of rule a radically different future for the neighborhood something other than Tsarist autocracy.

A 'Latin' Poland represented the West during the time of troubles occupying the Kremlin, trying to strip Russia of its Orthodox 'soul' and civilizational distinctiveness. Then the Russian nation rose up against the Western interveners drove them from the Kremlin and saved its identity. Solzhenitsyn reminded his readers. Incidentally, at the same moment, Boris Yeltsin introduced a new national holiday in place of the anniversary of the Bolshevik Revolution: the anniversary of the expulsion of the Poles from the Kremlin.

Secondly, the Russian state's territorial shape was expanded in a series of just wars to unite the heritage of Kyivan Rus. In this sense, Solzhenitsyn completely justified the partition of the Commonwealth by Russia together with the participation of Prussia and Austria. In Solzhenitsyn's vision, there is no room for separating these lands – and thus the whole of Ukraine and Belarus – from the embrace of Russian statehood.

Thirdly and finally: the great Empire that Russia ultimately built in the 19ᵗʰ century was fundamentally different from all others, particularly the Western empires. It was built to benefit the nations annexed to it, and as a result actually handicapped the Russian center. Some nations, like the rebellious Poles, did not appreciate this benefit, a fact Solzhenitsyn stated not without regret, confirming yet another cliché of the most primitive Tsarist propaganda.

Russia is thus a separate civilization, threatened by political and cultural aggression from the West, which is ready to exploit every 'Time of Troubles' period that the Russian state experiences; Russia is a great state, justly built and existing for the good of the 'annexed' peoples. These motifs, which found an authoritative defender in Solzhenitsyn, were widely read as confirming the diagnosis that the Russia of the 1990s was once again in a state of a *Great Smuta*, a new threat and that the West (at least some of its politicians) who were cynically exploiting this situation to ultimately reduce the significance of the Russian political and cultural community. This view was shared by an increasing number of representatives of the Russian elite, even those who shared the hopes at the beginning of that decade for a rapid 'normalisation' of Russia, understood by a Russia becoming similar in many aspects to life to the most economically developed countries of the West.

The sense of being able to achieve such a way out began to grow rapidly when, after the financial crisis of 1997, Russia recovered remarkably quickly and on its own merits, thanks largely to rising commodity prices for its energy exports. NATO was enlarged in 1999 to include former satellites of the USSR (Poland, Hungary and the Czech Republic, with the Baltic states already lined up), and the forces of that same pact were then used to launch a military strike against Orthodox, Slavic Serbia. A country widely perceived in Russia as its natural client and younger brother. Thus, came about the sense that Russia's conflict with the West was very much a tangible one and that Russian politics had to confront this reality head on. Russia, the 'natural defender of truth and justice,' was destined to perform this role again on the global stage while at the same time coming up to the state of readiness to effectively defend its own interests in its (similarly 'natural')

A horrific picture of the destruction in Kyiv in 2022 after Russian shelling: the surviving wall of a single-family house and a burnt-out apartment block. Civilians and residential buildings are the most frequent victims of Russian air strikes.

sphere of influence. This was the moment at which Boris Yeltsin handed over power to Vladimir Putin.

The time has come to construct a new historical memory. The specific 'historical wars' waged with its neighbors (especially Latvia, Estonia, Poland, Lithuania, formerly Georgia, now especially with Ukraine) by Russian propaganda spread over hundreds of books, propaganda documentaries and feature films, and dozens of portals dedicated to these tasks and millions of internet 'posts'. This is a topic for a separate, wide-reaching study; there is no space for it here. Let us, therefore, summarize, provisionally only, these reflections with a reminder of such a real-life scene. It was 16 January 2014. The 'Ukrainian crisis' was already entering into its decisive phase. On that day, Ukraine's *Verkhovna Rada*, controlled by President Yanukovych, adopted so-called dictatorial laws designed to curb freedom of speech and assembly. Ukraine was supposed to return to the Russian world (*Russkiy mir*). But what is this Russian world supposed to consist of? What was or is its essence – is it precisely this kind of legislation – a systematic, top-down restriction of freedom?

The most effective tool for answering this question is, history. This was the view of Vladimir Putin himself, who, on this very day, 16 January 2014, devoted more than two hours of his precious time to a meeting with representatives of a group developing the concept of a 'new educational and methodological complex (or framework) for native history'. To put it simply: he convened a briefing to discuss a new model for teaching history that would be uniform for all students in Russia. He repeatedly met on this matter with successive directors of the Russian Academy of Sciences Institute of History, with the Kremlin's 'court historian' (since the time of Gorbachev) Alexander Oganovich Chubarian and with 'state officials dealing with history' of minor rank. In the end, it was time for the final solution. The result was to be one textbook for all grades, divided into chronological sections for grades 5 to 11, through which history was to be taught. Of course, symbolically eight guests were invited to the meeting to seal this multi-year effort. They included the ministers of education and science as well as that of culture, the rectors of important universities, heads of television programs and even President Putin's personal chaplain, the Archimandrite of the Sretensky Monastery, Tikhon (Shevkunov).

443

The speaker of the working group was the second person of the state, the President of the Duma and the President of the renewed Russian Historical Society in one person – Sergei Naryshkin. He stressed the magnitude of the public consultations undertaken in developing a new, unified conception of Russian history – almost like the debate on the Stalinist constitution of 1936. 'This will rebuff those who say that the new textbook will resemble the old *Short Course in the History of the Communist Party of the Soviet Union. (Short Course – VKP(b))*, noted Chairman Naryshkin. And here came President Putin's typical retort: 'And why did you mention "VKP(b)" [using the abbreviated term], in a whisper? Are you afraid, or are you afraid that I will be frightened?' (*Vy samyi boytyes' ili boytyes', chto my ispugayemsya?*). This is a key remark: let us not be afraid of comparing our actions to Stalinist times. Let us not be fearful of anything! After this remark, Mr Chubarian, the academic, laid out the essence of the new synthesis of history: it is necessary to show how the country 'overcame difficult problems'. He enumerated them: The *Great Smuta* and the infamous 'Polish intervention' at the beginning of the 17th century, then the Napoleonic invasion of 1812, and finally, the most important, "the Great Patriotic War" of 1941–1945.

In short, the compulsory study of Russian history is based on the history of the threats that come in the form of successive invasions from the West – and on the lessons learned from the sacrifices by which these threats were 'overcome'. 'The difficult problem' of Stalin's rule can be explained precisely by the need to 'overcome' the threat of a foreign invasion during the Second War. Mr Chubarian, therefore, called Stalinism in its most criminal period of the 1930s a modernizing dictatorship. So, yes, a dictatorship, but it was nothing exceptional, no real totalitarianism there; Poland, for example, also had a dictatorship at the time, Pilsudski's, as was the case similarly in Lithuania, Hungary, or Romania… In the USSR, however, this dictatorship brought something priceless, effective 'modernization'… However, another problem is annexing other countries to Russia or the USSR. 'In some [neighboring] countries, this was considered to have been a colonial period,' thus laments the proponent of the new textbook project (although he assures us that Ukrainians, Belarusians, Armenians, Tajiks and Kyrgyz people do not think so). He also immediately suggests the correct answer to these wrongful accusations: Russian pupils will learn the consequences of

The President of Ukraine, Volodymyr Zelensky, became famous for his incredible courage in the face of Russia's criminal invasion of Ukraine. The acclaimed artist emerged as a world statesman of the highest order.

joining Russia and then the USSR and how much the newly joined nations gained by doing so.

President Putin thanked all in attendance for the vision presented. He again expressed frustration that the long process of certifying school textbooks is 'absolutely unacceptable', comparable with 'being spat upon in the face'. Vladimir Putin is most irritated by the ambiguous assessments of the USSR's involvement in the Second World War. Referring to the 'incorrect' interpretations of the Molotov-Ribbentrop Pact, he finds any mention of Stalin's strategic cooperation with Hitler, the invasion of Poland, the annexation of the Baltic republics, a bemoaning, a 'deliberate understatement of the role of the Soviet people in the fight against fascism' dismissively calling such phenomena, in the beautiful language of Joseph Stalin: *eto prosto biezobraziye, eto prosto kakoy-to idieologicheskiy musor* ('it is simply rascality, it is some kind of ideological trash'). 'And this is what we have to free ourselves from' the final conclusion of the historical deliberation. Well, the 'liberation' continues through further successive wars, unfortunately no longer only wars on paper; no longer 'historical' or cultural, instead quite real and tangible.

Can we emerge from this state of war and find reassurance in this challenging time? Where can we draw hope from and break this apparent fatalism in Polish-Russian relations driven by Kremlin ideology? I will answer in a few simple points.

Firstly, history must not be forgotten. This following argument is often used: let's not revisit these issues because they are just a burden in our relations; let us write off the past with a thick line. It seems that those who say this do not understand the vital issue in Polish-Russian relations of the last few decades, the time of the legacy of the Soviet Empire. We only have a chance of coming to an understanding with Russia and the Russians based on the rejection of this totalitarian legacy. Millions of Russians (or those whose ancestors were) victims of that system are being subjected to an increased wave of indoctrination. It instils a sense of pride in them, in the Empire of which they were and still remain slaves. There is a need for truth, a truth for which the overmatched but all the more to be respected voice of the 'Memorial' civil rights group struggles to make heard (a group recently banned on Putin's orders) an association thanks to whose efforts we also know a great deal about the crimes committed against us Poles.

Must we assume that Russians will always live a lie, that they will always be subject to the terrorist malign power of the stronger? We can make that assumption and simply turn our backs on Russia? If we do, then we must consider whether or not we can build a wall suitably impervious to protect us from Russia. Europe could erect such a wall in its entirety, but could we convince the whole of Europe to join in such a russophobic policy that would finally shatter the imperial structure of Russian identity?

The fight to remember the executioners and victims, the Empire and the right to independence of smaller nations, a battle that we are also waging in Poland and Europe, is also vital to help bring about change in Russia. President Lech Kaczyński spoke about this during the last conversation I had the honor of conducting with him for the 'Arcana' publication. He said that Russia and Putin, or any other leader of that country, would lose due to what has been the downfall of every emperor in history: a sense of hubris after a series of successes that seem to have no end. Under Vladimir Putin, Russia is accelerating so quickly to seize power over neighboring countries by the most brutal of means. A success which will eventually, and this is what President Lech Kaczyński said, arouse resistance, a counter-resistance. It will be as it has always been so far in history. As an empire becomes increasingly larger and more powerful, it not only crosses a certain barrier of its own capabilities but also crosses the difficult to discern barrier that of the patience of other strong players on the world who want to remain the strongest in the world. The USA gave way because it was convenient for them, and China is waiting because it believes it has time. Western Europe is in a state of crisis and confusion that it may not perhaps come out of, yet our Polish future also depends on it. The Islamic countries are also not waiting passively; they are expanding. Let us recall that Russia, the Russian Federation, is already a 25% Muslim country. And by 2050, based on demographic projections it will cross the 50% barrier; half of the citizens of the Russian Federation will then be of the Islamic faith.

These are not problems which will pass on their own; they are problems which will force the Russians, the hand of the Russian elite, problems which will also move their neighbors, including the serious, influential players on the world stage, all these actors to change their policy either within Russia or towards Russia. The most important thing for us Poles in this situation is not to lose sight of the truth about our history, who killed whom and in the name of what ideals or interests, who built a civil society and who chose and supported despotism. This is important. If we decide to remember this, then we will not have to be reminded of it at the expense of our own material interests and cost. Because, as we can see, a policy in which we give up courting historical truth does not lead, has not led to a safeguarding of Polish economic interests. Quite the contrary. Paraphrasing the statement of an American president, we can say at the end of this journey: *'It's history, stupid'*. It's a history we cannot sleep through because it will wake us up and rudely, as it has done so in the dramatic year of 2022.

**SCIENCE FOR
THE SOCIETY**

The Publication has been financed by funds from the Polish State
Budget under the program "Science for the Society" administered
by the Ministry of Education and Science Republic of Poland. Project
nr. NdS/551133/2022/2022 total grant 2 million PLN, total value of project 2 million PLN (Poland).

The project under the title of „Presenting the history of Poland for Western societal and cultural circles" will be composed of translations into
English and German, the printing and distribution of the following series
of books: "Poland and Russia", and five volumes of "The Annals
of Poland" by Professor Andrzej Nowak.

**POLSKA FUNDACJA
HUMANISTYCZNA**
IM. WINCENTEGO KADŁUBKA

ul. Szwedzka 38
PL 30-324 Kraków
tel.: (+48) 12 254 56 02,
260 32 90, 260 32 40,
254 56 26
e-mail: kontakt@pfhwk.pl

1st Edition
Kraków 2023

ISBN 978-83-7553-375-0